THE LAW OF COMPULSORY MOTOR VEHICLE INSURANCE

LLOYD'S INSURANCE LAW LIBRARY
Series Editors: Robert Merkin
and Malcolm A. Clarke

LLOYD'S INSURANCE LAW LIBRARY

Directors' and Officers' Liability Insurance
Adolfo Paolini and Deepak Nambisan

*Insurance Law and the Financial Services
Ombudsman Service*
Judith P. Summer

Reinsuring Clauses
Özlem Gürses

Insurance Disputes
Third Edition
The Right Honourable Lord Mance, Iain Goldrein
QC and Robert Merkin

The Law of Liability Insurance
Malcolm A. Clarke

*Lloyd's:
Law and Practice*
Julian Burling

*Systemic Risk and the Future of Insurance
Regulation*
Edited by Andromachi Georgosouli and
Miriam Goldby

Chinese Insurance Contracts
Law and Practice
Zhen Jing

The Law of Liability Insurance
Second Edition
Malcolm A. Clarke

Good Faith and Insurance Contracts
Fourth Edition
Peter MacDonald Eggers QC, Simon Picken and
Patrick Foss

The Law of Compulsory Motor Vehicle Insurance
Özlem Gürses

For more information about this series, please visit: www.routledge.com/Lloyds-Insurance-Law-Library/book-series/LILL

THE LAW OF COMPULSORY MOTOR VEHICLE INSURANCE

ÖZLEM GÜRSES

informa law
from Routledge

First published 2020
by Informa Law from Routledge
2 Park Square, Milton Park, Abingdon, Oxon OX14 4RN

and by Informa Law from Routledge
52 Vanderbilt Avenue, New York, NY 10017

Informa Law from Routledge is an imprint of the Taylor & Francis Group, an informa business

© 2020 Özlem Gürses

The right of Özlem Gürses to be identified as author of this work has been asserted by her in accordance with sections 77 and 78 of the Copyright, Designs and Patents Act 1988.

All rights reserved. No part of this book may be reprinted or reproduced or utilised in any form or by any electronic, mechanical, or other means, now known or hereafter invented, including photocopying and recording, or in any information storage or retrieval system, without permission in writing from the publishers.

Trademark notice: Product or corporate names may be trademarks or registered trademarks, and are used only for identification and explanation without intent to infringe.

British Library Cataloguing-in-Publication Data
A catalogue record for this book is available from the British Library

Library of Congress Cataloging-in-Publication Data
Names: Gürses, Özlem, author.
Title: The law of compulsory motor vehicle insurance / Ozlem Gurses.
Description: Abingdon, Oxon ; New York, NY : Routledge, 2020. |
   Includes bibliographical references and index. |
Identifiers: LCCN 2019013036 (print) | LCCN 2019018342 (ebook) |
   ISBN 9781315767062 (Ebook) | ISBN 9781138000674 (hardback)
Subjects: LCSH: Automobile insurance—Law and legislation—Great Britain. |
   Automobile insurance—Law and legislation—European Union countries. |
   International and municipal law—Great Britain.
Classification: LCC KD1892 (ebook) | LCC KD1892 .G87 2020 (print) |
   DDC 346.41/086232—dc23
LC record available at https://lccn.loc.gov/2019013036

ISBN: 978-1-138-00067-4 (hbk)
ISBN: 978-1-31576-706-2 (ebk)

Typeset in Times New Roman
by Apex CoVantage, LLC

CONTENTS

Preface	xv
Table of cases	xvii
Table of EU legislation	xxvii
Table of UK Statutes	xxix
Table of UK statutory instruments	xxxiii

CHAPTER 1	BRIEF HISTORY OF THE INSURANCE OBLIGATION AND INTERACTION WITH THE EU LAW	1
CHAPTER 2	THE INSURANCE OBLIGATION: OVERVIEW	16
CHAPTER 3	INSURANCE OBLIGATION: SCOPE (MEANING OF "PERMIT," "CAUSE," "MOTOR VEHICLE," "ROAD OR OTHER PUBLIC PLACE")	27
CHAPTER 4	REQUIREMENTS WITH RESPECT TO THE INSURANCE POLICY: FORM AND SCOPE	49
CHAPTER 5	THE MEANING OF "USE" OF A VEHICLE	67
CHAPTER 6	CIVIL LIABILITY	90
CHAPTER 7	CONTROL OF POLICY TERMS	105
CHAPTER 8	THIRD PARTY VICTIM'S RIGHT OF DIRECT ACTION AGAINST INSURERS	134
CHAPTER 9	CREDIT HIRE AGREEMENTS	178
CHAPTER 10	MOTOR INSURERS' BUREAU	197
CHAPTER 11	INJURIES SUFFERED IN THE EU	237

CHAPTER 12	THE PUBLIC POLICY DOCTRINE	252
CHAPTER 13	INSURANCE OF AUTOMATED VEHICLES	268

Index 277

DETAILED CONTENTS

Preface	xv
Table of cases	xvii
Table of EU legislation	xxvii
Table of UK Statutes	xxix
Table of UK statutory instruments	xxxiii

CHAPTER 1 BRIEF HISTORY OF THE INSURANCE OBLIGATION AND INTERACTION WITH THE EU LAW	1
Introduction	1
History (domestic law)	1
Third Parties (Rights Against Insurers) Act 1930	3
Objectives of motor third party liability insurance	4
The EU regime	5
A Member State's liability for a failure to implement a Directive	10
Limitation period	13
The principle of "consistent interpretation"	13
Direct effect	15

CHAPTER 2 THE INSURANCE OBLIGATION: OVERVIEW	16
Obligation to insure under the Road Traffic Act 1988	16
Obligation under EU Directives	17
Strict liability	17
Burden of proof	18
Certificate of insurance	18
Keeping a record of the certificate	20
When a vehicle does not meet insurance requirements	21
Void and voidable insurance contracts	22
Contracts with an exclusion clause	22
No obligation on the insurer to accept insurance proposals	23
Exceptions to compulsory insurance or security	23
EU law	24

DETAILED CONTENTS

CHAPTER 3   INSURANCE OBLIGATION: SCOPE (MEANING OF
"PERMIT," "CAUSE," "MOTOR VEHICLE," "ROAD
OR OTHER PUBLIC PLACE") 27

Permit and cause use 27
Conditional permission 28
Death of the person who gave the permission 30
The offender 30
A person using the vehicle in the course of employment 31
The meaning of "permit" under RTA section 151(8) 31
Extension clauses – permitted users for the scheduled vehicle 31
    Continuing ownership 34
Double insurance, contribution and rateable proportion clauses 37
Motor vehicle 39
    EU law 41
Road or other public place 42
    Road 42
    "On" the road 42
    Public access 42
    A definable way between two points 43
    Car parks 44
"Other public place" 44
    Offences other than RTA s 143 45
    Beaches 45
    EU law 46
    Compatibility with the EU law 47

CHAPTER 4   REQUIREMENTS WITH RESPECT TO THE INSURANCE
POLICY: FORM AND SCOPE 49

Insurer 49
Policy document 49
Deregulation Act 2015 50
The 2002 Regulations 50
Transfer 51
Risks that are not required to be covered 51
EU law: minimum amount of indemnity 51
The position of employees 53
    RTA 1988 section 145(4A) 54
    Employee driver 55
    Meaning of "carried" 56
    Insurance of an exempted institution 56
Vicarious liability 57
Subrogation in employment cases 59
Issues to be covered by section 145 60
    Personal injury 62

viii

DETAILED CONTENTS

Non-material damages	62
Who can claim compensation for non-material damages?	63
Injury to the person who was actually using the vehicle	64
Passengers	64
The owner when injured as a passenger in their own vehicle	65
"Any liability" arising out of the use of the vehicle	65

CHAPTER 5 THE MEANING OF "USE" OF A VEHICLE 67
Significance of defining the term "use"	67
Meaning	68
"Use" is not confined to "drive"	69
Causation	69
Normal function of the vehicle	70
Is "normal function" of a vehicle confined to use as a means of transport?	71
EU law	72
Reconciling domestic and EU law	74
"Moving" a motor vehicle	76
Immobility	78
Towage	79
Driver has no control of the vehicle towed	79
Vehicle not used under its own power	80
Is a passenger a user?	83
Common law	84
Controlling, managing or operating the vehicle	84
Joint venture	85
Person accepting a lift	85
Pre-determined joint purpose	85
Having "control or management" through ownership interest	87
EU law	88

CHAPTER 6 CIVIL LIABILITY 90
Introduction	90
Is breach of statutory duty actionable?	91
Motor insurance	92
The nature of liability	93
Causation	95
The owner is a passenger in his own vehicle	95
Exclusions from cover	95
The user must be impecunious	97
Interpretation of "permit" and "cause"	97
The effect of avoidance of the insurance contract	98
No extension to section 143(1)(a)	99
Monk v Warbey liability and the MIB	100
Economic loss	101
Limitation period	102

ix

DETAILED CONTENTS

CHAPTER 7 CONTROL OF POLICY TERMS	105
Insurer v third party victim	105
Domestic law	105
Conditions identified under section 148(2)	106
Passengers	106
Passenger's contribution to the accident	107
Insurers' liability to the assured where policy contains s 148 limitations	107
Terms that are not relevant to actual loss (IA 2015 s 11)	108
Suspensory conditions	110
Conditions and conditions precedents after the IA 2015	112
Restrictions referred to under the RTA 1988 s 148(2)	112
Conditions in relation to driving license	113
Claims provisions	113
Notification provisions	114
"As soon as possible"	114
Claim co-operation clauses	115
What is insured under compulsory motor third party liability insurance?	116
Permitted exclusions from cover	116
RTA 1988 section 145(4)	116
Social, domestic, pleasure purposes	117
The essential character of the journey	118
Borderline cases	119
Multiple characters of the journey	119
Motive to determine the essential character of the journey	121
Incidental deviations	121
Hire and reward	121
Car-sharing arrangements	122
Definition of assured	123
The EU dimension	123
Minimum coverage	125
The victim is the owner of the vehicle	125
(1) Owner is the driver injured by their own negligence	126
(2) Owner is a passenger and the driver is a person covered by the owner's insurance	126
(3) Owner is a passenger and the driver is not covered by the owner's insurance	126
(4–6) Owner is a pedestrian	127
Single premium	128
Exclusions for assured's deliberate act	129
Arbitration clauses	131
Void or voidable contracts	132
Unfair terms	133
CHAPTER 8 THIRD PARTY VICTIM'S RIGHT OF DIRECT ACTION AGAINST INSURERS	134
The regime under section 151 of the RTA 1988	134

DETAILED CONTENTS

Delivery of certificate	135
Liability covered by section 151(2)	136
Section 151(2)(a)	136
Section 151(2)(b)	136
Unlicensed driver exclusion – section 151(3)	137
Excluded liability – section 151(4)	137
Stolen or unlawfully taken	138
The state of mind under section 151(4)	139
Knew	139
Had reason to believe	140
Ex turpi causa	143
Policy restrictions and section 151	144
A claim through the assured or through section 151	145
Permitted exclusions	146
Monk v Warbey liability and section 145 of the RTA 1988	148
Right of recourse	151
Insurer's right of recourse against the owner who was a passenger	152
A judgment against an untraced driver and a section 151 claim	155
Notifying the insurer of the action against the assured	158
Timing	159
Formality and the content of the notice	160
Bringing of the proceedings	161
Is mere contact sufficient?	164
Waiver	165
Cancellation of the policy	167
Stay of execution	167
Seeking declaration to avoid the insurance contract	167
Motor Insurers' Bureau Articles of Association, Article 75	169
Notification of the third party claimant	172
Section 152 and EU law	173
Discretion on the court to set aside a default judgment	175
Primary direct actions against insurers under the EU law	175
CHAPTER 9 CREDIT HIRE AGREEMENTS	178
General principles of claiming damages when a vehicle is damaged	178
Cost of repair	178
Cost of hire	179
Car hire	180
Legal statutes of credit hire agreements	181
Champerty and public policy considerations	181
Contingent liability	182
Mitigation point	182
Calculating damages	184
Assessing the basic hire rate	185
Impecuniosity	186

DETAILED CONTENTS

Failure to mitigate the loss	189
Failure to examine the insurance documents	189
Proof of a need for a replacement vehicle	189
Offer for a replacement vehicle by the defendant's insurer	190
Delay in arranging a repair	191
Claimant's no claim discount	192
Where the claimant did not pay for the cost of hire himself	192
Fruit of the claimant's own insurance and insurer's subrogation	192
Insuring the credit hire charge	193
Ex turpi causa	194
Different forms of arrangement	195
CHAPTER 10 MOTOR INSURERS' BUREAU	197
The Motor Insurers' Bureau Agreements	197
Uninsured Drivers Agreement	199
Untraced Drivers Agreement	199
EU Directives	199
The legal status of the MIB Agreements	202
Is the MIB an emanation of the state?	203
Is the MIB independent of its members insurers?	205
Where the MIB is unnecessarily involved	206
Untraced or Uninsured Drivers Agreement	206
Uninsured Drivers Agreement	207
Scope	207
Relevant liability	207
Unsatisfied judgment	208
Authorities excluded	208
Other sources of recovery	209
The 2017 Supplementary Agreement	209
Passengers	210
Withdrawn consent	211
RTA s 151(8)	212
Where a claim is made by the dependants	212
Duties of the claimant	213
MIB's response	217
Untraced Drivers Agreement	217
Scope	217
Joint liability of identified and unidentified persons	218
Other sources of recovery	218
Damage to property	218
Passengers	219
Duties of the claimant	219
Compensation	219
Costs	221
Dispute resolution	222

DETAILED CONTENTS

Set-off	223
Enforcement of payment	224
The nature of claim against the MIB	224
Defences available to the MIB	225
Stolen vehicles	225
The meaning of "knew" in the context of the Directives	226
The law subsequent	228
Insurer's insolvency	230
Does the MIB protect the vehicle users?	234
Relying on a Directive in a claim against the MIB?	234

CHAPTER 11 INJURIES SUFFERED IN THE EU	237
Implementation of the Fourth Directive	239
Entitlement to compensation where the insurer is identified	240
Compensation body's response	241
Vehicle or insurer is not identified	242
Level of compensation – applicable law	243
Jurisdiction matters	246
Green Card	248

CHAPTER 12 THE PUBLIC POLICY DOCTRINE	252
Various applications of the doctrine	253
Limitations to the doctrine	255
Life insurance references	255
Careless driving and *ex turpi causa*	256
Joint illegal enterprise	257
Turpitude	258
Mental element	260
Causation	261
Turpitude not found – contributory negligence	264
The nature of claims against MIB and public policy	264
Claim against insurers under the 2010 Act	265
Vehicles used in the course of a crime	267

CHAPTER 13 INSURANCE OF AUTOMATED VEHICLES	268
Automated vehicles defined by the Act	269
Liability	270
Defences available for the insurer	272
Contributory negligence	272
Software	273
Subrogation	274
Motor Insurers' Bureau	274

Index	277

PREFACE

This book aims to explain the rules applicable to compulsory insurance covering civil liability for compensation of losses that arise out of traffic accidents. The recovery of the loss that is suffered by the person who is responsible for the accident (first party losses) falls outside the scope of the compulsory third party liability insurance and therefore is not covered by this work.

The interaction between different sources of law that establish the principles applicable to this type of insurance requires a very comprehensive understanding of the overall system as well as the role of each angle within it. This will involve not only separating the insurer's liability as against the victim but also as against the party to the contract of insurance or the person causing the damage. Moreover, the requirements for a compensation by the liability insurer in this context are to be analysed in a harmonised system which consists of domestic and European Union laws.

This book aims to explore this harmonised system and tries to present a methodology which will help the reader to follow how to assess a claim that arises out of a traffic accident. It explains the scope of such insurance obligation by focusing on whose responsibility it is to insure such liability, what the requirements are in terms of the content of the insurance policy, the restrictions to insurer's power either to exclude or limit liability, the influence of the relevant Directives of the European Union, the direct right of action by the victim of a traffic accident against the insurer and the role of the Motor Insurers' Bureau. The collaboration between a number of different statutory provisions and the court decisions inevitably led to a big number of cross references amongst different chapters.

The book also includes detailed discussions on what the law should be in order to provide consistency amongst the rules and principles identified, and how solutions to newly emerging issues can be found. As often happens, the principles applicable to compulsory motor third party liability insurance is ever evolving and fast developing. If and when the UK leaves the EU, it is yet to be observed to what extent the UK will still be bound by the rules developed by the EU law. This book analyses the law as applicable at time of writing whilst uncertainties over the scope of the withdrawal agreement are yet to be determined.

On 24 June 2019 the Secretary of State made the Motor Vehicles (Compulsory Insurance) (Miscellaneous Amendments) Regulations 2019 to come into force from 1 November 2019 (the 2019 Regulations). Since the 2019 Regulations were published at the very late stage of the publishing process of this book, it was not possible to modify the chapters that examined the areas that these Regulations covered. The most significant of the amendments introduced by the 2019 Regulations is modifying section 152(2) of the RTA

xv

1988 to the effect permitting the insurer to argue avoidance of the insurance contract towards the third party victim only if such avoidance took place "before the happening of the event which was the cause of the death or bodily injury or damage to property giving rise to the liability". In reading Chapter 8 especially, readers should take into account of the amendments made by these Regulations.

I would like to express my gratitude to Professor Robert Merkin for not only all of his constructive comments whilst writing this book but also his endless support throughout my career. The usual disclaimers apply.

Southampton
April 2019

TABLE OF CASES

Adams v Andrews [1964] 2 Lloyd's Rep 347 ....10.08
Adams v Commissioner of Police of the Metropolis [1980] RTR 289 ....3.53, 3.54, 3.56
Adams v Dunne [1978] RTR 281.. 2.23, 6.30
Ageas Insurance Ltd v Stoodley [2018] 4 WLUK 40..8.123
Agheampong v Allied Manufacturing (London) Ltd [2009] Lloyd's Rep IR 379....................9.53
Akers v Motor Insurers' Bureau [2003] Lloyd's Rep IR 427 .... 10.112, 10.113, 10.116, 10.117
Albert v Motor Insurers' Bureau [1972] AC 301 ....4.56
Alexander v Rolls Royce Motor Cars Ltd [1996] RTR 95 ....9.05, 9.18, 9.18
Allen v Mohammed [2017] Lloyd's Rep IR 73...........................6.23, 8.05, 8.58, 8.61, 8.62, 8.63,
                                                          8.64, 8.65, 8.68, 8.147, 8.149
Ambrosio Lavrador v Companhia de Seguros Fidelidade-Mundial SA (C-409/09) [2012]
    Lloyd's Rep IR 236...
Amicable Society for a Perpetual Assurance Office v Bolland (1830) IV Bligh,
    N. S. 194..12.02
Andersen v Hameed [2010] CSOH 99... 8.28, 8.41
Angelidaki v Organismos Nomarkhiaki Aftodiikisi Rethimnis (C-378/07) [2009] 3 CMLR 15.......1.34
Argo Systems FZE v Liberty Insurance Pte Ltd [2011] 2 Lloyd's Rep 61..............................8.119
Ashton v Turner [1981] QB 137 ....12.25
Aspen Insurance UK Ltd v Pectel Ltd [2009] Lloyd's Rep IR 440................................. 7.12, 7.42
Atkinson v The Newcastle and Gateshead Waterworks Company (1877) 2
    Ex. D. 44.. 6.05, 6.10
AXA Insurance UK Plc v Norwich Union Insurance Ltd [2008] Lloyd's
    Rep IR 122 .... 4.22, 4.23, 4.24, 4.25, 4.26, 4.37, 7.98
AXN v Worboys [2013] Lloyd's Rep IR 207............. 5.10, 5.11, 5.14, 5.20, 5.21, 5.22, 5.33, 7.60
B (A Minor) v Knight [1981] RTR 136.. 5.69, 5.71
Barrett v DPP [2010] RTR 2 ....3.63
Baugh v Crago [1975] RTR 453 ....2.10
Bayraz v Acromas Insurance Co County Court (Central London),
    6 February 2014 .... 8.147, 8.148
Becker v Finanzamt Munster-Innenstadt (8/81) [1982] 1 CMLR 499............. 1.36, 10.129, 10.130
Bee v Jenson (No 2) [2008] Lloyd's Rep IR 221 ....9.03, 9.18
Beechwood Birmingham Ltd v Hoyer Group UK Ltd [2011] QB 357.......... 9.17, 9.21, 9.39, 9.40
Bell Assurance Association v Licenses & General Insurance Corp & Guarantee
    Fund Ltd (1923) 17 Ll L Rep 100 .... 7.45, 7.49
Ben v Jenson (No.2) [2008] Lloyd's Rep IR 221.......................................9.10, 9.47, 9.48
Benjamin v Storr (1873–74) L.R. 9 C.P. 400 ....6.06
Bent v Highways & Utilities Construction Ltd [2010] EWCA Civ 292..................9.21, 9.27, 9.33

xvii

TABLE OF CASES

Beresford v Royal Insurance Co Ltd [1938] AC 586..............................12.06, 12.07, 12.11, 12.32
Biddle v Johnston [1965] 2 Lloyd's Rep 121...2.12, 7.75
Bluebon Ltd v Ageas (UK) Ltd (Formerly Fortis Insurance Ltd) [2017]
    EWHC 3301 (Comm)..7.22
Board Of Trade v Cayzer, Irvine And Co, Ltd [1927] AC 610...7.105
Borders v Swift [1957] Crim. L.R. 194...4.04
Boss v Kingston [1962] 2 Lloyd's Rep 431 ....3.23, 3.27, 3.28, 3.29, 3.31, 3.32, 3.33, 5.07
Bradburn v Great Western Railway Co (1874–75) L.R. 10 Ex. 1...9.03
Bretton v Hancock [2005] RTR 22 ....5.05, 5.76, 5.77, 6.03, 6.32, 6.33, 6.40, 6.42, 6.44, 6.45
Brewer v DPP [2005] RTR 5...3.64
Bright v Ashfold [1932] 2 KB 15 ....7.27
Bristol Alliance Ltd Partnership v Williams [2013]
    RTR 9..............2.12, 4.40, 6.23, 7.06, 7.52, 7.56, 7.97–7.102, 8.05, 8.09, 8.43, 8.47, 8.51–8.56, 8.90
British Waterways v Royal & Sun Alliance Insurance plc [2012] Lloyd's Rep IR 562..............5.74
British Westinghouse Electric and Manufacturing Co Ltd. v Underground
    Electric Railways Co of London Ltd [1912] AC 673 ....9.17
Brown v Roberts [1965] 1 QB 1..5.63, 5.66, 5.67
Browning v Phoenix Assurance Co Ltd [1960] 2 Lloyd's Rep 360............................ 3.01, 7.55
BTA Baltic Insurance Company' AS v Apdrošināšanas Nams' AS (C-648/17)
    ECLI:EU:C:2018:917 .... 5.08, 5.78, 5.79, 5.80, 13.16
Buchanan v Motor Insurers' Bureau [1954] 2 Lloyd's Rep 519...3.54
Bucknall v Jepson County Court (Leigh), 9 September 1998 [1998] CLY 1456 ....9.38
Bugge v Taylor [1941] 1 KB 198 ....3.53
Burdis v Livsey [2003] RTR 3...9.03
Burns v Currell [1963] 2 QB 433 ....3.42
Byrne v Motor Insurers' Bureau [2009] QB 66..........................1.26–1.32, 10.23, 10.26, 10.132
C.A. Silverton v Goodall [1997] PIQR P451 ....10.24
Commission of the European Communities v Italy C-518/06) [2009] 3 CMLR 22...................1.16
Cambridge v Motor Insurers' Bureau [1998] RTR 365...10.59
Cameron v Hussain [2017] EWCA Civ 366..8.124, 8.137, 8.140
Cameron v Liverpool Victoria Insurance Co Ltd [2019] UKSC 6............. 5.07, 6.23, 7.50, 8.137
Candolin v Vahinkovakuu- tusosakeyhtio Pohjola (C-537/03) [2006] Lloyd's
    Rep IR 209 ....7.11, 7.57, 7.87, 7.90, 8.73
Caple v Sewell [2002] Lloyd's Rep IR 627.. 7.61, 7.67
Carnill v Rowland [1953] 1 WLR 380 ....2.28
Carswell v Secretary of State for Transport [2011] Lloyd's Rep IR 644...... 1.05, 1.26, 1.28, 1.29,
    10.01, 10.02, 10.09, 10.18, 10.19, 10.28, 10.84, 10.85, 10.91
Ceylon Motor Insurance Association Ltd v Thambugala [1953] AC 584.........8.102, 8.105, 8.109
Charlton v Fisher [2002] QB 578..2.12, 3.63, 4.62, 8.43, 8.44, 8.46,
    8.48, 8.49, 8.52, 10.97, 12.33, 12.34
Chief Constable of Avon and Somerset v F [1987] 1 All ER 318...3.45
Churchill Insurance Co Ltd v Wilkinson (C-442/10) [2012] Lloyd's Rep IR 544 ....7.57
Churchill Insurance Co Ltd v Fitzgerald [2013] Lloyd's
    Rep IR 137 ....1.34, 1.35, 7.85, 8.71, 8.75–8.80
Churchill Insurance Co Ltd v Wilkinson (C-442/10) [2012] Lloyd's Rep IR 544 ....1.11,
    7.49, 7.87, 7.90, 7.92, 7.106, 8.14,
    8.32, 8.73, 8.75, 8.77, 8.78, 8.79, 10.98
Clark v Farley [2018] EWHC 1007 (QB)..12.16, 12.20, 12.27
Clarke v Clarke [2012] EWHC 2118 (QB).. 3.70, 3.71, 12.28, 12.29
Clarke v Kato [1999] RTR 153.. 3.53, 3.58, 3.60, 3.64, 3.69

xviii

TABLE OF CASES

Clarke v Vedel [1979] RTR 26...10.30
Cleaver v Mutual Reserve Fund Life Association [1892]
   1 QB 147 .... 12.05, 12.06, 12.09, 12.09, 12.11
Clelland v Quinn Direct 2011 G.W.D. 2–91... 9.26, 9.33
Cobb v Williams [1973] RTR 113... 5.09, 5.63, 6.18, 8.73
Coles v Hetherton [2015] RTR 7 ....9.01, 9.02, 9.04, 9.06, 9.47, 9.48
Colley v Shuker [2019] EWHC 781 (QB)...8.141,10.312
Comitato di Coordinamento per la Difesa della Cava v Regions Lombardia (C-236/92) [1994]
   Env LR 281 ....1.36
Commission of the European Communities v Italy (C-518/06) [2009] 3 CMLR 22 .... 1.16, 2.29
Compania Maritima San Basilio SA v Oceanus Mutual Underwriting Association
   (Bermuda) Ltd [1977] QB 49, ...10.106
Contingency Insurance Co Ltd v Lyons (1939) 65 Ll L Rep 53.....................................8.124
Cooper v Motor Insurers' Bureau [1983] RTR 412 affirmed by the Court of Appeal [1985]
   QB 575... 4.55, 4.59, 7.86, 10.35, 10.62
Copley v Lawn [2009] Lloyd's Rep IR 496 ....9.03, 9.41, 9.43
Corfield v Groves [1950] 1 All ER 488...................................... 6.14, 6.15, 6.25, 6.38, 6.49
Couch v Steel (1854) 3 El. & Bl. 402 .... 6.04, 6.05
Coward v Motor Insurers' Bureau [1963] 1 QB 259 ....10.19
Cox v White [1976] RTR 248 .... 3.55, 3.56
Cross v British Oak Insurance Company, Ltd [1938] 2 KB 167...................................8.100
Croxford v Universal Insurance Co Ltd [1936] 2 KB 253 ....8.124
Csonka v Magyar Allam (C-409/11) [2014] 1
   CMLR 14..............................1.16, 2.07, 7.49, 10.16, 10.119, 10.124, 10.125, 10.126, 10.127
Cunigunda, In the Estate of [1911] P 108.................................... 12.02, 12.06, 12.11
Daley v Hargreaves [1961] 1 WLR 487 .... 3.42, 3.43
Daniels v Vaux [1938] 2 KB 203.. 6.17, 6.51
Dansk Industri (DI) v Rasmussen's Estate (C-441/14) [2016] 3 CMLR 27 ....1.26
Davey v Towle [1973] RTR 328 ....2.11
Dawsons v Bonnin [1922] 2 AC 413 ....7.20
Delaney v Pickett [2013] Lloyd's Rep IR 24 .... 12.23, 12.24
Delaney v Secretary of State for Transport [2015] Lloyd's Rep IR 441 .... 7.77, 10.98, 12.35, 12.36
Delgado Mendes v Credito Agricola Seguros – Companhia de Seguros de Ramos Reais SA
   (C-503/16) [2018] Lloyd's Rep IR 16...7.92
Department of Trade and Industry v St. Christopher Motorists' Association Ltd [1974]
   1 WLR 99..9.56
Desouza v Waterlow [1999] RTR 71 ....8.95, 8.96, 8.98, 8.104, 8.108, 8.109
Digby v General Accident Fire and Life Assurance Corp Ltd [1943] AC 121................. 4.35, 4.57
Dimond v Lovell [2002] 1 AC 384..9.01, 9.02, 9.05, 9.08, 9.21, 9.23,
                                9.24, 9.26, 9.28, 9.34, 9.35, 9.49
Director of Public Prosecutions v Fisher [1992] RTR 93 ....2.08, 3.06, 3.08
Director of Public Prosecutions v Heritage [2002] EWHC 2139 (Admin)...............................2.08
Director of Public Prosecutions v Kavaz [1999] RTR 40 ....2.11
Dodson v Peter H Dodson Insurance Services [2001]
   Lloyd's Rep IR 278................................ 3.23, 3.28, 3.29, 3.30, 3.31, 3.32, 3.33
Doe d. Murray v Bridges (1831) 1 B. & Ad. 847...6.05
DPP v Saddington [2001] RTR 15 .... 3.44, 3.42
Drake Insurance Plc v Provident Insurance Plc [2004] QB 601.....................................3.34
Drake Insurance Plc, Re [2001] Lloyd's Rep IR 643..8.120
Drozdovs v Baltikums AAS [2014] RTR 14 .... 1.23, 4.48, 4.52, 4.53, 4.54

xix

TABLE OF CASES

Dunlop Pneumatic Tyre Co Ltd v Selfridge & Co Ltd [1915] AC 847......................3.17

Dunthorne v Bentley [1996] RTR 428.................5.09, 5.10, 5.11, 5.12, 5.13, 5.14, 5.28

Durrant v MacLaren [1956] 2 Lloyd's Rep 70..2.23, 6.30, 8.92

Eagle Star Insurance Co Ltd v Cresswell [2004] Lloyd's Rep IR 537......................7.12

Eagle Star Insurance Co Ltd v Provincial Insurance [1994] 1 AC 130.....................3.34

EB Central Services Ltd v Revenue and Customs Commissioners [2008] STC 2209..............1.35

Eden v Mitchell [1975] RTR 425..5.41, 5.61

Elizabeth v Motor Insurers' Bureau [1981] RTR 405.....................................10.81

Elliot v Grey [1960] 1 QB 367.......5.33, 5.35, 5.36, 5.43, 5.44, 5.48, 5.54, 5.55, 5.56, 5.58, 5.60

English v Western [1940] 2 KB 156...7.75

Evans v Lewis [1964] 1 Lloyd's Rep 258...2.24

Evans v Secretary of State for the Environment, Transport and the Regions (C-63/01) [2004]
RTR 32.............................. 1.29, 10.09, 10.20, 10.80, 10.84, 10.87, 10.92

Evans v TNT Logistics Ltd [2007] Lloyd's Rep IR 708....................................9.17

Everson v Flurry [1999] CLY 3411.............................. 9.21, 9.44, 9.54, 9.56

Faccini Dori v Recreb Srl (C-91/92) [1994] ECR I-3325.................................1.26

Farah v Abdullahi [2018] EWHC 738 (QB)...............................8.12, 8.137, 8.139

Farr v Motor Traders' Mutual Insurance Society [1920] 3 KB 669.............7.22, 7.23, 7.24

Farrell v Whitty (C-356/05) [2007] Lloyd's Rep IR 525.........1.17, 1.26, 1.36, 7.08, 10.25, 10.26,
10.129, 10.130, 10.132, 10.132

FBTO Shadeverzekenngen NV v Odenbreit (C-463/06) [2008] Lloyd's Rep IR 354..............11.40

Ferrymasters Ltd v Adams [1980] RTR 139..2.10

Fidelidade-Companhia de Seguros SA v Caisse Suisse de Compensation (C-287/16) [2017]
RTR 26............................ 7.57, 7.106, 7.107, 7.108, 8.136, 8.137, 8.138, 8.139, 8.141, 10.98

Fleming (t/a Bodycraft) v Customs and Excise Commissioners [2008] 1 CMLR 48..............1.35

Fleming v M'Gillivray 1945 SLT 301..6.53

Foster v British Gas Plc (C-188/89) [1991] 1 QB 405............................ 10.21, 10.132

Francovich v Italy Case C-6/90, [1991] ECR I-537............................. 1.26, 12.36

Freshwater v Western Australian Assurance Co Ltd [1933] 1 KB 515......................7.104

Friends Provident Life & Pensions Ltd v Sirius International Insurance Corp [2005]
2 Lloyd's Rep 517...7.12

Fundo de Garantia Automovel v Juliana (C-80/17) EU:C:2018:661......... 3.68, 5.29, 5.30, 10.16, 10.34

Gale v Motor Union Insurance Co Ltd [1928] 1 KB 35................... 3.35, 3.36, 3.38, 7.42

Gardner & Co Ltd v Cone [1928] Ch. 955..1.09

Gardner v Moore [1984] AC 548.....................4.61, 7.102, 8.46, 8.48, 8.52, 8.56,
12.01, 12.02, 12.06, 12.12, 12.14, 12.30–12.33

GFP Units v Monksfield [1972] 2 Lloyd's Rep 79...7.75

Ghaidan v Godin-Mendoza [2004] 2 AC 557..1.35

Giles v Thompson [1994] 1 AC 142.............................9.07, 9.11, 9.13, 9.14

Glenfinlas, The (Note) [1918] P 363...9.03

Golden Strait Corp v Nippon Yusen Kubishika Kaisha (The Golden Victory) [2007]
2 AC 353...9.10

Golding v London & Edinburgh Insurance Co Ltd (1932) 43 Ll L Rep 487..................7.104

Goodbarne v Buck [1940] 1 KB 771........................... 3.09, 6.27, 6.28, 6.29

Gorris v Scott (1873–74) L.R. 9 Ex. 125...6.10

Gosling v Howard [1975] RTR 429.............................5.02, 5.36, 5.37

Granada UK Rental & Retail v SPN Fareway [1995] CLY 3728.............................10.29

Gray v Blackmore [1934] 1 KB 95..2.12

Gray v Commissioner of Police of the Metropolis [2016] EWCA Civ 1360..................2.16

Gray v Thames Trains Ltd [2009] 1 AC 1339.............. 12.02, 12.03, 12.04, 12.08, 12.22

TABLE OF CASES

Greenlees v Allianz Insurance [2011] CSOH number 173..9.26
Griffin v Squires [1958] 1 WLR 1106 ....3.56
Guardian Assurance Co Ltd v Sutherland (1939) 63 Ll L Rep 220..8.124
Gurtner v Circuit [1968] 2 QB 587... 10.18, 10.19, 10.61, 10.95
Hall (Deceased), Re [1914] P 1 .... 12.02, 12.10, 12.11
Harbutt's "Plasticine" Ltd v Wayne Tank and Pump Co Ltd [1970] 1 QB 447 ....9.32
Hardy v Motor Insurers' Bureau [1964] 2 QB 745 .... 4.60–4.62, 7.96, 7.102, 8.45–8.48,
        8.52, 8.56, 10.18, 10.19, 10.36, 10.97, 12.02, 12.05, 12.06, 12.30, 12.32–12.34
Harrington v Link Motor Policies at Lloyd's [1989] RTR 345 ....8.95, 8.96, 8.97, 8.101–8.111
Harrington Motor Co Ltd Ex p. Chaplin, Re (1927–28) 29 Ll L Rep 102...................................1.08
Harrison v Hill 1932 J.C. 13 ....1.11, 3.53, 3.54, 3.55
Harvey v Motor Insurers' Bureau Queen's Bench Division (Mercantile Court)
    (Manchester), 21 December 2011 ....10.90
Hatton v Hall [1997] RTR 212.. 5.63, 5.71, 5.73, 5.74, 5.75
Haven Insurance Co Ltd v EUI Ltd (t/a Elephant Insurance) [2018] EWCA Civ 2494 ....8.132
Heap-Hammond v TNT UK Ltd County Court (Yeovil), 15 June 2007....................................9.44
Henderson v Dorset Healthcare University NHS Foundation Trust [2018] 3 WLR 1651........12.08
Herbert v Railway Passengers Assurance Co (1938) 60 Ll L
    Rep 143...2.04, 7.43, 8.94, 8.101, 8.104, 8.112, 8.113
Hewer v Cutler [1974] RTR 155 .... 5.02, 5.38, 5.40–5.45, 5.48, 5.54
Hewison v Meridian Shipping Services Pte Ltd [2003] PIQR p17....................................9.52
Hofsoe v LVM Landwirtschaftlicher Versicherungsverein Munster AG (C-106/17) [2018]
    Lloyd's Rep IR 608...11.41
Holliday v Henry [1974] RTR 101..3.51
Hood's Trustees v Southern Union General Insurance Co of Australasia Ltd (1928)
    31 Ll L Rep 23..1.08
Horton v Sadler [2007] 1 AC 307...10.59
Houghton v Scholfield [1973] RTR 239 ....3.53
Houghton v Trafalgar Insurance Co Ltd [1954] 1 QB 247................................ 7.34, 7.35
Howe v Motor Insurers' Bureau [2017] Lloyd's Rep IR 576 .... 11.25, 11.35
ICI Plc v Colmer (Inspector of Taxes 1.35
Inman v Kenny [2001] EWCA Civ 35.. 3.69, 3.71
Investors Compensation Scheme Ltd v West Bromwich Building Society (No.1)
    [1998] 1 WLR 896...3.30
Irving v Morgan Sindall PLC [2018] EWHC 1147 (QB) 9.14, 9.32
Island Records Ltd v Corkindale [1978] Ch. 122...6.04
JA Chapman & Co Ltd (In Liquidation) v Kadirga Denizcilik ve Ticaret AS [1998]
    Lloyd's Rep IR 377...3.32
Jacobs v Motor Insurers' Bureau [2011] Lloyd's Rep IR 355 ......10.08, 10.98, 11.25, 11.30, 11.42
Jacques v Harrison (1884) 12 QBD 165...8.142
James & Son v Smee [1955] 1 QB 78...3.02, 3.04, 3.06
James v British General Insurance Co Ltd [1927] 2 KB 311 .... 12.02, 12.05, 12.07, 12.14
John T Ellis Ltd v Hinds [1947] KB 475 .... 4.31, 4.33, 5.05, 5.07
John v Humphreys [1955] 1 WLR 325..2.11
Jones v Chief Constable of Bedfordshire [1987] RTR 332.......................................2.33
Jones v Welsh Insurance Corp Ltd (1937) 59 Ll L Rep 13 ....7.62, 7.68, 10.01
Joyce v O'Brien [2013] Lloyd's Rep IR 523...12.24
JRM (Plant) v Hodgson [1960] 1 Lloyd's Rep 538 ....2.27
Jureidini v National British & Irish Millers Insurance Co Ltd [1915] AC 499.......................7.104
Kampelmann v Landschaftsverband Westfalen-Lippe (C253/96) [1998] 2 CMLR 131 ....1.36

xxi

TABLE OF CASES

Keeley v Pashen [2005] Lloyd's Rep IR 289 .... 4.48, 7.60, 7.71, 8.42
Kelly v Cornhill Insurance Co. Ltd. [1964] 1 WLR 158 ....3.09
Kelly v Mackle [2009] NIQB 39 .... 9.10, 9.18, 9.24, 9.28
Kerridge v Rush [1952] 2 Lloyd's Rep 305 ....2.27
Kosmar Villa Holidays Plc v Trustees of Syndicate 1243 [2008] Lloyd's Rep IR 489. ....8.117
Lagden v O'Connor [2004] 1 AC 1067 .... 9.06, 9.07, 9.10, 9.15, 9.16, 9.18, 9.24, 9.28–9.35
Langman v Valentine [1952] 2 All ER 803 ....3.05
Lauri v Renad [1892] 3 Ch. 402 ....1.09
Law Guarantee Trust & Accident Society Ltd, Re [1914] 2 Ch. 617 ....1.08
Leathley v Drummond [1972] RTR 293 .... 2.11, 4.04
Leathley v Tatton [1980] RTR 21 .... 5.68, 5.71
Lees v Motor Insurers' Bureau [1952] 2 Lloyd's Rep 210 ....5.07, 4.18, 4.34
Legal and General Assurance Society Ltd. v Drake Insurance Co. Ltd. [1992] QB 887 .... 3.34, 3.39
Lewington v Motor Insurers' Bureau [2018]
    RTR 18 ....1.34, 1.35, 3.40, 3.42, 3.44, 3.48, 3.49, 7.77, 7.103
Lewis v Tindale [2018] EWHC 2376 (QB) 1.34, 3.66, 3.71, 5.16, 10.26, 10.130–10.133
Liesbosch, The [1933] AC 449 ....9.45
Limbrick v French [1993] PIQR 121 .... 2.10, 4.59
Lister v Romford Ice and Cold Storage Co Ltd [1957] AC 555 ....4.38
Litaksa Uab v Bta Insurance Co Se (C-556/13) [2015] RTR 21 ....7.95
Litster v Forth Dry Dock & Engineering Co Ltd [1990] 1 AC 546 .... 1.35, 10.99
Livingstone v Rawyards Coal Co (1880) 5 App. Cas. 25 ....9.01
Lloyd v Singleton [1953] 1 QB 357 .... 3.09, 6.29
Lloyd-Wolper v Moore [2004] RTR 30 ....2.10, 3.07, 3.14
London Corporation, The [1935] P 70 ....9.03
Lonrho Ltd v Shell Petroleum Co Ltd (No.2) [1982] AC 173 ....6.06
Louden v British Merchants Insurance Co [1961] 1 Lloyd's Rep 154 ....7.30
Lyons v May [1948] 2 All ER 1062 .... 2.08, 2.09
MacDonald v Carmichael 1941 J.C. 27 ....3.40
MacDonald v Carmichael 1953 SLT (Sh. Ct.) 117 ....3.43
Maden v Haller [2009] Lloyd's Rep IR 496 ....9.41
Maher v Groupama Grand Est [2010] Lloyd's Rep IR 543 ....11.40
Manifest Shipping Co Ltd v Uni-Polaris Insurance Co Ltd (The Star Sea) [2003]
    1 AC 469 ....10.110
Maple Leaf Macro Volatility Master Fund v Rouvroy [2009] 1 Lloyd's Rep 475 ....9.10
Marleasing SA v La Comercial Internacional de Alimentación SA (C-106/89) [1990]
    ECR I-4135 .... 1.34, 7.97, 8.32, 10.99, 11.25
Marsh v Moores [1949] 2 KB 208 ....3.05, 4.31, 5.07
Marshall v Southampton and South West Hampshire Area Health Authority (Teaching)
    (C-152/84); [1986] ECR 723 ....1.26
Martin v Dean [1971] 2 QB 208 ....6.23, 6.25, 6.55
Martindale v Duncan [1973] 1 Lloyd's Rep 558 .... 9.45, 9.46
Mastin v Blanchard [1995] CLY 3727 ....10.29
May v DPP [2005] EWHC 1280 (admin) 3.63
McAll v Brooks [1984] RTR 99 .... 9.17, 9.54
McBlain v Dolan 1998 SLT 512 ....8.98, 8.103, 8.107, 8.114, 8.115, 8.119, 8.123
McBride v UK Insurance Ltd [2017] Lloyd's Rep IR 352 ....9.24, 9.25, 9.26
McCall v Poulton [2009] Lloyd's Rep IR 45 ....1.26
McCormick v National Motor and Accident Insurance Union Ltd (1934) 49 Ll L Rep 361 ....3.16
McCracken v Smith [2016] Lloyd's Rep IR 171 .... 12.03, 12.16–12.20, 12.25, 12.29

xxii

TABLE OF CASES

McGoona v Motor Insurers' Bureau [1969] 2 Lloyd's Rep 34 .... 7.65, 7.74, 8.95, 8.96, 8.102
McGurk and Dale v Coster 22 March 1995 [1995] CLY 2912 .... 3.65
McHugh v Okai-Koi [2017] EWHC 1376 .... 12.27
McKnight v Davies [1974] RTR 4 .... 8.25, 8.26
McLeod (or Houston) v Buchanan [1940] 2 All ER 179 .... 2.08, 2.09, 3.02, 3.04, 6.08
McMinn v McMinn [2006] RTR 33 .... 8.10, 8.20–8.28, 8.32–8.39
Mendes Ferreira v Companhia de Seguros Mundial Confiança SA (C-348/98)
  ECLI:EU:C:2000:442 .... 7.10, 7.84
Merchants & Manufacturers Insurance Co Ltd v Hunt (Charles & John (An Infant)) [1941]
  1 KB 295 .... 8.122, 8.123, 8.124, 8.134
Mighell v Reading [1999] Lloyd's Rep IR 30 .... 10.23, 10.26
Miller v Hales [2007] Lloyd's Rep IR 54 .... 2.33, 4.18, 4.22, 4.23, 4.27, 4.28
Mills v Toner [1995] CLY 3725 .... 10.29
Milton Keynes BC v Nulty [2013] Lloyd's Rep IR 243 .... 7.12
MJ Harrington Syndicate 2000 v Axa Oyak Sigorta AS [2007] Lloyd's Rep IR 60 .... 7.12
Monk v Warbey [1935] 1 KB 75 .... 3.23, 5.77, 5.79, 6.01, 6.03, 6.07–6.16, 6.22, 6.24, 6.25,
                         6.28, 6.30–6.38, 6.40, 6.41, 6.44, 6.48–6.55, 8.57, 8.62–8.66, 8.82
Moore v Secretary of State for Transport [2007] PIQR p24 .... 1.33
Moreno v Motor Insurers' Bureau [2017] Lloyd's Rep IR 99 .... 10.128, 11.13, 11.24, 11.25,
                         11.29, 11.30, 11.31, 11.32, 11.33, 11.34
Morris v Ford Motor Co [1973] QB 792 .... 4.38, 4.39
Morris v Williams (1951) 50 LGr 308 .... 2.08
Motor & General Insurance Co. Ltd. v Cox [1990] 1 WLR 1443 .... 8.07
Motor Insurers' Bureau v Lewis [2019] EWCA Civ 909 .... 3.66, 5.16, 10.24, 10.26, 10.130
Motor Oil Hellas (Corinth) Refineries SA v Shipping Corp of India (The Kanchenjunga)
  [1990] 1 Lloyd's Rep 391 .... 8.117
Mumford v Hardy [1956] 1 WLR 163 .... 2.10
Napthen v Place [1970] RTR 248 .... 5.05
National Farmers Union Mutual Insurance Society Ltd v Tully 1935 SLT 574 .... 8.123, 8.124
Nawaz v Crowe Insurance Group [2003] RTR 29 .... 8.95, 8.101, 8.112, 8.113, 8.142
Neto de Sousa v Portugal (C-506/16) EU:C:2017:642; [2018] Lloyd's Rep IR 118 .... 1.17, 7.83,
                         8.74, 8.76
Newbury v Davis [1974] RTR 367 .... 3.06, 7.109
Nichol v Leach [1972] RTR 476 .... 5.50, 5.51, 5.59
Norman v Aziz [2000] RTR 107 .... 6.41, 6.52, 6.53
Nunez Torreiro v AIG Europe Ltd (C-334/16) [2018] Lloyd's Rep IR 418 .... 3.46, 3.66,
                         3.67, 5.26, 5.78, 5.79, 10.130
NUT v St Mary's Church [1996] T.L.R. 726. 16 December 1996 .... 10.24
O'Brien v Anderton [1979] RTR 388 .... 3.42
O'Mahony v Joliffe [1999] RTR 245 .... 5.73, 5.74, 5.75
Ocean Accident & Guarantee Corp Ltd v Cole [1932] 2 KB 100 .... 2.18
Oxford v Austin [1981] RTR 416 .... 3.55, 3.57, 3.65
Parry v Cleaver [1970] AC 1 .... 9.03, 9.47
Passmoor v Gibbons [1979] RTR 53 .... 4.31
Passmore v Vulcan Boiler & General Insurance Co Ltd (1936) 54 Ll L
  Rep 92 .... 7.54, 7.64, 7.65, 7.66, 7.69
Patel v London Transport Executive [1981] RTR 29 .... 7.53, 12.07, 12.08
Patel v Mizra [2017] AC 467 .... 12.7, 12.8, 12.27,
Pattni v First Leicester Buses Ltd [2012] Lloyd's Rep IR 577 .... 9.20, 9.22, 9.34
Payzu Ltd v Saunders [1919] 2 KB 581 .... 9.17

xxiii

TABLE OF CASES

Pearl Assurance Plc v Kavanagh [2001] CLY 3832 .... 3.07, 7.109

Percy v Smith [1986] RTR 252 ....3.42

Perehenic v Deboa Structuring County Court (Banbury), 7 July 1998 [1998]
CLY 1467 .... 9.07, 9.46

Persson v London Country Buses [1974] 1 Lloyd's Rep 415 .... 10.19, 10.92

Peters v General Accident Fire & Life Assurance Corp Ltd (1937) 59 Ll L Rep 148 ....10.01

Peters v General Accident Fire & Life Assurance Corp Ltd (1938) 60 Ll L Rep 311...............3.24

Petillo v Unipol Assicurazioni SpA (C-371/12) [2014] 3 CMLR 1 .... 1.16, 1.17, 4.48, 4.50, 4.51

Pfeiffer v Deutsches Rotes Kreuz Kreisverband Waldshut eV (Joined Cases C-397/01 to
C-403/01) [2004] ECR I-8835 ....1.26

Philcox v Carberry [1960] Crim. L.R. 563 ....2.11

Phillips v Rafiq [2007] 1 WLR 1351 ....10.53

Pickett v Roberts [2004] RTR 28 .... 10.47, 10.51

Pickstone v Freemans Plc [1989] AC 6 ....1.35

Pitts v Hunt [1991] 1 QB 24 .... 12.17, 12.22, 12.25

Porter v Addo [1978] 2 Lloyd's Rep 463 ....10.48

Pratt v Patrick [1924] 1 KB 488 ....5.63, 6.18, 8.73

Provincial Insurance Co Ltd v Morgan & Foxon [1933] AC 240....................................7.25

Prudential Insurance Co v Inland Revenue Commissioners [1904] 2 KB 658 .... 9.55, 9.56

Pryor v Chief Constable of Greater Manchester Police [2011] RTR 33 .... 2.15, 2.16

Pumbien v Vines [1996] RTR 37 .... 5.02, 5.04, 5.36, 5.42, 5.45, 5.52, 5.53, 5.54, 5.56, 5.58, 5.59

Quinn v Leathem [1901] AC 495..12.05

R v Baldessare (1931) 22 Cr App R 70..12.20

R v Secretary of State for Transport ex parte National Insurance Guarantee Corporation
[1996] C.O.D. 425; Times, June 3, 1996 ....4.23

R v Secretary of State for Transport, ex parte Factortame (No. 5) [2000]
1 AC 524... 1.26, 1.29, 1.32

R v Spence [1999] RTR 353 ....3.63

R&S Pilling (t/a Phoenix Engineering) v UK Insurance Ltd [2019]
UKSC 16... 2.12, 3.72, 5.04, 5.05, 5.09, 5.28, 5.34, 8.05

R (on the application of IDT Card Services Ireland Ltd) v Customs and Excise
Commissioners [2006] STC 1252..1.35

R v Phipps (Owen Roger) [1970] RTR 209 ....8.25

Rainy Sky SA v Kookmin Bank [2012] 1 Lloyd's Rep 34 ....3.30

Randall v Motor Insurers' Bureau [1968] 1 WLR 1900 ....3.52

Re v Jogee [2016] UKSC 8.. 12.15, 12.20, 12.21

Reay v Young [1949] 1 All ER 1102..3.05

Rendlesham v Dunne [1964] 1 Lloyd's Rep 192 ....7.39

Revill v Newberry [1996] 1 All ER 291...12.25

Richards v Cox [1943] 1 KB 139 ....4.34

Richards v Port of Manchester Insurance Co Ltd (1934) 50 Ll L Rep 132 .... 2.10, 2.24

Richardson v Baker [1976] RTR 56... 4.31, 4.32, 4.35, 4.36

Richardson v Pitt-Stanley [1995] QB 123 ....6.40

Ricketts v Thomas Tilling Ltd [1915] 1 KB 644 ....5.63

RoadPeace v Secretary of State for Transport [2018]
1 WLR 1293 ....7.57, 7.54, 8.90, 8.147, 8.151, 10.23

Rodrigues de Andrade v Proenca Salvador (C-514/16) [2018] Lloyd's
Rep IR 164 .... 1.16, 3.46, 3.66, 5.08, 5.22–5.26, 5.29, 5.31–5.33, 5.78, 10.130

Rogerson v Scottish Automobile & General Insurance Co. (1931) 41 Ll L Rep 1 .... 3.25, 3.26

Ross Hillman Ltd. v Bond [1974] QB 435.. 3.04, 3.06

xxiv

TABLE OF CASES

Ruiz Bernaldez (C-129/94) [1996] All ER (EC) 741 .... 1.16, 7.57, 7.77, 7.78, 7.80, 7.81, 7.100
Ryan Brain v Yorkshire Rider Ltd [2007] Lloyd's Rep IR 564 .... 9.07, 9.20, 9.21
Sahin v Havard [2017] Lloyd's Rep
    IR 110 .... 3.09, 6.03, 6.11, 6.19, 6.21, 6.23, 8.65–8.68, 8.81, 8.82
Sayce v TNT (UK) Ltd [2012] Lloyd's Rep IR 183 .... 9.41, 9.43
Scotland Tudhope v Every 1977 SLT 2 .... 5.02
Scott v Avery (1856) 5 H.L. Cas 811 .... 7.104
Seddon v Binions [1978] RTR 163 .... 7.55, 7.58, 7.59, 7.61, 7.66, 7.68, 7.69
Severn Trent Water v Williams [1995] CLY 3724 .... 10.29
Shave v Rosner [1954] 2 QB 113 .... 3.01, 3.04, 3.09
Sheldon Deliveries Ltd v Willis [1972] RTR 217 .... 3.06
Silverton v Goodall [1997] PIQR p451 .... 10.19, 10.59, 10.62, 10.63
Singh v Rathour [1988] RTR 324 .... 3.01, 7.55
Singh v Solihull Metropolitan Borough Council [2007] 2 CMLR 1279 .... 7.98
Singh v Yaqubi [2013] Lloyd's Rep IR 398 .... 9.07, 9.18
Slater v Buckinghamshire CC (C-162/13) [2015] Lloyd's Rep IR 142 .... 5.15
Smith v Relph [1963] 2 Lloyd's Rep 439 .... 3.11
Sobrany v UAB Transtira [2016] Lloyd's Rep IR 266 .... 9.08, 9.50, 9.51
Sotiros Shipping Inc and Aeco Maritime SA v Sameiet Solholt (The "Solholt") [1983]
    1 Ll. rep. 605 .... 9.17
South Staffordshire Tramways Co Ltd v Sickness & Accident Assurance Association Ltd
    [1891] 1 QB 402 .... 1.03
Spence v United Taxis County Court (Newcastle upon Tyne), 20 May 1997 [1998]
    CLY 1465 .... 9.38
St Helen's Colliery Co v Hewitson [1924] AC 59 .... 4.17
Starkey v Hall (1936) 55 Ll L Rep 24 .... 2.14
Stebbing v Liverpool & London & Globe Insurance Co [1917] 2 KB 433 .... 7.103
Stevens v Equity Syndicate Management Ltd [2015] RTR 24 .... 9.08, 9.20, 9.25, 9.26
Stevens v Jeacocke [1848] 11 QB 731 .... 6.04
Stinton v Stinton [1995] RTR 167 .... 5.63, 5.65, 5.70, 5.71, 5.74, 8.99, 8.103
Stych v Dibble [2013] Lloyd's Rep IR 80 .... 8.09, 8.15, 8.20–8.29, 8.32–8.39
Tapsell v Maslen [1967] Crim. L.R. 53; (1966) 110 S.J. 853 .... 2.08
Tattersall v Drysdale [1935] 2 KB 174 .... 1.11, 2.13, 3.15, 3.21, 3.27, 5.07
Telford and Wrekin BC v Ahmed [2006] EWHC 1748 (admin) 2.27
Thomas v Hooper [1996] RTR 37 .... 5.02, 5.36, 5.43, 5.46–5.55, 5.59, 5.60
Thompson v Lodwick [1983] RTR 76 .... 3.10
Tinline v White Cross Insurance Association Ltd [1921] 3 KB 327 .... 12.05, 12.14
Tinsley v Milligan [1994] 1 AC 340 .... 12.08
Total Graphics Ltd v A.G.F. Insur- ance Ltd [1997] 1 Lloyd's rep 599 .... 12.06
Tremelling v Martin [1971] RTR 196 .... 2.13
Tudhope v Every 1977 SLT 2 .... 5.36, 5.61
Turnbull v MNT Transport (2006) Ltd [2010] CSOH 163 .... 3.36, 3.38, 5.05, 5.39, 5.60
Tustin v Arnold (1915) 84 LJKB 2214 .... 7.46
Tweddle v Atkinson (1861) 1 B. & S. 393 .... 3.17
UK Insurance Ltd v R&S Pilling T/AS Phoenix Engineering [2019] UKSC 16 .... 5.27
Ul-Haq v CEVA logistics Ltd [2012] CLY 1903 .... 7.53
Umerji v Khan [2014] RTR 23 .... 9.15, 9.17
Vandepitte v Preferred Accident Insurance Corporation of New York [1933] AC 70 ...... 3.17, 3.19
Vandyke v Fender [1970] RTR 236 .... 4.17, 4.18
Vellino v Chief Constable of Greater Manchester [2002] 1 WLR 218 .... 12.02, 12.22

TABLE OF CASES

Verelst's Administratrix v Motor Union Insurance Co Ltd [1925] 2 KB 137 .... 7.42, 7.44

Vnuk v Zavarovalnica Triglav dd (C-162/13) [2015] Lloyd's Rep
   IR 142 .... 3.49, 3.66, 3.67, 5.09, 5.16, 5.24, 5.26, 5.27, 5.79, 7.58, 10.130

Vodafone 2 v The Commissioners for Her Majesty's Revenue & Customs [2010] Ch. 77 .... 1.35

W v Veolia Environmental Services (UK plc) [2012] Lloyd's Rep IR 419 .... 9.21, 9.51

Wake v Wylie [2001] RTR 20 .... 8.13, 8.95, 8.101, 8.104, 8.109, 8.110, 8.115, 8.119

Wakeling v Harrington [2007] EWCh 1184 (Ch) 9.14

Wallett v Vickers [2018] EWHC 3088 (QB) 12.12, 12.15, 12.17, 12.19, 12.21, 12.29

Ward v British Oak Insurance Co Ltd [1932] 1 KB 392 .... 1.09

Wastell v Woodward and Chaucer Syndicates Ltd [2017] Lloyd's
   Rep IR 474 .... 5.10, 5.18, 5.19, 5.22, 5.33, 8.68

Waters v Monarch Fire and Life Assurance Co (1856) 5 El. & Bl. 870 .... 3.19

Watkins v O'Shaughnessy [1939] 1 All ER 385 .... 3.10

Watson Norie v Shaw [1967] 1 Lloyd's Rep 515 .... 9.07

Weaver v Tredegar Iron & Coal Co Ltd [1940] AC 955 .... 4.17

Weddell v Road Transport and General Insurance Co, Ltd [1932] 2 KB 563 .... 3.36, 3.38

Weldrick v Essex & Suffolk Equitable Insurance Society Ltd, (1949–50)
   83 Ll L Rep 91 .... 8.95, 8.104, 8.109

West Midlands Travel Ltd v Aviva Insurance UK Ltd [2014] Lloyd's Rep IR 66 .... 9.19, 9.40

West Yorkshire Trading Standards Service v Lex Vehicle Leasing Ltd [1996] RTR 70 .... 4.31

White v London Transport [1971] RTR 326 .... 10.79

White v White [2001] RTR 25 .... 8.31, 8.34, 8.35, 8.37, 10.01, 10.07, 10.19, 10.104–10.117

Whyatt v Powell [2017] Lloyd's Rep IR 478 .... 10.114–10.118

Wigley-Foster v Wilson [2016] Lloyd's Rep IR 622 .... 10.125–10.127

Wilkinson v General Accident Fire and Life Assurance Corp [1967] 2 Lloyd's Rep 182 .... 3.24

Williams v Baltic Insurance Association of London [1924] 2 KB 282 .... 3.18, 3.19

Williams v Jones [1975] RTR 433 .... 5.36

Windle v Dunning & Son Ltd. [1968] 1 WLR 552 .... 4.31

Windsor v Chalcraft [1939] 1 KB 27 .... 8.142

Winter v DPP [2003] RTR 14 .... 3.44

WISE Underwriting Agency Ltd v Grupo Nacional Provincial SA [2004]
   Lloyd's Rep IR 764 .... 8.116

Wood v Capita Insurance Services Ltd [2017] 4 All ER 615 .... 3.30

Woodall v Pearl Assurance Co Ltd [1919] 1 KB 593 .... 7.104

Woodward v James Young (Contractors) Ltd 1958 J.C. 28 .... 3.40, 3.43

Wyatt v Guildhall Insurance Company [1937] 1 KB 653 .... 7.70

Zurich General Accident & Liability Insurance Co Ltd v Morrison [1942]
   2 KB 53 .... 8.124, 8.135

xxvi

TABLE OF EU LEGISLATION

Directive 72/166/EEC of 24 April 1972
    (First Directive) 1.15, 1.21, 11.43
    art 1(1) 3.46, 3.68, 5.30
    art 1(3) 11.18, 11.49
    art 1(4) 3.68
    art 2 ....1.16
    art 2(2) 11.32
    art 3 ....1.16, 2.34
    art 3(1) 1.17, 1.19, 1.21, 2.07, 5.16,
        5.30, 5.78, 7.77, 7.78, 10.34, 10.98
    art 4 .... 1.17, 2.34, 10.12
    art 6 ....1.16
    art 7 ....1.16
Directive 84/5/EEC of 30 December 1983
    (Second Directive) 1.21, 1.27,
        4.15, 10.09, 10.13, 10.16, 12.35
    art 1 ....10.109, 11.20
    art 1(1) 1.18, 4.12, 7.78, 7.99
    art 1(4) 8.30, 8.31, 8.32, 10.10,
        10.11, 10.17, 10.25, 10.34,
        10.98, 10.103, 10.110, 11.11, 12.36
    art 2 ....8.11
    art 2(1) 1.19, 8.30
    art 4(1) 10.20
Directive 88/357/EEC of 22 June 1988 ..... 1.21
Directive 90/232/EEC of 14 May 1990
    (Third Directive) 1.19, 1.21, 4.21, 10.11
    art 1 ....10.129
    art 1(1) 1.19
    art 2 ....1.20, 7.94
    art 4 ....10.11
    art 5(1) 1.20
Directive 2000/26/EC of the European
    Parliament and of the Council of 16 May
    2000 (Fourth Directive) 1.20, 1.21,
        10.16, 11.01, 11.02, 11.04
    recital 12 ....1.20

art 4(1) 1.20
art 4(4) 1.20
art 5(1) 11.04
art 5(2) 11.04
art 6 .... 10.17, 11.12, 11.13
art 6(2) 11.10, 11.11
art 7 .... 10.17, 11.12, 11.13
art 7(2) 11.11
Directive 2005/14/EC, of the European
    Parliament and of the Council of 11 May
    2005 (Fifth Directive) 1.21, 4.15
    art 1(3) 10.12
    art 1(3)(b) 10.12
    art 2 ....4.13
    art 2(4) 10.13
    art 2(6) 10.13
    art 4(2) 1.21
Directive 2009/103/EC of the European
    Parliament and of the Council of
    16 September 2009 (Consolidated
    Directive) 1.22, 2.06, 2.37, 3.48,
        4.15, 8.143, 10.16, 10.44,
        10.120, 11.29, 12.35
    art 1 ....5.26
    art 1(1) 3.46, 5.30, 5.78
    art 1(3) 2.35
    art 1(4) 4.45
    art 1(5) 11.44
    art 1A 5.26
    art 3 ....2.05, 2.07, 3.67, 7.49
    art 3(1) 1.22, 2.35, 3.68,
        7.77, 7.78, 10.98, 10.130, 11.20
    art 4 ....1.25
    art 5(1) 2.07, 2.35
    art 5(2) 2.35
    art 6 ....2.35, 11.20
    art 7 ....2.35

TABLE OF EU LEGISLATION

art 8 ....2.35

art 9 .... 4.14, 4.16, 7.84, 7.99, 10.130

art 10 .... 8.31, 8.32, 10.14,
10.17, 10.98, 10.119,
10.121, 10.122, 10.123

art 10(1) 7.80, 10.100

art 10(2) 8.30, 10.101, 10.103

art 11 ....7.78, 10.15

art 12 ....7.87, 7.88

art 12(1) 4.21, 4.58, 7.86,
8.73, 8.79, 10.129

art 12(2) 4.58

art 12(3) 4.42, 7.91, 7.93

art 13 ....8.19, 8.20

art 13(1) 6.20, 7.79, 7.92,
8.18, 8.30, 8.79, 10.45

art 13(1)(a) 7.80, 7.82, 8.11

art 13(1)(b) 7.82

art 13(3) 7.81

art 14 .... 4.44, 7.94, 7.95

art 16 ....2.36, 2.39

art 17 ....7.80

art 18 ....8.02, 8.144

art 20 ....11.02

art 20(1) 11.03

art 21 ....11.02

art 21(1) 11.03

art 22 ....11.02, 11.06

art 23 ....11.02, 11.04

art 23(4) 11.04

art 24 ....11.02

art 24(1) 10.17, 11.03, 11.05

art 24(2) 11.10, 11.13

art 25 ....11.02

art 25(1) 10.17, 11.11, 11.13, 11.24

art 26 ....11.02

art 28A(2) 2.39

Regulation 1215/2012 of the European
Parliament and of the Council of
12 December 2012 (Brussels Recast
Regulation) 11.36

art 4 ....11.37

art 4(1) 11.37

art 5 ....11.37

art 5(1) 11.37

art 6 ....11.37

art 10 ....11.38, 11.39

art 11 ....11.38, 11.39

art 11(1)(b) 11.39, 11.40

art 12 ....11.38, 11.39, 11.39

art 13 ....11.38

art 13(1) 11.39

art 13(2) 11.39, 11.40

art 14 ....11.38

art 15 ....11.38

art 16 ....11.38

Regulation (EU) 2016/679 of the European
Parliament and of the Council of
27 April 2016 ....1.25

Regulation (EU) 2016/792 of the European
Parliament and of the Council of
11 May 2016 ....4.16

TABLE OF UK STATUTES

Arbitration Act 1996
s 12..8.132
s 67..8.132
s 91..7.105
Automated and Electric Vehicles
    Act 2018 ....13.02, 13.03,
                    13.04, 13.05, 13.15,
                    13.16, 13.18, 13.25
s 1(1)...13.06
s 2.......................13.13, 13.14, 13.19, 13.23
s 2(1)..13.08, 13.14
s 2(1)(a)..13.13
s 2(2)..13.14, 13.17
s 2(3)..13.10, 13.11
s 2(4)..13.17
s 2(5)..13.19
s 2(6)..13.21
s 2(7)..13.14
s 3(1)..13.19
s 3(2)..............................13.12, 13.13, 13.20
s 4...13.21
s 4(1)..13.21
s 4(2)..13.21
s 4(4)..13.22
s 5...13.23
s 5(1)(a)..13.24
s 5(3)..13.23
s 5(4)..13.23
s 5(5)..13.24
s 7...13.06
s 8(1)(a)..13.03
s 8(1)(b)..13.13
s 8(2)..13.09
s 8(3)(b)..13.20
s 21(1)..13.02
s 21(3)..13.02
Civil Liability (Contribution) Act 1978......6.53

Consumer Credit Act 1974 ....9.49
s 8...9.49
ss 11–19..9.49
s 15...9.49
s 60...9.49
s 61...9.49
s 65...9.49
s 127...9.49
Consumer Insurance (Disclosure and
    Representations) Act 2012
s 6...7.23
s 10...7.23
Consumer Rights Act 2015......................7.109
Sch 2 ....7.109
Sch 4 ....7.109
Contagious Diseases (Animals) Act 1869
s 75...6.11
Contracts (Rights of Third parties)
    Act 1999 .... 10.18, 10.19, 10.91
Criminal Law Act 1967
s 14...9.11
s 14(2)..9.11
Deregulation Act 2015 .... 4.05, 8.06, 8.120
Sch 3 ....4.06
Sch 3 ....4.07, 4.08
Employers' Liability (Compulsory Insurance)
    Act 1969 .... 4.17, 4.20, 4.21,
                    4.22, 4.22, 4.26, 4.30, 4.34
s 1(1)...4.22
s 145(4A)...4.37
European Communities Act 1972
s 2(4)...10.109
Fatal Accidents Act 1976.................6.14, 12.21
s 1..10.53
s 1(3)..10.54
Highways Act 1896...................................1.05
Insurance Act 2015...................................7.12

xxix

TABLE OF UK STATUTES

s 9(2) 7.23
s 10 ... 7.13–7.18, 7.21, 7.24, 7.26, 7.40, 7.42
s 10(2) 7.13
s 11 ... 7.14–7.18, 7.24, 7.27–7.32, 7.39, 7.40
s 11(1) 7.18, 7.19, 7.20, 7.31
s 11(2)(a) 7.31
s 11(3) 7.18–7.21, 7.24, 7.26, 7.32,
7.35, 7.36, 7.42
s 15 .... 7.16, 7.28
s 16 .... 7.28
s 16(1) 7.23
s 17 .... 7.28
Law Reform (Contributory Negligence)
Act 1945 .... 6.16, 13.19
s 2 .... 13.19
s 3(2) 13.19
Liability (Compulsory Insurance)
Act 1969 .... 4.20
Life Assurance Act 1774 .... 3.16, 3.19, 3.21
Limitation (Scotland) Act 1973 .... 10.73
Limitation Act 1980
s 2 .... 1.33, 6.46
s 10A 13.24
s 11 .... 6.47, 8.110
s 11(5) 6.16
Married Women's Property Act 1882
s 11 .... 12.09
Motor Car Act 1903 .... 1.05
National Insurance (Industrial Injuries)
Act 1946 .... 4.20
Road Traffic Act 1930 .... 1.06, 1.07,
1.08, 1.11, 4.61, 6.09,
6.14, 6.49, 7.27, 7.47,
7.70, 10.01, 12.14
s 35 .... 5.35, 5.60, 6.01, 6.08, 6.13, 6.29
s 35(1) 2.08, 2.09, 5.67, 6.28
s 36(1)(b)(i) 4.19
s 36(4) 3.20, 4.18
s 121(1) 3.50, 3.53
ss 143–156 .... 1.12
s 143(2) 1.13
s 151 .... 1.13
Road Traffic Act 1934 ...... 1.07, 8.01, 8.135, 8.93
s 12 .... 7.52
Road Traffic Act 1960 .... 1.07, 4.61
s 145 .... 4.19
s 201(2) 2.08
s 203(3)(a) 8.46
s 203(4)(B) 4.19

s 257(1) 3.50
Road Traffic Act 1962 .... 8.93
Road Traffic Act 1971 .... 1.07
Road Traffic Act 1972 .... 4.19, 4.20, 8.93
s 40(5) 5.61
s 44(1) 5.47
s 143 .... 10.35
s 143(1) 2.08. 5.47
s 145(4)(a) 4.19
s 196(1) 3.50
Road Traffic Act 1988 .... 1.07, 2.04, 2.12, 3.05,
3.71, 4.04, 8.126, 8.127, 8.135, 8.71,
8.93, 9.53, 10.33, 13.12, 13.25
s 47 .... 5.52
s 87(1) 2.14
s 95 .... 10.133, 13.25
s 95(2) 4.01, 10.02, 10.05
s 103 .... 3.64
s 143 .... 2.07, 2.14, 2.22, 2.32,
3.64, 3.65, 4.34, 5.04, 5.35,
5.52, 5.61, 5.80, 6.01, 6.08, 6.11,
6.13, 6.26, 6.27, 6.34, 7.102, 7.49, 7.99,
8.43, 8.56, 8.82, 10.133, 10.32, 10.35
s 143(1) 2.01, 2.08, 2.08,
3.12, 3.62, 5.76, 6.01, 10.35
s 143(1)(a) 4.37, 5.03, 5.05, 6.35, 8.66
s 143(1)(b) 3.01, 3.14, 6.12, 6.22,
6.28, 6.34, 6.36, 6.39,
6.43, 6.49, 8.57, 8.58, 8.63, 8.65, 8.66
s 143(2) 1.01, 2.01, 2.24,
2.26, 3.12, 3.23, 4.33,
6.01, 8.43, 8.51, 8.58, 8.65
s 143(3) 2.08, 3.12
s 143(4) 2.08
s 144 .... 2.20, 2.31, 2.32, 2.33,
10.32, 10.38, 13.17
s 144(1) 2.19, 2.31
s 144(1)(a) 2.31
s 144(1)(b) 2.31
s 144(2) 13.10
s 144(2)(b) 4.27
s 144A 2.21
s 144A 2.22
s 144B 2.20
s 144C(1) 2.21
s 144C(2) 2.21
s 144C(9) 2.21
s 144D 2.22
s 145 .... 4.21, 4.30, 4.34,

TABLE OF UK STATUTES

4.40, 4.43, 4.47, 5.10, 5.81,
6.21, 6.22, 6.36, 6.45, 7.41,
7.72, 7.75, 7.96, 7.97, 7.99,
7.102, 8.05, 8.43, 8.61, 8.64,
10.32, 10.36, 10.133, 13.13

s 145(1) 4.01
s 145(2) 4.01
s 145(3) 4.22, 5.09, 5.15,
5.17, 5.19, 7.102, 10.131
s 145(3)(a) 3.72, 4.27, 4.37,
4.41, 4.42, 4.44, 4.55, 5.01,
5.20, 5.82, 7.86, 8.44, 8.45,
8.46, 8.56, 10.35, 13.13
s 145(3)(b) 4.46
s 145(3)(c) 4.47
s 145(3A) 13.13, 13.9
s 145(4) 4.11, 7.51, 7.52, 7.56
s 145(4)(a) 4.19, 4.20, 4.22,
4.23, 4.27, 4.29, 4.34
s 145(4)(b) 13.17
s 145(4A) 4.21, 4.22, 4.23,
4.24, 4.26, 4.27, 4.30
s 145(5) 10.05, 13.25
s 146 .... 2.03
s 147 .... 4.06
s 147(1) 2.12, 4.05, 8.06
s 147(1A) 4.02, 4.03
s 147(1B) 4.02, 4.03
s 147(1C) 4.02
s 147(1D) 4.03
s 147(2) 4.05
s 148 .... 7.02, 7.82, 7.102, 7.109, 13.21
s 148(1) 7.02
s 148(2) 7.02, 7.04, 7.06, 7.52, 7.56
s 148(2)(a) 7.31
s 148(2)(b) 7.32
s 148(2)(c) 7.33
s 148(2)(d) 7.33
s 148(2)(e) 7.36
s 148(2)(f) 7.37
s 148(2)(g) 7.38
s 148(2)(h) 7.38
s 148(4) 7.02, 7.05, 8.47, 8.148
s 148(5) 7.03, 7.41
s 148(6) 7.03, 7.39, 8.71
s 148(7) 3.20, 3.22, 4.06, 7.75
s 149 .... 7.07
s 150 .... 7.70, 7.72, 7.74
s 150(1) 7.72
s 150(2) 7.73

s 151 .... 3.13, 3.22, 4.07, 4.28,
4.29, 4.33, 5.80, 5.82, 6.02,
6.11, 6.22, 7.75, 7.98, 7.99,
7.102, 8.01, 8.03, 8.04, 8.05,
8.07, 8.43, 8.45, 8.47, 8.48,
8.50, 8.51, 8.53, 8.54, 8.56,
8.69, 8.82, 8.82, 8.88, 8.89, 8.123,
8.134, 8.137, 8.142, 8.146, 8.149,
10.31, 12.31, 12.34, 13.22
s 151(1) 8.06
s 151(2) 7.108, 8.05, 8.08, 8.101, 8.16,
8.57, 8.67, 8.88, 13.14
s 151(2)(a) 8.05, 8.09, 8.14, 8.47,
8.52, 8.59, 8.82
s 151(2)(b) 6.19, 6.21, 6.23, 6.35,
6.36, 7.82, 8.10–8.17, 8.47,
8.54, 8.54, 8.57–8.67, 8.72,
8.84, 8.88, 10.53, 13.26
s 151(3) 7.39, 7.82, 8.14, 8.16, 8.54, 8.69
s 151(4) 8.15–8.20, 8.28, 8.30, 8.32,
8.33, 8.35, 8.36, 8.40,
8.42, 8.54, 8.90, 10.45
s 151(5) 8.47, 8.54, 8.92
s 151(7) 8.16, 8.47, 8.69, 8.88
s 151(7)(a) 7.39, 8.69
s 151(7)(b) 8.69
s 151(8) 3.07, 3.13, 3.22, 5.80,
6.19, 7.89, 7.90, 7.93, 7.109,
8.16, 8.47, 8.69–8.80, 8.84,
8.88, 10.52, 10.53, 13.22
s 151(8)(b) 3.14
s 152 .... 4.08, 6.31, 8.54, 8.89, 8.95,
8.111, 8.114, 8.120, 8.123,
8.134, 8.136, 8.141, 10.31
s 152(1) 8.96, 8.111, 8.119
s 152(1)(a) 7.97, 8.108, 8.110,
8.112, 8.114, 8.115, 8.118, 8.92
s 152(1)(b) 8.121
s 152(1)(c) 8.120
s 152(2) 8.114, 8.122, 8.138, 8.141, 8.82
s 152(3) 8.135
s 152(4) 8.135
s 153(1) 4.08
s 153(3) 8.01
s 154(1)(a) 2.17
s 154(1)(b) 2.17
s 154(2) 2.17
s 157 .... 4.47
s 158 .... 4.47
s 159 .... 4.47

xxxi

TABLE OF UK STATUTES

s 160......................................4.47
s 161(1)..........................4.02, 4.47
s 165(1)..................................2.13
s 165(2)..................................2.13
s 165(3)..................................2.14
s 165(4)..................................2.13
s 165A..............................2.14, 2.16
s 165A(3)................................2.14
s 165A(3)(b)............................2.15
s 165A(4)................................2.14
s 165A(5)................................2.14
s 171(2)..................................2.14
s 174......................................2.18
s 183(3)..........................4.26, 4.37
s 185(1)..............1.34, 3.40, 3.48, 5.55
s 185(1)(c)..............................3.49
s 185(2)..................................5.55
s 189......................................3.40

s 192(1)..................................3.50
Sch 2AI..................................2.22
Terrorism Act 2000
  s 1..............................8.127, 10.44
Theft Act 1968..........................8.21
  s 12....................................8.24
  s 12(1)................................8.40
Third Parties (Rights Against Insurers)
  Act 1930 .... 1.08, 1.09, 1.10,
      6.08, 8.48, 8.49, 8.49, 10.01, 12.34
Third Parties (Rights Against Insurers)
  Act 2010 .... 1.10, 6.02, 6.08,
      8.01, 8.04, 10.01, 10.96, 12.31–12.34
Vehicle Excise and Registration
  Act 1994 ....7.04, 7.38
Workmen's Compensation
  Act 1897 ....4.17, 4.20

TABLE OF UK STATUTORY INSTRUMENTS

Cancellation of Contracts Made in a
   Consumer's Home or Place of Work etc
   Regulations 2008, SI 2008
   No 1816 ....9.51
Civil Procedure Rules 1998, SI 1998
   No 3132 ....8.100, 8.142
   r 6.16 ....8.84
Consumer Credit (Agreements) Regulations
   1983, SI 1983 No 1553 ....9.49
Employers' Liability (Compulsory
   Insurance) Exemption (Amendment)
   Regulations 1992, SI 1992
   No 3172 ....4.22
European Communities (Rights against
   Insurers) Regulations 2002,
   SI 2002/3061 ....1.13, 4.09, 1.20, 6.02,
                             8.03, 8.147,
                      8.147, 8.149, 12.31
   reg 2(1) 8.144–8.146
   reg 3 ....8.148
   reg 3(2) 8.144–8.146, 8.149, 8.150
Motor Vehicles (Compulsory Insurance)
   (Information Centre and Compensation
   Body) Regulations 2003, SI 2003
   No 37 .... 1.20, 11.12, 11.25, 11.29
   reg 1 ....11.12
   reg 2(1) 11.18
   reg 9(2) 11.19
   reg 10 ....10.17, 11.13
   reg 11 ....11.15, 11.16
   reg 11(1)(b) 11.15
   reg 11(1)(c) 11.17
   reg 11(1)(c)(i) 11.15
   reg 11(1)(c)(ii) 11.15
   reg 11(2) 11.15
   reg 11(3) 11.15
   reg 12 ....11.15

reg 12(1)(a) 11.16
reg 12(1)(b) 11.16
reg 12(1)(c) 11.16
reg 12(2) 11.16
reg 12(3) 11.17, 11.22
reg 12(4)(a) 11.17
reg 12(4)(b) 11.17, 11.32
reg 12(5)(a) 11.17
reg 12(5)(b) 11.17
reg 13 ....11.18, 11.21
reg 13(1) 11.18, 11.19
reg 13(2) 11.13
reg 13(2)(b) 11.13, 11.22,
                 11.24, 11.30, 11.32
reg 14 ....11.22, 11.22
reg 14(2) 11.22
reg 15(2)(a) 11.23
reg 15(2)(b) 11.23
Motor Vehicles (Compulsory Insurance)
   Regulation 2000, SI 2000
   No 726 ....3.61, 3.62, 3.69
Motor Vehicles (Compulsory Insurance)
   Regulations 2016, SI 2016 No 1193
   reg 2(2) 7.51
Motor Vehicles (Compulsory Insurance)
   (Miscellaneous Amendments)
   Regulations 2019, SI 2019/
   1047 ....8.124, 8.141
Motor Vehicles (Construction and Use)
   Regulations 1973, SI 1973 No 24
   reg 99(1) 5.61
Motor Vehicles (International Motor
   Insurance Card) Regulations 1971,
   SI 1971/792 ....11.46
Motor Vehicles (Third Party Risks)
   Regulations 1972, SI 1972
   No 1217 ....2.03, 2.12

reg 6 .... 2.12
reg 10 .... 2.19
reg 10(3) 2.19
reg 10(4) 2.19
reg 12 .... 4.10
Motor Vehicles (Third-Party Risks Deposits)
    Regulations 1992, SI 1992
    No 1284 .... 2.03

Unfair Arbitration Agreements (Specified
    Amount) Order 1999, SI 1999
    No 2617 .... 7.105
Unfair Terms in Consumer Contracts Regulations
    1999, SI 1999 No 2083 .... 7.109
    reg 6 .... 7.109
    Sch 2 .... 7.109
Vehicles (Compulsory Insurance) Regulations
    1992, SI 1992 No 3036 .... 4.21

CHAPTER 1

Brief history of the insurance obligation and interaction with the EU law

Introduction

1.1 Motor vehicle insurance is a type of compulsory insurance the absence of which renders the use of a motor vehicle a criminal offence under the Road Traffic Act 1988.[1] The rules that govern the compulsory liability insurance for motor vehicle accidents (Motor Third Party Liability (MTPL)) do not derive from the domestic legislation or the common law court cases only. The Directives of the European Union[2] aiming to harmonise the rules applicable to insurance of civil liability with respect to motor vehicle accidents also influence the interpretation of such rules considerably. Therefore, the sources of the principles applicable to insurance of civil liability for motor vehicle accidents may be summarised mainly as the domestic statutory provisions, the relevant EU Directives, the common law court cases interpreting the domestic provisions and the decision of the Court of Justice of the European Union (CJEU) interpreting the relevant EU Directives.

1.2 The starting point to analyse the scope of the compulsory liability insurance for motor vehicle accidents is to determine the meaning of "use" as this phrase unlocks the key for the compulsory insurance requirement. However, before exploring the meaning of this term a brief history of compulsory motor vehicle liability insurance will be provided.

History (domestic law)

1.3 Insurances were offered in the nineteenth century for "indemnifying the owners of horses and vehicles against their Common Law liability for accidents arising through the negligence of their drivers."[3] The policies had been initially domestic, but with the growth of the commercial use of vehicles the first commercial policy was observed in 1901.[4] From 1903 onwards car users increased rapidly which led to a proportionate rise in motor vehicle accidents between 1912 and 1928.[5] In the 1920s the life of a car was estimated as four–five years.[6] At those times the premiums were assessed on a per capita basis with regard given to the number of drivers employed and the amount of indemnity

---

1 RTA 1988 s 143(2).

2 They will be referred to as "relevant Directives" throughout the book. A detailed description of the scope of each related Directive will be provided further in this chapter.

3 J. Alfred Eke, *The Principles of Insurance and Their Application*, 1926, London, p 66.

4 R.M. Merkin/M. Hemsworth, *The Law of Motor Insurance*, 2nd ed, 2015, Sweet & Maxwell [1–11].

5 Eke, *The Principles of Insurance and Their Application*, 1926, London, p 71–72. Whilst the number fatal accidents were 390 in 1912, the number went up to 768 in 1928.

6 *Edney v De Rougemont* (1927) 28 Ll L Rep 215.

required for any one accident.[7] Two different types of cover were available.[8] First, insuring third party risks only, ie covering the assured's liability for personal injury and damage to property of the public. Second, in addition to the third party liability, it was possible to purchase insurance for damage to the assured's own vehicles and harness and fatal injury to his horses. In *South Staffordshire Tramways Co Ltd v Sickness & Accident Assurance Association Ltd*[9] a tramcar was insured for "claims for personal injury in respect of accidents caused by vehicles for twelve calendar months from 24 November 1887," to the amount of "£250 in respect of any one accident." When the insured tramcar was overturned as a result of which 40 passengers were injured, the word "accident" was interpreted by the Court as meaning "in respect of any single injury to person or property accidentally caused."

1.4 The policies excepted from the cover for instance damage to any viaduct, bridge, road or anything beneath, by the weight of the vehicle; earthquake, war, riot or civil commotion; wear and tear, depreciation, mechanical fracture, and/or breakdown of any part of the vehicle unless caused by external impact and loss arising out of the explosion of the boiler of the vehicle.[10] Personal injury claims by passengers in the vehicle was excluded unless specifically provided for and an additional premium paid to cover the risks.[11]

1.5 On the other hand, the increasing number of victims of automobile accidents had created social problems.[12] Traffic on the highways was regulated by the out-dated Highways Act 1896 and the Motor Car Act 1903. It had become apparent that people who were injured by the negligent driving of motor cars were in a parlous situation if the negligent person was unable to pay damages. As a result, the injured party was deprived of appropriate compensation.[13]

1.6 In 1928, a Royal Commission was appointed to examine the whole problem of transportation. First Report of the Royal Commission on Transport ("The Control of Traffic on Roads")[14] emphasised the urgency of the need for legislative steps to regulate this area of law.[15] On the basis of recommendations which the Commission embodied in its first report, after a careful survey, the government proposed a Bill which became the Road Traffic Act 1930 (RTA 1930). This Act imposed, for the first time, a statutory obligation on the users of all motor vehicles to provide security against their legal liability for the death of or bodily injury caused to third parties. The Road Traffic Act 1930 received Royal Assent on 1 August 1930. The Act was a comprehensive statute providing for (a) the regulation of motor vehicles and traffic on roads (eg by classification of automobiles, licensing of drivers, driving offences and penalties etc); (b) the protection of third parties

---

7 Eke, p 67.

8 Eke, p 67.

9 [1891] 1 QB 402.

10 Eke, p 77. For more information about exclusion clauses observed in the motor vehicle policies issued before the RTA 1930 see Merkin/Hemsworth, [1–12].

11 Eke, p 77.

12 For some detailed statistical information as to the number of registered vehicles, accidents and victims involved in those accidents in the early twentieth century see E. D. Weiss, "Legislation and Road Accidents," 2 *Mod. L. Rev.* 139 (1938); see also P. Bartrip, "No-Fault Compensation on the Roads in Twentieth Century Britain," 69 *Cambridge L.J.* 263 (2010), p 264–265.

13 *Carswell v Secretary of State for Transport* [2011] Lloyd's Rep IR 644, [7].

14 19 July 1929. Cmd. 3365, p 3.

15 F. Deak, "Compulsory Liability Insurance under the British Road Traffic Acts of 1930 and 1934," 3 *Law & Contemp. Probs.* 565 (1936), p 566.

against risks arising out of the use of automobiles; (c) amending the highway laws; and (d) the grant of power to local authorities to regulate public service vehicles.

1.7 The RTA 1930 was then amended by the Road Traffic Act 1934, and then the relevant legislation was amended by the Consolidation Acts of 1960 and 1971 and 1988. Currently the Road Traffic Act 1988 (RTA 1988) is in force and governs the compulsory insurance requirement in its Part VI.[16]

Third Parties (Rights Against Insurers) Act 1930

1.8 The RTA 1930 was supplemented by the Third Parties (Rights Against Insurers) Act 1930 (TPA 1930). Prior to the adoption of the TPA 1930 it was held by the Courts that a third party victim had no right of direct action against the insurer in the case of the assured becoming bankrupt or insolvent or the case of a winding up order being issued.[17] As a result, the insurance indemnity had to be part of the insolvent assured's asset from which the victim had to try to recover his loss. Consequently, if the assured had a claim against the insurers, the payment by the insurer under the insurance contract was to be made to the liquidators and the third party victim would claim it as *pari passu* with the other creditors. The injustice of this rule had been acknowledged by the Court of Appeal in *Re Harrington Motor Co Ltd Ex p. Chaplin*,[18] in which a taxicab belonging to the assured company knocked down the victim pedestrian by the negligence of a driver of one of its cabs. The victim recovered judgment against the company for £324. The judgment was given on 28 January 1927, and on 15 February an order was made for its compulsory winding up. At the time of the accident the company had a third party liability insurance under which the insurer paid to the liquidator on 14 April 1927. The victim's argument that the amount awarded for him by the judgment did not form part of the assets of the company available for distribution among the creditors in the winding up was rejected by Eve J whose judgment was affirmed by the Court of Appeal. There was no such principle of equity supporting the claim, the liquidators did not owe any fiduciary duties to the victim, and neither the assured nor the liquidator can be treated as a trustee for him in enforcing the claim against the insurers. Although it was strenuous and able,[19] the Court felt obliged to dismiss the claim because of the absolute break in the absence of a contractual relationship between the insurer and the victim.[20] The Court of Appeal however expressed that "if any alteration is to be made in it that must be made by the proper authorities and by the proper means." Parliament then addressed this issue by the TPA 1930 which did not create privity between the third party victim and insurer but enabled the former to vest in the assured's contractual rights against the insurer in some certain cases which the assured's financial difficulties create.

---

16 For an overview of the compulsory motor third party liability insurance see J. Davey, "A Compulsory Diet of Chicken and Eggs: The EU Motor Insurance Directives as a Shadow Tort Regime," *Research Handbook on EU Tort Law*, Ed. by P. Giliker, 2017, p 239–244.

17 *Re Harrington Motor Co Ltd Ex p. Chaplin* (1927–28) 29 Ll L Rep 102; *Hood's Trustees v Southern Union General Insurance Co of Australasia Ltd* (1928) 31 Ll L Rep 237.

18 [1928] Ch. 105.

19 *Re Harrington Motor Co Ltd Ex p. Chaplin* [1928] Ch. 105.

20 Applied *Re Law Guarantee Trust & Accident Society Ltd* [1914] 2 Ch. 617.

1.9 The TPA 1930 did not apply retrospectively. In an action brought against the insurers by a motor vehicle accident victim the Court of Appeal confirmed[21] that no statute shall be construed so as to have a retrospective operation unless its language is such as plainly to require such a construction.[22]

1.10 The TPA 1930 was not confined to motor insurance cases as it had general application. It created a statutory subrogation that upon assured's insolvency the third party victims who can make a claim against the assured stepped into the assured's shoes with regards to the assured's claim against the insurers under the insurance contract. The Third Parties (Rights Against Insurers) Act 2010 (TPA 2010),[23] which replaced the TPA 1930, retained this position and also has general application. Notably, because of the developments in the motor vehicle compulsory insurance regime that is analysed throughout this book, the TPA 2010 is less significant for motor accident victims than the victims of other types of liability of the assured.

Objectives of motor third party liability insurance

1.11 The RTA 1930 was described as "social legislation."[24] The long title of the RTA 1930 was "An Act… to make provision for the protection of third parties against risks arising out of the use of motor vehicles." The main aim of the Act was the protection of the public[25] by providing that there should be a body of insurers behind every driver of a vehicle,[26] and hence, guaranteeing that an injured person will obtain the compensation that he or she is awarded against the negligent driver.[27] The following consolidating Acts retained such objective and the compulsory insurance requirements.

1.12 Part VI of the RTA 1988 regulates "Third Party Liabilities." The rules governing "Compulsory insurance or security against third-party risks" are to be found under sections 143–156 of the RTA 1988.

1.13 In summary, under the current regime, the protection of the public is provided by:

(1) imposing an obligation on all drivers to insure against third party liability under sanction of the criminal law;[28]

(2) conferring on a successful claimant a right of action against the assured's insurer after obtaining a judgment against the assured;[29]

---

21 In *Ward v British Oak Insurance Co Ltd* [1932] 1 KB 392 the claimant was injured by a motor lorry on 17 November 1927, obtained judgment against the company whose driver caused the accident on 21 March 1929. A liquidator was appointment for the company as a result of a voluntary winding up on 27 December 1927. In such a case where tortfeasors became bankrupt or went into liquidation while money was due to them from insurers who had secured them against claims in respect of their torts, the 1930 Act did not apply since the injury happened before the Act was passed.

22 *Lauri v Renad* [1892] 3 Ch. 402; *Gardner & Co Ltd v Cone* [1928] Ch. 955.

23 The TPA 2010 came into force on 1 August 2016.

24 Deak, "Compulsory Liability Insurance under the British Road Traffic Acts of 1930 and 1934," 3 *Law & Contemp. Probs.* 565 (1936), p 570.

25 *Harrison v Hill* 1932 J.C. 13, 16, see also Lord Sands at p 17.

26 *Tattersall v Drysdale* [1935] 2 KB 174.

27 *Churchill Insurance Co Ltd v Wilkinson* [2010] Lloyd's Rep IR 591, Waller LJ, [3].

28 RTA 1988 s 143(2).

29 RTA 1988 s 151.

(3) the two Agreements between the Motor Insurers' Bureau (MIB) and the Secretary of State for the Environment having been voluntarily entered into, in the case of a guilty driver who may either be uninsured altogether or turn out to be untraceable so that it is not known whether he is insured or not and if so by whom;[30] and

(4) the European Communities (Rights against Insurers) Regulations 2002/3061 which implements the relevant Directives of the European Parliament and of the Council, in the case of a further direct right of action by a victim of a traffic accident against insurers (with no pre-condition of a judgment awarding damages in favour of the claimant and against the assured motorist).

All of the issues listed above are analysed in this book.

The EU regime

1.14 A series of EU Directives[31] progressively defined the obligations of Member States concerning the insurance of civil liability in respect of the use of vehicles. These Directives are not directly applicable in all Member States; the Member States' obligation is to ensure that the result to be achieved by the relevant Directive is achieved. The choice and form of methods of achieving that result is left to Member States.[32] Between 1972 and 2009 in total six Directives were passed in relation to MTPL insurance. It is necessary to mention the historical progression of the relevant Directives.

1.15 The First Directive adopted in order to facilitate the movement of travellers between Member States was Council Directive 72/166/EEC of 24 April 1972[33] on the approximation of the laws of Member States relating to insurance against civil liability in respect of the use of motor vehicles and to the enforcement of the obligation to insure against such liability.

1.16 One of the aims of the First Directive was to simplify the cross-border traffic between European Member States by abolishing the control of the Green Card.[34] The free movement of motor vehicle drivers is an autonomous freedom of Community law.[35] This First Directive established a system based, first, on the abolition of checks on insurance Green Cards on the crossing of internal borders in the European Community and, second, on the obligation on each of the Member States to ensure that third party liability in respect of the use of motor vehicles is covered by insurance.[36] Hence, national rules on compulsory motor insurance had to be harmonised to pursue mainly the following objectives[37]: (1) to ensure the free movement of vehicles normally based on European

---

30 www.mib.org.uk.

31 The relevant Directives of the European Parliament and of the Council will briefly be mentioned as the EU Directives throughout this book.

32 Art 249 of the EC Treaty.

33 This Directive will be referred to as "First Directive" throughout this book.

34 For the Green Card scheme please refer to Chapter 11.

35 *Ruiz Bernaldez Case* (C-129/94) [1996] All ER (EC) 741, [19].

36 Directive 72/166/EEC preamble; Articles 2 and 3. *Commission of the European Communities v Italy* (C-518/06) [2009] 3 CMLR 22.

37 *Csonka v Magyar Allam* (C-409/11) [2014] 1 CMLR 14 [26]; *Rodrigues de Andrade v Proenca Salvador* (C-514/16) [2018] Lloyd's Rep IR 164, [32]; *Petillo v Unipol Assicurazioni SpA* (C-371/12) [2014] 3 CMLR 1 [26].

Union territory and of persons travelling in those vehicles,[38] and (2) to guarantee that the victims of accidents caused by those vehicles receive comparable treatment irrespective of where in the European Union the accident occurred. Those objectives have continuously been pursued and reinforced by the EU legislature.[39]

1.17 Notably the obligation to provide insurance cover against civil liability for damage caused to third parties by motor vehicles is distinct from the extent of the compensation to be afforded to them on the basis of the civil liability of the insured person. The Directives referred to here do not seek to harmonise the rules of the Member States governing civil liability.[40] In principle the Member States remain free to determine, in particular, which damage caused by motor vehicles is to be compensated and the extent of such compensation as well as the persons who are entitled to it.[41] As referred to above the initial concern of the First Directive was the free movement of vehicles between the Member States. The disparities between national requirements in the insurance of civil liabilities in such accidents had the danger of impeding the free movement of motor vehicles and persons within the European Community. With these considerations the First Directive established the basic obligation of Member States to ensure the existence of insurance cover. Article 3(1) provided:

> Each Member State shall, subject to Article 4, take all appropriate measures to ensure that civil liability in respect of the use of vehicles normally based in its territory is covered by insurance. The extent of the liability covered and the terms and conditions of the cover shall be determined on the basis of these measures.

Hence, the Member States must ensure that the civil liability arising under their domestic law is covered by insurance which complies with the provisions of the Directives. The Member States must exercise their powers in that field in compliance with EU law, and the national provisions which govern compensation for road accidents may not deprive Directives of their effectiveness.

1.18 Major disparities between the laws of the different Member States that were nevertheless still being observed after the First Directive continued to worry the Council that they might have a direct effect upon the establishment and the operation of the common market. Following that Second Council Directive, Directive 84/5/EEC of 30 December 1983,[42] on the approximation of the laws of the Member States relating to insurance against civil liability in respect of the use of motor vehicles was adopted. The Second Directive extended the insurance referred to in Article 3(1) of the First Directive to property damage.[43] The main purpose of this Directive was to improve guarantees of compensation for victims of motor accidents by ensuring a minimum level of protection

---

38 Vehicles normally based in the territory of a third country were still subject to the checks for either Green Card or a certificate of frontier insurance establishing that the vehicle was insured against civil liability in respect of the use of vehicles, throughout the territory in which the Treaty establishing the European Economic Community is in force. First Directive, Articles 6 and 7.

39 *Rodrigues de Andrade v Proenca Salvador* (C-514/16) [2018] Lloyd's Rep IR 164, [33].

40 *Farrell v Whitty* (C-356/05) [2007] Lloyd's Rep IR 525, [2]; *Neto de Sousa v Portugal* (C-506/16) [2018] Lloyd's Rep IR 118, [29]; *Petillo v Unipol Assicurazioni SpA* (C-371/12) [2014] 3 CMLR 1 [29].

41 *Petillo v Unipol Assicurazioni SpA* (C-371/12) [2014] 3 CMLR 1 [30].

42 This Directive will be referred to as "Second Directive" throughout this book.

43 Art 1(1).

for them throughout the Community. The details of the Second Directive will be referred to in the relevant chapters.

1.19 The Third Directive, Council Directive 90/232/EEC of 14 May 1990[44] on the approximation of the laws of the Member States relating to insurance against civil liability in respect of the use of motor vehicles, once more emphasised that motor vehicle accident victims should be guaranteed comparable treatment irrespective of where in the Community accidents occur. Having noted the gaps in the compulsory insurance cover of motor vehicle passengers in certain Member States, the Directive provided: "Without prejudice to the second subparagraph of Article 2(1) of [the Second Directive], the insurance referred to in Article 3(1) of [the First Directive] shall cover liability for personal injuries to all passengers, other than the driver, arising out of the use of a vehicle."[45] Article 3(2) of the First Directive required Member States to comply with the compulsory insurance requirement with respect to loss or injury occurred in their own territory, whereas, the Third Directive extended the obligation to cover the entire territory of the Community.[46] In line with this, every insurance policy should, moreover, guarantee for a single premium, in each Member State, the cover required by its law or the cover required by the law of the Member State where the vehicle is normally based, when that cover is higher.[47] The Third Directive required Member States to ensure that necessary measures were taken to enable victims of traffic accidents are able to ascertain promptly the identity of the insurance undertaking covering the liability arising out of the use of any motor vehicle involved in the accident.[48]

1.20 A further attempt to promote the sound functioning of the single market with respect to motor vehicle insurance was carried out via the Fourth Directive, Directive 2000/26/EC of the European Parliament and of the Council of 16 May 2000[49] on the approximation of the laws of the Member States relating to insurance against civil liability in respect of the use of motor vehicles and amending Council Directives 73/239/EEC and 88/357/EEC. This Fourth Directive introduced significant enhancements to the rights of victims of road traffic accidents. This can be seen as the "mirror image" of the Green Card System. While the Green Card System protects victims of accidents caused by foreign vehicles, the system of the Fourth Directive envisages protecting "visiting" victims, suffering a road traffic accident in another Member State than their Member State of residence. As stated under Art 1(1), the objective of the Fourth Directive was to lay down special provisions applicable to injured parties entitled to compensation in respect of any loss or injury resulting from accidents occurring in a Member State other than the Member State of residence of the injured party which are caused by the use of vehicles insured and normally based in a Member State. In order to pursue such goal insurers were required to appoint claims representative in each Member State of the EEA.[50] This solution would enable damage suffered by injured parties outside their Member State of

---

44 This Directive will be referred to as "Third Directive" throughout this book.
45 Art 1(1).
46 Art 2.
47 Art 2.
48 Art 5(1).
49 This Directive will be referred to as "Fourth Directive" throughout this book.
50 Art 4(1).

residence to be dealt with by procedures familiar to them and in their own language.[51] The requirement of appointing a claims representative shall not preclude the right of the injured party or his insurance undertaking to institute proceedings directly against the person who caused the accident or his insurance undertaking.[52] The claims representative must be able to receive and handle claims addressed by victims, resident in the Member State where the claims representative is established and having suffered an accident in another Member State of the EEA than the victim's own Member State of residence. This protection system will however not alter the rules determining the law applicable to the road traffic accident.[53]

1.21 The First Directive required compulsory motor third party liability insurance in respect of the use of vehicles normally based in Member States' territory. The Fifth Directive, Directive 2005/14/EC,[54] amended this as follows[55]:

> – the territory of the State of which the vehicle bears a registration plate, irrespective of whether the plate is permanent or temporary [or]
> in cases where the vehicle does not bear any registration plate or bears a registration plate which does not correspond or no longer corresponds to the vehicle and has been involved in an accident, the territory of the State in which the accident took place.

By the Fifth Directive the Member States ceased to be allowed to exclude liability for injury suffered by passengers in case the passenger knew or should have known that the driver was intoxicated.[56] Article 4(2) clarified that the insurance referred to in Article 3(1) of Directive 72/166/EEC shall cover personal injuries and damage to property suffered by pedestrians, cyclists and other non-motorised users of the roads who, as a consequence of an accident in which a motor vehicle is involved, are entitled to compensation in accordance with national civil law.

1.22 The Consolidated Motor Insurance Directive,[57] Directive 2009/103/EC, brings together the five earlier Directives mentioned above.[58] The recitals of the 2009 Directive reiterate the objectives set out in the previous Directives. Its main concern is to reinforce and consolidate the internal market in motor insurance. Article 1 provides definitions for "vehicle," "injured party," "National Insurers' Bureau," "territory in which the vehicle is normally based," "Green Card," "insurance undertaking" and "establishment." Article 3(1) concerns the insurance obligation for civil liability with respect to the use of motor vehicles within the territory of the European Community. The Directive then consolidates all the

---

51 Recital 12.

52 Art 4(4).

53 The measures provided by the Fourth Directive were implemented in the UK by the European Communities (Rights against Insurers) Regulations 2002/3061 and the Motor Vehicles (Compulsory Insurance) (Information Centre and Compensation Body) Regulations 2003 (SI 2003/37).

54 Directive 2005/14/EC, of the European Parliament and of the Council of 11 May 2005 amending Council Directives 72/166/EEC, 84/5/EEC, 88/357/EEC and 90/232/EEC and Directive 2000/26/EC of the European Parliament and of the Council relating to insurance against civil liability in respect of the use of motor vehicles.

55 Art 1(1).

56 Art 4(1)

57 The "Consolidated Directive" hereinafter.

58 Directive 2009/103/EC of the European Parliament and of the Council of 16 September 2009 relating to insurance against civil liability in respect of the use of motor vehicles, and the enforcement of the obligation to insure against such liability.

other measures provided by the previous Directives. The relevant Articles will be referred to throughout this book wherever the Directives address those issues.

1.23 European Union law must be interpreted and applied uniformly in the light of the versions existing in all the languages of the European Union.[59] Where there is a divergence between the various language versions of a European Union text, the provision in question must thus be interpreted by reference to the general scheme and the purpose of the rules of which it forms part.[60] This is the most overwhelming ratio that the CJEU refers to in the interpretation of the Directives which will be observed throughout this book.

1.24 To assess the effectiveness, efficiency and coherence of the motor insurance legislation, the Commission Work Programme 2016 announced an evaluation of the Directive. An evaluation was carried out, which included a public consultation held from 28 July until 20 October 2017.[61] The conclusion of the evaluation was that most elements of the Directive remain fit for purpose, while certain amendments in specific areas would be appropriate. On 24 May 2018 the European Commission has published a proposal for Directive amending the Consolidated Directive. The proposal addressed mainly five issues:

- enhancing the protection of traffic accident victims where the insurer is insolvent;
- improving the recognition of claims history statements, especially in a cross-border context;
- insurance checks to combat uninsured driving;
- harmonisation of minimum amounts of cover; and
- the scope of the Directive.

1.25 The proposed amendments will be referred to throughout this book where relevant. One of those amendments relevant to the information provided above is replacing Article 4 of the Consolidated Directive with the following:

Article 4 Checks on insurance

(1)   Member States shall refrain from making checks on insurance against civil liability in respect of vehicles normally based in the territory of another Member State and in respect of vehicles normally based in the territory of a third country entering their territory from the territory of another Member State.

However, they may carry out such checks on insurance provided that those checks are non-discriminatory, necessary and proportionate to achieve the end pursued, and

(a)   are carried out as part of a control which is not aimed exclusively at insurance verification or

(b)   they form part of a general system of checks on the national territory and do not require the vehicle to stop.

---

59 *Drozdovs v Baltikums AAS* [2014] RTR 14, [39].
60 Ibid.
61 https://ec.europa.eu/info/sites/info/files/2017-motor-insurance-consultation-document_en.pdf.

(2) On the basis of the law of the Member State to which the controller is subject, personal data may be processed where necessary for the purpose of combatting uninsured driving of vehicles travelling in Member States other than where they are normally based as set out in Article 1. This law shall be in accordance with Regulation (EU) 2016/679*[62] and shall also lay down suitable measures to safeguard the data subject's rights and freedoms and legitimate interests.

A Member State's liability for a failure to implement a Directive

1.26 It is inherent in the system of the Treaty for the European Union that when harm is caused to individuals because domestic law fails to comply with EU requirements, the defaulting State is potentially liable to the individual if the EU measure in question is designed to confer clear and enforceable rights.[63] If individuals were unable to obtain compensation in such circumstances, the full effectiveness of Community rules would be impaired and the protection of the rights which the Community rules grant would be weakened.[64] This is especially applicable where the availability for enforcing the rights granted for the individuals depends on a prior action on the part of the State.[65] Within this context, national Courts are under an obligation to achieve full and effective protection of rights derived from European law and to ensure that those rules are fully effective.[66] In determining a member State's liability[67] to an individual for a failure to implement a Directive, a national Court will look for the satisfaction of the following constituent elements[68]:

(i) The Directive must have been intended to confer rights on individuals.[69]

---

62 *Regulation (EU) 2016/679 of the European Parliament and of the Council of 27 April 2016 on the protection of natural persons with regard to the processing of personal data and on the free movement of such data, and repealing Directive 95/46/EC (General Data Protection Regulation) (OJ L 119, 4.5.2016, p 1).

63 *Francovich v Italy* (C-6/90) [1995] ICR 722, [35]; *Carswell v Secretary of State for Transport* [2011] Lloyd's Rep IR 644. In *Francovich v Italy* (C-6/90) the relevant Directive was Council Directive 80/987 which was intended to guarantee employees a minimum level of protection under Community law in the event of the insolvency of their employer, without prejudice to more favourable provisions existing in the Member States. In particular it provided for specific guarantees of payment of unpaid wage claims. Italy failed to bring into force the laws, regulations and administrative provisions necessary to comply with the Directive within a period which expired on 23 October 1983. F had worked for CDN but had received only sporadic payments on account of his wages. CDN was ordered by the Court to pay approximately 6 million lire to F. F claimed to be entitled to obtain from the Italian State the guarantees provided for in Directive 80/987 or, in the alternative, compensation.

64 *Francovich v Italy* (C-6/90) [1995] ICR 722, [33].

65 Ibid, [34].

66 *McCall v Poulton* [2009] Lloyd's Rep IR 454, [111]; *Byrne v Motor Insurers' Bureau* [2009] QB 66, [21].

67 *Francovich* liability was described as an interference with deeply rooted legal traditions and core conceptions on the separation of powers, parliamentary sovereignty, and judicial independence, author and hierarchies. M. F. Granger, "Francovich Liability Before National Courts: 25 Years On, Has Anything Changed?" *Research Handbook on EU Tort Law*, Ed. by P. Giliker, 2017, p 95. Granger provides a broad overview of the application of Francovic damages in a number of EU Member States. In this book this chapter focuses only on the liabilities that may arise with respect to compulsory motor third party liability insurance.

68 *Francovich v Italy* (C-6/90) [1995] ICR 722; *R v Secretary of State for Transport, ex parte Factortame (No. 5)* [2000] 1 AC 524.

69 It is worth noting here that a Directive cannot of itself impose obligations on an individual and cannot therefore be relied upon as such against an individual. *Farrell v Whitty* (C-413/15) [2018] Lloyd's Rep IR 103, [31]. *Marshall v Southampton and South West Hampshire Area Health Authority (Teaching)* (C-152/84); [1986] ECR 723, [48]; *Faccini Dori v Recreb Srl* (C-91/92) [1994] ECR I-3325, [20]; *Pfeiffer v Deutsches Rotes Kreuz,*

(ii) The content of those rights must be capable of being identified on the basis of the provisions of the Directive.

(iii) Where the Member State exercises its discretion to implement the Directive, but the boundaries of the discretion are exceeded there is a breach by the Member State. This will only attract damages if the Member State's failure to transpose the Directive is "sufficiently serious."

(iv) There must be a direct causal link between the breach in question and any loss or damage sustained.

1.27 The first two elements will be analysed for every Directive separately. For instance, there is no doubt that the Second Directive satisfies the first two requirements in (i) and (ii) above.[70] The meaning of the third element should be clarified given that it will determine whether or not a Member State complied with its obligations or failed to implement the necessary measures as required by the EU law in the context of MTPL insurance.

1.28 A Member State's failure to transpose the Directive is "sufficiently serious" when the State "manifestly and gravely" disregarded the limits of its discretion.[71] The measure to compare the two systems is "the test equivalence" rather than identicality.[72] The principle of "equivalence" raises two sub-questions:

(i) Is there a "similar domestic action"?

(ii) Are the rules applicable to the Community right "not less favourable"?[73]

For instance, in the context of the Second Directive and the MIB Agreements, the European Court of Justice held in *Evans v Secretary of State for the Environment, Transport and the Regions*[74] that

> It is ... clear that the Community legislature's intention was to entitle victims of damage or injury caused by unidentified or insufficiently insured vehicles to protection equivalent to, and as effective as, that available to persons injured by identified and insured vehicles.

This is an unambiguous statement of the need to ensure equivalence with the system for insured drivers.[75]

1.29 The burden of proof is satisfied[76] if, in its proper domestic context, a national procedural provision renders the application of the relevant European law rights either impossible or excessively difficult.[77] It therefore appears that differences may be tolerated,

---

Kreisverband Waldshut eV (Joined Cases C-397/01 to C-403/01) [2004] ECR I-8835, [108] and *Dansk Industri (DI) v Rasmussen's Estate* (C-441/14) [2016] 3 CMLR 27, [30].

70 *Byrne v Motor Insurers' Bureau* [2009] QB 66 [33].

71 *Brasserie du Pecheur SA v Federal Republic of Germany, Regina v Secretary of State for Transport* (Joined Cases C-46/93 and C-48/93) [1996] QB 404. facts *Reg. v H.M. Treasury, Ex parte British Telecommunications Plc.* (C-392/93) [1996] QB 615; *Reg. v Ministry of Agriculture, Fisheries and Food, Ex parte Hedley Lomas (Ireland) Ltd.* (C-5/94) [1997] QB 139; *Dillenkofer v Federal Republic of Germany* (C-178/94) [1997] QB 259; *Denkavit Internationaal B.V. v Bundesamt fur Finanzen* (C-283/94) [1996] ECR I-5063.

72 *Byrne v Motor Insurers' Bureau* [2009] QB 66, [21]; *Carswell v Secretary of State for Transport* [2011] Lloyd's Rep IR 644.

73 *Byrne v Motor Insurers' Bureau* [2009] QB 66, [22]; *Carswell v Secretary of State for Transport* [2011] Lloyd's Rep IR 644, [16].

74 (C-63/01) [2004] Lloyd's Rep IR 391.

75 *Byrne v Motor Insurers' Bureau* [2009] QB 66, [44].

76 *Carswell v Secretary of State for Transport* [2011] Lloyd's Rep IR 644, [66].

77 Ibid, [17], [66]

that every single disparity is not significant. The threshold is high, and it requires a value judgment[78] by the national Court by taking into consideration a number of factors such as the clarity and precision of the rule breached, the degree of excusability of an error of law and the existence of any relevant judgment on the point.[79] *Evans v Secretary of State for the Environment, Transport and the Regions*[80] concerned the Motor Insurers' Bureau's Untraced Drivers Agreement 1972, which has subsequently been revised in a number of important respects by the 2003 Agreement. The CJEU carried out a comprehensive review of the legality of the Untraced Drivers Agreement, and it is an authoritative statement of the legal context in which the Untraced Drivers Agreement had to be considered.[81]

1.30 A number of issues discussed by the CJEU and those issues are referred to in Chapter 10. For the purposes of the present topic the CJEU accepted that the MIB Agreements should allow the claim of costs and interest but left it to the national Court to decide if the UK failed to implement the Directive in this respect. In the domestic dispute,[82] the judge struck out the victim's claim on its facts and in any case now the latest versions of the relevant Agreements permit the claim of interest and cost.

1.31 A further challenge was seen in *Byrne v Motor Insurers' Bureau*[83] where the claimant sustained injuries when a car ran into him in 1993, when he was 3 years old. The vehicle was never traced and at the time the claimant's parents, who did not seek legal advice, were unaware of the existence of the MIB scheme. It was 2001 when they became aware of the scheme for the first time and in October 2001 a claim was submitted against the MIB. However, the claim was made outside the three-year time limit set by clause 1(1)(f) of the Untraced Drivers Agreement 1972.[84] Proceedings against the MIB and the Secretary of State for Transport were begun in March 2006. By considering "the relative precision of the requirement, following *Evans*; the serious consequences of failure to comply; and the clear warning given in *Evans* of the need to make the comparison," the Court of Appeal was also satisfied that the infringement of the victim's right was sufficiently serious for the purposes of *Francovic* damages.

1.32 It is also clear from the cases that it is not necessary to establish fault or negligence on the part of the Member State going beyond what is relevant to show a sufficiently serious breach.[85] In *Byrne v Motor Insurers' Bureau* the Court of Appeal[86] agreed with Flaux J[87] at first instance where the judge said, "The fact that a Member State acted in good faith is not an answer if the lack of thoroughness, although inadvertent, is a sufficiently serious breach." Liability may still be established without any intentional infringement; the state of mind of the infringer may matter to the effect that a deliberate intention to infringe

---

78 *Byrne v Motor Insurers' Bureau* [2009] QB 66, [45].

79 See Lord Clyde in *R v Secretary of State for Transport, ex parte Factortame (No. 5)* [2000] 1 AC 524, 554–557; *Byrne v Motor Insurers' Bureau* [2009] QB 66, [21]; *Evans v Secretary of State for the Environment, Transport and the Regions* (C-63/01) [2004] Lloyd's Rep IR 391, [86].

80 (C-63/01) [2004] Lloyd's Rep IR 391.

81 [2009] QB 66, [44].

82 *Evans v Secretary of State for the Environment, Transport and the Regions* [2006] EWHC 322 (QB).

83 [2009] QB 66.

84 The Agreement, unlike the Limitation Act 1980, contained no provision suspending the limitation period during the claimant's minority.

85 *R v Secretary of State for Transport, ex parte Factortame (No. 5)* [2000] 1 AC 524.

86 [2009] QB 66.

87 [2008] Lloyd's Rep IR 61, [74].

would obviously weigh heavily in the scales of seriousness. Further, the behaviour of the infringer after it has become evident that an infringement has occurred and the position taken by one of the Community institutions in the matter may also be of importance.

Limitation period

1.33 The applicable limitation period in a claim against the UK for a failure to implement a Directive is six years under the Limitation Act 1980 s 2. It was held that a claim for damages by relying on the *Francovic* principles is not a separate and distinct cause of action that accrued after the date of the original cause of action.[88] In order to determine the date from when the relevant six-year period commences, it is necessary to establish when the relevant loss occurred. In the context of a claim for the reason that the UK failed to implement the Directives to provide compensation for the victims of untraced drivers, the relevant period starts running from the date when the claimant became the victim of an untraced driver and thus found himself subject to the restriction upon the rights contemplated for such victims by the relevant Directive. This rule was established in *Moore v Secretary of State for Transport*.[89] The claimant was seriously injured in a motor accident when he was at the age of 28 and a professional actor with the Royal Shakespeare Company. The accident took place on 19 April 1995, and the driver was untraced. Having been unsatisfied with the compensation awarded by the MIB, the claimant turned to the Secretary of State for Transport for Francovich damages, for having failed properly to implement the Second Motor Insurance Directive.[90] The claimant for Francovich damages was held to have been time barred given that the action was brought on 3 February 2006 whereas the relevant loss occurred at the date of the accident.

The principle of "consistent interpretation"

1.34 The Directives are not directly applicable in the Member States but need to be implemented into national legislation. It is a Member State's EU law obligation under Article 5 EEC to take all appropriate measures to achieve the result envisaged by the Directive.[91] This duty is binding on all the authorities of Member States including, for matters within their jurisdiction, the Courts.[92] Consequently, when a national Court interprets a provision of national law it is required to do so as far as possible in the light of the wording and purpose of Community law, in order to achieve the result sought by Community law.[93] The phrase "reading down" is used to express the principle of consistent interpretation.[94] The national Court must use interpretive methods recognised by its own

---

88 *Moore v Secretary of State for Transport* [2007] PIQR P24.
89 [2007] Lloyd's Rep IR 469.
90 The Untraced Drivers Agreement operative at that time was the 1972 Untraced Drivers Agreement.
91 *Marleasing SA v La Comercial Internacional de Alimentacion SA* (C-106/89) [1992] 1 CMLR 305, [8].
92 Ibid.
93 *Marleasing SA v La Comercial Internacional de Alimentacion SA* (C-106/89) [1992] 1 CMLR 305, [8]; *Lewis v Tindale* [2018] EWHC 2376 (QB), [42] (in the context of the location of the accident – whether private or public land); *Lewington v Motor Insurers' Bureau* [2018] RTR 18, [2] (in the context of the definition of motor vehicle under section 185(1) of the RTA 1988).
94 *Lewis v Tindale* [2018] EWHC 2376 (QB), [42].

national law.[95] Furthermore, this consistent interpretation obligation is limited by the principles of legal certainty and non-retroactivity, and the national Court must not use that obligation as the basis for re-interpreting other existing national laws.[96]

1.35 The obligation on the English Courts to construe domestic legislation consistently with Community law obligations is both broad and far-reaching. Such nature of the principles of consistent interpretation has been explained by a number of reported cases on the interpretation of domestic statutes in several different contexts including human rights and corporation tax.[97] It is accepted that the principles set out in those cases applied equally to the interpretation of national laws which implement the EU Directives.[98] Those principles that have been clarified by the Court cases were summarised by counsel for HMRC in *Vodafone 2 v Revenue and Customs Commissioners*[99] and subsequently have been reiterated by the judges in a number of other cases.[100] Accordingly, the obligation of consistent interpretation

(a)   is not constrained by conventional rules of construction;

(b)   does not require ambiguity in the legislative language;

(c)   is not an exercise in semantics or linguistics;

(d)   permits departure from the strict and literal application of the words which the legislature has elected to use;

(e)   permits the implication of words necessary to comply with Community law obligations; and

(f)   is not affected by the precise form of the words to be implied.

1.36 The abovementioned reported Court cases also highlighted the following two constraints:

(a)   The meaning should "go with the grain of the legislation." In other words, an interpretation must not lead to an interpretation being adopted which is inconsistent with the fundamental or cardinal feature of the national legislation since this would cross the boundary between interpretation and amendment.

(b)   The meaning should be "compatible with the underlying thrust of the legislation being construed." It cannot require the Courts to make decisions for which they are not equipped or give rise to important practical repercussions which the Court is not equipped to evaluate.

In the UK the RTA must be interpreted so as to accord with it.

---

95 *Churchill Insurance Co Ltd v Fitzgerald* [2013] Lloyd's Rep IR 137, [47].

96 *Churchill Insurance Co Ltd v Fitzgerald* [2013] Lloyd's Rep IR 137 [48]; *Angelidaki v Organismos Nomarkhiaki Aftodiikisi Rethimnis* (C-378/07) [2009] 3 CMLR 15 [199].

97 *Vodafone 2 v The Commissioners for Her Majesty's Revenue & Customs* [2010] Ch. 77 [37]; *ICI Plc v Colmer (Inspector of Taxes* (income and corporation tax); *Pickstone v Freemans Plc* [1989] AC 66 (work of equal value); *Litster v Forth Dry Dock & Engineering Co Ltd* [1990] 1 AC 546 (unfair dismissal); *R. (on the application of IDT Card Services Ireland Ltd) v Customs and Excise Commissioners* [2006] STC 1252 (VAT); *EB Central Services Ltd v Revenue and Customs Commissioners* [2008] STC 2209 (VAT); *Fleming (t/a Bodycraft) v Customs and Excise Commissioners* [2008] 1 CMLR 48 (VAT); *Ghaidan v Godin-Mendoza* [2004] 2 AC 557 (Sexual orientation discrimination).

98 *Churchill Insurance Co Ltd v Fitzgerald* [2013] Lloyd's Rep IR 137, [49].

99 [2010] Ch. 77.

100 *Churchill Insurance Co Ltd v Fitzgerald* [2013] Lloyd's Rep IR 137; *Lewington v Motor Insurers' Bureau* [2018] Lloyd's Rep IR 562.

Direct effect

1.37 This issue will be revisited in Chapter 10 with references to the case law authorities that discussed this matter. It suffices here to state that the CJEU ruled in *Becker v Finanzamt Munster-Innenstadt*[101] and was later applied consistently[102] that

> wherever the provisions of a Directive appear, as far as their subject-matter is concerned, to be unconditional and sufficiently precise, those provisions may, in the absence of implementing measures adopted within the prescribed period, be relied upon as against any national provision which is incompatible with the Directive or in so far as the provisions define rights which individuals are able to assert against the state.

---

101 (8/81) [1982] 1 CMLR 499.
102 *Comitato di Coordinamento per la Difesa della Cava v Regions Lombardia* (C-236/92) [1994] Env. L.R. 281; *Kampelmann v Landschaftsverband Westfalen-Lippe* (C253/96) [1998] 2 CMLR 131; *Farrell v Whitty* (C-356/05) [2007] Lloyd's Rep IR 525.

CHAPTER 2

The insurance obligation

Overview

Obligation to insure under the Road Traffic Act 1988

2.1 Under the Road Traffic Act 1988 (RTA 1988) s 143 (1)

(a) using a motor vehicle on a road or other public place[1] or
(b) causing or permitting any other person to use a motor vehicle on a road or other public place

without having in force in relation to the use of the vehicle such a policy of insurance or such a security in respect of third party risks as complies with the requirements of Part VI of the RTA 1988 is a criminal offence.[2]

2.2 Permitting the use of a vehicle, as will be discussed below, is not the same as using the vehicle.[3]

2.3 The objective of the section is to grant protection for those who sustain injury or damage caused by the use of a motor vehicle on a road or in a public place by providing for compulsory insurance in respect of third party risks. As an alternative to taking out a compulsory policy, a person may obtain a security in respect of third party risks. The security must comply with the RTA 1988 s 146 and satisfy the requirements listed under the Motor Vehicles (Third Party Risks) Regulations 1972[4] and the Motor Vehicles (Third-Party Risks Deposits) Regulations 1992.[5]

2.4 Whether or not the policy cover includes the person who was actually using the vehicle at the relevant time will be determined by the insurance policy, but this has to be considered also together with the RTA 1988[6] and the EU Directives.

---

1 The words "public place" were not included in the original version of the RTA 1988. In *Clarke v Kato* [1998] 4 All ER 417, as discussed in Chapter 3, the House of Lords held that the word "road" did not include a car park or similar public place. For the purpose of complying with Council Directive 72/166/EEC, as modified by Council Directives 84/5/EEC and 90/232/EEC, section 143, among others, was then amended by the Motor Vehicles (Compulsory Insurance) Regulations 2000/726 Reg 2 which added "public place" to both subsections (a) and (b) and hence extended the insurance requirement to the use of vehicles in public places other than roads. This modification came into force on 3 April 2000.

2 RTA 1988 s 143(1)–(2).

3 *Sahin v Havard* [2017] Lloyd's Rep IR 110, Longmore LJ, [20].

4 SI 1972/1217.

5 SI 1992/1284.

6 *Herbert v Railway Passengers Assurance Co* (1938) 60 Ll L Rep 143. This requires an understanding of how the whole scheme operates under RTA 1988, and the following chapters will present how the insurance policy is read together with the EU Directives and the RTA 1988.

Obligation under EU Directives

2.5 The Consolidated Directive Article 3 requires each Member State to take all appropriate measures to ensure that civil liability in respect of the use of vehicles normally based in its territory is covered by insurance. As referred to in Chapter 1 the Member States' obligation is to ensure that the result to be achieved by the relevant Directive is achieved. Each Member State shall take all appropriate measures to ensure that the insurance cover includes any loss or injury occurs in another Member State. The choice and form of methods of achieving that result is left to Member States.[7]

2.6 Under the Consolidated Directive the Member States should also ensure that where the loss occurs during a direct journey between two territories in which the Treaty is in force the loss or injury shall be covered in accordance with the national laws on compulsory insurance in force in the Member State in whose territory the vehicle is normally based. It may be nevertheless possible to seek compensation in the Member State where the accident occurred. This is analysed in Chapter 11.

2.7 The Consolidated Directive Article 3[8] requires Member States to establish, in their domestic legal systems, a general obligation to insure vehicles.[9] Section 143 of the RTA 1988 complies with this. Derogations are permitted under Article 5, and the RTA 1988 includes some exceptions to the compulsory motor vehicle insurance. Those exceptions will be referred to below.

Strict liability

2.8 The proof of an act or default as precisely defined by the RTA 1988 s 143(1)[10] is sufficient to find the offence under s 143(2).[11] Subject to the exceptions listed under sub-sections (3) and (4), this is an offence of strict liability[12] that the lack of knowledge on no insurance cover is not a defence.[13]

2.9 Intention to commit the breach of the statute need not be shown.[14] In *Lyons v May*[15] the owner of a motor-lorry requested a garage proprietor who had repaired the vehicle to deliver it at the owner's premises. The owner's third party policy covered himself and persons in his employ. The garage proprietor, who was not in the employ of the lorry owner, had no third party policy to cover his driving of the lorry. There was no inquiry as to such insurance by the lorry owner who was held to be guilty of an offence under the RTA 1930 s 35(1).

---

7 Art 249 of the EC Treaty.

8 Previously, Art 3(1) of the First Directive, Council Directive 72/166/EEC.

9 *Csonka v Magyar Allam* (C-409/11) [2014] 1 CMLR 14 [24].

10 Similar provisions appeared in the former Acts: RTA 1930 s 35(1), RTA 1960 s 201(2), RTA 1972 s 143(1).

11 *McLeod (or Houston) v Buchanan* [1940] 2 All ER 179.

12 *Director of Public Prosecutions v Fisher* [1992] RTR 93.

13 *Director of Public Prosecutions v Heritage* [2002] EWHC 2139 Admin; *Tapsell v Maslen* [1967] Crim. L.R. 53; (1966) 110 S.J. 853. The prosecution are not obliged to prove knowledge of the fact that the user is without insurance; the offence is not one involving *mens rea* in that respect. *Lyons v May* [1948] 2 All ER 1062; *Morris v Williams* (1951) 50 LGR 308.

14 *McLeod (or Houston) v Buchanan* [1940] 2 All ER 179.

15 [1948] 2 All ER 1062.

2.10 If the policy covers the owner but the person who uses the vehicle with his permission is not covered, clearly the offence is committed.[16] An offence is committed where also the owner[17] permits the use of the vehicle with an honest and mistaken belief that the borrower has insurance whereas he does not.[18] If the owner argues that he was induced to permit the vehicle by a misrepresentation by the borrower the statutory responsibility still lies on him; the claim for misrepresentation against the misrepresentor is a matter between them.[19]

Burden of proof

2.11 As also seen above with regards to the certificate, the burden is on the driver of proving that he was covered by insurance whilst driving. In *Davey v Towle*[20] the motorist was driving C's vehicle at C's request. When he was stopped by the police officer he was unable to produce either his driving licence or an insurance certificate. The police officer issued a form which permitted the motorist to produce the documents within an identified period of time at Barton police station which the motorist failed to comply with. He then defended himself by arguing that it was not his fault that no documents were presented, he had spoken to C after being stopped by the police, and C had said that he would take the documents to the police station. It was held that the failure of C to take the certificate to the police station could not have any effect whatever on the charge against the defendant motorist, who himself failed to do what was required of him.[21]

Certificate of insurance

2.12 Under section 147(1) of the RTA 1988 a certificate of insurance is required to be delivered by the insurer to the assured. The certificate must satisfy the prescribed form and contain the necessary particulars as identified by the statute. The form of certificates and ancillary matters are governed by the Motor Vehicles (Third Party Risks) Regulations 1972.[22] Every certificate of insurance or certificate of security shall be issued not later than four days after the date on which the policy or security to which it relates is issued or renewed.[23] Such certificate triggers[24] the commencement of the compulsory insurance as required under Part VI of the RTA 1988. The contract of insurance is constituted by

---

16 *Richards v Port of Manchester Insurance Co Ltd* (1934) 50 Ll L Rep 132. *Mumford v Hardy* [1956] 1 WLR 163. The insurer will still provide cover for the victim's loss with a right of recourse against the driver and the assured owner. See Chapter 8 and the RTA 1988 s 151.

17 A person who permits the use under section 143 may not be the owner, however, for simplicity "owner" will be used to express the person who permits or causes someone to use the vehicle without insurance.

18 *Baugh v Crago* [1975] RTR 453; *Ferrymasters Ltd v Adams* [1980] RTR 139; *Limbrick v French* [1993] PIQR 121. *Limbrick* was decided under the 1972 Act, the wording of which was almost identical in this respect.

19 *Lloyd-Wolper v Moore* [2004] RTR 30.

20 [1973] RTR 328. Applied *John v Humphreys* [1955] 1 WLR 325; *Philcox v Carberry* [1960] Crim. L.R. 563; *Leathley v Drummond* [1972] RTR 293.

21 See also *Director of Public Prosecutions v Kavaz* [1999] RTR 40.

22 SI 1972/1217.

23 Reg 6.

24 R.M. Merkin, *Colinvaux's Law of Insurance*, 11th ed (main work and supplement series), 2017, Sweet & Maxwell [23–05].

and contained in the policy.[25] The certificate itself does not replace the contract of insurance that is required by the Act,[26] but it confirms that the insurers provide the cover that the RTA 1988 requires.[27] Recently Lord Hodge confirmed in *R&S Pilling (t/a Phoenix Engineering) v UK Insurance Ltd*[28] that the certificate, whose function is evidence of the existence of the policy, is not to be interpreted as a separate contractual basis.[29] Hence, the certificate is not a contractual document and is incapable of undermining the policy itself.[30] Where the policy contains an exclusion clause which is not seen in the certificate, it does not deprive the policy wording of effect.[31]

2.13 A driver may be asked by a police constable to produce a certificate proving that the driver is covered by the required insurance.[32] A driver may produce either the certificate or a duplicate copy of it.[33] If the driver does not produce the certificate or other evidence of insurance when asked, he may do so within seven days at a police station that was specified by him at the time when its production was required.[34] The production must be for a reasonable time to enable the constable to examine it and take details.[35] Moreover, in the case of the production at a police station the policyholder must produce it in person,[36] as sending it by post is not sufficient for this purpose.[37]

2.14 If a person fails to produce such evidence of insurance the constable may seize the vehicle.[38] If the owner fails to produce the certificate or other documents as stated under section 165(2)(a) the owner will be guilty of an offence.[39] Further, a police constable may seize the vehicle if he has reasonable grounds for believing that the vehicle is being driven in contravention of section 87(1) or 143 of the RTA 1988.[40]

2.15 A wrongful seizure, however, may entitle the owner of the vehicle for damages in tort for wrongful interference with goods. In *Pryor v Chief Constable of Greater Manchester Police*[41] the driver was using the car with the permission of the owner and presented the certificate of insurance to the police constable who made an inquiry with the insurer. The insurer wrongly informed that that cover was dependent on the vehicle also having its own insurance cover. According to the certificate shown, the driver who was driving with the owner's permission was covered. The Court accepted the claim for damages as there had been no failure to produce the required evidence under s 165A(3)(b).

---

25 *Biddle v Johnston* [1965] 2 Lloyd's Rep 121.

26 Ibid.

27 *Charlton v Fisher* [2002] QB 578, 583; *R&S Pilling (t/a Phoenix Engineering) v UK Insurance Ltd* [2019] UKSC 16 [28]–[29].

28 [2019] UKSC 16.

29 Ibid, [28]–[30].

30 *Bristol Alliance Ltd Partnership v Williams* [2013] RTR 9.

31 *Bristol Alliance Ltd Partnership v Williams* [2013] RTR 9; *Gray v Blackmore* [1934] 1 KB 95.

32 RTA 1988, s 165(1)(2); s 170: In the case of an accident. *Tattersall v Drysdale* [1935] 2 KB 174.

33 Motor Vehicles (Third Party Risks) Regulations 1972/1217, Reg 7(1).

34 RTA 1988 s 165(4). In the case of accident within seven days after the occurrence of it (s 170(7).

35 *Tremelling v Martin* [1971] RTR 196.

36 RTA 1988 s 165(4)(a); *Starkey v Hall* (1936) 55 Ll L Rep 24.

37 *Starkey v Hall* (1936) 55 Ll L Rep 24.

38 RTA 1988 s 165A(3)–(5).

39 RTA 1988 s 165(3); s 171(2).

40 RTA 1988 s 165A.

41 [2011] RTR 33.

2.16 *Pryor* was distinguished in *Gray v The Commissioner of Police of the Metropolis*[42] where on the facts the Court held that the police constable had had reasonable grounds for believing that the vehicle was being driven without insurance[43] and the requirements under section 165A for seizure of the vehicle were met. *Gray* confirmed that the burden is on the driver to produce the best evidence of his insurance in the form of a hard copy or an electronic copy, and there is no obligation on the police officer to provide electronic equipment to the driver himself to enable him to produce electronically the certificate.

2.17 When a claim is made against a driver by the victim of an accident and the victim demands such information, the driver must state whether he was insured by a policy having effect for the purposes of Part VI of the RTA 1988 or had in force a security having effect for those purposes in respect of that liability.[44] If he is insured, he must give such particulars with respect to that policy or security as were specified in any certificate of insurance or security delivered in respect of that policy or security.[45] If without reasonable excuse, a person fails to comply with the provisions of these subsection requirements, or wilfully makes a false statement in reply to any such demand as is referred to above, he is guilty of an offence.[46]

2.18 It is an offence to make a false statement or withhold any material information for the purpose of obtaining the issue of a certificate of insurance or certificate of security under Part VI of the RTA which was mentioned above.[47] Additionally, an insurer will be guilty of an offence by issuing a certificate of insurance which to his knowledge is false in a material particular. It was argued in *Ocean Accident & Guarantee Corp Ltd v Cole*[48] the insurer issued, with knowledge, a false certificate for the assured. In this case the policy, which provided that it might be renewed during any period for which the insurer might accept payment for the renewal of the policy and no liability should arise until the premium due had been paid and accepted, expired on 3 June 1931. The policyholder paid the premium on 11 June, and a certificate was issued by the insurer on that date stating that the certificate was valid from 4 June. The Court interpreted that as soon as the insurer had accepted a premium, their liability had attached for the period for which they had accepted payment for the renewal of the policy, namely, from 3 June 1931.

Keeping a record of the certificate

2.19 The Motor Vehicles (Third Party Risks) Regulations 1972 provide that insurers must keep a record of the following information for seven years[49]:

- the number of the policy or security;
- the name and address of the person to whom the policy or security is issued; either the name of every person whose liability is covered by the policy or

---

42 [2016] EWCA Civ 1360.
43 The driver subsequently adduced evidence that he was insured.
44 RTA 1988 s 154(1)(a).
45 RTA 1988 s 154(1)(b).
46 RTA 1988 s 154(2).
47 RTA 1988 s 174.
48 [1932] 2 KB 100.
49 Reg 10; commencing on the expiry of the relevant policy or security (Reg 10(4)).

security, or if that is not reasonably possible, a description of the persons whose liability is covered by the policy or security;

- the registration number of every vehicle insured or a description of the vehicles which are identified in the policy or security other than by reference to a registration number;
- the date on which the policy or security comes into force and the date that it expires;
- (in the case of a policy) the conditions on which the insurance cover is determined; and
- (in the case of a security), the conditions on which the security will be implemented.[50]

When a vehicle does not meet insurance requirements

2.20 Under section 144B it is an offence when a vehicle does not meet the insurance requirements. The insurance requirement is satisfied when (a) the policy or security, or the certificate of insurance or security which relates to the vehicle, identifies the vehicle by its registration mark as a vehicle which is covered by the policy or security or (b) the vehicle's owner is specified in the insurance policy or security. There are a number of exceptions to the offence set out in the new section 144B. Some of these are similar to the exceptions in section 144 of the RTA which apply to the section 143 offence of using a vehicle without insurance. Other exceptions may apply where the registered keeper no longer keeps the vehicle; it is not kept for use on a road or other public place or has been stolen. The exceptions apply only if a prior statement (such as a statutory off-road "SORN" declaration) has been made to the appropriate authorities as required by regulations.

2.21 If a section 144A offence is committed, the Secretary of State can give a fixed penalty notice on a person whom he believes has committed the offence. The notice gives the offender the opportunity to pay a fixed penalty (currently £100) to discharge the offence.[51] If £100 is paid before the expiry of 21 days no proceedings are commenced against the offender.[52]

2.22 Additionally, section 144D introduced Schedule 2AI under which the Secretary of State can make regulations which enable an authorised person to clamp vehicles upon reasonable suspicion that a section 144A offence has been committed and to enable the removal and disposal of such vehicles, including the time and manner in which such vehicles may be disposed of. Regulations may exempt a vehicle with a current disabled person's badge, or which meets other prescribed conditions, from being clamped. The Regulations may enable a person to obtain release of a clamped or an impounded vehicle if he or she pays any due charges and can show (a) that in driving the vehicle away he

---

50 Under Reg 10(3), "Any person who has deposited and keeps deposited with the Accountant-General of the Supreme Court [the sum for the time being specified in section 144(1) of the Road Traffic Act 1988] shall keep a record of the motor vehicles owned by him and of any certificates issued by him or on his behalf under these Regulations in respect of such motor vehicles and of the withdrawal or destruction of any such certificates."

51 RTA 1988 section 144C(1)(2).

52 Regulations may substitute a different amount for the amount for the time being specified as £100 (s 144C(9)).

or she will not be committing an offence under section 143 of the RTA and (b) that the registered keeper is not guilty of an offence under section 144A. Regulations may also make it a criminal offence to interfere with a clamp or associated notice, use a vehicle in breach of statutory requirements in connection with disabled persons or give any false declaration to secure release of a vehicle.

Void and voidable insurance contracts

2.23 If a contract of insurance is avoidable, and at the time the vehicle is used the policy has not been avoided, the contract is in force and the user is not guilty of being without insurance at the relevant time.[53] A contract which is voidable may be enforced between the parties until it is avoided. However, once avoided, the contract is treated as it was never made.

2.24 Void contracts are different to above as no insurance contract comes into existence and the offence in the RTA 1988 s 143(2) is committed.[54]

Contracts with an exclusion clause

2.25 A person may be uninsured because the insurance contract contains an express exclusion clause for the claim in question. This matter should be approached with care. First of all, some exclusion clauses are restricted in that they cannot be relied upon towards a third party victim of a motor traffic accident.[55] The insurer, however, after compensating the victim's loss, may recoup[56] against the assured by virtue of those policy exclusions which can be enforced towards him.

2.26 Some exclusions on the other hand are enforceable against both the assured and the third party victim in which case no insurance cover is available for the accident. It follows that the offence under s 143(2) has been committed.[57]

2.27 In *Telford and Wrekin BC v Ahmed*[58] the policy excluded the use on "ply for hire" operations from the insurance cover. The defendant, who was plying for hire a hackney carriage for which a licence to ply for hire had not been obtained, was found guilty of an offence of using the vehicle without insurance.[59] Insurance certificates contained a footnote in the following form: "Advice to Third Parties. Nothing in the certificate affects your right as a third party to make a claim." The Court held that the note merely gave notice of the consequences of arrangements made under the aegis of the Motor Insurers' Bureau for the compensation of third parties for the liabilities of an uninsured driver. It did not affect what was in fact covered by the policies. As noted in *Telford*, it is a matter of construction of the policy terms to find if the motorist is insured.

---

53 *Durrant v MacLaren* [1956] 2 Lloyd's Rep 70; *Adams v Dunne* [1978] RTR 281.

54 *Richards v Port of Manchester Insurance Co Ltd* (1934) 50 Ll L Rep 132; *Evans v Lewis* [1964] 1 Lloyd's Rep 258.

55 See Chapter 7 and RTA 1988 s 148 and the Consolidated Directive Art 13.

56 RTA 1988 s 151(7).

57 See Chapter 2.

58 [2006] EWHC 1748 (Admin).

59 See also *JRM (Plant) v Hodgson* [1960] 1 Lloyd's Rep 538 where the policy excluded cover for "use whilst drawing a trailer" and *Kerridge v Rush* [1952] 2 Lloyd's Rep 305 where "drawing a greater number of trailers in all than is permitted by law" was excluded.

2.28 The relevant exclusion may have two different meanings. In *Carnill v Rowland*[60] the issue was the interpretation of the words "a sidecar permanently fixed." The insurers accepted that they were "on risk" when the cycle was fitted with a chassis and a third wheel but with the body of the sidecar temporarily absent. The Court accepted the insurers' interpretation of the wording in the light of the facts and the policyholder was not guilty of an offence.

No obligation on the insurer to accept insurance proposals

2.29 In *Commission of the European Communities v Italy*[61] the Commission of the European Communities challenged Italian legislation that required motor insurers providing such cover in Italy to accept compulsory insurance risks on the basis of contract terms and insurance rates which were established in advance by them. Guidance was given by Italian law as to the calculation of premiums. The Commission's argument was that the relevant domestic law hinders intra-Community trade in so far as it reduces the ability of insurance undertakings, having their head office in another Member State, to implement their strategic market choices independently. The CJEU held that the domestic law leaves intact the right of access to the Italian market as regards MTPL insurance resulting from that authorisation. The Court recognised that the obligation to contract restricts the freedom of establishment and the freedom to provide services which economic operators, in principle, enjoy. The Court nevertheless upheld the legislation as enough justification was found for its enforcement. The very purpose of MTPL insurance is to guarantee compensation for victims of road traffic accidents. The domestic law hence served such a social protection objective. Moreover, the number of road traffic accidents declared to insurance undertakings is particularly high in certain areas in the south of Italy. That situation has led to a considerable increase in the financial risks incurred by those undertakings in that region. The domestic law was held to be appropriate to ensure the achievement of the objective which it pursues and did not go beyond what it necessary to attain it.

2.30 English law does not provide such an express restriction on the ability of an insurer to reject an insurance proposal for MTPL; insurers are free to accept or reject the assured's proposal for insurance.

Exceptions to compulsory insurance or security

2.31 The RTA 1988 section 144 refers to two different types of exception. The first exception which appears under subsection (1) relies on some certain amount of deposit that would be kept at the specified institution for the owner of a vehicle. Accordingly, if that person deposits and keeps deposited with the Accountant General of the Senior Courts the sum of £500,000,[62] at a time when the vehicle is being driven under the owner's control,

---

60 [1953] 1 WLR 380.

61 (C-518/06) [2009] 3 CMLR 22.

62 This amount is the minimum and subject to amendments by the Secretary of State (after the approval of the House of Parliament) who may by order made by statutory instrument substitute a greater sum 144(1)(A)(B).

absence of insurance or security would not result in a criminal offence. In other words, the money deposited will replace the insurance-security requirement.

2.32 Irrespective of the depositing requirement mentioned above, vehicles that are owned by some certain defined institutions are excepted from section 143 at a time when the vehicle is being driven under the owner's control. These institutions include[63] for instance the council of a county or county district in England and Wales, the Common Council of the City of London, a vehicle owned by a local policing body or a police authority.[64]

2.33 The excepted institutions or body of authorities under section 144 may nevertheless take out compulsory motor vehicle insurance. As seen in *Miller v Hales*,[65] which is discussed in more detail below, the Kent Constabulary had a motor vehicle policy with the defendant insurers and the policy was held to cover the claim for the injuries suffered by a police constable. It is further to be noted that when a police officer is on duty, using his own motor vehicle for police purposes and not covered by his own third party insurance or security, he is covered by the exception from requirement of third party insurance or security as set out in section 144 of RTA 1988.[66]

EU law

2.34 Article 4 of the First Directive made it possible for Member States to derogate from Article 3 of the Directive in respect of vehicles belonging to certain persons, or certain types of vehicle, or vehicles having a special plate. However, such derogations were subject to the condition that Member States take the appropriate measures to ensure that compensation is paid in respect of any loss or injury caused in the territory of other Member States by vehicles belonging to such persons.

2.35 The Consolidated Directive grants the same permission with the addition of what had been introduced by the Fifth Directive.[67] Accordingly, derogation from such obligation is permitted in respect of certain natural or legal persons, public or private; a list of such persons shall be drawn up by the State concerned and communicated to the other Member States and to the Commission.[68] This permission is subject to the condition that appropriate measures to ensure that compensation is paid in respect of any loss or injury caused in its territory and in the territory of other Member States by vehicles belonging to such persons are taken by Member States. This includes designating an authority or body in the country where the loss or injury occurs responsible for compensating injured parties. Derogation is also permitted in respect of certain types of vehicle or certain

---

63 For a full list see RTA 1988 s 144.

64 At a time when it is being driven under the owner's control, or to a vehicle at a time when it is being driven for police purposes by or under the direction of a constable. For the full list see section 144 of the RTA 1988.

65 [2007] Lloyd's Rep IR 54.

66 *Jones v Chief Constable of Bedfordshire* [1987] RTR 332.

67 The Fifth Directive provided that the Member States shall ensure that, for certain vehicles that belong to public or private persons and are therefore excluded from compulsory MTPL insurance, a compensation system is in operation. Additionally, for vehicles excluded from the MTPL insurance obligation because of holding certain plates, Member States shall ensure that they are treated in the same way as vehicles for which the insurance obligation provided for in Article 3(1) has not been satisfied so that, if needed, compensation would be provided by the national compensation body. Art 1(3).

68 Art 5(1).

vehicles having a special plate.[69] Such vehicles would be treated as if not insured.[70] As a result, the guarantee fund of the Member State in which the accident has taken place shall have a claim against the guarantee fund in the Member State where the vehicle is normally based.[71] Article 6 aims to ensure that National Insurers' Bureau collects and provides the necessary information about the territory that the vehicle is normally based, and it is registered as well as the insurance information. Vehicles that are normally based in third countries are subject to checks when they enter into a Member States that any loss or injury caused by those vehicles is covered throughout the EU by insurance as required by the Directive.[72] Such vehicles must provide either a Green Card or an insurance certificate proving the insurance mentioned above.[73]

2.36 Member States are required to take necessary measures that single premium is charged by the insurance bodies to insure vehicles in the entire territory of the Community.[74]

2.37 Where citizens move across borders, in order to facilitate switching to a new insurance provider, the current Article 16[75] of the Consolidated Directive provides that Member States must ensure the policyholder has the right to request a claims history statement covering the last five years. Upon the receiving policyholders' request, the insurer shall provide that statement to the policyholder within 15 days (Article 16 paragraph 2).

2.38 There is no requirement on insurers to take such statements into account when calculating premiums. The Commission believed that to facilitate the authentication of claims history statements by insurers it is beneficial that content and format are the same across the EU.[76] Hence, the proposal[77] dated 24 May 2018 to the effect amending the Consolidated Directive adds the following sentence at the end of the second subparagraph: "They shall do so using the form of the claims history statement."

2.39 Further, the Commission highlighted that although statements may be required as provided by Article 16 of the Consolidated Directive, the statements are not taken into account by the insurers when citizens move across borders and when they are issued by an insurer in another Member State, sometimes their authenticity is questioned.[78] As a result the Commission proposed the following to be added to Article 16 of the Consolidated Directive:

> Member States shall ensure that insurance undertakings or the bodies as referred to in the second subparagraph, when taking account of claims history statements issued by other insurance undertakings or other bodies as referred to in the second subparagraph, do not treat policyholders in a discriminatory manner or surcharge their premiums because of their nationality or solely on the basis of their previous Member State of residence.
>
> Member States shall ensure that insurance undertakings publish their policies in respect of their use of claims history statements when calculating premiums.

---

69 Art 5(2).
70 Compensation for accidents caused by uninsured vehicles is examined in Chapter 10.
71 Compensation for accidents caused by uninsured or untraced drivers is analysed in Chapter 10.
72 Art 7.
73 Art 8.
74 Art 14.
75 "Statement relating to the third party liability claims."
76 https://ec.europa.eu/info/law/better-regulation/initiatives/ares-2017-3714481_en#pe-2018-3261.
77 See Chapter 1 for the background of this proposal.
78 https://ec.europa.eu/info/law/better-regulation/initiatives/ares-2017-3714481_en#pe-2018-3261.

THE INSURANCE OBLIGATION

The Commission shall be empowered to adopt implementing acts in accordance with Article 28a(2) specifying the contents and form of the claims history statement referred to in the second subparagraph. That statement shall contain information about all of the following:

(a) the identity of the insurance undertaking issuing the claims history statement;
(b) the identity of the policyholder;
(c) the vehicle insured;
(d) the period of cover of the vehicle insured:
(e) the number and value of the declared third party liability claims during the period covered by the claims history statement.

The objective of this proposed amendment is to benefit citizens moving across borders.

CHAPTER 3

Insurance obligation

Scope (meaning of "permit," "cause," "motor vehicle," "road or other public place")

Permit and cause use

3.1 Section 143(1)(b) of RTA 1988 states, "A person must not cause or permit any other person to use a motor vehicle on a road or other public place . . ." without the insurance cover required by the statute. Two different actions are in question here: (1) to permit and (2) to cause another person to use a motor vehicle. The word "consent" may be used interchangeably with "permission."[1] Giving leave and licence to somebody to use the vehicle is described as "to permit"[2]: A allows his friend B to use his motor car.[3]

3.2 Permission may be given expressly or inferred from the arrangement between the relevant parties to it. In *McLeod (or Houston) v Buchanan*[4] it was held that where a policy covers for business use only and if the owner permits another to use the vehicle without any restrictions, this impliedly permits all uses including for purposes not covered by any insurance.[5] *Buchanan* is to be conferred with some other precedents in which it was held that a permission to use is not, unless more is proved, a permission to use in contravention.[6]

3.3 It is a matter of fact to prove if the permission includes any restrictions. This issue will be analysed in more detail below.

3.4 Both "to permit" or "to cause" require proof of *mens rea* in knowledge of the facts rendering the user unlawful.[7] However, the two expressions differ in a number of respects. The user involves some express or positive mandate "to cause" the use of the vehicle,[8] in the form of ordering or directing someone to use the vehicle.[9] If A tells

---

1 *Singh v Rathour* [1988] RTR 324, referring to *Browning v Phoenix Assurance Co Ltd* [1960] 2 Lloyd's Rep 360.

2 *Shave v Rosner* [1954] 2 QB 113, [116], Lord Goddard. In the context of the Motor Vehicles (Construction and Use) Regulations, 1951, Reg 72(1): "Every motor vehicle . . . shall at all times be in such condition . . . that no danger is caused . . . to any person . . . on a road." By Regulation 101 any person who "uses or causes or permits to be used on any road a motor vehicle . . . in contravention of . . . the preceding Regulations" commits an offence.

3 *Shave v Rosner* [1954] 2 QB 113, [116], Lord Goddard.

4 [1940] 2 All ER 179.

5 *McLeod (or Houston) v Buchanan* [1940] 2 All ER 179.

6 *James & Son v Smee* [1955] 1 QB 78.

7 *Ross Hillman Ltd. v Bond* [1974] QB 435. In the case of a company it must be proved that some person for whose criminal act the company is responsible permitted as opposed to committed the offence. *James & Son v Smee* [1955] 1 QB 78.

8 *McLeod (or Houston) v Buchanan* [1940] 2 All ER 179; *Ross Hillman Ltd. v Bond* [1974] QB 435.

9 *Shave v Rosner* [1954] 2 QB 113, [116], Lord Goddard; *McLeod (or Houston) v Buchanan* [1940] 2 All ER 179; *Ross Hillman Ltd. v Bond* [1974] QB 435.

his chauffeur to bring his car round and drive A to his work, A is causing the car to be used.[10] "To permit," in this respect, is a looser and vaguer expression than "to cause."[11]

3.5 Each case turns on its own facts. In *Reay v Young*[12] an offence was committed where a husband, who was insured, allowed his wife, who was uninsured, to drive the car, he himself being present. The wife was not driving as his servant. This is to be distinguished from a case where an employee, during the course of his employment and whilst the vehicle is on its authorised route, permits an uninsured person to drive the insured vehicle that is under his control. In *Marsh v Moores*[13] the insurance was taken out by the employer and provided cover "in the event of an accident caused by or through or in connexion with the vehicle against all sums which the company shall become legally liable to pay in respect of the death or bodily injury to any person or damage to property." J was employed as a driver and he allowed P to drive the vehicle while it was proceeding on the route of its authorised journey. J was giving a lesson in driving sitting beside P and ready to operate the hand brake. No accident took place but the matter arose because the vehicle was overtaken by the police who then ascertained that P was not the holder of a driving licence. The Court held that the RTA 1930 did not require that there should be a policy of insurance in existence covering the personal liability of the driver of the vehicle if there was already a policy in respect of third party risks covering the user of the car at the material time. J was the servant of the company who was entrusted with the driving of the car on the day in question. It was an unauthorised act by J to allow P to drive, but it was within the scope of his authority of controlling the vehicle. It was left open in *Reay v Young* whether or not the husband was controlling the driving and so that he was the driver of the car – both husband and wife pleaded guilty in that case. In *Marsh*, it was held that if a third party had been injured as a result of an accident at the relevant time J would be liable, at least in part, along with P and J's employers would, in turn, be legally responsible vicariously for the negligence of their servant acting within the scope of his authority. Such loss would have fallen within the scope of the insurance and therefore no offence of uninsured driving was committed.

Similarly, in *Langman v Valentine.*[14] the second respondent, who was sitting in the seat next to that of the driver and had his left hand on the steering wheel and right hand on the hand-brake was held to be driving the vehicle. The policy that insured the second respondent would have covered if a victim had been injured by an accident when the first respondent was taking a driving lesson in this form from the second respondent. The mere fact that the former had no policy was immaterial where the latter was driving simultaneously.

Conditional permission

3.6 If a permission is given subject to a condition, failing to fulfil it may nullify the permission. In *Newbury v Davis*[15] D had granted H permission to use the vehicle, subject

---

10 *Shave v Rosner* [1954] 2 QB 113, [116], Lord Goddard.
11 *McLeod (or Houston) v Buchanan* [1940] 2 All ER 179.
12 [1949] 1 All ER 1102.
13 [1949] 2 KB 208.
14 [1952] 2 All ER 803.
15 [1974] RTR 367.

to his insuring it. H however used the vehicle with no insurance in force. The Court interpreted H's use as without D's permission. A similar ruling is seen in *Sheldon Deliveries Ltd v Willis*[16] where a limited company, who could act only through its servants, had its express instructions disobeyed by an employee driver. The company had no knowledge that the employee was using the vehicle contrary to the instructions, and that knowledge of fact[17] was required for conviction so there was no conviction. *Director of Public Prosecutions v Fisher*[18] did not refer to *Sheldon* but distinguished *Newbury* and added that considering the serious consequences that a traffic accident might cause to the third party victims, *Newbury v Davis* should be read with extreme caution.[19] The facts of *Director of Public Prosecutions v Fisher*[20] were slightly different that when lending the car to L the defendant's condition was, knowing that L was disqualified, that L could find a driver who was insured for the journey. R, who was uninsured, drove the vehicle for L who never enquired if R was insured. It was held that in order to establish a conditional permission, the defendant would have at least to have been found to have given it directly to the would-be driver. The Court's concern was that a person who lends his car to another could then avoid liability merely by saying something to the other to the effect, "Please see to it that you are insured before using the car."[21]

3.7 On the other hand, *Newbury v Davies* was followed once more in *Pearl Assurance Plc v Kavanagh*[22] where the assured K permitted H to drive her vehicle only if H arranged his own insurance cover. H, who drove the vehicle without insurance, was involved in an accident. The Court held that K's permission, which was subject to a condition which was not fulfilled, was not a permission at all.[23] Moreover, later, the Court of Appeal confirmed in *Lloyd-Wolper v Moore*[24] that the assured owner may protect himself by making the permission subject to the performance or fulfilment of a condition.

3.8 The facts of *Fisher* are clearly different from the other cases that went to the different directions to *Fisher*. It might be said that the owner of a vehicle may argue that he had given a conditional permission which was not fulfilled and he may defend himself in an action depending on the content and the nature of the permission. The defendant must know the fact that his vehicle is being driven by someone else, and if the defendant does not know such a fact then the offence is not committed. As again noted above, the lack of knowledge on whether the driver is insured is not a defence, but the lack of the actual driving is a defence. In *Fisher* it could be a clearer reason if the Court had emphasised that the defendant had known that because L was disqualified some other people would have been driving for L and hence, the Court required that the condition must have been communicated to the actual driver.

---

16 [1972] RTR 217.

17 See *Ross Hillman Ltd. v Bond* [1974] QB 435 and *James & Son v Smee* [1955] 1 QB 78 mentioned above.

18 [1992] RTR 93.

19 *Director of Public Prosecutions v Fisher* [1992] RTR 93.

20 [1992] RTR 93.

21 *Director of Public Prosecutions v Fisher* [1992] RTR 93, 97–98, Watkins LJ.

22 [2001] CLY 3832.

23 This was an action by K's insurer against K under section 151(8) of the RTA 1988 which is discussed in Chapter 8.

24 [2004] RTR 30.

Death of the person who gave the permission

3.9 The permission is personal to the person who has been granted it.[25] Continuing permission must be assumed until shown to have been terminated.[26] Unless any limitation is stated expressly, the permission does not automatically lapse on the death of the person who granted it, but the executrix can terminate the permission.[27] In *Kelly v Cornhill Insurance Co. Ltd*[28] the policy covered "(1) any person driving the insured car on the order of or with the permission of the insured and who has not been refused any motor vehicle insurance or continuance thereof by any insurer." The father who took out this policy died on 2 June 1959, after he gave permission to his son to drive the vehicle. While driving the car the son was involved in an accident in February 1960, causing damage to the property of third parties. Lord Dilhorne rejected to read the word "permission" in the policy as "permission which the insured was at all relevant times in a position to cancel or revoke."[29] Further, there was no reason by operation of law to regard a permission for an unlimited duration to have been either revoked or cancelled upon death of the permitter.[30]

The offender

3.10 Permission to use a vehicle can be given by the owner or another person, for instance a hirer of the vehicle.[31] The vital question is whether the alleged offender is in a position to forbid the use of the vehicle.[32] Hence, in *Thompson v Lodwick*[33] it was held that the defendant who agreed to supervise the driving and sat in the front passenger seat whilst the owner of the vehicle, who had the provisional driving licence, was driving it without insurance, was held not to be in a position to forbid the use of this vehicle. Moreover, in *Watkins v O'Shaughnessy*[34] the defendant was held not to be in a position to control and hence to permit the driver to use the vehicle once he sold it to the driver.

3.11 This matter is important also when, under an insurance policy, the persons entitled to drive included "the policyholder and any other person who was driving on the policyholder's order or with his permission." When the vehicle is sold, in principle, the owner ceases to have insurable interest in it and any permission given by him before the sale cannot be extended after it.[35] If the new owner uses the vehicle without insurance, he cannot argue that he was using it with the previous owner's permission.[36]

---

25 *Kelly v Cornhill Insurance Co. Ltd.* [1964] 1 WLR 158.
26 Ibid.
27 Ibid.
28 [1964] 1 WLR 158.
29 Ibid, 162.
30 Ibid, 162.
31 *Sahin v Havard* [2017] Lloyd's Rep IR 110.
32 *Lloyd v Singleton* [1953] 1 QB 357; *Shave v Rosner* [1954] 2 QB 113; *Goodbarne v Buck* [1940] 1 KB 771.
33 [1983] RTR 76.
34 [1939] 1 All ER 385.
35 *Smith v Relph* [1963] 2 Lloyd's Rep 439.
36 Ibid.

A person using the vehicle in the course of employment

3.12 If the driver is an employee who neither knew nor had reason to believe that there was not in force in relation to the vehicle such a policy of insurance or security as is mentioned in the RTA 1988 s 143(1), the employee may not be charged for the criminal offence under the RTA 1988 s 143(2). The relevant conditions to be satisfied are that the vehicle must be used by an employee in the course of his employment and the vehicle must not belong to the employee and was not in his possession under a contract of hiring or of loan. These conditions are listed under the RTA 1988 s 143(3) and are cumulative.[37] Hence, a taxi driver who hired a vehicle from M Taxi Rental was found guilty under s 143(2) although being uninsured was not his failure. He was uninsured because M had failed to notify the insurer of this particular driver's name to be noted on the policy.[38] The Court found no difficulty in finding the breach as he had hired the taxi and was acting as an independent contractor.

The meaning of "permit" under RTA section 151(8)

3.13 The scope of the RTA 1988 s 151 is discussed in Chapter 8. Briefly, the insurer is under the obligation to indemnify the victim of a traffic accident even though the driver does not fall within the insurance cover. The law treats the insurance contract, with regards to the third party's claim, as if provided cover for the driver in question. Under section 151(8) the RTA 1988 provides that the insurer has a right of recourse, after indemnifying the third party victim's loss, against the driver or any person who is insured under the policy and caused or permitted the use of the vehicle which gave rise to the liability.[39]

3.14 The word "permitted" in s 151(8)(b) is to be interpreted the same way as the word "permits" in s 143(1)(b).[40] In *Lloyd-Wolper v Moore*[41] before taking out the motor vehicle insurance the father expressly misrepresented a number of matters which induced the insurer to enter into the contract. His son involved in an accident and having indemnified the third party victim, the insurer, under section 151(8), returned to the insured father. Two of the matters misrepresented by the father were that his son was 17 and he had driving licence, whereas he was 16 at the relevant time and was not eligible for the licence at that age. If the son had been insured, there would have been no recourse claim under section 151(8) of the RTA 1988. However, the son was uninsured and the father committed the offence under section 143.

Extension clauses – permitted users for the scheduled vehicle

3.15 It had been common for motor policies to extend the policy cover beyond the assured by express clauses.[42] For instance in *Tattersall v Drysdale*[43] the relevant clause

---

37 *R. (on the application of Chaplin) v Wood Green Crown Court* [2012] EWHC 3773 (Admin), [8].
38 *R. (on the application of Chaplin) v Wood Green Crown Court* [2012] EWHC 3773 (Admin)
39 RTA 1988 S 151(8)(b).
40 *Lloyd-Wolper v Moore* [2004] RTR 30.
41 [2004] RTR 30.
42 *Tattersall v Drysdale* [1935] 2 KB 174, at 181.
43 [1935] 2 KB 174.

provided "the insurance shall extend to indemnify any person who is driving on the assured's order or with his permission in respect of any legal liability as aforesaid."

3.16 However, enforceability of such clauses had been challenged by the two then applicable principles of English law: (1) the traditional doctrine of privity of contract and (2) it was questioned whether the insurable interest requirement under the Life Assurance Act 1774[44] applied to motor policies with respect to such extension clauses.[45]

3.17 These problems were illustrated well in *Vandepitte v Preferred Accident Insurance Corporation of New York*.[46] The insurance that was taken out by R covered third party risks, and that the indemnity should be available to any person operating the car with the permission of the assured. R's daughter J was involved in an accident when she was driving the car with her father's permission. The insurers rejected the victim's claim and the Privy Council decided for the insurers, having adopted a strict interpretation of the traditional doctrine of privity that was applicable at the time,[47] Lord Wright held that the mere generality of the language was not in itself sufficient to find a contract between J and the insurers. Moreover, R had no authority from J to insure on her behalf and at no time did she purport to adopt or ratify any insurance even if made on her behalf. Furthermore there was no consideration proceeding from J. Finally, Lord Wright found no evidence that R had any intention to create a beneficial interest for J under the contract as a trustee,[48] either specifically or as member of a described class. The outcome was that R was the contracting party in law, but he had no insurable interest in J's personal liability.

3.18 A similar issue came before Roche J in *Williams v Baltic Insurance Association of London*.[49] B was driving her brother's car with his consent. B's brother had effected insurance by which the insurers agreed to indemnity him against damage to, or loss of, his motor car, and (by clause 2) "against all sums for which the insured (or any licensed personal friend or relative of the insured while driving the car with the insured's general knowledge and consent) shall become legally liable in compensation for . . . accidental bodily injury caused to any person."

3.19 The policy was held to have plainly covered B only. The problem with regards to a claim by B with respect to an accident caused by B's sister arose out of the Life Assurance Act 1774: the assured had no interest in his sister's liability and therefore cannot recover; that B, who might be said to be interested, could not recover, because

---

44 14 Geo. 3, c. 48.

45 *McCormick v National Motor and Accident Insurance Union Ltd* (1934) 49 Ll L Rep 361.

46 [1933] AC 70. The traditional doctrine of privity was reformed by the 1999 Act. However, the doctrine still applies to the contracts that fall outside the scope of the 1999 Act and in the cases where the 1999 Act is excluded by the parties. *Vandepitte* hence will not apply when the 1999 Act applies. However, even in the common law *Vandepitte* was overruled by *Fraser River Pile & Dredge Ltd v Can-Dive Services Ltd* [2000] 1 Lloyd's Rep 199. *Vandepitte* was regarded as "unreasonable application of the doctrine of privity to contracts of insurance and inconsistent with commercial reality." [2000] 1 Lloyd's Rep 199 at pp 207 and 208, respectively.

47 Lord Wright referred to and applied *Dunlop Pneumatic Tyre Co Ltd v Selfridge & Co Ltd* [1915] AC 847 and *Tweddle v Atkinson* (1861) 1 B. & S. 393.

48 The rule is that a party to a contract can constitute himself a trustee for a third party of a right under the contract and thus confer such rights enforceable in equity on the third party. The trustee then can take steps to enforce performance to the beneficiary by the other contracting party as in the case of other equitable rights. The action should be in the name of the trustee; if, however, he refuses to sue, the beneficiary can sue, joining the trustee as a defendant.

49 [1924] 2 KB 282.

her name was not inserted in the policy. Roche J held that[50] this was an insurance on the motor car, being on a policy on goods it fell outside the scope of the 1774 Act.[51] B's sister was interested as the driver of the motor car in respect of the motor car itself. By an analogy, a person is interested in a marine adventure who (inter alia) may incur liability in respect thereof. B effected the insurance and he was insured, but it was an insurance for himself and the other persons mentioned in clause 2. Nevertheless, in *Vandepitte* the Court said it was not clear whether Roche J in *Williams* treated the driver of the car as directly insured or as a cestui que trust. As found in *Vandepitte*, the policy in *Williams* was of "honour policy" under which an insurer would provide an indemnification for business reputation.

3.20 The RTA 1930 s 36(4)[52] provided

> Notwithstanding anything in any enactment, a person issuing a policy of insurance under this section shall be liable to indemnify the persons or classes of persons specified in the policy in respect of any liability which the policy purports to cover in the case of those persons or classes of persons.

3.21 A broad interpretation of this section was adopted in *Tattersall v Drysdale*[53] where Goddard J said, "The Act was aimed at the protection of the public by providing that there should be a body of insurers behind every driver of a car."[54] In *Tattersall* G was the director of a motor dealers company. T left his car with G for sale. Whilst driving the Riley car that was lent to him by G, T had an accident. T had been insured with L; G (and the car Riley) was insured with E. Both policies provided that the insurance is extended to indemnify a person driving the insured car with the assured's permission provided that such person is not entitled to indemnity under any other policy. The question was whether T was still insured under the L policy at the time of the accident. L policy was not in force because T had sold his car, and the extension in the L policy fell with the rest of the policy. The words "Notwithstanding anything in any enactment" were meant to exclude any consequences that might otherwise result from the operation of the Life Assurance Act, 1774. T was held to have been covered by the extension clause in the E policy.

3.22 Currently the RTA 1988 s 148(7) provides almost identical wording and renders a motor policy containing an extension clause a series of bilateral contracts each between the insurer and a named or permitted driver.

The RTA 1988 s 148(7) can apply only where the policy contains an extension clause. Where the policy does not contain an extension clause as such the insurer would still have to compensate the victim's loss as if the driver was covered by the insurance under the RTA 1988 s 151. The difference between a policy which has an extension clause and the loss is covered by the insurer and the coverage without an extension clause is that in the latter the insurer may recoup against the user and the person insured under section 151(8).[55]

---

50 Referring to *Waters v Monarch Fire and Life Assurance Co* (1856) 5 El. & Bl. 870.
51 Section 4 of the Act.
52 Now the RTA 1988 s 148(7) which will be referred to below.
53 [1935] 2 KB 174, 181.
54 Ibid.
55 See Chapter 8.

3.23 Extension clauses vary greatly and it is ultimately a matter of construction of the individual policy whether the claim in question is covered by an extension clause in an insurance contract.[56] The outcome of such construction of insurance contracts has its implications on the criminal offence under section 143(2) of the RTA 1988 and civil liability for the owner under *Monk v Warbey*. Hence, the importance of being covered by an extension clause is not to be undermined.

Continuing ownership

3.24 A motor vehicle insurance policy is not assignable without the permission of the insurer, and the new owner of the vehicle in principle is not automatically insured by the seller's insurers.[57] Consequently, the policy lapses when the insured vehicle is sold.[58] The fact that the purchaser had not paid the whole of the purchase price is irrelevant for that purpose.[59] In *Peters v General Accident Fire & Life Assurance Corp Ltd*[60] the policyholder was described in the policy schedule as C who sold the car to P who then had an accident whilst driving the vehicle purchased. P was not insured under this policy and his action against the insurer was rejected. P was driving the car as the new owner, not as a person who was driving it with the permission of C.

3.25 Moreover, unless the policy otherwise provides, it is not possible to shift the insurance from car to car during the currency of the policy without the insurer's knowledge.[61]

3.26 *Rogerson v Scottish Automobile & General Insurance Co.*[62] highlights the differences between the meanings of "instead of" and "succession" in the context of extension clauses. In *Rogerson* the insurance contract covered the assured's legal liability in respect of his use of any motor car (other than a hired car), provided that such car is at the time of the accident being used instead of "the insured car." During the currency of the policy, without informing the insurance company, the assured exchanged his first insured car for another car of a similar type, and shortly afterwards, while driving the substituted car, he was involved in an accident. The wording of the policy was interpreted as covering only while there was an existing insured car and the assured was temporarily using another car in substitution for the insured car. Accordingly, if the assured has parted with the property in the insured vehicle and buys another car, he is using his new purchase in succession to the insured car, not instead of it.

3.27 The following cases confirmed that the assured has the privilege or further protection while using another car only temporarily as it is the scheduled car which is always the subject of the insurance.[63] A use other than temporary would not be using the vehicle as an alternative but as a replacement which falls outside the scope of the extension clause. This method of interpretation was once more confirmed in *Boss v Kingston*[64] in

---

56 *Dodson v Peter H Dodson Insurance Services* [2001] Lloyd's Rep IR 278; *Boss v Kingston* [1962] 2 Lloyd's Rep 431.
57 *Peters v General Accident Fire & Life Assurance Corp Ltd* (1938) 60 Ll L Rep 311.
58 *Wilkinson v General Accident Fire and Life Assurance Corp* [1967] 2 Lloyd's Rep 182.
59 *Peters v General Accident Fire & Life Assurance Corp Ltd* (1938) 60 Ll L Rep 311.
60 Ibid.
61 *Rogerson v Scottish Automobile & General Insurance Co.* (1931) 41 Ll L Rep 1.
62 (1931) 41 Ll L Rep 1.
63 *Tattersall v Drysdale* [1935] 2 KB 174.
64 [1962] 2 Lloyd's Rep 431.

which the defendant driver, B, had had a Triumph motorcycle which he had been insured for. The relevant contract of insurance provided "the company will also indemnify the insured while driving a motor-cycle not belonging to him and not hired to him under a hire-purchase agreement as though such motor-cycle was a motor-cycle described in the schedule." B had sold the Triumph and had an accident whilst driving H's motorcycle. H's insurance policy responded only when H was the driver. The Court held that B's policy lapsed when he sold the Triumph. The premium was fixed by reference to the named vehicle and the cover for the assured driving a motorcycle not belonging to him and not hired to him under a hire-purchase was to effect temporary cover whilst the named vehicle was out of use. Where the seller parts with the possession of the vehicle but retains the right to use of it would be different.

3.28 On the other hand, in *Dodson v Peter H Dodson Insurance Services*[65] the Court of Appeal expressed that *Boss v Kingston* was open to substantial doubt. As seen above, the narrow interpretation of the extension clauses meant that the use of an alternative vehicle is insured only where the assured parted with the scheduled insured vehicle on a temporary basis. If the policy lapses because of a permanent parting with the vehicle insured, the cover for using an alternative vehicle ceases together with the insurance contract. The word "temporary," although, did not appear in the actual wording of the policies; the Courts, by way of interpretation, read the relevant clauses as if such word was included. On the other hand, in *Dodson v Peter H Dodson Insurance Services*[66] the Court of Appeal rejected to read "temporary" in the clause unless the policy wording expressly stated that.

3.29 In *Dodson* the contract was for a period from 11 September 1992 to 11 September 1993. The claimant sold the vehicle on 17 April 1993. On 16 May 1993 he was involved in an accident when he was driving his mother's car with her permission. The policy provided: Clause 1(1): "The company will indemnify the insured in respect of legal liability for death of or bodily injury to any person and damage to property caused by or in connection with (a) the insured vehicle (b) the driving by the insured (with the owner's permission) of any motor car or motorcycle neither owned nor held under a hire-purchase agreement by the insured." In line with the previous authorities, the insurers argued that the policy lapsed when he sold the insured vehicle. The Court drew attention to the lack of such wording in the policy that neither expressly required that the insured vehicle was "out of use" nor that the use of any other vehicle should be "temporary." The Court further drew attention to the fact that the extension clause contained no notification requirement with regard to using another vehicle. In any event, the Court was ready to adopt the *contra proferentem* rule in case of any real ambiguity: the insurers' general terms and conditions were put forward contractually, and they were seeking to read an unexpressed restriction of their liability into such wording. *Dodson v Peter H Dodson Insurance Services*[67] did not overrule *Boss v Kingson* but distinguished it.

3.30 The previous authorities emphasised the following matters: the possession of the scheduled vehicle, insurable interest in the vehicle and being a replacement rather than being a temporary alternative to the scheduled vehicle. *Dodson*, however, seems to

---

65 [2001] Lloyd's Rep IR 278, [41].
66 [2001] Lloyd's Rep IR 278.
67 Ibid.

focus on the express wording of the extension clause. The matter therefore is which of these considerations should prevail with respect to the protection of third parties. It is submitted that neither of them can be preferred on its own. The reasons are twofold: On the one hand, the interpretation of contractual terms, as has long been adopted by the English Courts, includes the background circumstances and factual matrix.[68] It follows that, where motor vehicle insurers put forward their general terms and conditions to motor vehicle assureds the express policy restrictions should be preferred over restricted interpretations of extension clauses. In comparison with the assured's position with the insurers, it can doubtless be argued that the latter can insert express restrictions to extension clauses. There are numerous different examples of extension clauses; however, the abovementioned facts do not over stretch the coverage by such clauses. Rather, they seem to be in line with the ordinary course of use of vehicles in ordinary life. Therefore what *Dodson* proposed may be supported on the *contra proferentem* point of view. The word "temporarily" parting with the possession of the vehicle identified in the policy does not appear in the clause and adding such a word is controversial.

3.31 On the other hand, the Court's reason in *Dodson* does not persuasively answer how, in the light of the established principle that the policy lapses when the scheduled vehicle is sold, their interpretation can stand. In *Dodson* the cover was provided

> in respect of legal liability for death of or bodily injury to any person and damage to property caused by or in connection with (a) the insured vehicle (b) the driving by the insured (with the owner's permission) of any motor car or motor cycle neither owned nor held under a hire-purchase agreement by the insured.

In *Boss v Kingston* the policy provided:

> (1) The company will indemnify the insured in the event of an accident caused by or through or in connection with any motor-cycle described in the schedule . . . against liability at law for damages . . . in respect of death or bodily injury to any person or damage to property. (2) In terms of and subject to the limitations of and for the purposes of the policy the company will also indemnify the insured while driving a motor-cycle not belonging to him and not hired to him under a hire-purchase agreement as though such motor-cycle was a motor-cycle described in the schedule.

3.32 Nevertheless, *Dodson* distinguished *Boss v Kingston*. Perhaps not surprisingly, the Court of Appeal expressly confessed the difficulty in satisfactorily distinguishing *Boss* without creating unacceptable uncertainty.[69] It is an established principle of law that the insurance premium is, unless policy otherwise provides, indivisible and the whole premium is due once the policy is incepted.[70] Since the premium is indivisible in case the policy is later cancelled with a prospective effect, there is no total failure of consideration and the premium is not returned to the assured. Only if the policy provides expressly a prorata return of the premium or the premium payment obligation will cease in the case the policy is terminated, the premium is returned or the future obligations to pay the premium ceases, respectively.

---

68 *Investors Compensation Scheme Ltd v West Bromwich Building Society (No.1)* [1998] 1 WLR 896; *Rainy Sky SA v Kookmin Bank* [2012] 1 Lloyd's Rep 34; *Wood v Capita Insurance Services Ltd* [2017] 4 All ER 615.
69 [2001] Lloyd's Rep IR 278, [41].
70 *JA Chapman & Co Ltd (In Liquidation) v Kadirga Denizcilik ve Ticaret AS* [1998] Lloyd's Rep IR 377.

3.33 In *Dodson* the Court of Appeal stated that if cover lapses automatically upon or after disposal of the insured vehicle without replacement the insured will be left (i) without cover under clause 1(1)(b) at the very moment when he is likely to require it and (ii) without any *right* to any return of premium.[71] This is, however, what the true position is under the currently applicable law. Further, the non-payment of premium was not an issue in *Dodson*. Further, the Court of Appeal found *Boss* open to substantial doubt but stressed the difficulty in distinguishing *Boss* without creating unacceptable uncertainty in the area of law.[72] Though with hesitation, their Lordships preferred to reinforce the message that assureds are entitled to more clear wordings than the wordings in question in this and similar cases over the risk of uncertainty.[73]

Double insurance, contribution and rateable proportion clauses

3.34 The reason for the assured taking out double insurance may be mystery[74] or an oversight on the expiry date of the previous policy by the assured; nevertheless, it is not alien to see double insurance in motor insurance cases. In the case of double insurance, whether there is a right to contribution between the two insurers depends upon independent principles of equity that "burdens should be shared equally."[75]

3.35 A particular person's use of a vehicle may fall under two different insurance policies both of which may be worded in a way literal reading of which would cancel each other out and leave the user with no insurance cover. In *Gale v Motor Union Insurance Co Ltd*[76] Roche J discussed the connection between rateable proportion clauses in two different policies. G was insured under a policy of the Motor Union Company in respect of his own car. L, who was driving G's car with G's consent, was involved in an accident. L was insured with the Accident Corporation. Both Motor Union and Accident Corporation policies provided that if, at the time of the happening of any accident, any other insurance covers the same accident, then the insurer shall be liable no more than a rateable proportion of any sum or sums payable in respect thereof for compensation. It appears at first sight that such clauses should cancel each other (by neglecting in each case the proviso in the other policy) with the result that, on the ground in each case that the loss is covered elsewhere, it is covered nowhere. Roche J held that the clauses provided that if the assured is completely protected elsewhere by insurance then he is not to be entitled to recover under these policies or either of them. But in cases where these policies provide for a proportionate or partial indemnity neither gives a full indemnity or complete protection. The provision as to rateable contribution qualifies and explains the preceding clause negativing liability. It is agreed that rateably in the circumstances means that each company pays half. Additionally, a motorist may also be insured under

---

71 [2001] Lloyd's Rep IR 278, [39].
72 [2001] Lloyd's Rep IR 278, [41].
73 Ibid, [42].
74 *Legal and General Assurance Society Ltd. v Drake Insurance Co. Ltd.* [1992] QB 887.
75 See *Legal and General Assurance Society Ltd. v Drake Insurance Co. Ltd.* [1992] QB 887, [891–892] where Lloyd LJ explains the reasons for contribution in double insurance in a very concise and clear way. See also *Drake Insurance Plc v Provident Insurance Plc* [2004] QB 601; *Eagle Star Insurance Co Ltd v Provincial Insurance* [1994] 1 AC 130.
76 [1928] 1 KB 359.

two different policies not because he took out two different contracts for the same risk with two different insurers, but circumstances permit him to be covered under different insurances. For instance the risk that occurred because of an employee's negligence may fall within two different liability insurance covers taken out by the employer, such as public liability and motor vehicle insurance.

3.36 Alternatively, a motorist who uses a vehicle with owner's permission may be covered by an extension clause in the owner's policy as permitted user and at the same time he may also have his own insurance which provides cover when using vehicles other than the one identified in the policy that the motorist himself has taken out. It may be the case that each of these policies provides cover only if the risk is not covered under any other policy. In other words, the policy cover might be excluded where another policy covers the same risk. When the two policies are potentially engaged, then they will cancel each other out which would produce a wholly unreasonable result. The two insurance companies accept premiums, but then the risk is left uncovered because the two deny indemnity on the basis that each purports to leave the risk solely with the other.[77] The reasonable construction of the policy requires each policy to engage by a rateable proportion.[78]

3.37 As seen below normally policies provide a rateable proportion clause rather than cancelling each other out. A typical example of those clauses is

> If at any time any claim arises under this Policy there is any other existing insurance covering the same loss damage or liability the Company shall not be liable to pay or contribute more than its rateable proportion of such claim.

3.38 Rateably in the circumstances means that each company is responsible to pay half.[79] But even when one of the policies in question provides a rateable proportion but the other does not, the Court is likely to interpret it in a way rateably proportioning the loss.[80] In *Weddell v Road Transport and General Insurance Co, Ltd*[81] Weddell held a motor car policy which insured any relative or friend who drives the vehicle with Weddell's consent. Condition 4 provided that the insurer would not contribute any more than its rateable proportion of any loss if any other insurance covers the accident in question. Weddell's brother had an accident while driving the vehicle with Weddell's consent. The driver was insured with respect to the car he owned; such insurance did not contain a rateable proportion clause but provided

> Section L: driving other cars. The indemnity granted under section A herein is hereby extended to cover the insured whilst driving any private motor-car not belonging to him for pleasure or professional purposes if no indemnity is afforded the insured by any other insurance.

It was held that the reasonable construction requires holding both companies liable, although Weddell's brother's insurance did not contain a rateable proportion clause. If

---

77 *Turnbull v MNT Transport (2006) Ltd* [2010] CSOH 163.

78 *Turnbull v MNT Transport (2006) Ltd* [2010] CSOH 163; *Weddell v Road Transport and General Insurance Co, Ltd* [1932] 2 KB 563; *Gale v Motor Union Insurance Co Ltd* [1928] 1 KB 359.

79 *Gale v Motor Union Insurance Co Ltd* [1928] 1 KB 359.

80 *Turnbull v MNT Transport (2006) Ltd* [2010] CSOH 163; *Weddell v Road Transport and General Insurance Co, Ltd* [1932] 2 KB 563; *Gale v Motor Union Insurance Co Ltd* [1928] 1 KB 359.

81 [1932] 2 KB 563.

one of the policies' maximum limit is lower than its rateable share the assured bears the excess.[82]

3.39 The purpose of this type of clause is to achieve the effect of contribution at the payment stage, ie that if there are other insurers on risk then the insurer in question does not pay and seek contribution, but only pays the amount that it would have paid after contribution. It was therefore held that a rateable proportion clause is an attempt by contract with the assured to recreate the equity and forestall the need for its application.[83] The risk of the insolvency of the other insurers is thus cast on the assured. Where, on the other hand, contribution is sought by an insurer, as appears from *Legal and General Assurance Society Ltd. v Drake Insurance Co. Ltd.*,[84] whether the insurer has also a right of recourse against his assured will be taken into account. In *Legal and General* it was held that where an insurer has a right of recourse against the assured, and fails to exercise it, his payment to the third party is to be regarded as voluntary and the insurer will be unable to exercise contribution rights against any other insurer in respect of the payment. This position was doubted by the Court of Appeal in *Drake* where his Lordships considered it appropriate for the Supreme Court to examine the matter when it arises again.

Motor vehicle

3.40 RTA 1988 section 185 provides definitions for "'motor vehicle' and other expressions relating to vehicles." A motor vehicle is "a mechanically propelled vehicle intended or adapted for use on roads."[85] Certain vehicles are not to be treated as motor vehicles.[86] It is not enough that a vehicle can be used on a road; it must be "intended or adapted" for such use.[87] The words "intended or adapted for use on roads" in this section was developed in particular from 1941 onwards in criminal prosecutions for driving without insurance or without road tax.[88]

3.41 The word "adapted" may mean altered[89] or fit and apt[90] to the effect covering the vehicle as initially constructed or subsequently altered[91] for use on roads, but the meaning of "adapted" is yet uncertain. The statute does not say "used on roads," but "intended or adapted for use on roads"[92] which was interpreted as "for ordinary road purposes."[93]

3.42 So far the common law cases mostly focused on the word "intended," and an objective test has been settled to determine its meaning. Intention does not refer to the intention of any particular person; it is not the intention of the user of the vehicle either

---

82 *Turnbull v MNT Transport (2006) Ltd* [2010] CSOH 163.

83 *Drake Insurance Plc v Provident Insurance Plc* [2004] QB 601, [125] Rix LJ.

84 [1992] QB 887.

85 RTA 1988 s 185(1).

86 RTA 1988 s 189.

87 See discussions in *Woodward v James Young (Contractors) Ltd* 1958 J.C. 28; *MacDonald v Carmichael* 1941 J.C. 27.

88 *Lewington v Motor Insurers' Bureau* [2018] RTR 18, [23].

89 *Burns v Currell* [1963] 2 QB 433.

90 Ibid.

91 See discussions in *Woodward v James Young (Contractors) Ltd* 1958 J.C. 28; *MacDonald v Carmichael* 1941 J.C. 27.

92 *Woodward v James Young (Contractors) Ltd* 1958 J.C. 28.

93 Ibid.

at the moment of the alleged offence or for the future.[94] The objective of the test, which is also called the Burns test,[95] is to determine whether a reasonable person looking at the vehicle would say that one of its users would be a road user.[96] The existing common law test has a degree of flexibility.[97] It was held that a go-kart, a self-propelled vehicle with an engine, was not a motor vehicle within the meaning of the Act.[98] Applying the same objective test a miniature motorcycle with a 22 cc engine on a public road[99] and a forklift truck, a mechanically propelled vehicle and registered and taxed for use on the road as a works truck,[100] were both held to be motor vehicles. In respect of the latter the Court held that the intention was to use the vehicle on the road when it suited the owner's business purposes.

3.43 The Scottish Courts decided in *MacDonald v Carmichael*[101] that, on the facts of the case, a dumper truck used in civil engineering works was not a motor vehicle. *Mac-Donald v Carmichael* was followed in *Daley v Hargreaves*[102] where dumpers, mechanically propelled vehicles used in construction works, were held not intended or adapted for use on roads within the meaning of the Act then in force. *Daley* was strictly on the particular facts of the case and is not intended to apply to dumpers generally.[103] *MacDonald v Carmichael* was distinguished in *Woodward v James Young (Contractors) Limited*[104] which concerned a Ferguson motor tractor with a two-wheeled trailer attached and was intended for use on roads.[105] It was a tractor of the ordinary kind used by members of the agricultural Community.

3.44 A Go-ped is also a motor vehicle that passes the objective text. In *DPP v Saddington*[106] this was so held although a Go-ped probably would not be used on a road in ordinary circumstances; any qualification is to be narrowly construed.[107] However, the Court noted that the test is not whether a reasonable person would use a Go-ped on a road[108] but whether a reasonable person would say, contemplating some general use on the roads, that one of its uses would be use on the roads.[109] In *Winter v DPP*[110] the City Bug – the front wheel of which was modified so as to allow pedals to be fitted, and did not drive a chain but push the front wheel itself – was held to be a motor vehicle. Reflecting the purposive interpretation of a statute,[111] it was held that "fitted with pedals

---

94 *Burns v Currell* [1963] 2 QB 433, 440, Lord Parker CJ; *Daley v Hargreaves* [1961] 1 WLR 487.

95 *DPP v Saddington* [2001] RTR 15. Phil LJ said, at [13], the Burns test has been applied for approaching 40 years, and should not readily be departed from.

96 *Burns v Currell* [1963] 2 QB 433.

97 *Lewington v Motor Insurers' Bureau* [2018] RTR 18, [31].

98 *Burns v Currell* [1963] 2 QB 433.

99 *O'Brien v Anderton* [1979] RTR 388.

100 *Percy v Smith* [1986] RTR 252.

101 1953 SLT (Sh. Ct.) 117.

102 [1961] 1 WLR 487.

103 Ibid, 492, Salmon J.

104 1958 J.C. 28.

105 As distinguished from a Diesel dumper.

106 [2001] RTR 15.

107 *Lewington v Motor Insurers' Bureau* [2018] RTR 18, [63].

108 The Court noted that the distributors' advice not to use the Go-ped on the roads will in practice be ignored to a considerable extent. [2001] RTR 15, [20].

109 [2001] RTR 15, [19].

110 [2003] RTR 14.

111 *Lewington v Motor Insurers' Bureau* [2018] RTR 18, [34].

by means of which it is capable of being propelled" meant that the vehicle was "reasonably capable of being propelled" by the pedals.

3.45 Once a vehicle has been manufactured as one which is intended or adapted for use on a road, it would require very substantial and dramatic alteration to cease to be a motor vehicle. A change of this nature was found in *Chief Constable of Avon and Somerset v F*[112] where the motorcycle in question had been manufactured for road use but adapted for "scrambling" on private land by the removal of its registration plate, reflectors, lights and speedometer.

EU law

3.46 The Consolidated Directive, Directive 2009/103/EC, defines "vehicle" as "any motor vehicle intended for travel on land and propelled by mechanical power, but not running on rails, and any trailer, whether or not coupled."[113] The motor vehicles referred to in Article 1(1) of the First Directive are, irrespective of their characteristics, intended normally to serve as means of transport. An agricultural tractor[114] and a military vehicle with Anibal wheels[115] will fall under this definition.

3.47 However, being classified as a vehicle is only a starting point to identify the insurance obligation against civil liability with regards to the use of motor vehicles. The other elements will be analysed below.

3.48 At this point it is worth noting a further issue of interpretation of section 185(1) of the RTA 1988 in line with the Consolidated Directive. In this respect, in *Lewington v Motor Insurers' Bureau*,[116] on appeal, Bryan J held that the arbitrator erred in ruling that it is not possible to reconcile the wording of s 185 with the Consolidated Directive.

3.49 In *Lewington* the claimant, C, suffered serious injuries caused by the negligence of a driver who stole a dumper truck, drove it on a public road and caused a crash. The driver ran off and has never been traced. C claimed against the Motor Insurers' Bureau (MIB) for compensation under the Untraced Drivers Agreement 2003. The MIB argued and the arbitrator held that the dumper truck was not a "motor vehicle" within the definition of section 185(1)(c) of the RTA 1988 and so insurance for it was not compulsory. Having emphasised the broad interpretation of the word "use" in *Vnuk v Zavarovalnica Triglav dd*,[117] which is analysed in Chapter 5, the judge distinguished matters which relate to "the normal use of a vehicle, such as moving from A to B or whatever, and the vehicle being used in a way where it is not being used as a vehicle as such."[118] Accordingly, if someone has climbed on to a tractor with a view to picking some apples from an apple tree under which the tractor has previously been parked, the vehicle is being used as a ladder, not as a vehicle. In the course of doing so a bucket that the person is holding falls and injures somebody, that is not a use of a vehicle that is consistent with

---

112 [1987] 1 All ER 318.
113 First Directive, Council Directive 72/166/EEC Art 1.1 and Directive 2009/103/EC Art 1.1 contain identical definitions of "vehicle."
114 *Rodrigues de Andrade v Proenca Salvador* (C-514/16) [2018] Lloyd's Rep IR 164.
115 *Nunez Torreiro v AIG Europe Ltd* (C-334/16) [2018] Lloyd's Rep IR 418.
116 [2018] RTR 18.
117 (C-162/13) [2015] Lloyd's Rep IR 142.
118 [2018] RTR 18, [53].

the normal function of that vehicle.[119] Having applied the Burns test the judge held that the dumper was a vehicle within the meaning of section 185.

Road or other public place

Road

3.50 The concept of road has been subject to several adjustments. For the purposes of the compulsory third party liability insurance road has been defined as "any highway and any other road to which the public has access, and includes bridges over which a road passes."[120]

"On" the road

3.51 An interesting argument was raised in *Holliday v Henry*[121] in which a vehicle that was placed on a roller skate so that its wheels were not in actual contact with the road surface was held to be on the road. Lord Widgery CJ commented that otherwise if one put a piece of newspaper under each wheel, the vehicle would be no longer on the road.

3.52 Some cases are borderline. In *Randall v Motor Insurers' Bureau*[122] a lorry injured the claimant whilst he was on a private property which was a piece of land at the back of the school, belonging to the school. Entrance to this land was from Hillsborough Road. At the time of the accident the rear part of the lorry including the wheel which ran over the claimant's leg, was still, just, on private property but it was held that the greater part of the lorry was on the road, and the lorry as a whole was using the road. The lorry was being driven further on to the road in order to drive away along the road – which caused the injury.

Public access

3.53 The road may or may not be public; the definition is intended to cover all kinds of roads,[123] highways and "any other" roads. It was held in *Harrison v Hill*[124] that the road which was not a public road but members of the public frequently walk upon was a road within the meaning of the RTA 1930 s 121(1). A private land to which the public does not have access falls outside the definition of road but a road which belongs to the class of private road and all that can be said with regard to its availability to the public

---

119 Ibid.
120 RTA 1930, s 121(1); RTA 1960, s 257(1); RTA 1972, s 196(1); RTA 1988 s 192(1).
121 [1974] RTR 101.
122 [1968] 1 WLR 1900.
123 *Clarke v Kato* [1999] RTR 153.
124 1932 J.C. 13. *Harrison v Hill* was applied in *Houghton v Scholfield* [1973] RTR 239 in the context of a cul-de-sac which was held to be a road to which the public had access and in *Bugge v Taylor* [1941] 1 KB 198 in the context of the forecourt of a hotel. *Adams v Commissioner of Police of the Metropolis* [1980] RTR 289 in the context of private road known as Aberdeen Park, London N5.

is that the public "has access" to it is a road within the statutory definition referred to above.[125]

3.54 The phrase that "to which the public has access" has been proved to be controversial. The public in this context means the public generally[126] who may be pedestrians or drivers of motor vehicles.

3.55 "Access" does not mean that the public has a positive right of its own to access, nor does it mean that there exists no physical obstruction against physical access.[127] It means that the public actually and legally enjoys access to it.[128] The primary intention of the place is again irrelevant.[129] In this respect the permission may be explicit or implicit, and it is irrelevant whether the access should be by consent of the owners of the road rather than tolerance.[130]

3.56 Whether the public has access to it is to be determined as a matter of fact and degree in each case.[131] In *Griffin v Squires*[132] the Court expressed some doubts that the sole test to apply to determine if a place is a road is if it is a place to which the general public has access. The Court was in favour of the view that there be something else which as a matter of common sense and ordinary meaning is a road but it was not explained by the judges what the additional requirements could be.[133]

A definable way between two points

3.57 *Griffin* was referred to in *Oxford v Austin*[134] as being a useful guidance. Kilner Brown J set the question in the context of a car park as "whether or not there is a definable way between two points over which vehicles could pass." Once this is determined the second question is whether or not the public, or a section of the public, has access to that which has the appearance of a definable way.

3.58 In *Clarke v Kato*[135] Lord Clyde said, "I would hesitate to formulate a comprehensive definition whereby a place may be identified as a road, but some guidance should be found by considering its physical character and the function which it exists to serve." His Lordship defined road as: "It leads from one place to another and constitutes a route whereby travellers may move conveniently between the places to which and from which it leads."[136]

3.59 As mentioned below this definition was crucial to define whether a car park was a road.

---

125 *Harrison v Hill* 1932 J.C. 13.

126 *Harrison v Hill* 1932 J.C. 13; *Buchanan v Motor Insurers' Bureau* [1954] 2 Lloyd's Rep 519; *Adams v Commissioner of Police of the Metropolis* [1980] RTR 289.

127 *Harrison v Hill* 1932 J.C. 13.

128 *Harrison v Hill* 1932 J.C. 13; *Oxford v Austin* [1981] RTR 416, 419.

129 *Oxford v Austin* [1981] RTR 416, 419.

130 *Cox v White* [1976] RTR 248.

131 *Cox v White* [1976] RTR 248; *Adams v Commissioner of Police of the Metropolis* [1980] RTR 289.

132 [1958] 1 WLR 1106.

133 It was held that it was a matter for the magistrates to decide as a matter of fact whether this car park in the ordinary sense could be treated as a road. [1958] 1 WLR 1106.

134 [1981] RTR 416.

135 [1999] RTR 153.

136 [1999] RTR 153, 160.

Car parks

3.60 The House of Lords heard conjoined appeals in *Clarke v Kato*; both cases concerned accidents that took place in two different car parks. As well as the physical characteristics such as a road's location which should be identifiable as a route or way or shape that it may be continuous or in the case of a cul-de-sac, the Court found it necessary to consider the function of the place in order to see if it qualifies as a road.[137] Lord Clyde held that the accidents concerned in this appeal did not take place in roads; the car parks concerned in the Appeal were not places designed or dedicated for the passage of vehicles. The emphasis was put on the differences in function between road and car park. Whilst the former is to enable movement along it to a destination, although incidentally a vehicle on it may be stationary, the latter is to enable vehicles to stand and wait and incidentally a car may be driven across it. His Lordships expressed sympathy for the unfortunate victims of these two accidents but stated that the legislature must decide as matter of policy whether an alteration of the law is to be made and precisely how that alteration ought to be achieved.

3.61 The Motor Vehicles (Compulsory Insurance) Regulations 2000[138] extended the application of the compulsory insurance requirement to "or other public place." This will be covered in the following paragraphs.

"Other public place"

3.62 The legislative change was introduced by the Motor Vehicles (Compulsory Insurance) Regulations 2000[139] which added the words "or other public place" to the RTA 1988 s 143(1). As a result, the use of a motor vehicle is now required to be insured against liability incurred in any "public place" as well as on any road.

3.63 A number of authorities have discussed the meaning of "public place," and it appears from those authorities that the test for a public place is the same as the test for a place to which the public has access, as contained in the definition of road.[140] The roadway inside a caravan park constituted both a public place and a road.[141] A car park which was attached to commercial premises and had a gated entrance that was only open during the day was held to be a public place.[142] This car park displayed a sign that use of the car park was "for customers only," and it was accessible from a main public road where there were no restrictions placed on members of the public on entry to the car park.[143] A public house car park and a hospital car park were held to be public places.[144]

---

137 Ibid.

138 SI 2000/726. The Regulations came into force on 3 April 2000.

139 Ibid.

140 Colinvaux, [23–011].

141 *Barrett v DPP* [2010] RTR 2. It was a large, privately owned caravan park situated between the main road and the beach. There was a public footpath through the caravan park giving access to the beach, along which the general public had a right of way on foot.

142 *May v DPP* [2005] EWHC 1280 (Admin).

143 See however, *Charlton v Fisher* [2002] QB 578 in which the incident occurred in the car park of a hotel and the Court of Appeal said, without discussing in detail as the main issue was the public policy defence, that it occurred off road. Hence, the claimant's claim fell outside the compulsory liability insurance regime.

144 See discussions in *May v DPP* [2005] EWHC 1280 (Admin).

On the other hand, in *R v Spence*[145] a small car park which consisted of a yard outside a small office building, flanked on three sides by a wall, a hedge and a fence was held not to be a public place. The fourth side had bollards that prevented access from the road. A swing gate, which was open by day and closed at night, permitted entrance. The car park was used by employees, customers and other business visitors who were held to be a special class as distinct from members of the general public.[146] *R v Spence* was distinguished in *May v DPP*[147] in which photographs which showed that all members of the public were invited by signs to enter the premises and park in the context of a retail commercial enterprise, quite different from the small office building in *Spence*. The phrase "to which the public has access" is not synonymous with "from which the public is not excluded."[148] A street is an example of a public land; the front garden or front area of a private house is an example of a private land. When clearly delimited as such, a private garden is not a place to which the public has access, merely because public access is not physically obstructed by a fence, wall or gate, or legally prohibited by a notice or by any combination of them.[149] In order to be a public place evidence must show that anyone who wants to, as a member of the public, does in fact have access to it, either by an invitation or toleration.[150]

Offences other than RTA s 143

3.64 "Other public place" was added to RTA 143 to extend the compulsory insurance requirement for the use of a vehicle. For other offences, for instance RTA 1988 s 103, which do not use the word "other public place" but only mention driving on a "road" *Clarke v Kato* will still be applicable. In *Brewer v DPP*,[151] a railway station car park was held not to be a "road." The only feature which was capable of rendering the car park a road was that staff drove cars through the car park on their way to the staff car park, but that was insufficient to render the car park capable of being a road. Accordingly a private car park is not a road unless it satisfies the definition provided by *Clarke v Kato*. It could be a public place if "access to public" is found and it may fall within the meaning of the RTA 1988 s 143.

Beaches

3.65 Here it is worth noting *McGurk and Dale v Coster*[152] in which an accident occurred at one part of the beach that was used as a car park for which the local authority charged an entry fee to drivers and displayed notices specifying a speed limit. Drivers were advised

---

145 [1999] RTR 353.
146 *R v Spence* [1999] RTR 353.
147 [2005] EWHC 1280 (Admin).
148 *Harriot v DPP* [2006] Crim. L.R. 440, [16], Mitting J.
149 Ibid.
150 *Harriot v DPP* [2006] Crim. L.R. 440. *Harriot v DPP* was not a case that discussed the meaning of "public place" under the RTA; however, Sedley LJ noted that, for legal certainty, the interpretation of public place should be the same "whether the charge is driving a motor vehicle there, being drunk and disorderly there, or carrying a bladed article there." [2006] Crim. L.R. 440, [11].
151 [2005] RTR 5.
152 22 March 1995 [1995] CLY 2912.

to keep within 50 yards of the sand dunes and providing that entry to the beach was for the purpose only of proceeding to and from a parking place. However, the issue which persuaded the Court that the car park here was not road was that such parking places were not specifically marked on the sand. The Court applied *Oxford v Austin* and decided that there was no definable way between two points and the beach car park did not therefore have the character of a road. The notice instructing the public to keep within 50 yards of the sand hills was not sufficient to ascertain a definable way for the purposes of the test in *Oxford v Austin*. After the amendment to the RTA 1988 s 143 such a car park, depending on the findings of public access, will fall under the section.

EU law

3.66 *Vnuk v Zavarovalnica Triglav dd* (C-162/13)[153] concerns the meaning of "use of a vehicle"[154] as well as the "physical location" of the accident within the meaning of the compulsory MTPL insurance.[155] *Vnuk* was interpreted by the subsequent decisions as a case that ruled that the concept of "use of vehicles" is not limited to road use,[156] but covers any use of a vehicle that is consistent with the normal function of that vehicle.[157] Thus, the interpretation that "the obligation of compulsory insurance extends to the use of vehicles on private land" was implicit in *Vnuk* and explicit in the later decisions.[158] Subsequently, the CJEU held that there is no restriction in the Directives on the use of such vehicles on certain terrain or on certain roads.[159] There is hence no basis for limiting the compulsory insurance requirements on the basis of the characteristics of the terrain on which the motor vehicle is used.[160] Member States are precluded from restricting the insurance cover in areas that are not "suitable for use by motor vehicles."[161]

3.67 In *Nunez Torreiro v AIG Europe Ltd*[162] T, an officer in the Spanish army, was injured when a military vehicle in which he was travelling as a passenger overturned while on night-time military manoeuvres. At the time the vehicle was on private land that the public was excluded from and on terrain suitable for tracked vehicles but not wheeled vehicles. With a reference to *Vnuk* the CJEU held that the concept of "use of vehicles" in Article 3 of the Consolidated Directive is not limited to travel on public roads but covers any use of a vehicle that is consistent with the normal function of that vehicle. The coverage is for any use of a vehicle as a means of transport irrespective of the terrain. Article 3 of the Consolidated Directive, as held by the Court, did not permit an exclusion from compulsory insurance cover injuries and damage that resulted from

---

153 [2015] Lloyd's Rep IR 142.

154 The meaning of "use" is the subject of Chapter 3 of this work.

155 *Lewis v Tindale* [2018] EWHC 2376 (QB), [38]. Approved by the Court of Appeal: *Motor Insurers Bureau v Lewis* [2019] EWCA Civ 909.

156 *Rodrigues de Andrade v Proenca Salvador* (C-514/16) [2018] Lloyd's Rep IR 164, [34]; *Nunez Torreiro v AIG Europe Ltd* (C-334/16) [2018] Lloyd's Rep IR 418.

157 Ibid.

158 *Lewis v Tindale* [2018] EWHC 2376 (QB), [96]. Approved by the Court of Appeal: *Motor Insurers Bureau v Lewis* [2019] EWCA Civ 909.

159 *Rodrigues de Rodrigues de Andrade v Proenca Salvador* (C-514/16) [2018] Lloyd's Rep IR 164, [42], [36]; *Nunez Torreiro v AIG Europe Ltd* (C-334/16); [2018] Lloyd's Rep IR 418, [31].

160 *Rodrigues de Andrade v Proenca Salvador* (C-514/16) [2018] Lloyd's Rep IR 164, [35].

161 *Nunez Torreiro v AIG Europe Ltd* (C-334/16) [2018] Lloyd's Rep IR 418.

162 (C-334/16) [2018] Lloyd's Rep IR 418.

the driving of motor vehicles on roads or terrain that were not "suitable for use by motor vehicles," with the exception of roads or terrain which, although not suitable for that purpose, were nonetheless "ordinarily so used."

3.68 In *Fundo de Garantia Automovel v Juliana*[163] the question was whether Article 3(1) of the First Directive requires the taking out of a contract of insurance against civil liability in relation to the use of a motor vehicle when the vehicle concerned is parked on private land, solely by the choice of the owner, who no longer intends to drive the vehicle. J, for health reasons, stopped driving her motor vehicle and kept it parked in the yard of her house. She had not taken any formal steps to withdraw it from use. J's son, D, was involved in an accident by J's car when he was driving it without his mother's permission or knowledge. Three people died as a result of the accident. D was not insured to drive his mother's vehicle. The national compensation body paid compensation to the victims and then brought the present proceedings against J and her son for reimbursement of the sum of €437,345.85. J argued that she had not been under an obligation to take out civil liability insurance with respect to her vehicle because she had not intended to use it. The Supremo Tribunal de Justiça (Supreme Court) referred to the abovementioned question as well as the question of whether the national compensation body has the right of subrogation against the owner of the vehicle regardless of whether the owner was responsible for the accident. Alternatively, if the subrogation right is enforceable only when the accident occurred whilst the owner had actual control of the vehicle. The CJEU held that the obligation to insure does not depend on whether the vehicle is actually being used as a means of transport at a given time. So long as it is capable of being driven, that corresponds of "vehicle" within the meaning of Article 1(1) of the First Directive. The fact that she no longer intended to drive it is of no relevance in that regard. What mattered was the vehicle concerned is still registered in a Member State and is capable of being driven but is parked on private land. The CJEU emphasised that national legislation may provide that the compensation body can recoup against the owner of the vehicle involved in the accident as well as the person/s responsible for the accident. Article 1(4) of the Second Directive does not preclude national legislation to this effect.

Compatibility with the EU law

3.69 *Clarke v Kato* was applied in *Inman v Kenny*[164] which concerned an accident that took place in 1995 and therefore fell outside the scope of the Motor Vehicles (Compulsory Insurance) Regulations 2000. In *Inman v Kenny* an uninsured motorcyclist had deliberately ridden off a metalled path (which was a road) onto a grassy path (which was not a road) and where the claimant was injured.

3.70 A similar event occurred in *Clarke v Clarke*[165] in which J was struck and injured by a Jeep motor vehicle being driven by P, J's sister-in-law, which has left him paraplegic. The accident was the culmination of a long-standing feud between two families. On the day of the accident C encountered P on a narrow lane, their cars were parked on a gravelled entrance to a farm, and a fight ensued. At some point, P drove the vehicle onto an adjacent paddock and C was struck by the vehicle. In light with *Inman*, it was

---

163 (C-80/17) EU:C:2018:661.
164 [2001] EWCA Civ 35.
165 [2012] EWHC 2118 (QB).

held that the fact that the chain of events started on a road did not mean that the injuries occurred on a road.

3.71 The cases of *Clarke* and *Inman* were binding and applied in *Lewis v Tindale* in which Soole J held that under Part VI of the RTA 1988 the accident occurred in this case on a private land and was not a liability which was required to be insured against. However, after *Clarke* and *Inman* had been decided but before *Lewis v Tindale* was litigated, the CJEU extended the application of the relevant Directives to private land. Having considered the recent developments as highlighted in the text above, Soole J concluded that the RTA 1988 does not comply with the Directives and that there is a requirement to insure against liability for the use of vehicles on private land. Hence, it was not possible to construe the RTA 1988 consistently with the Directives. It follows that an interpretation which excises the geographical limitation to a "road or other public place" clearly goes against the grain and thrust of legislation which provides that limitation. Consequently, the solution is an amendment, not an interpretation.[166] The Court of Appeal approved Soole J's judgment that what was held in *Lewis* was clearly right. The UK complies with its obligations under the Directives through the RTA 1988 and as observed with regards to the addition of "other public place," clearly, a further statutory amendment is needed in order to be compatible with the compulsory insurance requirement as aimed for by the relevant Directives.

3.72 Lord Hodge also agreed in *R&S Pilling (t/a Phoenix Engineering) v UK Insurance Ltd*[167] that the RTA 1988 s 145(3)(a) is not compatible with the EU law but the section cannot be read down. The relevant "use" under the RTA 1988 is use "on a road or other public place," and not the extended cover – to a private place – which the CJEU jurisprudence now requires.

---

166 *Lewis v Tindale* [2018] EWHC 2376 (QB), [58]. Additionally, Soole J discussed the legal nature of the MIB the conclusion of which led the MIB to be liable to the claimant at least up to the minimum amount of insurance cover required by the Directives. This second issue of *Lewis v Tindale* is referred to in Chapter 10.

167 [2019] UKSC 16 [40]–[41].

CHAPTER 4

Requirements with respect to the insurance policy

Form and scope

Insurer

4.1 In order to comply with the requirements of Part VI of the RTA 1988, a policy of insurance must be issued by an authorised insurer.[1] "Authorised insurer" means, as defined by section 95(2),[2] an insurer who is a member of the Motor Insurers' Bureau.[3]

Policy document

4.2 The "policy of insurance" includes a covering note;[4] hence, the existence of insurance cover may be proved in the form of a cover letter.[5] The insurer who issued a policy of insurance covering the liability as required under Part VI of the RTA 1988 must deliver to the person by whom the policy is effected a certificate (certificate of insurance) in the prescribed form and containing such particulars of any conditions subject to which the policy is issued and of any other matters as may be prescribed.[6] This matter is also referred to in Chapter 2.

4.3 A certificate of insurance may be delivered electronically[7] if the person agreed to its electronic transmission.[8] If a certificate is made available on a website, the insurer must ensure that the certificate remains continuously accessible to the person on the website until the expiry of the last day on which the policy to which it relates has effect.[9] Where the certificate has become defaced or has been lost or destroyed, upon assured's request, the insurer shall issue to him a fresh certificate.[10] A defaced certificate should be returned to the insurer before a fresh certificate is issued.[11]

---

1 RTA 1988 s 145(1)(2).

2 "Authorised insurer" under section 145 has the same meaning as in section 95 (See s 145(5)).

3 As mentioned in Chapter 10 the MIB is a company limited by guarantee and incorporated under the Companies Act 1929 on 14 June 1946.

4 RTA 1988 s 161(1). [1]

5 Colinvaux, [23–024].

6 RTA s 147(1).

7 Upon the agreement of the assured the insurer may either transmit it to an electronic address specified by the assured for the purpose of delivery or the insurer may make the certificate available to the assured by placing an electronic copy of it on a website. RTA 1988 s 147(1B)(1C).

8 RTA 1988 s 147(1A)(1B).

9 RTA 1988 s 147(1D).

10 Reg 13.

11 Reg 13.

4.4 A certificate of insurance, unlike a cover note, is not a "policy of insurance" for the purpose of the RTA 1988. Whilst a certificate of insurance may be accepted as evidence of existence of insurance cover,[12] in appropriate cases the Court may call for the policy itself.[13]

Deregulation Act 2015

4.5 Before it was amended by the Deregulation Act 2015, section 147(1) of the RTA 1988 used to provide: "A policy of insurance shall be of no effect for the purposes of this Part of this Act unless and until there is delivered by the insurer." The subsection now provides: "An insurer issuing a policy of insurance for the purposes of this Part of this Act must deliver" so that delivery of the certificate or security is no longer required for the policy or security to be legally effective.[14]

4.6 Certificates are still required as explained above; however, the insurance cover's effectiveness does not any longer depend of their issuance. Deregulation Act 2015 Schedule 3 amended section 148 of the RTA 1988. Before it was amended, certain policy terms could not be relied upon "where a certificate of insurance or certificate of security has been delivered under section 147 of [RTA 1988] to the person by whom a policy has been effected or to whom a security has been given." In its current form the section provides: "Where a policy or security is issued or given for the purposes of this Part of this Act. It is therefore now sufficient that a policy has been issued or a security has been given.

4.7 Schedule 3 of the Deregulation Act 2015 also amended section 151 of the RTA 1988 to the effect that the duty of an insurer to satisfy a judgment obtained by a third party against the assured applies when "a policy or security is issued or given for the purposes of this Part of this Act," but not where "a certificate of insurance or certificate of security has been delivered." In other words, the issue of a certificate is no longer a condition that has to be satisfied in order to allow a third party to bring a direct action against an insurer in respect of an unsatisfied judgment obtained against the assured.

4.8 Similarly, section 153 (1) of the RTA 1988 was amended with respect to the victim's claim against the insurer in the case of assured's bankruptcy. The Deregulation Act 2015 repealed the necessity of surrendering certificate after the cancellation of the policy or security under section 152 of the RTA 1988. It now suffices for the insurer to escape from liability if, amongst other things, "before the happening of the event which was the cause of the death or bodily injury or damage to property giving rise to the liability, the policy or security was cancelled by mutual consent or by virtue of any provision contained in it."

The 2002 Regulations

4.9 Where an action is brought directly against an insurer under the terms of the European Communities (Rights against Insurers) Regulations 2002[15] the retention

---

12 *Borders v Swift* [1957] Crim. L.R. 194.

13 *Leathley v Drummond* [1972] RTR 293.

14 Similarly, section 147(2) used to provide, "A security shall be of no effect for the purposes of this Part of this Act unless and until there is delivered by the person giving the security," and was substituted by "A person giving a security for the purposes of this Part of this Act must deliver."

15 This is analysed in Chapter 8.

or otherwise certificate was and is of no significance. The 2002 Regulations permit a direct action whether or not the victim has first obtained judgment against the assured, the only requirement being that there was a policy in force at the time of the accident. If the policy has been brought to an end by that date, whether or not the certificate had been surrendered, then the direct action is unavailable.

Transfer

4.10 Before the policy or security is transferred, except in the case of a certificate of insurance delivered by electronic means, the holder of it shall return the certificate to the company that issued it.[16] Where a certificate of insurance is suspended or ceased to be effective with the consent of the assured, it must be returned within seven days – except when it is delivered electronically.[17]

Risks that are not required to be covered

4.11 Section 145(4) provides a list of risks that are not required to be covered by the compulsory motor insurance policy under Part VI of the RTA 1988. Accordingly,

(1) bodily injury or death suffered by an employee arising out of or in the course of his employment
(2) liability in respect of damage to the vehicle
(3) any contractual liability
(4) liability in respect of damage to goods carried for hire or reward in or on the vehicle or in or on any trailer (whether or not coupled) drawn by the vehicle
(5) any liability of a person in respect of damage to property in his custody or under his control.

Additionally, with regards to the coverage provided for liabilities of the assured motorist in respect of damage to property the maximum amount of cover required is £1,200,000 for any one accident involving the vehicle.

In respect of claims for loss of life or personal injury as a result of traffic accidents, there is no statutory ceiling on the amount of liability, and the UK has opted for unlimited liability.

EU law: minimum amount of indemnity

4.12 The Second Directive Article 1(2) set out the minimum level of compensation that the compulsory insurance provide in each Member State, who were free to set higher amounts for compensation. For personal injury claims the limit was set 350,000 ECU[18] per victim, and 100,000 ECU per claim was set in the case of damage to property irrespective of the number of victims. Member States were permitted to, in

---

16 Motor Vehicles (Third Party Risks) Regulations 1972. Reg 12.
17 Motor Vehicles (Third Party Risks) Regulations 1972. Reg 12.
18 The unit of account as defined in Article 1 of Regulation (EEC) No 3180/78 and used before being replaced by the Euro on 1 January 1999, at parity.

place of the above minimum amounts, provide for a minimum amount of 500,000 ECU for personal injury where more than one victim is involved in a single claim or, in the case of personal injury and damage to property, a minimum overall amount of 600,000 ECU per claim whatever the number of victims or the nature of the damage.

4.13 Article 2 of the Fifth Directive amended the monetary amounts previously set by the Second Directive. Accordingly, each Member State shall require insurance to be compulsory at least EUR 1,000,000 per victim or EUR 5,000,000 per claim, whatever the number of victims in the case of personal injury. In the case of damage to property the minimum limit was set as EUR 1,000,000 per claim, whatever the number of victims.

4.14 These limits remain unchanged for now under Article 9 of the Consolidated Directive. These amounts are subject to a review every five years after 11 June 2005 in line with the European Index of Consumer Prices (EICP) established pursuant to Regulation (EC) No 2494/95. The latest review took place on 10 May 2016.[19]

As a result of the review, the amounts laid down in Euro are as follows:

- In the case of personal injury, the minimum amount of cover is increased to €1,220,000 per victim or €6,070,000 per claim, whatever the number of victims.
- In the case of material damage, the minimum amount is increased to €1,220,000 per claim, whatever the number of victims.

4.15 Certain Member States are benefiting from a transitional period[20] for the application of the Consolidated Directive 2009/103/EC and are subject to lower minimum amounts than the higher amounts laid down in the Directive. Therefore these minimum amounts are still not the same across all Member States. The Member States benefitting from a transitional period fall into three groups, with three different transitional periods, and therefore the calculation has been carried out separately for each group. A review applicable to those countries took place on 4 July 2018.[21]

As a result of the review, the amounts laid down in Euro are as follows.

For the Member States for which the transition period ended in December 2011 (Slovakia and Slovenia):

- In case of personal injury, the minimum amount of cover is increased to EUR 1,050,000 per victim or EUR 5,240,000 per claim, whatever the number of victims.
- In case of material damage, the minimum amount is increased to EUR 1,050,000 per claim, whatever the number of victims.

For the Member States for which the transition period ended in May 2012 (Czech Republic, Greece and Latvia), and those for which the transition period ended in June 2012 (Bulgaria, Estonia, Italy, Lithuania, Malta, Poland, Portugal and Romania):

---

19 https://eurlex.europa.eu/legalcontent/EN/TXT/?uri=CELEX%3A52016DC0246.

20 This is due to transition periods in accordance with Article 1(2) of the Directive 84/5/ECC, as amended by Directive 2005/14/EC, and has allowed some Member States to delay applying the full minimum amounts.

21 https://eur-lex.europa.eu/legal-content/EN/TXT/?uri=OJ%3AJOC_2018_233_R_0001.

- In case of personal injury, the minimum amount of cover is increased to EUR 1,050,000 per victim or EUR 5,210,000 per claim, whatever the number of victims.
- In case of material damage, the minimum amount is increased to EUR 1,050,000 per claim, whatever the number of victims.

For other Member States, for which Directive 2009/103/EC entered into application with no transitional period, the minimum amounts were already revised in 2016 as stated above.

4.16 The European Commission's proposal to amend the Consolidated Directive which is mentioned in Chapter 1 proposed replacing the current Article 9 by the following:

1. Without prejudice to any higher guarantees which Member States may prescribe, each Member State shall require the insurance referred to in Article 3 to be compulsory in respect of the following minimum amounts:
   (a) for personal injuries: EUR 6 070 000 per accident, irrespective of the number of victims, or EUR 1 220 000 per victim;
   (b) for damages to property, EUR 1 220 000 per claim, irrespective of the number of victims.
   For Member States that have not adopted the euro, the minimum amounts shall be converted into their national currency by applying the exchange rate as at [Publications Office – set the date the date of entry in force of this Directive] published in the Official Journal of the European Union.
2. Every five years from [date of entry into force of this Directive], the Commission shall review the amounts referred to in paragraph 1 in line with the harmonised index of consumer prices (HICP) established pursuant to Regulation (EU) 2016/792 of the European Parliament and of the Council**.[22]
   The Commission shall be empowered to adopt delegated acts in accordance with Article 28b concerning the adaptation of those amounts to the HICP within six months after the end of each five year period.
   For Member States that have not adopted the euro, the amounts shall be converted into their national currency by applying the exchange rate of the date of the calculation of the new minimum amounts and as published in the Official Journal of the European Union.

The position of employees

4.17 A statutory compulsory insurance scheme with respect to claims against employers for injuries suffered by employees as a result of accidents arising out of and in the course of employment is governed by the Employers' Liability (Compulsory Insurance) Act 1969 (ELCIA 1969). Historically, the Workmen's Compensation Act 1897 and its successors provided such a statutory scheme between 1897 and 1948. The House of Lords held in *St Helen's Colliery Co v Hewitson*[23] that, upon the true interpretation of the expression "arising out of and in the course of the employment," the workmen's compensation scheme did not apply to an employee who was injured when travelling to work in a vehicle provided by his employer if he was not obliged to use that transport. For

---

22 ** Regulation (EU) 2016/792 of the European Parliament and of the Council of 11 May 2016 on harmonised indices of consumer prices and the house price index, and repealing Council Regulation (EC) No 2494/95 (OJ L 135, 24.5.2016, p 11).

23 [1924] AC 59; *Weaver v Tredegar Iron & Coal Co Ltd* [1940] AC 955.

employer's liability, the employee must have an *obligation* to travel in it[24] that rendered insufficient either to have the right to or be permitted to travel in the vehicle.

4.18 Section 36 of the RTA 1930 provided that insurance was not required to cover (a) liability in respect of death or injury of a person "arising out of and in the course of his employment" by the insured or (b) "except in the case of a vehicle in which passengers are carried for hire or reward or by reason of or in pursuance of a contract of employment, liability in respect of death of or bodily injury to persons carried in or upon or entering or getting on to or alighting from the vehicle at the time of the occurrence of the event out of which the claims arise." At the relevant time, the claims that fall under (a) were expected to be covered by the Workmen's Compensation Acts.[25] Subsection (b) aimed to cover for liability in respect of the death of or injury to workmen who were not protected under the Workmen's Compensation Act schemes.[26]

4.19 The RTA 1960 adopted the same provisions but by the Motor Vehicles (Passenger Insurance) Act 1971 the second exception mentioned above was abolished. The exception for liability in respect of death or injury of a person "arising out of and in the course of his employment" by the insured, was re-enacted in section 145 of the Road Traffic Act 1972, in reliance of the employers' liability insurance scheme. Currently the RTA 1988 s 145(4)(a)'s wording provides:

> the policy shall not . . . be required . . . to cover liability in respect of death, arising out of or in the course of his employment, of a person insured by the policy or of bodily injury sustained by such a person arising out of and in the course of his employment.[27]

4.20 Insurance of liabilities which is excluded by section 145(4)(a) of RTA 1988 and (previously excluded by RTA 1972) had not been compulsory until the ELCIA 1969 came into force[28] in 1972.[29] Before the ELCIA 1969, the position had been that unless the employer had happened to have a liability policy there would have been no ultimate protection for an injured employee in the event of his employer's insolvency.

RTA 1988 section 145(4A)

4.21 With the ELCIA 1969 coming into force, the employers' liability insurers were required to indemnify the employer in the event that an employee was killed or injured by negligence attributable to the employer in the course of the employee's employment. However, the MTPL insurance related matters became more complex with the adoption of the European Union of the Third Motor Insurance Directive, Council Directive 90/232/EC, which required Member States to provide compulsory motor insurance for "all

---

24 *Vandyke v Fender* [1970] RTR 236, 241.

25 *Lees v Motor Insurers' Bureau* [1952] 2 Lloyd's Rep 210, 212; *Miller v Hales* [2007] Lloyd's Rep IR 54, [8], Jack J; *Vandyke v Fender* [1970] RTR 236, 241.

26 Gilbert, 105.

27 This exclusion appeared in all the relevant acts that imposed compulsory motor vehicle insurance. RTA 1930 s 36(1)(b)(i); RTA 1960 s 203(4)(B); RTA 1972 s 145(4)(a).

28 Employers' liability insurance became compulsory with effect from 1 January 1972 when the Employers' Liability (Compulsory Insurance) Act 1969 came into force.

29 In the meantime, in 1946 (with effect from July 1948) the Workmen's Compensation Act had been repealed by the National Insurance (Industrial Injuries) Act 1946. Various industrial benefits paid by the State were provided by this Act.

passengers, other than the driver, arising out of use of a vehicle."[30] This meant that if an employee was being carried as a passenger and was injured as the result of negligent use of the vehicle by or on behalf of the employer, he had to be insured under the Road Traffic Act 1988. In order to comply with the Third Directive, consequently, subsection (4A) was inserted[31] in section 145 of the 1988 Act, which provides that:

> In the case of a person
>
> (a)   carried in or upon a vehicle, or
> (b)   entering or getting on to, or alighting from a vehicle,
>
> the provisions of paragraph (a) of subsection (4) do not apply unless cover in respect of the liability referred to in that paragraph is in fact provided pursuant to a requirement of the Employers' Liability (Compulsory Insurance) Act 1969.

4.22 Consequential changes were made to the ELCIA 1969 to exclude this situation from compulsory employers' liability cover.[32] Before the change, if an employer was liable to an employee who was injured when being carried in the employer's vehicle, that liability was covered by compulsory employers' liability insurance if the employee's travel arose out of and was in the course of his employment. Under the current regime the employer's motor vehicle insurance covers injuries suffered by the employee under the circumstances described in section 145(4A). In other words, section 145(4A) brings a limited category of cases back within subsection 145(3).[33] The effect of these developments is that section 145(4)(a) takes the approach of excluding employees and section 145(4A) excludes from the exclusion employee passengers.[34]

Employee driver

4.23 The word "carried" in section 145(4A) is not statutorily defined. But it was held that the meaning of (b) should not affect the meaning of (a), and the words of section 145(4A) are not apt to include the driver of the vehicle because the intended reference was to persons who were passengers.[35] Consequently, an employee might be injured in a vehicle but might not be covered by his employer's motor insurance policy because he was not a passenger.

---

30 Now Consolidated Directive Article 12(1).

31 By the Motor Vehicles (Compulsory Insurance) Regulations 1992, SI 1992 No 3036.

32 The Employers' Liability (Compulsory Insurance) Exemption (Amendment) Regulations 1992 were made in December 1992 and came into force on 1 July 1994, and made an exception to the circumstances in which the Employers' Liability (Compulsory Insurance) Act 1969 require cover. The Regulations exempt an employer from any obligation imposed by section 1(1) of the ELCIA 1969 to insure against liability for bodily injury sustained by an employee when the employee is "(i) carried on or upon a vehicle, or (ii) entering or getting on to, or alighting from a vehicle, in the circumstances specified in that subsection and where that bodily injury is caused by, or arises out of, the use by the employer of a vehicle on the road; and the expressions "road," "use" and "vehicle" have the same meanings as in Part VI of the Road Traffic Act 1988."

33 *AXA Insurance UK Plc v Norwich Union Insurance Ltd* [2008] Lloyd's Rep IR 122, 125.

34 *Miller v Hales* [2007] Lloyd's Rep IR 54, [19], Jack J.

35 *R v Secretary of State for Transport ex parte National Insurance Guarantee Corporation* [1996] C.O.D. 425; Times, June 3, 1996; *Miller v Hales* [2007] Lloyd's Rep IR 54, [16], Jack J; *AXA Insurance UK Plc v Norwich Union Insurance Ltd* [2008] Lloyd's Rep IR 122.

Meaning of "carried"

4.24 RTA 1988 section 145(4A) did not adopt a "cover all" approach with respect to liability for all injuries to employees suffered in the course of employment and arising from use of the employer's vehicle on the road.[36] The ordinary and natural meaning of "carried in or upon a vehicle" connotes that the person is being transported or moved from one place to another.[37]

4.25 Whether a person is being carried is not determined by looking at the position at a single point of time, but by taking a broader view of why he is "in or upon a vehicle."[38] As a result, a person does not immediately cease to be "carried" once his vehicle ceases (temporarily or permanently) to be in motion.[39] Similarly, he may be being "carried" when he has entered a vehicle and is waiting for it to start.[40] In these situations he would be in or upon the vehicle for the purpose of being carried.

4.26 It was therefore held that the injury suffered by a workman who was injured when he fell off the bucket which was raised by a hoist attached to a van was outside the scope of the wording of "carried in or upon a vehicle" in section 145(4A). The workman was to remove some overhead street Christmas lightning and was required to stand in the bucket (a platform at the end of the boom) whilst carrying out the work. It was common ground that the apparatus formed a part of the lorry, in accordance with the RTA 1988 s 183(3) which extends the meaning of "motor vehicle" to associated equipment and machinery. When the lorry with this attached equipment was parked and the worker was raised in the bucket, another lorry drove past and hit the boom, causing the worker to fall out of the bucket and to suffer personal injury. It was held that the workman was not being carried in or upon a vehicle and therefore was not required to be insured under the RTA 1988 s 145(4A). This injury was required to be insured by the compulsory liability insurance under the ELCIA 1969.

Insurance of an exempted institution

4.27 A comprehensive discussion of the RTA 1988 s 145 subsections 3(a), 4(a) and 4A can be found in *Miller v Hales*[41] in which M was a police constable who was chasing a motorcycle with a pillion passenger that drove past ignoring signs to stop. The rider, H, stopped on a dead end road after a long pursuit and M put one handcuff on him. H, however, managed to escape, ran into the police car that had been left with the keys in it. The other man got in on the passenger side and they locked the doors so that M was unable to open them. While M was at the rear of the car it reversed violently. M fell beneath it and was dragged some distance before he became free, suffering very serious injuries. Exemptions from the compulsory MTPL insurance under the RTA 1988 are mentioned in Chapter 1. One of the exceptions listed under the RTA s 144(2)(b) is vehicles owned by a police authority and driven under the owner's control or vehicles "being

---

36 *AXA Insurance UK Plc v Norwich Union Insurance Ltd* [2008] Lloyd's Rep IR 122, 127–128.
37 Ibid, 127.
38 Ibid.
39 Ibid.
40 Ibid.
41 [2007] Lloyd's Rep IR 54.

driven for police purposes by or under the direction of a constable or an employee of a police authority."

4.28 Although exempted, in *Miller v Hales*, the relevant Constabulary chose to have a motor vehicle policy with QBE International Insurance Limited instead of being self-insured and the issue in *Miller v Hales* was a RTA 1988 section 151 claim by M against the insurer. H was clearly not permitted to drive the police car; however, as analysed in Chapter 8 section 151 requires a judgment to be honoured by the insurer as if the insurance contract insured all persons.

4.29 The first question was about M's employment and whether the RTA 1988 s 145(4)(a) had the effect that no cover was required and therefore was not provided, because M was to be treated as acting in the course of employment when he was injured. The judge answered this question by holding that a constable was not an employee but an officer. That meant M had no contract of employment. This ruling resolved the matter between the parties and if H was to be treated as insured under section 151 of the RTA 1988, the insurer was liable to M.

4.30 Jack J also discussed, although *obiter*, if M had been an employee, could M argue his claim falls under the RTA 1988 s 145(4A) as an insurance cover was not available pursuant to a requirement of the ELCIA 1969?[42] On the facts, as a matter of common sense, Jack J found that M's intention was to get the car door open so he could get H out. His intention was not then to get into the car. Under s 145(4A) an attempt to enter must be an attempt to enter to be a passenger. Whereas, as held *obiter* by Jack J, M's action could not be described as entering the vehicle or attempting to enter the vehicle as a passenger, that is, someone who would be carried by it. Had M been an employee acting in the course of his employment, s 145(4) would have removed the protection of the RTA 1988 and the protection would not have been reinstated by s 145(4A).

Vicarious liability

4.31 An employer (master) is using his vehicle if the vehicle is being used by his servant (employee) on the employer's business.[43] If an employee driver drives a motor vehicle for his employer, the employer will be vicariously liable for the consequences of the employee's negligence so long as he is driving as the servant of the employer[44] and is acting in the scope of his authority.[45]

---

42 Jack J noted that a police authority will have persons working for it apart from constables but it is not required to insure under the ELCIA 1969. This is presumably on the same basis that it is not required to take out the compulsory MTPL insurance under the RTA 1988, namely that it will be good for the money. *Miller v Hales* [2007] Lloyd's Rep IR 54, [8].

43 *Richardson v Baker* [1976] RTR 56; *Passmoor v Gibbons* [1979] RTR 53.

44 *West Yorkshire Trading Standards Service v Lex Vehicle Leasing Ltd* [1996] RTR 70; See also *Windle v Dunning & Son Ltd.* [1968] 1 WLR 552 in which the "user" of a vehicle was interpreted restrictively. The defendants hired three lorries from W. Ltd., haulage contractors. W. Ltd. operated the vehicles, and the drivers were their servants. With regards to the relevant offence under the RTA 1960 the defendants were held not to be using the vehicles and that the responsibility for such use rested with the driver or his employer.

45 *John T Ellis Ltd v Hinds* [1947] KB 475; *Marsh v Moores* [1949] 2 KB 208.

4.32 In *Richardson v Baker*[46] the argument was that the employee had been instructed to drive from London to Felixstove but had not been instructed to drive *the*[47] vehicle that he in fact did. It was held that so long as the vehicle was being used on the master's business he was using the vehicle even though he had not in fact specifically authorised the employee to undertake such use.

4.33 A person who sends his driver out with his motor vehicle on business causes[48] his driver to use the vehicle.[49] If the owner of a car who has covered his own liability by a policy lends it to a friend he will commit an offence unless either his own policy extends to cover liability incurred by the friend while driving, or the friend has a policy that will indemnify him while he is driving another person's car.[50] The existing policy of the owner of the vehicle might have to cover the loss under section 151, however, it is submitted that the offence under the RTA 1988 s 143(2) is nevertheless committed. Otherwise, the purpose of imposing criminal offence for uninsured used of a vehicle would be jeopardised if, so long as there is insurance cover, although not expressly insured, any user of a vehicle would be covered and that would excuse the fact that the offence was committed.

4.34 The employees' position regarding sections 143 and 145 of the RTA 1988 was stated in Chapter 4. The question arose in the past in circumstances where a driver employee injured another employee employed by the same person in the course of their employment.[51] Assume that in the absence of the compulsory insurance under the ELCIA 1969, could the victim make a claim against the MIB? Under the RTA 1988 section 145(4)(a) such a claim would fall outside the compulsory MTPL insurance and consequently, will not be regarded as a relevant liability that the MIB would be liable to compensate.[52]

4.35 However, it may all ultimately depend on the policy wording. In *Richards v Cox*[53] it was held that the policy insured separately the owner and the driver who was the owner's servant. Hence, the insurer was liable for the injury caused by the employee driver to another employee of the owner. If the owner had driven and made a claim, the policy would not have covered[54] that loss, but the injured servant was not the employee driver's servant.

4.36 In *Richards v Cox* the policy wording was as follows:

> In the terms of and subject to the limitations of and for the purposes of this section the company will treat as though he were the insured person any person who is driving such vehicle on the insured's order or with his permission provided (A) that such person is not entitled to indemnity under any other policy.

4.37 As the statutory position is achieved today employers have to insure their liabilities arising out of or in the course of employment and the issue is likely to be between

---

46 [1976] RTR 56.
47 Emphasis added.
48 For meaning of "cause" see Chapter 3.
49 *John T Ellis Ltd v Hinds* [1947] KB 475, 484.
50 *John T Ellis Ltd v Hinds* [1947] KB 475, 485.
51 *Lees v Motor Insurers' Bureau* [1952] 2 Lloyd's Rep 210; *Richards v Cox* [1943] 1 KB 139.
52 *Lees v Motor Insurers' Bureau* [1952] 2 Lloyd's Rep 210.
53 [1943] 1 KB 139. Applied *Digby v General Accident Fire and Life Assurance Corporation, Ltd.*, [1943] AC 121.
54 That liability would be required to be covered by the employer's liability insurance.

motor vehicle and employers' liability insurers if each argues that the other insurer is liable. A clear example of this is *AXA Insurance UK Plc v Norwich Union Insurance Ltd*[55] in which an employee was injured when he was about to remove some overhead Christmas lightning. At the time of the accident he was in a bucket which was attached to a hoist with an elevating platform and a boom. This equipment was all part of the lorry (by which the worker travelled on that morning) in accordance with s 183(3) of the 1988 Act which extends the meaning of "motor vehicle" to associated equipment and machinery. When the lorry with this attachment was parked and the worker was raised in the bucket, another lorry drove past and hit the boom, causing the worker to fall out of the bucket and to suffer personal injury. The parties agreed that for the purposes of the RTA 1988 s 143(1)(a) the employer or the worker was at the material time the user of the lorry in the road. Moreover, for the purposes of the RTA 1988 s 145(3)(a) the injury suffered by the worker was caused by or arose out of such use of the vehicle on the road. The matter at stake was whether the employer's motor vehicle or the employers' liability insurers will be liable for the loss. As referred to in paragraph 4.26 above this fell outside the RTA 1988 s 145(4A) and was to be insured under the ELCIA 1969.

Subrogation in employment cases

4.38 Where an employee caused injury to another employee in the course of his employment, after compensating it can the employer or its insurer recoup against the employee who caused the injury? Technically, as established by the majority of the House of Lords in *Lister v Romford Ice and Cold Storage Co Ltd*,[56] there is no implied term in a contract of employment that an employee who injures a co-worker is immune from proceedings for indemnification by his employer who is vicariously liable. Further, an employer is not under an implied obligation to insure for the benefit of its employees in respect of their potential liabilities. In *Lister*, which was later described as being an unfortunate case whose ill effects have been avoided only by an agreement, the son who was employed to drive a motor vehicle injured his father whom he had taken as his mate.[57] The company, after compensating the father's loss, sued the driver for damages for breach of an implied term that he would exercise reasonable care in the performance of his duties as servant. The claim was upheld by the majority of the House of Lords. However, the Minister of Labour in 1957 appointed an inter-departmental committee to study the implications of the decision. The committee expressed its view as dealing with the matter by voluntary methods, such as extension of the "gentleman's agreement" within the insurance field. Following the report, the then deputy chairman of the British Insurance Association wrote a letter, dated 23 October 1959, to all members of the association and invited the addressees, in their common interest to confirm adherence to a revised[58] "gentleman's agreement" as follows:

> Employers Liability Insurers agree that they will not institute a claim against the employee of an insured employer in respect of death of or injury to a fellow employee, unless the weight

---

55 [2008] Lloyd's Rep IR 122.
56 [1957] AC 555.
57 *Morris v Ford Motor Co* [1973] QB 792, 801, Lord Denning.
58 The reference to a revised agreement relates to an earlier agreement in 1953.

of evidence clearly indicates (1) collusion or (2) wilful misconduct, on the part of the employee against whom the claim is made. The agreement shall apply in priority to the provisions of any claims agreements operating between insurers who subscribe to this agreement.

4.39 The majority of the Court of Appeal refused to extent *Lister* to the issue in *Morris v Ford Motor Co.*[59] where the facts fell outside the scope of the gentleman's agreement referred to above.[60] In *Morris* M was employed by a firm of cleaners and was injured whilst working at the motor factory owned by Ford. The injury was due to the negligence of one of Ford's servants, R, who drove a fork-lift truck without keeping a proper lookout. M claimed damages against Ford; Ford then served a third party notice against the firm of cleaners claiming an indemnity. Under the cleaning contract, the firm of cleaners had contracted to indemnify Ford against any liability to M, even though it was caused by the negligence of Ford's own servants. The firm of cleaners then claimed against R. Under the *Lister* principle if Ford had sued R, they would have got judgment against him for the full amount which they had had to pay to M. It would have followed that the cleaners would "stand in the shoes of Ford" and to exercise against R all the rights which Ford has against him.

Lord Denning applied the principle of equity and held that holding R personally liable would be unfair and would imperil good industrial relations.[61] No one had expected that R would be personally liable; the damages were expected to be borne by the insurers. James LJ agreed with Lord Denning that was operative in an industrial setting in which subrogation of the third party to the rights and remedies of the defendants against their employees would be unacceptable and unrealistic. Hence, a term was implied that the cleaners and Ford excluded the subrogation right in their indemnity agreement. Stamp LJ dissented by rejecting that the right of subrogation, which arises from the contract of indemnity itself, could not be excluded by an implied agreement.

Issues to be covered by section 145

4.40 The RTA 1988 s 145 is a neutral provision,[62] the purpose of which is to specify what the "requirements in respect of policies of insurance" are.[63]

4.41 Section 145(3)(a) sets out the policy requirements, and they are subject to the exceptions stated above. Accordingly, the policy

> (a) must insure such person, persons or classes of persons as may be specified in the policy in respect of any liability which may be incurred by him or them in respect of the death of or bodily injury to any person or damage to property caused by, or arising out of, the use of the vehicle on a road [or other public place] in Great Britain.

---

59 [1973] QB 792.

60 This claim did not come under the "gentleman's agreement," because the injured man, M, was not an employee of Ford but was an employee of the firm of cleaners.

61 [1973] QB 792, 798.

62 It does not stipulate that the user must take out a policy of insurance complying with the Act nor does it say that the "authorised insurer" has to issue a policy which complies with the Act. *Bristol Alliance Ltd Partnership v Williams* [2013] RTR 9, Ward LJ, [37].

63 *Bristol Alliance Ltd Partnership v Williams* [2013] RTR 9, Ward LJ, [37].

4.42 The RTA 1988 s 145 (3)(a) requires the compulsory MTPL insurance to cover the liability mentioned in the subsection to "any person." In the EU regime the Consolidated Directive expressly states that the insurance obligation includes covering civil liability for personal injuries and damage to property suffered by pedestrians, cyclists and other non-motorised users of the roads as a consequence of an accident in which a motor vehicle is involved.[64]

4.43 The key area under the RTA 1988 s 145 is the meaning of the word "use" which is mainly to be insured under a MTPL insurance. The matters that have arisen with regards to the clarification of the meaning of "use" necessitate it to be analysed in detail in the next chapter.

4.44 It was mentioned in Chapter 1 that the relevant Directives never sought to harmonise the scope and forms of liability within Member States. The rights of a victim to seek compensation vary depending upon where an injury takes place. Article 14 of the Consolidated Directive provides that the insurance cover required of a vehicle must be the greater of that demanded by the law of the Member State in which the accident occurred, or that demanded by the law of the Member State in which the vehicle was normally based. Each Member State is required to provide by its domestic law that any compulsory policy against civil liability arising out of the use of a vehicle covered, on the basis of a single premium, the entire territory of the EU, and to ensure that the scope of cover provided was either that of the Member State in which the vehicle was normally based, or that of the Member State in which it was used, whichever was greater. This is implemented by the RTA 1988 s 145(3)(aa) which states that the policy

(aa)   must, in the case of a vehicle normally based in the territory of another member State, insure him or them in respect of any civil liability which may be incurred by him or them as a result of an event related to the use of the vehicle in Great Britain if, –

(i)   according to the law of that territory, he or they would be required to be insured in respect of a civil liability which would arise under that law as a result of that event if the place where the vehicle was used when the event occurred were in that territory, and

(ii)   the cover required by that law would be higher than that required by paragraph (a) above.

4.45 Article 1(4) of the Consolidated Motor Insurance Directive 2009 defines where a vehicle is "normally based" which is

• in cases where no registration is required for a type of vehicle but the vehicle bears an insurance plate, or a distinguishing sign analogous to the registration plate, the territory of the State in which the insurance plate or the sign is issued; or

• in cases where neither registration plate nor insurance plate nor distinguishing sign is required for certain types of vehicle, the territory of the State in which the person who has custody of the vehicle is permanently resident.

---

64 Art 12(3).

4.46 The RTA 1988 section 145(3)(b) then provides a vehicle normally based in Great Britain must be insured in respect of any liability which may be incurred in respect of the use of the vehicle, in the territory other than Great Britain and Gibraltar of each of the Member States of the Communities according to

(i)   the law on compulsory insurance against civil liability in respect of the use of vehicles of the State in whose territory the event giving rise to the liability occurred; or

(ii) if it would give higher cover, the law which would be applicable under this Part of this Act if the place where the vehicle was used when that event occurred were in Great Britain.

Personal injury

4.47 Insurance obligation under section 145 includes cover for "emergency treatment."[65] Payment for emergency treatment and hospital treatment of traffic casualties is regulated by sections 157–161 of the RTA 1988.

4.48 The words "personal injury" refer to both physical and psychological suffering. As a result, in the domestic context, it was held that the psychiatric illness suffered as a result of a motor accident may constitute "bodily injury."[66] The CJEU held that with regards to the meaning of "personal injury," reference must be made to the general scheme and purpose of that provision and of the Directive.[67] It follows that the meaning of "personal injuries" covers any type of damage, insofar as compensation for such damage is provided for as part of the civil liability of the insured under the national law applicable in the dispute.[68]

Non-material damages

4.49 Whether or not non-material damages are recoverable is a matter for domestic law as civil liability for traffic accidents is determined by national law and the Directives relevant to this book do not seek to harmonise Member States national rules applicable to civil liability for traffic accidents.[69] It follows that a national law may either allow or disallow recovery for non-pecuniary losses, and the Directives do not interfere in such rules.

4.50 Consequently, Member States' national laws may provide specific compensation schemes which may stipulate compensation with a ceiling lower than provided by the Directives for compulsory insurance cover.[70] This was discussed in *Petillo v Unipol Assicurazioni SpA*[71] in the context of national legislation which lays down a specific compensation scheme for non-material damage resulting from minor physical injuries

---

65 RTA 1988 s 145(3)(c).
66 *Keeley v Pashen* [2005] Lloyd's Rep IR 289.
67 *Drozdovs v Baltikums AAS* [2014] RTR 14, [40].
68 *Drozdovs v Baltikums AAS* [2014] RTR 14; *Petillo v Unipol Assicurazioni SpA* [2014] 3 CMLR 1 [34].
69 See Chapter 1.
70 For limitations see above [4.12] onwards.
71 [2014] 3 CMLR 1.

caused by road traffic accidents, limiting the compensation payable for that damage in comparison with the compensation allowed for identical damage arising from causes other than those accidents.

4.51 Where national law civil liability rules permit recovery for non-material losses, the Member States' obligation under the Directives arise and they are required to ensure that compulsory insurance covers compensation for non-material losses as well as those material. As held in *Petillo v Unipol Assicurazioni SpA*,[72] the non-material losses may be permitted by the national law to a financial ceiling that falls below the minimum insurance requirement under the Directives. The point to be emphasised here is that the civil liability rules that contain such a financial limitation fall outside the coverage of Directives who then do not prevent such ceilings from civil liability rules.

4.52 However, where a national law permits recovery from the person responsible for the accidents without a limitation as such, the Directives again require the Member State to ensure that compulsory insurance covers at least the minimum amounts laid down in the Directives.[73] The logic is that so long as the national law permits recovery for an injury for an amount whose ceiling is not lower than the limitations for compensation provided by the Directives, whether material or non-material damages, if they are permitted under national law, they should be covered by compulsory liability insurance at least to the amount that is provided by the Directives.

Who can claim compensation for non-material damages?

4.53 *Drozdovs v Baltikums AAS*[74] was a joint case in which claims as a result of accidents that occurred in the Czech Republic and Latvia were considered. In the first case H was killed in the Czech Republic in a road traffic accident caused by P. H was married and had a daughter. H's wife and daughter sued P for compensation for the "non-material" damage arising as a result of the loss of their husband and father. In the second case the parents of V died in a road traffic accident in Riga (Latvia). The accident was caused by the driver of a motor vehicle insured by the company AAS Baltikums (Baltikums). The guardian of V brought an action against Baltikums claiming payment of compensation for the non-material damage suffered by V owing to the death of his parents at his young age.

4.54 It was held that when national law enables the victim to recover for non-material damages, anyone entitled to compensation under national civil law for such damage is entitled to the benefit of the Directives. Compulsory insurance against civil liability in respect of the use of motor vehicles must cover compensation for non-material damage suffered by the next of kin of the deceased victims of a road traffic accident, in so far as such compensation is provided for as part of the civil liability of the insured party under the national law applicable in the dispute in the main proceedings.[75] In other words, those who are protected by the Directives are not limited to persons directly involved in the event causing the harm.

---

72 Ibid.
73 *Drozdovs v Baltikums AAS* [2014] RTR 14, [46], [58].
74 [2014] RTR 14.
75 *Drozdovs v Baltikums AAS* [2014] RTR 14, [48].

Injury to the person who was actually using the vehicle

4.55 The RTA 1988 section 145(3)(a) provides that the policy

> (a) must insure such person, persons or classes of persons as may be specified in the policy in respect of any liability which may be incurred by him or them in respect of the death of or bodily injury to any person.

The words "bodily injury to any person" are restricted so as to exclude the driver of the vehicle at the time of the imagined risk. The significance of this matter with respect to the claims against the MIB is illustrated in *Cooper v Motor Insurers' Bureau*[76] where K asked C to road test K's motorcycle. During the course of that test the brakes failed and C collided with a motor car on the highway. Having suffered very severe injuries C claimed against the MIB to recover the judgment that was obtained against uninsured K. As affirmed by the Court of Appeal, Barry Chedlow QC held that the compulsory insurance must be against third party risks and must cover the liabilities of the user and the person who causes or permits user. It hence follows that there must be an intention to restrict the scope of the phrase "any person" in section 145(3)(a) so as to exclude the driver of the vehicle at the time of the imagined risk.[77] As a result, only C's liability was relevant liability that fell within the statutory compulsory insurance regime but K's liability to C was not.

Passengers

4.56 Insurance cover for third party liability to passengers had not been compulsory[78] under the scheme provided by the 1930 and 1960 Acts except for "in the case of a vehicle in which passengers are carried for hire or reward or by reason of or in pursuance of a contract of employment."[79] Hence, where public transport was concerned it was eminently reasonable that the operator of such vehicles should have insured passengers,[80] eg a taxicab that carried passengers as a matter of business. This exception led to a number of disputes on the meaning of "hire or reward" when a privately owned vehicle rather than a public transport was concerned[81] and the rule was that there must be more than a mere social kindness to make the use of the vehicle that of carrying for hire or reward.[82]

---

76 [1983] RTR 412 affirmed by the Court of Appeal [1985] QB 575.

77 *Cooper v Motor Insurers' Bureau* [1985] QB 575, 580–581. Cooper was decided under section 143 of the RTA 1972 which was similarly worded to section 143 of the RTA 1988 with a change to subsection numbers.

78 The reason behind this rule is, presumably, the belief that passengers, like the driver himself, can properly be left to look after themselves. A difference between public transport and a passenger who is carried say for a lift but not hire or reward is, in the former the public has no right or means to assess the driver's identity or qualifications or characteristics, the passenger has more control in the latter. It was found not justified to impose private car owners to insure all potential passengers. *Albert v Motor Insurers' Bureau* [1972] AC 301, 317, Lord Donovan.

79 RTA 1960 s 203(4).

80 *Albert v Motor Insurers' Bureau* [1972] AC 301, 318–319, Lord Donovan.

81 A number of examples may be brought into question here. A and B may for their weekly game of golf travel to the golf course in A's car driven by A, and B make his contribution by paying for A's lunch or for the petrol that is bought on the journey. A party of men living in the same village and going to work in a city may take turns at driving the party in their respective cars. A number of mothers agree that in turn one of them will take all their children to school. A party of people, one of whom owned a car, decided to go on holiday together in the car and agreed to share the car expenses.

82 *Albert v Motor Insurers' Bureau* [1972] AC 301.

4.57 Policy wordings might have required some different interpretation. For instance, in *Digby v General Accident Fire and Life Assurance Corp Ltd*[83] the policyholder was injured when travelling in her car as a passenger whilst it was being driven by her chauffeur. The claim against the insurer was successful because the policy provided cover "against all sums which the policyholder should 'become legally liable to pay in respect of any claim by any person.'"

4.58 Insurance coverage for passengers is compulsory under the current regime.[84] It had been decided by the CJEU that the word "passengers" within the meaning of the compulsory insurance regime applicable within the EU covered passengers who were family members of the user of the vehicle and passengers who were carried in the vehicle free of charge. Consequently, derogations from the Directives to the effect either limiting or excluding the insurance cover from these last two mentioned groups were not permitted – they were required to be treated like any other third party victims.[85] The Consolidated Directive now requires insurance for liability for personal injuries to all passengers, other than the driver, arising out of the use of a vehicle.[86] It is not permitted to exclude insurer's liability in respect of their personal injuries suffered by the members of the family of the policyholder, driver or any other person who is liable under civil law in the event of an accident, and whose liability is covered by the insurance referred to in Article 3.[87]

The owner when injured as a passenger in their own vehicle

4.59 A question arose as to whether *Cooper v Motor Insurers' Bureau*[88] would be extended to a case where the passenger was himself the owner of the vehicle and was injured by the negligent use of the vehicle by another, who was not the servant of the owner. This was the matter in *Limbrick v French*[89] where *Cooper* was distinguished. The driver had the owner's permission to drive; however, the owner had not known that the driver was not insured. The owner victim did not know that the driver (her boyfriend) who was driving her car with her permission was not insured. In fact, she told her boyfriend that her insurance did not cover him and he said that he had been insured. The Court found it crucial that the MIB's liability was a liability of the uninsured driver which included the risk of personal injury to the passenger of the car at the relevant time.[90] This was required to be indemnified under Part VI of the 1972 Act (now Part VI of the 1988 Act).

"Any liability" arising out of the use of the vehicle

4.60 As far as the injuries suffered by victims of motor vehicle accidents are concerned, the policy of insurance which a motorist is required by statute to take out must cover

---

83 [1943] AC 121.
84 RTA 1988 s 145(3)(a); the Consolidated Directive Art 12(1).
85 *Mendes Ferreira v Companhia de Seguros Mundial Confiança SA* (C-348/98) ECLI:EU:C:2000:442.
86 Art 12(1).
87 Art 12(2).
88 [1985] QB 575.
89 [1993] PIQR P121.
90 As mentioned above, permitting someone to use a vehicle without insurance is strictly a criminal offence. Here, the matter was not the owner's criminal liability, as the owner pleaded guilty to that offence, but the uninsured driver's and therefore the MIB's civil liability against the victim.

REQUIREMENTS WITH RESPECT TO THE INSURANCE POLICY

any liability which may be incurred by him arising out of the use of the vehicle by him. As discussed in Chapter 12 the word "any" here is interpreted broadly, that it is wide enough to cover, in general terms, any use by the motorist of the vehicle, whether it is an innocent or a criminal use.[91] If the motorist makes a criminal use of the vehicle after the policy is taken out, he is not himself entitled to recover on the policy for damages that he had paid to the victim, but if he does not pay the damages, then the injured third party can recover against the insurers under the relevant section of the RTA that grants a direct action against insurers.[92] It is a liability which the motorist, under the statute, was required to cover.[93] For this reason, although the assured cannot claim against the insurer under these circumstances, a third part victim can. In other words, the injured third party is not affected by the disability attached to the motorist himself.[94]

4.61 The facts of *Hardy v Motor Insurers' Bureau* are given in Chapter 12 The Court of Appeal held that the liability of motorist (Phillips) to the victim (Hardy) was a liability which Phillips was required to cover by a policy of insurance, even though it arose out of his wilful and culpable criminal act.[95] Although Phillips would not have been entitled to claim under the insurance policy, the injured third party would not be disabled from recovering from them. Phillips was not insured and the claim was addressed to the MIB and it was held that the MIB must pay the injured third party, even though Phillips was guilty of felony. These principles confirmed in a case where the victim was ran down by the motorist who deliberately drove his vehicle on the pavement where the victim was walking.[96]

4.62 It was later explained by Rix LJ in *Charlton v Fisher*[97] that the right available for the third party victim under the MIB Agreement grounds upon a separate right provided by it rather than the insurance contract between the motorist and the insurer – in any event the motorist was uninsured in *Hardy*. The right is independent to that of the assured. Therefore, even if *ex turpi causa* may be argued against a claim by the motorist, that does not defeat the third party victim's claim which does not derive from the motorist's right against the insurer or the MIB but it is independent. This matter is also discussed in Chapter 12.

---

91 *Hardy v Motor Insurers' Bureau* [1964] 2 QB 745.
92 Ibid.
93 Ibid.
94 Ibid.
95 The 1946 MIB Agreement provided, "If judgment in respect of any liability which is required to be covered by a policy of insurance or a security under Part II of the Road Traffic Act, 1930 (Part VI of the Road Traffic Act 1960 when the case was decided), is obtained against any person or persons in Great Britain and any such judgment is not satisfied," then the Motor Insurers' Bureau will pay it to the person in whose favour the judgment was given. The question in *Hardy* was whether the liability of Phillips to Hardy was a liability which came under the agreement. The MIB argued that this liability of Phillips was a liability for the consequences of his own wilful and deliberate criminal act. Since no person can insure himself in respect of his own wilful crime, this is not a claim which is to be insured under the RTA and consequently which is not to be compensated by the MIB.
96 *Gardner v Moore* [1984] AC 548. The case was decided under the RTA 1972 and the 1972 MIB Agreements. The same principles applied in Hardy under the RTA 1930 and 1946 MIB Agreements.
97 *Charlton v Fisher* [2002] QB 578.

CHAPTER 5

The meaning of "use" of a vehicle

Significance of defining the term "use"

5.1 Identifying the "user" of a motor vehicle is the matter at the heart of motor vehicle insurance. Under the RTA 1988 s 145(3)(a) the compulsory liability insurance must cover "the use of a vehicle." The crucial question is whether or not at a particular time a motor vehicle is being used.

5.2 It is the user's obligation to insure his/her use of the vehicle. The liability of "user" as identified under the RTA 1988 is the relevant liability that is covered by the MIB in the absence of insurance.[1] If the owner of the vehicle allows an uninsured person to use the vehicle civil liability may be imposed on the owner.[2] The offences under the RTA 1988 with regard to "not having a valid insurance" or "not having a valid certificate" are attached to the use of the vehicle.[3] Hence, identifying if the person who caused the loss was the user of the vehicle in question and if the accident that caused the injury amounted to the use of the vehicle are the starting points of the analysis of the compulsory motor vehicle insurance in the UK.

5.3 Does the term "use" of a vehicle include anything which is consistent with the normal function of the vehicle? Further, what functions of a vehicle fall under its "normal function"? The RTA 1988 s 143(1)(a) states "a person must not use a motor vehicle on a road [or other public place]" without having the insurance or security required by the Act. The section does not distinguish whether the vehicle is in motion or stationary, whether

---

1 See Chapter 10.

2 See Chapter 6.

3 The word "use" appears in many different sections, schedules and regulations in relation to the compulsory insurance and also the offences with respect to using the vehicle without insurance or without having a valid test certificate. The Courts emphasised the point at stake as the mischief that the relevant legislative instrument aims to protect. With regards to the instruments that have been adopted in relation to the third party compulsory insurance, "use" should have the same meaning in the interpretation of those legislative rules. However, the views so far have gone to two different directions: see for instance *Hewer v Cutler* [1974] RTR 155, 159 and *Scotland Tudhope v Every* 1977 SLT 2 confirmed that the mischief against which this enactment prohibiting user without a valid test certificate was not the same as that of using a vehicle without insurance. This view proposed that since the vehicle in question was, at the time of the alleged offence, incapable of being moved because its rear wheels were locked, none of the particular dangers against which the mandatory requirement to hold a valid test certificate was intended to protect the public could conceivably have emerged. On the other hand in *Thomas v Hooper* Glidewell LJ held that "use" in both sections (sections 44 and 143 of the RTA 1972) had the same meaning for this purpose. *Pumbien v Vines* [1996] RTR 37, [45–46] and *Gosling v Howard* (Note) [1975] RTR 429 also confirmed that the mischief which the prohibition was catering for were the same. This book adopts the view that the object of these provisions is to protect the safety and property of other road users; therefore, use is to be interpreted in the same way under the above-mentioned sections.

the owner's intention to use or not to the vehicle is relevant or whether when a vehicle is towed by another vehicle that falls under the meaning of "use" in this context. Moreover, a question may be raised if carrying out some repairs on a motor vehicle amounts to its use? In this regard could a distinction be proposed between when repairs are carried out because the vehicle broke down during the course of a journey or when it was not making a journey but it did not pass its MOT. The uses on the road or other public place of diverse categories of vehicle vary greatly. This chapter attempts to provide a critical overview of the meaning of "use" as expressed by the statute and read by the common law courts as well as the CJEU.

Meaning

5.4 In determining what amounts to "use" of a vehicle emphasis should be put on the purpose of the RTA 1988 s 143 which is "to protect the safety and property of other road users."[4]

5.5 The user principle is itself very broad.[5] The RTA 1988 s 143(a) says nothing about driving; it refers to the use of the vehicle. The "user" concept is not confined to ownership[6] and goes much further than the physical act of driving[7] or operating.[8] There are authorities which approved that a person who rides in his car while being driven by someone else is using, although is not driving, the vehicle.[9]

5.6 The broad reading of the word "use" in this context reflects the reality that a motor vehicle can pose a danger for others in its vicinity whether or not it is being driven; for example, from a fire or explosion due to petrol, oil or lubricants leaking or if its hand brake fails while parked.

5.7 What has to be covered by insurance is the use of the vehicle, not the person using the vehicle.[10] It is true that typically a motor vehicle insurance policy insures the assured in respect of the ownership and user of a particular car, and the premium is calculated by considering the characteristics of the vehicle and the owner.[11] However, there is nothing that prevents a user who is not the owner of the vehicle to be insured with respect of its use. The compulsory MTPL insurance requires cover in respect of third party risks only and accordingly that there is no necessity for the assured to have any insurable interest in the vehicle.[12]

5.8 It is worth noting here that the European Court of Justice stated that the concept of "use of vehicles" within the meaning of the compulsory MTPL insurance covered by the

---

4 *Pumbien v Vines* [1996] RTR 37; *R&S Pilling (t/a Phoenix Engineering) v UK Insurance Ltd* [2019] UKSC 16.

5 *Bretton v Hancock* [2005] RTR 22, Rix LJ, [299].

6 *Napthen v Place* [1970] RTR 248.

7 *R&S Pilling (t/a Phoenix Engineering) v UK Insurance Ltd* [2019] UKSC 16 [34].

8 *Turnbull v MNT Transport (2006) Ltd* [2010] CSOH 163, [27]; *R&S Pilling (t/a Phoenix Engineering) v UK Insurance Ltd* [2019] UKSC 16.

9 *John T Ellis Ltd v Hinds* [1947] KB 475, 484; *Bretton v Hancock* [2005] RTR 22.

10 *Cameron v Liverpool Victoria Insurance Co Ltd* [2019] UKSC 6 [5], Lord Sumption; *Lees v Motor Insurers' Bureau* [1952] 2 Lloyd's Rep 210, 211; *John T Ellis Ltd v Hinds* [1947] KB 475; *Marsh v Moores* [1949] 2 KB 208.

11 *Tattersall v Drysdale* [1935] 2 KB 174.

12 *Boss v Kingston* [1962] 2 Lloyd's Rep 431, Lord Parker CJ.

Directives is an autonomous concept of EU law which cannot be left to the assessment of each Member State.[13] That interpretation has to take into account not only its wording but also its context and the objectives pursued by the rules of which it was part.[14]

"Use" is not confined to "drive"

5.9 A person uses a vehicle on a road if he has the use of it on a road.[15] Authorities confirmed and it has recently been emphasised more heavily both in the European[16] and domestic[17] contexts that such use is not confined to the act of driving the vehicle.[18] In *Dunthorne v Bentley*[19] about ten minutes before the accident, B had been driving her car but then parked with the hazard lights flashing as she was running out of petrol. She was seen by a colleague who stopped her motor car on the opposite side of the road. Following some shouted conversation, B ran cross the road,[20] into the claimant's path whose car struck B. B was fatally injured and the claimant suffered a serious head injury. The Court of Appeal held that B was using the car within the meaning of the RTA 1988 s 145(3) even though at the time of the accident she was not driving it. B would not have been crossing the road had her car not run out of petrol and because she was seeking help to continue her journey.

Causation

5.10 Section 145 of the RTA 1988 requires insurance to cover "the death of or bodily injury to any person or damage to property caused by, or arising out of, the use of the vehicle on a road or other public place." It is a matter of fact and degree to determine if the relevant loss arose out of the use of a vehicle on a road or other public place.[21]

5.11 Historically, it was stated that a policy wording that provides cover for losses that have been "caused by or through or in connection with the insured car" expressed a wider coverage than the Road Traffic Act provided.[22] Further, the case law has established that the phrase "arising out of" does not dictate a proximate cause test.[23] It expresses somewhat a weaker causal connection and contemplates more remote consequence than is embraced by "caused by."[24]

5.12 In *Dunthorne v Bentley* mentioned above, a collision took place between the claimant's vehicle and B when B, after stopping her car upon running out of petrol, was running across the road to speak with her colleague who stopped on the other side of

---

13 *Rodrigues de Andrade v Proenca Salvador* (C-514/16) [2018] Lloyd's Rep IR 164, [31]; *BTA Baltic Insurance* Company' AS *v* Apdrošināšanas Nams' AS (C-648/17) ECLI:EU:C:2018:917 [31].
14 [2015] Lloyd's Rep IR 142.
15 *Dunthorne v Bentley* [1996] RTR 428. For meaning of road see Chapter 3.
16 *Vnuk v Zavarovalnica Triglav dd* (C-162/13) [2015] Lloyd's Rep IR 142.
17 *R&S Pilling (t/a Phoenix Engineering) v UK Insurance Ltd* [2019] UKSC 16.
18 *Cobb v Williams* [1973] RTR 113.
19 [1996] RTR 428.
20 In order to obtain help, in particular, it appears, to get petrol to restart the car.
21 *AXN v Worboys* [2013] Lloyd's Rep IR 207; *Wastell v Woodward and Chaucer Syndicates Ltd* [2017] Lloyd's Rep IR 474, [19]; *Dunthorne v Bentley* [1996] RTR 428, 433, Rose LJ.
22 Gilbert, 16.
23 *AXN v Worboys* [2013] Lloyd's Rep IR 207.
24 *Dunthorne v Bentley* [1996] RTR 428.

the road. In a claim brought against B's estate it was held that the collision was caused by her negligence when seeking help to continue the journey in her car. B was using her car at the time of the accident. Rather than viewing her crossing the road in isolation, the Court considered what use of the car was being made by B at the time or immediately before the accident occurred.[25] She would not have been crossing the road had her car not run out of petrol, causing her to seek help to continue her journey.

5.13 It follows that a driver of a parked car walking to the boot to get a can of petrol would be engaged in an activity arising out of the use of the car.[26] Consequently, the words "arising out of use of the vehicle" would cover a case of an assured meeting with fatal injuries when filling the petrol tank or engaged in work on his car.[27]

5.14 The meaning of the words "arising out of" has been a matter of dispute in a number of occasions. A further clarification provided by the common law courts is that the term "arising out of" has a somewhat weaker causal connection than the words "caused by" that the former contemplates more remote consequences than those determined by the latter.[28]

5.15 Caution must be taken however in expanding the cover of the phrase so that "arising out of" is not given a strained meaning outside the purpose of the statutory requirement. This can be illustrated by *Slater v Buckinghamshire CC*.[29] P, who had suffered Down's syndrome, was knocked down by a car when he was about to be taken by a minibus to go to the centre where P used to spend weekdays. The minibus stopped on the far side of the road from P's house to pick him up. An escort who crossed to the middle of the road shouted P "Stay there," because there was a car coming. P however ran to the road and was hit by a car. The driver of the car was blameless. In an action against the minibus driver it was held that the accident was neither caused by nor arose out of the use of the minibus. It occurred when it did and where it did because P was making his way to board the minibus. To interpret "arising out of the use" to include the circumstances giving rise to P's accident would be to give an utterly strained meaning outside the purpose of RTA 1988 section 145(3). What *Slater* makes clear is the importance of the causal link between the vehicle that is used at the time of the accident and the injury suffered. If the vehicle has no link with the accident that occurred, it cannot be argued that the accident and the injury have occurred as a result of the use of the vehicle.

Normal function of the vehicle

5.16 At the time of writing this chapter *Vnuk v Zavarovalnica Triglav dd*[30] gives authoritative guidance on the first paragraph of Article 3 of the Consolidated Directive.[31] *Vnuk* was referred to in Chapter 3 with regards to the meaning of motor vehicle. Another area that the *Vnuk* case introduced further clarification with regards to the compulsory MTPL insurance is that it extended the meaning of use to a wider level than it had been

---

25 *Dunthorne v Bentley* [1996] RTR 428, 432, Rose LJ.
26 *Dunthorne v Bentley* [1996] RTR 428, 432, Rose LJ.
27 G. W. Gilbert, *Motor Insurance*, London, Sir Isaac Pitman & Sons, Ltd, 1933, 19.
28 *AXN v Worboys* [2013] Lloyd's Rep IR 207.
29 [2004] Lloyd's Rep IR 432.
30 (C-162/13) [2015] Lloyd's Rep IR 142.
31 *Lewis v Tindale* [2018] EWHC 2376 (QB), [44]; *Motor Insurers' Bureau v Lewis* [2019] EWCA Civ 909.

applied before. The accident occurred when a tractor to which a trailer was attached was reversing in the courtyard of the farm to position the trailer in that barn. The tractor was used when bales of hay were being stored in the loft of a barn. Whilst reversing the tractor struck the ladder on which V had climbed and caused V to fall. In an action by V against the insurers of the tractor the CJEU held that Article 3(1) of the First Directive[32] was to be interpreted as meaning that the concept of "use of vehicles" covered *any use of a vehicle that was consistent with the normal function of that vehicle.*[33] That concept might therefore cover the manoeuvre of a tractor in the courtyard of a farm in order to bring the trailer attached to that tractor into a barn.[34]

Is "normal function" of a vehicle confined to use as a means of transport?

5.17 The words "use of the vehicle on a road or other public place" under section 145(3) are not to be qualified as "use of the vehicle *as a motor vehicle* on a road." The combination of domestic and EU law interpretation of the words "caused by or arising out of use of the vehicle" has reached that one of the main relevant questions is whether, at the time of the accident, what the vehicle was being used for was consistent with the normal function of the vehicle.

5.18 In the domestic context the Courts disfavoured qualifying the use of the vehicle only to be used as a motor vehicle in the sense that it must be used for transport at the time of the accident in order to fall under the compulsory MTPL insurance.[35] The emphasis was put on the danger that such a qualification would privilege certainty of outcome over the breadth and flexibility that the statutory formulation provides.[36] In *Wastell v Woodward and Chaucer Syndicates Ltd*[37] Master Davidson said that for the purpose of section 145(3) a vehicle is not required to be used qua *motor vehicle.* The relevant issue to be determined was "what was the relevant use of the vehicle on the road" and then "whether the accident arose out of that use."

5.19 In *Wastell v Woodward and Chaucer Syndicates Ltd* the matter at stake was a vehicle that was being used as a hamburger van. It was parked in a lay-by. J, who was running it with his partner S, had adjusted a sign that he had placed on the opposite side of the road. When he was crossing the road to get back to his van he was hit by a motorcycle. J was killed, and the driver of the motorcycle was badly injured. In an action by the motorcycle driver against J's insurer the Court held that the accident arose out of the use of the hamburger van. *Slater v Buckinghamshire CC*[38] mentioned above was distinguished as Master Davidson emphasised that the interpretation of "use" of a vehicle varies greatly. Section 145 (3) states "the use of the vehicle on a road or other public place in Great Britain." The judge found it attractive at first that if the statute was qualified by the words "use of the vehicle *as a motor vehicle* on a road etc," such a qualification would offer a test which was simple to apply and which was closely aligned

---

32 Now Consolidated Directive Article 3.
33 Emphasis added.
34 That was matter for the referring Court to determine.
35 *Wastell v Woodward and Chaucer Syndicates Ltd* [2017] Lloyd's Rep IR 474, [16].
36 Ibid.
37 [2017] Lloyd's Rep IR 474.
38 [2004] Lloyd's Rep IR 432.

with the principal purpose of any motor vehicle, namely locomotion.[39] On the other hand, it would privilege certainty of outcome over the breadth and flexibility which the statute in its unadorned formulation provides.[40] The law has developed in a way focusing on the particular use of the vehicle, be that a tractor, an ice cream van, a flatbed lorry, an ambulance, a car or whatever. The precedent cases, in the view of Master Davidson, did not require that the vehicle be used qua *motor vehicle* in order for the statute to be engaged. The question was set by Master Davidson as "What was the relevant use of the vehicle on the road?" and "whether the accident arose out of that use." This is clearly a very broad and flexible interpretation of the words "use" which led to the conclusion that the hamburger van fell within the scope of section 145(3).

5.20 A further example is *AXN v Worboys*[41] in which the Court discussed the meaning of "arise out of" to a great extent. Worboys, after finishing his legitimate work as a taxi driver, offered to take women who were alone at night to their destinations. Once they accepted his offer, during their journeys, Worboys engaged them in conversation and persuaded them with lies to accept alcoholic drinks. The drinks, unknown to his passengers, contained sedatives and when they had taken effect, he carried out sexual assaults on his sedated victims. The victims brought claims against Worboys for damages alleging assault by poisoning, sexual assault and false imprisonment. The victims argued that they had a right of direct claim against the motor vehicle insurers who insured Worboys' liability in respect of the matters of which complaint was made. The question against the insurers was whether the bodily injuries suffered by the victims arose out of the use of Worboys' vehicle on a road or other public place within the meaning of RTA 1988 s 145(3)(a).

5.21 It was held that the chain between Worboys' use of the taxi and the claimants' injuries was broken by Worboys' acts of using sedatives with drinks and committing sexual assaults. The Court found no link between the injuries suffered by the claimants and the *use* of the taxi on a road at the time when the claimants were poisoned and assaulted. Their claimants' injuries arose not because of any wish to continue the journey, but instead because Worboys wanted to poison the claimants so as to facilitate and implement his wish to sexually assault them. This was a factor, which was not connected with the use of the taxi on a road.

EU law

5.22 It appears that, as also confirmed by the CJEU, the relevant period of time to assess the purpose of use of the vehicle is the time of the accident.[42] The discrepancy between the authorities, however, has been observed in terms of whether the normal function of the vehicle is confined to be used as a means of transport. *Wastell* above decides it is not. *Worboys*, however, seems to support this restriction. In the context of the EU law, the CJEU has recently held that the determining test will be whether, at the

---

39 *Wastell v Woodward and Chaucer Syndicates Ltd* [2017] Lloyd's Rep IR 474 [16].
40 [2017] Lloyd's Rep IR 474 [16].
41 [2013] Lloyd's Rep IR 207.
42 *Rodrigues de Andrade v Proenca Salvador* (C-514/16) [2018] Lloyd's Rep IR 164, [39]–[42].

time of the accident involving such a vehicle, that vehicle was being used principally as a means of transport.[43]

5.23 In *Rodrigues de Andrade and another v Proença Salvador*[44] although an agricultural tractor falls within the definition of motor vehicle, the CJEU held that it was not used as a means of transport at the time of the accident. In *Rodrigues* A was one of four workers applying herbicide to vines on the sloped terraces on the farm. The herbicide was contained in a drum with a spraying device mounted on the back of a tractor. It was necessary to run the engine of the tractor in order to operate the spraying device, but the tractor itself was stationary. There had been heavy rain that day and the land was slippery. A combination of the weight of the tractor, the vibrations of the engine, the movement of the herbicide hose and the condition of the land caused a landslip. The tractor fell down the terraces, reached the workers and landed on A with tragic fatal consequences. A claim was made against the employer's liability insurers for material and against motor insurers for non-material damages.

5.24 As mentioned in Chapter 3, the CJEU ruled that a tractor fell within the definition of "vehicle," in that it was a "motor vehicle intended for travel on land and propelled by mechanical power." The question was whether it was being "used." In *Vnuk* the vehicle in question was also a tractor which was in the courtyard of a farm and was reversing when the accident occurred. In *Rodrigues*, the tractor was stationary but being not in motion was not material to decide the case. The focus appears to be on the meaning of "normal function of a vehicle" which, in *Rodrigues*, was held to be "any use of a vehicle as a means of transport."

5.25 In *Rodrigues* the purpose of the use of the tractor was to generate, as a machine for carrying out work, the motive power necessary to drive the pump of the herbicide sprayer. The tractor was stationary, but the engine was turned on to power the spray. Whether or not the tractor was stationary or the engine was running did not, in itself, preclude the use of that vehicle at that time from falling within the scope of its function as a means of transport.[45] The tractor was nevertheless held not to have been used as a means of transport because the purpose of the use was to generate power for the herbicide sprayer.

5.26 The European Commission's proposal to amend the Consolidated Directive is referred to in Chapter 1. In the light of the decisions of *Vnuk v Zavarovalnica Triglav dd*,[46] *Rodrigues de Andrade v Proença Salvador*,[47] and *Nunez Torreiro v AIG Europe Ltd*[48] the Commission proposed adding 1a to Article 1 of the Directive. Article 1a describes "use of a vehicle" meaning

> any use of such vehicle, intended normally to serve as a means of transport, that is consistent with the normal function of that vehicle, irrespective of the vehicle's characteristics and irrespective of the terrain on which the motor vehicle is used and of whether it is stationary or in motion.

---

43 Ibid, [40].
44 (C-514/16) [2018] Lloyd's Rep IR 164.
45 *Rodrigues de Andrade v Proenca Salvador* (C-514/16) [2018] Lloyd's Rep IR 164, [39].
46 (C-162/13) [2015] Lloyd's Rep IR 142.
47 (C-514/16) [2018] 4 WLR 75.
48 (C-334/16) [2018] Lloyd's Rep IR 418.

Reconciling domestic and EU law

5.27 Undoubtedly, the *Vnuk* case has expanded the meaning of "use" within the scope of the compulsory MTPL insurance regime. Recently, in *UK Insurance Ltd v R&S Pilling T/AS Phoenix Engineering*[49] the Supreme Court rejected to stretch the word "use" to the carrying out of significant repairs to a vehicle on private property. In view of the Supreme Court "having the use of" makes good sense in the context of vehicles which have been left on a road or in a public place, where members of the public are likely to encounter them, but less sense if applied without qualification to vehicles located on private property.[50] The Supreme Court held that there must be a reasonable limit to the length of the relevant causal chain and the fire damage that arose whilst H was repairing his motor vehicle outside his employer's premises was not caused by H's use of his vehicle. Furthermore, a vehicle which is on its side being repaired on private property, such as a garage, is not being used "as a means of transport" as the CJEU jurisprudence requires.[51]

5.28 Additionally, in *R&S Pilling (t/a Phoenix Engineering) v UK Insurance Ltd*[52] the policy wording provided the following cover: "We will cover you for your legal responsibility if you have an accident in your vehicle." The Court of Appeal read the wording as if it said, "We will cover you for your legal responsibility if there is an accident involving your vehicle." The Supreme Court, however, overruled this construction and held that the Court of Appeal's interpretation removed the statutory causal link between the use of the vehicle on a road or other public place and the accident and expanded the cover significantly beyond the express terms of the clause, the requirements of the RTA 1988 as well as that which EU law currently requires.[53] Lord Hodge stated that the appropriate corrective construction would read the clause as, "We will cover you for your legal responsibility if you have an accident in your vehicle or if there is an accident caused by or arising out of your use of your vehicle on a road or other public place and . . ."

In this respect the Supreme Court was invited to, but rejected to hold that *Dunthorne v Bentley*[54] was wrongly decided. Lord Hodge found *Dunthorne* as a borderline case and said it "did not turn on a point of law but on the application of the law to a particular set of facts . . . having regard to the close connection in time, place and circumstance between the use of the car on the road and the accident."[55]

5.29 The relevant period of time to assess the purpose of use of the vehicle is the time of the accident.[56] However, this should not be taken in isolation.[57] As more recently held by the CJEU, *Rodrigues*

> does not in any way mean that the determination of whether there is an obligation to take out such insurance should be dependent on whether or not the vehicle at issue is actually being used as a means of transport at a given time.[58]

---

49 [2019] UKSC 16.
50 Ibid, [53].
51 Ibid, [53].
52 [2019] UKSC 16 [40]–[41].
53 Ibid, [50].
54 [1996] RTR 428.
55 Ibid, [44].
56 *Rodrigues de Andrade v Proenca Salvador* (C-514/16) [2018] Lloyd's Rep IR 164, [39]–[42].
57 *Dunthorne v Bentley* [1996] RTR 428, 432, Rose LJ.
58 *Fundo de Garantia Automovel v Juliana* (C-80/17) EU:C:2018:661, [41].

5.30 In *Fundo de Garantia Automovel v Juliana*[59] the CJEU held that Article 3(1) of the First Directive requires the taking out of a contract of insurance against civil liability in relation to the use of a motor vehicle when the vehicle concerned is parked on private land, solely by the choice of the owner, who no longer intends to drive the vehicle. The case will be referred to again in Chapter 10 with regards to the national compensation body's right of recoupment with regards to the compensation paid for an injury caused by an uninsured driver. Here it suffices to note that J, for health reasons, stopped driving her motor vehicle and kept it parked in the yard of her house. She had not taken any formal steps to withdraw it from use. J's son, D, was involved in an accident by J's car when he was driving it without his mother's permission or knowledge. Three people died as a result of the accident. D was not insured to drive his mother's vehicle. The CJEU held that the obligation to insure does not depend on whether the vehicle is actually being used as a means of transport at a given time. So long as it is capable of being driven, that corresponds of "vehicle" within the meaning of Article 1(1) of the First Directive.[60] The fact that she no longer intended to drive it is of no relevance in that regard. What mattered was the vehicle concerned is still registered in a Member State and is capable of being driven but is parked on private land.

5.31 *Rodrigues de Andrade v Proença Salvador* is likely to be treated as a case which turned on its own facts. In *Rodrigues* the CJEU differentiated the use as a means of transport and as a machine for carrying out work which was other than transport. The determining question was whether, at the time of the accident involving such a vehicle, that vehicle was being used *principally*[61] as a means of transport. Accordingly, the foremost purpose of the use of the vehicle concluded whether it was being used as a vehicle within the meaning of the compulsory MTPL insurance. According to *Rodrigues*, a machine for carrying out work at the time of the accident, which is other than means of transport, cannot be covered by the concept of use.

5.32 *Rodrigues* appears to have adopted a narrow approach in classifying the purpose of use of the vehicle within its own remit. It was not in fact the tractor itself but only the tractor's engine that was being used to provide the power necessary to operate the spraying machine. Presumably the power needed for the spraying machine could have been provided by some other means. Hence, at the time of the accident, the tractor was not used for transport but as a source of power for spraying herbicide by another machine. If the accident took place when the tractor was carrying either the workers or the necessary machines from one place to another, that would have clearly fallen within the meaning of "use" in the context of compulsory MTPL insurance.

5.33 Reconciling *Rodrigues* with *Wastell* where a hamburger van was held to be in use as a motor vehicle is not easy. Similar to *Rodrigues*, in *Wastell* at the time of the accident, the van was not used as a means of transport but was used to sell hamburgers. *Worboys*, however, is in line with *Rodrigues* because the abuse was not caused by or did not arise out of the use of the vehicle. Worboys' vehicle was used for the assault, but the key issue was that the assault was his personal intention to assault irrespective of the use of the vehicle. Assault could have taken place at any other places. He simply used it to

---

59 (C-80/17) EU:C:2018:661.
60 Now Article 1(1) of the Consolidated Directive.
61 Emphasis added.

attract vulnerable victims. In other words, he took advantage of the convenience that his profession as a cab driver provided for him that the victims got on his vehicle late at night with no suspicion that the taxi ride would end with an assault by the driver in a way that happened in the case. Not surprisingly, the causal link between the use of the vehicle as a means of transport by *Worboys* and the assault was not established. Both in *Rodrigues* and *Worboys* the respective vehicles were being used for a purpose other than means of transport; the purpose for which the vehicles were used could have been achieved by some other means. *Wastell* is distinguishable at this point because of the circumstances under which the accident took place. It is certainly arguable that, similar to *Worboys* and *Rodrigues*, hamburger could be sold in another premise than through a hamburger van. However, *Wastell* does not only depend on for what purpose that the hamburger van was used but should be read together with for what purpose J was crossing the road. The relationship between the hamburger van being on the road and the accident seems to have been closer than the same relationship between the assault and the vehicle being on the road in *Worboys*. *Wastell* appears to have relied on the accident having taken place on the road more than the use of the hamburger van as a motor vehicle for the purposes of transport on the road. *Wastell* may also be explained by the view adopted in the UK that "use" includes to "have the use of a motor-vehicle on the road" as explored above.[62]

"Moving" a motor vehicle

5.34 Whether a vehicle was stationery or mobilised at the relevant time is not conclusive in determining the purpose of its use. A vehicle may create a hazard for other road users in either case.[63]

5.35 The word "use" includes "moving"[64] but is not to be equated with propulsion or movement.[65] The main objective of adopting the RTA 1930 s 35 was to ensure that third party victims of traffic accidents were to be compensated.[66] Implementing a purposive interpretation of the section[67] it was held that the word "use" was equivalent to "have the use of a motor-vehicle on the road."[68]

5.36 *Elliot v Grey* is one of the most often cited cases on this matter.[69] The car in question in this case broke down on 20 December 1958. Its carburettor broke, its self-starter would not work, and its starting handle would not fit into the starting handle hole because its worm end would not fit. The owner kept it parked outside his house, removed the battery of the car and suspended the policy of insurance. The car could not be mechanically propelled because its engine would not work and by that date the petrol

---

62 *Elliot v Grey* [1960] 1 QB 367, 372, Lord Parker CJ.
63 *R&S Pilling (t/a Phoenix Engineering) v UK Insurance Ltd* [2019] UKSC 16 [45].
64 *Elliot v Grey* [1960] 1 QB 367, 371–372, Lord Parker CJ.
65 *Andrews v HE Kershaw Ltd* [1952] 1 KB 70; *Director of Public Prosecutions v Heritage* [2002] EWHC 2139 Admin; *Turnbull v MNT Transport (2006) Ltd* [2010] CSOH 163.
66 See *Elliot v Grey* [1960] 1 QB 367, 372, Lord Parker CJ.
67 Section 35 of the RTA 1930 appeared in Part II "Provision against third-party risks arising out of the use of motor vehicles"; the equivalent section, section 143 of the RTA 1988 appears under Part VI titled "Compulsory insurance or security against third-party risks."
68 *Elliot v Grey* [1960] 1 QB 367, 372, Lord Parker CJ.
69 Some of the cases referred to *Elliot v Grey* are: *Williams v Jones* [1975] RTR 433; *Pumbien v Vines* [1996] RTR 37; *Gosling v Howard* [1975] RTR 429; *Thomas v Hooper* [1986] RTR 1.

in its tank had evaporated away. In February 1959 another motor car collided with it. Lord Parker CJ said:

> In the absence, at any rate, of a finding that it was immovable as, for instance, the wheels were removed or something of that sort, I cannot bring myself to think that this car was not fairly and squarely within the words which I have used, "have the use of a motor-vehicle on the road."[70]

It follows that if a motor vehicle could be moved, albeit not driven, the owner had the use of it on a road within the meaning of the compulsory insurance requirement.[71] The word "use" means to have the advantage of a vehicle as a means of transport; including *any period or time between journeys*[72] suggests availability.[73] In *Elliot* the car could not be driven, but there was nothing to suggest that it could not be moved. Lord Parker CJ[74] noted that it was on the top of a hill and a little boy could release the brake and the car could go careering down the hill.

5.37 In *Gosling v Howard*[75] it was argued unsuccessfully that *Elliot* should be distinguished where a vehicle was parked "in a position well off the carriageway of a rural road and was only in a very technical sense on a road at all."[76] The vehicle was in perfect running order; hence, there was no basis to distinguish *Elliot*.

5.38 The car was held not to be in use in *Hewer v Cutler*,[77] the ratio of which has been questioned by a number of cases subsequently. In *Hewer* the vehicle was *wholly and effectively*[78] immobilised in the way that it was parked on a road. It was the key feature of the vehicle that no oil pressure was left in the torque converter; the owner disconnected a certain linkage in the gear box so that the rear (driving) wheels of the car were unable to rotate. The vehicle not only could not be driven but could not be moved until such time that the linkage was reconnected.

5.39 Some cases may be more clear-cut compared to the cases referred to above. For instance, in *Turnbull v MNT Transport (2006) Ltd*[79] D, while taking a mandatory rest break during a long haul journey, had temporarily disconnected the trailer from its tractor unit after parking the trailer on a public road. The claimant rode his bicycle into the detached trailer unit. It was held that the parked trailer was still the tractor unit's "one trailer" within the policy definition and there was no good reason to hold that D was not "using" the trailer at the material time. The journey had only been temporarily interrupted for a rest period mandatory under statute, and the loaded trailer would be moving on to its destination on the following day. If needed, the Court was also ready to apply the *contra proferentem* rule and interpret the policy wording to be construed in a manner favourable to the assured.

---

70 Disapproved in Scotland. See *Tudhope v Every* 1977 SLT 2.
71 *Elliot v Grey* [1960] 1 QB 367.
72 Emphasis added.
73 *Elliot v Grey* [1960] 1 QB 367, 372, Lord Parker CJ. Approved and applied in *Williams v Jones* [1975] RTR 433.
74 [1960] 1 QB 367, 372.
75 [1975] RTR 429.
76 See *Gosling v Howard* [1975] RTR 429, [431].
77 [1974] RTR 155.
78 Emphasis added.
79 [2010] CSOH 163.

Immobility

5.40 Some disagreements as to the identification of the true ratio of *Hewer v Cutler* have been observed amongst the judicial views. According to Kilner Brown J,[80] *Hewer* was a case in which the Court found in effect an impossibility of use: there was a mechanical immobilisation.

5.41 In *Eden v Mitchell*[81] the vehicle, the tyres of which were defective, was otherwise capable of being mobilised and was held to be in use for the compulsory insurance purposes.[82] Hence, it was to be distinguished from *Hewer*. Kilner Brown J identified the relevant true test as whether or not such steps had been taken as to make it impossible for anyone to use this vehicle.

5.42 On the other hand, Mitchell J held in *Pumbien v Vines*[83] that the distinction of mobility or immobility did not have great relevance to the use of the vehicle with respect to the compulsory insurance requirement under the statute. In the view of Mitchell J, the judgment in *Hewer* did not turn on the reason for the immobility of the vehicle but was founded simply upon the de facto position on the relevant date. Mitchell J described the situation where a vehicle is in a state that it can be repaired and then driven as reversible immobility.[84]

5.43 In *Thomas v Hooper*,[85] on the other hand, Glidewell J said, "The decisions [in *Elliot* and *Hewer*] went different ways because in the one case the vehicle could be moved whereas in the other it could not."

5.44 One can only speculate if, in *Elliot*, the judgment would have gone to a different direction if the vehicle had not been parked on a hill. It is submitted that the starting point should be the objectives of imposing the compulsory MTPL insurance and especially protecting the victim and ensuring that the victim is compensated. The cases mentioned above discussed the meaning of "use" in a number of different offences under the Road Traffic Acts applicable at the relevant time. The objective of those provisions is all the same – that they are to ensure that the obligation to take out and maintain compulsory MTPL insurance is complied with. In this respect, it is submitted that the interpretation of "use" should not be loose but it should cover positions of a vehicle where it may endanger public safety and may cause injury to third parties. This would provide an interpretation in line with the meaning of "use" as understood by the EU law. The principle that "use" is a broader concept than only "driving" a vehicle also supports this submission. As a result, parking a vehicle in areas where the compulsory MTPL insurance is required amounts to using the vehicle irrespective of the reason for being stationary.

5.45 Whether a vehicle is in use should not be determined without considering the location of the vehicle and the definition of motor vehicle and whether it has risk of endangering public safety. A vehicle may be stationary because it was parked whilst the

---

80 *Eden v Mitchell* [1975] RTR 425.
81 [1975] RTR 425.
82 The tread pattern of the tyres was so worn down that there was not a sufficient depth. In respect of each defective tyre he was charged with contravention of section 40(5) of the Road Traffic Act 1972 by use on a road of a motor vehicle which failed to comply with Regulation 99(1)(f) of the Motor Vehicles (Construction and Use) Regulations 1973.
83 [1996] RTR 37, 45.
84 *Pumbien v Vines* [1996] RTR 37, 46 Mitchell J.
85 [1986] RTR 1, 5.

hand brake is on, or it is broken and needs a repair or the owner does not plan to use it for a while and the battery is removed. The question of whether the vehicle can or cannot be mobilised is not determinative in identifying whether or not the vehicle is in use. As illustrated by the above discussion, there is no clear-cut guidance to ascertain the degree of immobility that is required to excuse the absence of compulsory MTPL insurance. In any case it should be noted that the majority view in the judiciary is, unlike Mitchel J in *Pumpbien,* that *Hewer* established a generally applicable rule in the meaning of use of a vehicle. This is explored in the immediately following paragraphs below.

Towage

Driver has no control of the vehicle towed

5.46 The meaning of the word "use" was also questioned when a vehicle was being towed by another vehicle. A vehicle may be towed with a driver steering the vehicle towed or with a driver sitting on the driver's seat but not being able to steer or control the vehicle at all. His only function in the latter case is simply to warn the driver who is towing the vehicle. Falling into the latter category, *Thomas v Hooper*[86] was a decision on its own facts and it is not seen as creating a generally applicable rule.[87]

5.47 In *Thomas v Hooper*[88] a white Morris Marina van was abandoned in a layby near Exeter. P bought the van and decided to move it from the layby to his address. At that time the steering was locked, the brakes were seized on, its wheels were unable to turn round at all, and many parts of the van needed replacing. The engine was in such a condition that it could not be started without extensive work being carried out on it. The Morris was chained to a Bedford van bumper to bumper. The chain was wrapped round the rear bumper of the Bedford and the front bumper of the Morris in such a manner that the bumpers were touching, but if the Bedford swerved suddenly, the vehicles would separate. P drove the Bedford whilst his friend sat in the driver's seat of the Morris. It was not possible to exercise any control over the Morris by its driver;[89] hence, the Morris was being dragged along the ground by the Bedford. The defendant who was sitting in the driver's seat of the Morris was charged with using the Morris on the road, contrary to the then applicable legislation, sections 44(1) and 143(1) of the Road Traffic Act 1972. However the decision was in his favour but with a note that "the facts of this case are most unusual and this is a decision on its own facts."[90]

5.48 In *Thomas v Hooper*[91] the Court found the *Elliot* and *Hewer* cases were unhelpful as in those cases the decision turned on whether the vehicle could or could not be moved, whereas in *Thomas* the vehicle was not stationary at the relevant time. It was in motion, though not under its own propulsion. It could not be steered, it could not be braked, and the wheels were locked and not capable of turning. In the words of Glidewell LJ it was

---

86 [1986] RTR 1.
87 *Pumbien v Vines* [1996] RTR 37, [45].
88 [1986] RTR 1.
89 Accordingly, he was rightly acquitted by the justices of driving it without a driving licence.
90 [1986] RTR 1, [6].
91 Ibid, [5].

"in many ways not what one would regard as a motor car at all. It was in a sense an inanimate hunk of metal and was being towed along the road rather like a sledge."[92]

5.49 As seen, when a vehicle is not stationary, the discussion includes "the control or management" of it to determine if it is being used. In *Thomas* the important point was that it was incapable of being controlled because the mechanisms by which a motor car is normally controlled were all inoperative.[93] If the vehicle was being towed by another vehicle along the road whilst the engine was not working but with the steering being operated and the brakes working, the vehicle would be being used on the road by whoever was at the steering wheel. As the judge highlighted in *Thomas*, this was not the case for the Morris van. The operative test was "there must be an element of controlling, managing or operating the vehicle as a vehicle." The facts in *Thomas* did not pass the relevant test. It seems that the Morris van was regarded no more than an item towed.

Vehicle not used under its own power

5.50 A vehicle does not necessarily have to be used under its own power in order to be used on a road for present purposes.[94] In this respect *Thomas v Hooper*[95] is to be compared and contrasted with *Nichol v Leach*.[96] Whilst in the former, as described by the judge, the vehicle was towed as a *"sledge,"*[97] in the latter the tow was not because the vehicle could not be moved but because it suited the claimant. In *Nichol* a mini saloon car was purchased as a "scrap vehicle" and was rebuilt by the defendants for racing on autocross circuits. The Mini was towed by a MGB sports car on a public road by means of a rope. The MGB was driven by Leach, and the Mini was steered by Linsell. There was no policy of insurance in force in respect of the Mini, there was no licence on the Mini. The Mini had an engine and was capable of moving on a road under its own power, and indeed it was used by the defendants for racing at the autocross meeting later on the same day that it was towed. Its windows had been stripped out, but it retained a windscreen, it had a revolution-counter instead of a speedometer, the passenger seat had been removed, and the driver's seat had been fitted with a seat belt. It was held that the car was produced as an ordinary motor car intended to run on roads, and it retained its character throughout. It did not cease to be a vehicle intended for use on roads merely because its present owner saw no prospect of driving it on a road under its own power.

5.51 Returning to our starting point above, the difference between *Nichol* and *Thomas* is that in the latter the vehicle was incapable of being *controlled*[98] by the defendant as it was being towed as a sledge. The only purpose for which the defendant could be in the vehicle was to give warning if any danger arose. It therefore appears that mobility or immobility of a vehicle may matter when it is not being driven itself but when it is treated as something else than a motor vehicle which is incapable of moving as a motor

---

92 Ibid, [6].
93 Ibid, [6].
94 *Cobb v Whorton* [1971] RTR 392, 395; *Nichol v Leach* [1972] RTR 476, [479].
95 [1986] RTR 1.
96 [1972] RTR 476.
97 Emphasis added.
98 Emphasis added.

vehicle. In *Thomas* it was treated as a sledge, or as a piece of item that was being towed. On the other hand, where a vehicle towed is itself capable to be used as a motor vehicle which moves on the areas that the compulsory insurance regime applies, it falls within the definition of "use." In this respect, *Thomas* and *Nichol* do not seem to be in conflict, but there is more to discuss before coming to such a conclusion.

5.52 *Thomas v Hooper*[99] was heavily criticised in *Pumbien v Vines*[100] in which Mitchell J ran through a detailed analysis of the authorities decided previously. In *Pumbien* the defendant purchased the vehicle in February 1992; from March 1992 he stopped using it and parked it on the road. The vehicle was in full working order, but the defendant did not use it after that, and he voluntarily cancelled the policy of insurance. The MOT test certificate relating to the vehicle expired in August 1992. On 10 November 1992 the vehicle was sold to T who collected it on 13 November 1992 for a dismantling. At the time that it was purchased on 10 November its tyres were deflated, the handbrake was on and the rear brakes were seized, and the gearbox had drained of oil through a leak in the transmission pipe. It would not have been possible to move the vehicle without first freeing the brakes, replacing the transmission pipe and oiling the gearbox, but this was possible. It was clear that in that state the vehicle, though clearly repairable, could neither be driven nor towed unless it was literally dragged. In the words of Mitchell J this was a reversible immobility that the vehicle was on a road, it was a "motor vehicle" as defined in the RTA 1988, and the defendant was under the obligations imposed upon him by sections 47 and 143 of the RTA 1988.

5.53 Whilst to be clearly distinguished, what appears to be common in *Pumbien* and *Thomas* is that the vehicles in question required some considerable external operations. Where they differed was extent of the repair needed: some more serious operations were needed in *Thomas* than those in *Pumbien*. Otherwise the vehicles could not be moved by their own power.

5.54 It was referred to above that in *Thomas* the Court preferred to distinguish *Elliot* and *Hewer*. On the other hand, although the vehicle was stationary in *Pumbien*, and following the logic in *Thomas* one might expect the same distinction, Mitchell J preferred the test established by *Elliot v Grey*.[101] Mitchell J disapproved going one step further and adding the test of "controlling or managing" the vehicle as the true or appropriate test if the conduct which is said to constitute a "use" within the provisions is leaving the vehicle parked on a road as opposed to dragging it along behind and roped to the bumper of another vehicle. In *Elliot* a vehicle was in "use" and therefore required to be insured for the purposes of the RTA 1988 even when it stood on a road with an engine which did not work and without petrol and a battery providing it could be moved for example by pushing or releasing the brake.

5.55 The test applied in *Thomas*, in the view of Mitchell J, was irreconcilable with the ratio decidendi in *Elliot v Grey*. Mitchell J said that a vehicle is a "motor vehicle" within the definition to be found in section 185(1) and (2) the vehicle is on a road, the owner of that vehicle has the use of it on a road whether at the material time it can move

---

99 [1986] RTR 1.
100 [1996] RTR 37.
101 [1960] 1 QB 367.

on its wheels or not.[102] A motor vehicle which is in good condition but which has been immobilised to prevent its wheels from rotating should still attract the insurance requirements under the RTA 1988. It should not be permitted to avoid the insurance requirement simply by immobilising the vehicle to the extent that the wheels cannot rotate. The one is neither more nor less of a hazard than the other when standing stationary on a road.

5.56 As noted above, *Pumbien v Viens* together with *Elliot*, although strict, lay down the most appropriate test for the use of the vehicle. As this book will adopt throughout, the objectives of the adoption of the Road Traffic Acts since 1930 should not be omitted in the interpretation of the Acts' provisions. As a matter of common sense the question obviously will be raised whether a vehicle has a potential to involve in a motor vehicle accident on a public road as a result of which innocent third parties may suffer losses. If the answer is yes prima facie that case should fall within the insurance requirements of the Road Traffic Act.

5.57 It might be argued that public liability insurance would provide coverage even if the relevant occurrence falls outside the statutory compulsory MTPL insurance requirement, for instance because the vehicle was immobilised or can be moved only when it is towed by another vehicle. However, it must be borne in mind that the MTPL insurance is compulsory, whereas public liability insurance is not. If the objective is to protect third party victims against use of motor vehicles on a road or other public place or even on a private land as the recent EU law developments have ruled, the interpretation should be in favour of finding a use where possible.

5.58 As stated by Mitchell J, whether or not a vehicle is a motor vehicle does not depend on whether it can be moved on its wheels or by means of towing if it is on a road. The vehicle must be on a road for a purpose. If a motor vehicle needs a repair it may be on the road because it is being taken to a garage for this purpose. Whether the function of the driver is steering or warning the driver in the other vehicle that performs the towage, the vehicle is potentially a vehicle on a road that may cause an accident and injure third parties. With respect to the threats involved, whether a vehicle is steered by the driver or the driver simply sits on the driver seat to warn the towing driver there is no difference. The test in *Elliot v Grey* is broad enough to encompass all these matters. For the purposes of having "the use of a motor-vehicle on the road" there should be no difference between when a vehicle is stationary or mobile. The danger is adopting otherwise, to avoid the statutory insurance requirement and the offences by simply immobilising the vehicle and still retaining it on a public road.

5.59 Further, similar to *Nichol*, the van in *Thomas* also initially had been produced with the intention to drive, as a motor vehicle. It did not cease to be a motor vehicle because the wheels would not rotate. As described in *Pumbien* it was a state of reversible immobility. When the question of danger to the public is concerned, it is artificial to distinguish between being towed because it is inoperative or being towed because the owner preferred it to be towed. In *Elliot* the risk of the vehicle moving down the hill in case the handbrake is off may also apply to *Thomas* although the wheels were not rotating – as it was reversible immobility. By its nature a motor vehicle is a motor vehicle whether it is being towed or driven under its own power.

---

102 Emphasis added.

5.60 *Thomas* would have been analysed differently if the Morris van had been carried as a cargo on another vehicle rather than being towed on its own wheels. *Thomas* was concerned with the question of whether the condition of a vehicle was so seized up as to deprive it of the character of a "mechanically propelled vehicle."[103] Towage did not change the nature of the van being a vehicle. One should not lose sight that the principle of the whole scheme of the Road Traffic Acts is to make third party insurance compulsory so as to protect accident victims.[104] Whether the wheels were locked solid or not, the vehicle on a public road was patently a source of danger to other people.[105] A stationary vehicle can pose a danger for others in its vicinity whether or not it is being driven; for example, a fire or explosion may occur because of the petrol content, it may leak some oil, or its brake may fail whilst parked. Clearly, the van in *Thomas* posed the same sort of danger.

5.61 This argument finds also its support from the rule that it is irrelevant that the defendant gave evidence to the effect that he had been ill for five days and that he had no intention of driving the vehicle with defective tyres.[106] Whether to repair or not, whether intending to use it or not for a while is a subjective decision of the owner at the time, and it cannot be an objective test to determine if the vehicle was in use.[107]

5.62 Having the control or management of the vehicle, however, is an appropriate test when the user is some person other than the driver. This will be explored in the next paragraphs.

Is a passenger a user?

5.63 The concept of the use of the vehicle on a road is not confined to the owner of the vehicle.[108] Moreover, someone can use a vehicle without being its driver.[109] The owner is to be taken as using a vehicle when he is a passenger and allows another person to drive the vehicle.[110] In such a case the owner wants to make a journey, hence, he is in the vehicle that is being used in order that he might make that journey.[111] This is not a case in which the owner is using the vehicle vicariously through someone else who is driving it, because he is regarded as using the vehicle directly.[112] It is also true that every passenger, in ordinary language, uses the vehicle they are driven in. However, a restricted interpretation of "user" within the meaning of the RTA 1988 section 143 is naturally necessary when a liability of a passenger as a user is in question. Otherwise almost every passenger in cars, cabs and buses, inadvertently but potentially, could have been committing

---

103 *Turnbull v MNT Transport (2006) Ltd* [2010] CSOH 163, [27].

104 See *Elliot v Grey* [1960] 1 QB 367 in which the Lord Parker CJ was influenced in his decision by the fact that section 35 of the RTA 1930 section appears in Part II of the Act under the heading of "Provision against third-party risks arising out of the use of motor vehicles."

105 *Turnbull v MNT Transport (2006) Ltd* [2010] CSOH 163, [27]. If his Lordship had needed to do so, Lord Emslie was ready to prefer *Elliot* and *Pumbien* over *Thomas*.

106 *Eden v Mitchell* [1975] RTR 425. The issue was a contravention of Regulation 99(1) of the Motor Vehicles (Construction and Use) Regulations 1973 and section 40(5) of the Road Traffic Act 1972 by way of the vehicle's tyres not being in a sufficient depth.

107 *Tudhope v Every* 1977 SLT 2 (Scottish view).

108 *Brown v Roberts* [1965] 1 QB 1, [11] Megaw J.

109 *Stinton v Stinton* [1995] RTR 167, Nourse LJ, [176]; see also *Ricketts v Thomas Tilling Ltd* [1915] 1 KB 644.

110 *Cobb v Williams* [1973] RTR 113; *Pratt v Patrick* [1924] 1 KB 488.

111 *Cobb v Williams* [1973] RTR 113.

112 Ibid.

criminal offences in accepting lifts in ignorance of the precise insurance position of the vehicle.[113]

5.64 Reflecting these concerns, there have been a number of UK cases that discussed if a passenger is user and hence, damage caused by a passenger is subject to compulsory insurance. As a result of these discussions a number of rules have emerged to apply to the case where a passenger is involved in an accident. However, now, all of these developments have to be considered with some of the very recent CJEU cases on this matter. The following paragraphs will first explain what the common law position has been and following that they will cover the EU law developments. At time of writing, it is not certain yet whether or not and also the UK will still follow the developments in the EU rules on this matter once the UK leaves the EU. Therefore, this chapter will set out the common law and the CJEU's interpretation of the matter separately.

Common law

5.65 In order to identify if a passenger is user, some guidance has been set, although not exhaustively,[114] by the common law on the basis of two different tests. Each of the two is a question of fact and degree. Accordingly, one way to identify if a passenger is the user is to ask if the passenger had any control or management of the vehicle at the relevant time. The alternative method is to question if the passenger was in a joint enterprise with the driver in the journey in question.

Controlling, managing or operating the vehicle

5.66 For a passenger to be a user it is necessary to establish an element of controlling, managing or operating the vehicle at the relevant time.[115] It has not been precisely defined what this element encompasses.[116] It is, however, clear that it is a question of fact and degree whether in any given case there is a sufficient element of control or management to constitute the passenger a user.

5.67 The leading case on this matter is *Brown v Roberts*,[117] in which B was injured whilst she was walking on a pavement, at which moment a passenger from a van that was being drawn up at the kerb opened the door. B was struck by the door, thrown sideways across the pavement and fell fracturing her left hip bone. The passenger, R, was not taking due and proper care for pedestrians on the pavement whilst opening the door of the van. The liability insurance with regards to the van did not include the legal liability of any passenger carried in the van. The only way to hold the insurer liable would have been to classify R as user of the van the argument of which was raised by B but was rejected by the Court. The Court recognised that for the purpose of the RTA 1930 s 35(1) there may be more than one person who is using a vehicle at any given time. The Court further acknowledged that driving a vehicle is not an essential element of using it. Nevertheless,

---

113 *Hatton v Hall* [1997] RTR 212, 217–218, Henry LJ.
114 *Stinton v Stinton* [1995] RTR 167, Nourse LJ, [177].
115 *Brown v Roberts* [1965] 1 QB 1, [15].
116 In *Brown v Roberts* the Court found it unnecessary to define it [1965] 1 QB 1, [15].
117 [1965] 1 QB 1.

neither of these characteristics of "use" was sufficient to classify R as a user of the van. The Court looked for "an element of controlling, managing or operating the vehicle at the relevant time," which was missing in the relationship between R and the van.[118]

Joint venture

5.68 An element of controlling, managing or operating the vehicle at the relevant time may be found where there is a joint venture to use the vehicle for a particular purpose or where the passenger procures the making of the journey. Such an element of control was present in *Leathley v Tatton*[119] where a friend of the defendants got into the driving seat of a car which did not start without being pushed by the defendant. Once the vehicle moved the defendant climbed into the passenger seat. For the Court this was a clear case where the defendant and his friend were acting in a joint enterprise, the purpose of which was to set the car going and see how the car in fact functioned. Where the defendant was sitting was not the determining factor. Although not sitting on the driver's seat, the defendant was using the car directly for his own purposes.

Person accepting a lift

5.69 A joint venture in the sense stated above was not found in *B (A Minor) v Knight*[120] where S was giving a lift to the defendant at the time of the accident. The defendant did not know when he accepted the lift that the van was being driven without the owner's consent, but that came to his knowledge during the journey and before the accident. He nevertheless remained on board as he did not fancy the idea of walking home. It was held that there was no element of joint enterprise; the defendant had no control over the use of the vehicle. He simply accepted a lift and became an innocent bystander. It would be artificial for the Court to hold that the defendant was a user only on the basis that the fact that S was driving it without the owner's consent.[121]

Pre-determined joint purpose

5.70 Whether there is an element of joint enterprise may be determined by also taking into account the pre-journey intention of the parties involved.[122] Therefore, where two persons agree on a joint venture to use a vehicle for a particular purpose they will have exercised an element of control or management in its use or operation.[123] This was illustrated in *Stinton v Stinton* where C knew that his brother, who was uninsured, was going to drive the vehicle in the evening that they went out for an evening's drinking with a third person. An accident occurred when C's brother was driving the vehicle. C was sitting as a passenger at the relevant time and he made a claim against the MIB for the

---

118 *Brown v Roberts* [1965] 1 QB 1, [15].
119 [1980] RTR 21.
120 [1981] RTR 136.
121 It should be noted that this was a criminal case and the Court particularly avoided being artificial in this context.
122 *Stinton v Stinton* [1995] RTR 167.
123 *Stinton v Stinton* [1995] RTR 167, 175.

injuries he suffered. The MIB successfully argued that C himself was also the user of the vehicle.

5.71 The relevant joint venture element does not exist when the passenger does not know all the plans of the driver and hence, may not be regarded as having sufficient control or management of the vehicle. This rule was regarded as good law in *Hatton v Hall*[124] where Henry LJ said both *Leathley v Tatton* and *B (A Minor) v Knight*[125] were clearly right and his Lordship distinguished *Stinton v Stinton*.[126]

5.72 In *Hatton* H was carrying out some work at the claimant's house. At the end of a working day the claimant invited H to have a drink. The claimant chose a public house that was ten miles away from the house and H suggested that they go on his motorcycle. On the way back from a public house the claimant was riding the motorcycle as a pillion passenger and was giving directions to H. An accident occurred when H, who was uninsured, negligently drove off the road. The MIB contested the liability under the exemption contained in clause 6(1)(c)(ii) of the 1972 Uninsured Drivers Agreement.[127] The Court of Appeal approved Waller J's judgment at first instance that a trip to a public house by motorcycle on a summer's evening did not involve a sufficient vesting of control or management of the motorcycle in the pillion passenger to make him a user of that vehicle on that trip.

5.73 The Court of Appeal held that it "seems to us to be good sense as well as good law"[128] that not all plans shared between driver and passenger give the passenger sufficient management of the vehicle to make him a user of the vehicle. It was explained in *O'Mahony v Joliffe*[129] that the position in *Hatton* was "merely an agreement to travel somewhere on an uninsured vehicle." In *Hatton*, hence, there was a joint venture but it did not involve an element of control or management to make the passenger a user; he was a passenger simply accepting a lift. With respect, it is submitted that it is not easy to reconcile how *Stinton* can be distinguished from *Hatton*.

5.74 *O'Mahony v Joliffe*[130] is a further example of which the Court found the passenger having the control of the vehicle as referred to above. In *O'Mahony* the claimant and her boyfriend decided together to drive the bike to go somewhere where they would have a private moment. The claimant was riding as pillion when her boyfriend lost control and crashed. No other vehicle was involved. Simon Brown LJ found *Stinton v Stinton* indistinguishable.[131] It was a jointly conceived plan to combine periods of illicit joy-riding with intervals of dalliance between. The actual riding of the vehicle was an integral part of the thrill of the venture and both were involved a joint decision making.

---

124 [1997] RTR 212.

125 [1981] RTR 136.

126 *Hatton v Hall* [1997] RTR 212, Henry LJ, [221–225].

127 Motor Insurers' Bureau (Compensation of Victims of Uninsured Drivers) Agreement 1972 clause 6(1)(c)(ii) provided: "MIB shall not incur any liability under clause 2 of this Agreement . . . where . . . (c) . . . the person suffering . . . bodily injury in respect of which the claim is made was allowing himself to be carried in a vehicle and . . . (ii) . . . being a person using the vehicle, he was using . . . the vehicle . . . without there being in force in relation to such use a contract of insurance as would comply with Part VI of the Road Traffic Act 1972, knowing or having reason to believe that no such contract was in force."

128 [1997] RTR 212, 224–225.

129 [1999] RTR 245.

130 Ibid.

131 [1999] RTR 245, 254. *O'Mahony v Joliffe* was applied in *British Waterways v Royal & Sun Alliance Insurance plc* [2012] Lloyd's Rep IR 562.

Unlike *Hatton*, the claimant actually assisted in setting the vehicle in motion and at one point during the outing the claimant herself actually rode the bike.

5.75 These cases reveal that it is a matter of fact and degree in every case whether the passenger had sufficient control of the vehicle to be regarded as a user of it. It is submitted that although in *O'Mahony*, passenger's actual driving of the vehicle at one point during the journey was a stronger element of joint riding compared to the other cases mentioned above, it is hardly persuasive that in *Hatton* the passenger did not have sufficient control of the motorcycle to be regarded as a user of it. Therefore, although the test is clearly set to determine if a passenger is a user, the test, as seen, has not been applied by the same rigidity by the Courts. In *Hatton* the Court stated that if a bank-robber is a pillion passenger on a getaway motorcycle, it may be inferred that he has a greater degree of management and control over the driver than the pillion passenger in *Hatton*.[132] A passenger who employs a driver to drive against the clock to catch an aeroplane will similarly have a power to control and/or manage the vehicle.[133] However, it is different if a father agreed to drive his 18-year-old son and 80-year-old mother-in-law, neither able to drive, to visit his wife in hospital.[134] Clearly, the first two examples that the Court gave were distinguishable from the last, but, with respect, the agreements between the claimant and H in *Hatton* is closer to the previous group but not the latter. Once again, this analysis confirms how dramatic effect the analysis of "control and management" of the vehicle can make and how the degree of assessment of the facts may differ.

Having "control or management" through ownership interest

5.76 *Bretton v Hancock*[135] is analysed in Chapter 6 with respect to the civil liability for contravention of the RTA 1988 s 143(1). The relevance of *Bretton* to the "use" of a motor vehicle is that in *Bretton* H owned the car that was purchased by her fiancé who paid for the purchase price of the vehicle. H and her fiancé were co-habitants; H was insured, but she did not know that her fiancé was uninsured. She had been told by her fiancé that he had insured himself to drive the car against third party risks. H was injured while travelling as a passenger when a collision with another vehicle occurred whilst her fiancé was driving the car.

5.77 One of the questions was if H was a "user" of the car at the time of the accident. The fact that she and her fiancé were living together in her house and that she paid all the household outgoings persuaded the Court that the two of them were at least to share in the ownership of the car. It was held that she had an interest in the car,[136] and she also had sufficient control of it on the relevant occasion to constitute use of the vehicle on her part. Without her having an interest in the car, she would not have been able to insure it comprehensively. It suffices here to say that *Bretton* confirmed that the owner of a vehicle is a co-user while being carried as a passenger. This case is also an illustration

---

132 *Hatton v Hall* [1997] RTR 212, 224–225.

133 Ibid.

134 Ibid.

135 [2005] RTR 22.

136 On appeal it was conceded that the question of user was to be determined by reference to the question of whether she had an interest in the car.

of an unsuccessful attempt in unusual circumstances to extend *Monk v Warbey* to a claim for pure economic loss which is discussed in Chapter 6.

EU law

5.78 As the EU law has developed especially in recent years, the motor vehicles referred to in Article 1(1) of the Consolidated Directive cover, irrespective of their characteristics, any use of a vehicle as a means of transport.[137] In this respect, in the view of the CJEU, the act of opening the door of a vehicle amounts to use of the vehicle which is consistent with its function as a means of transport. In particular this allows persons to get in or out of the vehicle or to load and unload goods which are to be transported in the vehicle or which have been transported in it.[138] That conclusion is not affected by the fact that the vehicles at issue were, at the time of the accident, stationary and that they were in a car park.[139] Consequently, the concept of use in this respect covers a case where a passenger causes damage to another vehicle whilst opening a vehicle door. In *BTA Baltic Insurance Company' AS v Apdrošināšanas Nams' AS*[140] a passenger of a vehicle parked in a supermarket car park ("the first vehicle") damaged the left rear side of the neighbouring vehicle ("the second vehicle") when opening the right rear door. Having emphasised that as has been consistently ruled since *Vnuk*, the scope of the concept of "use of vehicles," within the meaning of Article 3(1) of the First Directive, does not depend on the characteristics of the terrain on which the vehicle is used,[141] the Court did not have any difficulties in ruling that this was a type of civil liability in respect of the use of vehicles that must be covered by insurance.

5.79 As noted in Chapter 1 it is still the case at time of writing that the UK is under the duty to implement the EU Directives as well as ensuring that the compulsory insurance is provided at least to the extent the Directives stipulate. The domestic rules are to be interpreted consistently with the relevant Directives.[142] A comparison of the common law position as explained above and the *BTA Baltic Insurance* ruling reveals a clear conflict between the UK and EU regimes. In *BTA Baltic Insurance* the Court did not discuss whether the passenger had control of the vehicle. The Court applied straightforwardly the outcomes of the EU law's interpretation by especially *Vnuk*, *Rodrigues* and *Núñez Torreiro*. These cases have mainly established what the Court relied on in its reasoning in *BTA Baltic Insurance* in which the CJEU found no difficulties in ruling that the second vehicle's insurer can claim from the first vehicle's insurer so long as the passenger's act to open the door falls under the "use" in respect of the compulsory insurance.

5.80 As far as the UK law is concerned, however, the matter is more complicated for the concerns expressed at the outset that if the passenger is not insured, the passenger as well as the owner commit the offence under section 143. As referred to before,[143] for

---

137 *Rodrigues de Andrade v Proenca Salvador* (C-514/16) [2018] Lloyd's Rep IR 164.
138 *BTA Baltic Insurance* [36].
139 Ibid [37].
140 (C-648/17) ECLI:EU:C:2018:917.
141 *Rodrigues de Andrade v Proenca Salvador* (C-514/16) [2018] Lloyd's Rep IR 164, [35]; and of 20 December 2017, *Núñez Torreiro*.
142 See Chapter 1 for the Principle of Consistent Interpretation.
143 See Chapters 3 and 7.

the purposes of the compulsory MTPL insurance, what is required to be insured is the user. Failing to insure use of the vehicle by a passenger does not necessarily require to hold the owner liable under *Monk v Warbey* because the owner's insurer would satisfy the victim's claim under section 151 of the RTA 1988 with a right of recourse against the owner and the user of the vehicle under s 151(8).[144] When practicalities are considered, the only solution seems to be for the insurance policies to cover any user including passenger users. This practice may lead the premium to increase for compulsory MTPL insurance. However, there does not seem to be any other alternative solutions in the light of *BTA Baltic Insurance*.

5.81 In order to guarantee that the insurance policies include coverage for use by passengers, a legislative change to the RTA 1988 s 145 with respect to the requirements of the insurance cover would be appropriate. If the section provides that the insurance policy should include the use by passengers that would also resolve the controversy which is now created by *BTA Baltic Insurance*.

5.82 Alternatively the legislative change may be added to section 145(3)(a) "use" within the meaning of this section includes passenger use, so that statutorily the policies would be required to insure use by passengers. Such a legislative change would enable a third party victim to claim directly against the insurer under section 151. Where the policy does not include use by passengers, as noted above, the insurer would still have to satisfy the judgment against the passenger user, with a right of recourse against the owner and the passenger. In other words, the passenger would be treated as any other user of the vehicle who is currently subject to the compulsory MTPL insurance requirement.

---

144 See Chapter 8.

CHAPTER 6

Civil liability

Introduction

6.1 The RTA 1988 s 143 forbids a person using a motor vehicle without having an insurance or security as required by the Act. Further, the RTA 1988 regulates that a person must not cause or permit any other person to use a motor vehicle on a road unless there is insurance or security as required by the Act. Section 143 (2) of the RTA 1988 provides that "if a person acts in contravention of subsection (1) above he is guilty of an offence." In addition to this statutory sanction for contravening the insurance obligation under the RTA 1988, in *Monk v Warbey*[1] the Court accepted a claim in tort against the person who breached the RTA 1930 s 35 (now the RTA 1988 s 143) by allowing an uninsured person to use the vehicle.

6.2 As analysed throughout this book the scheme, in a nutshell, operates as follows: a victim of a motor vehicle accident may claim the loss suffered as a result of the accident from the user of the vehicle if the user negligently caused the injury. Ideally, the legislation aims to ensure that the driver is insured so that the driver's financial position will have no impact on the compensation of the third party's loss. If the user is insured there is a right of direct action against the insurer either under section 151 of the RTA 1988 or under the European Communities (Rights against Insurers) Regulations 2002/3061.[2] Moreover, although it may not be as significant in MTPL insurance as it is in other types of liability insurance contract, where the assured is insolvent the Third Parties (Rights Against Insurers) Act 2010 (TPA 2010) allows the victim to bring a direct claim against the assured's insurer. Because of the availability of the first two options, neither of which requires the assured's insolvency as a pre-requisite to the direct claim against the insurer, the TPA 2010 is unlikely to be needed in the motor insurance context.[3] If the user is uninsured or untraced, the victim may seek compensation from the MIB.[4] The broad interpretation of the scope of the compulsory MTPL insurance has been referred to in other chapters of this book. Under these circumstances one may question why there may be a need to discuss if seeking damages by a civil law action from the person who permitted an uninsured person to use the vehicle is available.

---

1 [1935] 1 KB 75.
2 See Chapter 8 for victim's right to claim directly from the user's insurer.
3 See also Merkin/Hemsworth, [5–192].
4 See Chapter 10.

90

6.3 There may be a case in which there is no right of action against the MIB or some unusual facts may lead the third party victim, as the last resort, to bring an action against the person who allowed an uninsured person to use the vehicle.[5] The problem does not arise often. However, a number of disputes that have arisen until today revealed that the matters that may lead to a discussion of the *Monk v Warbey* liability have not extinguished. Moreover, it is still relevant with regards to the right of recourse that either the owner's insurer or the MIB would exercise against the uninsured user and the person who permitted the uninsured use of the vehicle.

Is breach of statutory duty actionable?

6.4 Whilst previously it had been disapproved,[6] it was held in *Couch v Steel* that where there is a breach of a statutory duty resulting in damage to an individual, an action for damages will lie.[7] In *Couch v Steel*[8] a seaman of a merchant ship sued to recover damages for injuries sustained by him by reason of the omission of the defendant, a shipowner, to provide proper medicines for the ship's company. The action was successful. The ruling in *Couch v Steel* was described as a liberal approach to the imposition of civil liability for breach of a statutory duty.[9] Further, by way of construction, the purpose of imposing a criminal remedy by the statute justified a right of civil action for damages.[10]

6.5 The Courts, however, have not always been in favour of a right of civil action for damages where a statute provided a specified remedy for its non-compliance.[11] In *Atkinson v The Newcastle and Gateshead Waterworks Company*[12] Lord Cairns expressed grave doubts that *Couch v Steel* created a generally applicable rule. His Lordship questioned whether the authorities cited by Lord Campbell in *Couch* justified the broad general proposition that appeared to have been there laid down, that, wherever a statutory duty was created, any person who could show that he had sustained injuries from the non-performance of that duty, could bring an action for damages against the person on whom the duty was imposed.[13] Denison J was more dismissive about the right of civil action in *Stevens v Evans*[14] where the judge said, "It is a rule 'that upon a new statute which prescribes a particular remedy; no remedy can be taken, but the particular remedy prescribed by the statute.'"[15]

---

5 One may argue that given the compensation provided by the MIB this question has lost its importance. However, as *Sahin v Havard* [2017] Lloyd's Rep IR 110 and *Bretton v Hancock* [2005] RTR 22 illustrate, the matter may still arise despite all the efforts to ensure that the victim's loss is compensated by either the MTPL insurer or the MIB.

6 *Stevens v Jeacocke* [1848] 11 QB 731.

7 *Couch v Steel* (1854) 3 El. & Bl. 402.

8 (1854) 3 El. & Bl. 402.

9 M. A. Jones/A. M. Dugdale/M. Simpson *Clerk & Lindsell on Torts*, 22nd ed, 2018, Sweet & Maxwell [9–13].

10 *Island Records Ltd v Corkindale* [1978] Ch. 122.

11 *Stevens v Jeacocke* [1848] 11 QB 731.

12 (1877) 2 Ex. D. 441.

13 Ibid, 448.

14 (1761) 2 Burrow 1152, at 1157.

15 *Doe d. Murray v Bridges* (1831) 1 B. & Ad. 847, 859 Lord Tenterden CJ.

6.6 Lord Diplock, however, delivered two exceptions to the rule that "performance of the statute may be enforced by the way described by the statute, not by any other means including a civil action for damages."[16] The two classes of exception are:

(1) where upon the true construction of the Act it is apparent that the obligation or prohibition was imposed for the benefit or protection of a particular class of individuals, as in the case of the Factories Acts and similar legislation. This exception is construed in the light of the scope and purpose of the statute and in particular for whose benefit it is intended. When a duty of this kind is imposed for the benefit of particular persons there arises at common law a correlative right in those persons who may be injured by its contravention.

(2) where the statute creates a public right (ie a right to be enjoyed by all those of Her Majesty's subjects who wish to avail themselves of it) and a particular member of the public suffers "particular, direct, and substantial" damage "other and different from that which was common to all the rest of the public."[17]

Motor insurance

6.7 In the MTPL insurance context the Court of Appeal in *Monk v Warbey*[18] allowed the traffic accident victim's claim for damages against the owner of the vehicle. The real reason for the Court's finding for the claimant in *Monk v Warbey* was said to be Parliament's implied intention that victims of negligent driving should not go uncompensated with the introduction of compulsory insurance.[19] In other words the Court of Appeal sought to "add force and life to the cure and remedy according to the true intent of the makers of the Act."[20]

6.8 In *Monk v Warbey*, at the time of the accident, M was driving the car on behalf of K who borrowed the car from her fiancé, W. W was insured against third party risks, but both K and M were uninsured. Consequently, the claimant had two defendants who were not in a position to pay those damages and who were uninsured. The absence of insurance also meant that there was no right of action under the then Third Parties (Rights Against Insurers) Act 1930.[21] The last option available for the victim was, therefore, a civil action against W for permitting an uninsured person to use the vehicle in contravention of section 35 of the RTA 1930 (now the RTA 1988 s 143). The cumulative effect of the objective of the Act, the overwhelming consideration of protection of the victim against impecunious users of motor vehicles, the public nature of interests that the 1930 Act aims to protect, persuaded the Court of Appeal to approve the claimant's action.[22] The Court of Appeal found nothing in the Act to show that a personal action was precluded by reason

---

16 *Lonrho Ltd v Shell Petroleum Co Ltd (No.2)* [1982] AC 173, 185.

17 *Benjamin v Storr* (1873–74) L.R. 9 C.P. 400, 406–407, Brett J.

18 [1935] 1 KB 75.

19 C. R. Symmons, "The Impact of Third Party Insurance Legislation on the Development of the Common Law," 4 *Anglo-Am. L. Rev.* 426 (1975), p 429.

20 D. J. Llewelyn Davies, "The Interpretation of Statutes in the Light of Their Policy by the English Courts," 35 *Colum. L. Rev.* 519 (1935), p 528.

21 The Third Parties (Rights Against Insurers) Act 1930 was replaced by the Third Parties (Rights Against Insurers) Act 2010 as of 1 August 2016.

22 Approved also in *McLeod (or Houston) v Buchanan* [1940] 2 All ER 179.

of the existence of the special remedy provided for a breach. A personal right of action for a breach of the RTA 1930 s 35 lied on the assumption that the policy of insurance was one which would give a third party some measure of indemnity in the event of the person using the car being guilty of negligence.

6.9 Greer LJ emphasised that the unavailability of recovery for damages that third party victim suffered was the very contingency in respect of which the claimant was intended to be protected by the RTA 1930.[23] Moreover, the damages in this case flew directly from that breach.[24] Greer LJ said[25]:

> Prima facie a person who has been injured by the breach of a statute has a right to recover damages from the person committing it unless it can be established by considering the whole of the Act that no such right was intended to be given. So far from that being shown in this case, the contrary is established. To prosecute for a penalty is no sufficient protection and is a poor consolation to the injured person though it affords a reason why persons should not commit a breach of the statute.

6.10 Maughan LJ referred to *Atkinson v The Newcastle and Gateshead Waterworks Company*[26] as mentioned above, but his Lordship added that "the question whether that rule [if the Act provides a special remedy for a contravention of its provisions the prima facie rule is that that is the only remedy] applies in any particular case depends upon the purview of the legislation and the language employed."[27] Maughan LJ held that whether the intention of the statute was to preclude private remedy had to be decided by considering whether the harm sought to be remedied by the statute was one of the kind which the statute had been intended to prevent.[28] Moreover, the fact that the claim was brought by a person pointed out on a fair construction of the Act as being one whom the Legislature desired to protect strongly tended to support the view that this statute had not intended to preclude a civil action.

The nature of liability

6.11 The victim's right of claiming damages in addition to the statutory criminal remedy for breach of the RTA 1988 s 143 is now named as *Monk v Warbey* liability.[29] Given the availability to seek compensation from the insurer under section 151 of the RTA 1988 and from the MIB under the Motor Insurers' Bureau Agreements, the *Monk v Warbey* liability may not arise in the future in the same way it did in that case. However, as mentioned before, the circumstances that fall under the compulsory MTPL insurance are so diverse that the *Monk v Warbey* liability is still possible to argue on the facts.

---

23 [1935] 1 KB 75, 82, Greer LJ.

24 Ibid.

25 [1935] 1 KB 75, 81.

26 (1877) 2 Ex. D. 441.

27 [1935] 1 KB 75, 84.

28 In *Gorris v Scott* (1873–74) L.R. 9 Ex. 125 the action against the shipowner for the loss of the sheep that washed overboard was unsuccessful. The argument was that the defendant shipowner neglected to take a precaution required by an Order of the Privy Council made under the authority of the Contagious Diseases (Animals) Act, 1869, s 75. It was held that the object of the statute and the order was to prevent the spread of contagious disease among animals, and not to protect them against perils of the sea.

29 *Sahin v Havard* [2017] Lloyd's Rep IR 110, Longmore LJ, [14].

6.12 The basis of the claim against the owner who permitted an uninsured person to drive the vehicle is contravention of section 143(1)(b) of the Road Traffic Act 1988. The person primarily liable is the tortfeasor, who drove negligently and caused loss to the victim.[30] Where there is a breach of the statutory duty under section 143 (1)(b), and the person primarily liable for the loss is unable to satisfy the loss, *Monk v Warbey* enables the victim to proceed directly against the person who committed the breach.[31]

6.13 The damages awarded against the owner is the amount which is assessed against the driver of the vehicle for his tortious act, but the *Monk v Warbey* claim is addressed against the owner by reason of the owner's breach of the statutory duty by permitting an uninsured person to use the vehicle contrary to the Road Traffic Act.[32] This is supported by Maugham LJ's evaluation of the matter in *Monk v Warbey*[33] where his Lordship identified the necessary question as "whether on the true construction of the Road Traffic Act, an action may properly be brought by *a third party for damages caused by a breach of the statutory obligation*[34] imposed by s 35 [now the RTA 1988 s 143] upon the owner of a motor car in the somewhat unusual circumstances of this case."[35]

6.14 The breach of the statutory duty occurs at the time the user of the vehicle becomes uninsured as the owner is, at that moment, permitting the uninsured user to use the vehicle. When the accident, the tortious act by the driver, occurs, the victim has two different causes of action: against the uninsured driver and against the person who permitted the uninsured to drive. Under the *Monk v Warbey* liability, the victim would bring an action against the owner when the driver is impecunious[36] but there is no reason why he should not be able to bring an action against the owner and the driver at the same time. In *Corfield v Groves* the action was brought by the victim's wife under the Fatal Accidents Acts 1846–1908.[37] Hilberry J held that the breach of the statutory duty was a continuing breach operative at the time of the accident (the time of the tortious act), and the moment the tortious act occurred the deceased man had his cause of action for the tort. At the date of his death and before she ever issued her writ, there immediately accrued to the widow a right to claim under the Fatal Accidents Acts against the tortfeasor for negligently causing her husband's death. Her claim was enforceable against the owner of the vehicle under the decision in *Monk v Warbey* for any damages which she then sustained by reason of the breach by the owner of her statutory duty. That breach existed at the time of the tortious act, to fulfil the requirements of the RTA 1930. The damage had, in fact, accrued to her inasmuch as at the time of the tortious act the driver was an uninsured person and in such a financial position that nothing was obtained from him, even by bankruptcy proceedings.

6.15 The deceased victim's wife had her cause of action against the owner irrespective of the fact that at the time of the tort her damages could not be quantified.[38]

---

30 *Corfield v Groves* [1950] 1 All ER 488, 489.
31 Ibid.
32 Ibid.
33 [1935] 1 KB 75.
34 Emphasis added.
35 [1935] 1 KB 75, 83.
36 *Corfield v Groves* [1950] 1 All ER 488, 489.
37 Now Fatal Accidents Act 1976.
38 Although, in theory, her damages are quantified as on the day of the accruing of her complete cause of action. *Corfield v Groves* [1950] 1 All ER 488, 489–490.

Causation

6.16 No damages will be awarded under the *Monk v Warbey* liability if the damage suffered by the claimant was not caused by the breach of the statutory duty. In *Daniels v Vaux*[39] the negligent driver was not insolvent, but the claimant did not issue a claim form against the user within the limit of six months allowed by the Law Reform (Miscellaneous Provisions) Act, 1934.[40] Hence, the damage suffered was not as a result of the owner's breach of the statutory duty in the way that permitting her son to use the vehicle without insurance but the claimant's own failure that resulted in the lapse of the limitation period.

6.17 *Daniels v Vaux*[41] would also be applicable where, if, in theory, the claim can be raised against the MIB, but the MIB refuses the victim's claim because the victim failed to satisfy the procedural conditions set out under the MIB Agreements.

The owner is a passenger in his own vehicle

6.18 There are authorities which decided that the owner is to be taken as using a vehicle when he is a passenger and allows another person to drive the vehicle.[42] If that is true it follows that the owner and the user both were using the vehicle at the time of the accident and therefore when a victim suffers loss as a result of an accident caused by that vehicle, a claim may be made against the owner's insurer. In such a case the owner will still commit the criminal offence of permitting an uninsured use of the vehicle; however, because of the availability of the compensation by the insurer, it will not be necessary to discuss the *Monk v Warbey* liability. What is discussed in this chapter is where the owner or any other person who permitted uninsured use of the vehicle is not the user of the vehicle.

Exclusions from cover

6.19 Exclusions from the compulsory MTPL insurance cover are examined in Chapter 7 and a right of direct action against a MTPL insurer is analysed in Chapter 8. It suffices here to state that, where the person who permitted uninsured use is insured (whether owner or any other person insured and have the authority to permit someone else to use the vehicle),[43] the insurer, under section 151(2)(b), will be asked to satisfy the third party victim's claim as such use was required to be insured. Towards the third party victim, the use is to be treated as an insured use, despite the exclusion in the insurance contract, and the insurer may then recoup against the person who permitted the uninsured use as well as the actual user of the vehicle.[44]

---

39 [1938] 2 KB 203.

40 Now, under the Limitation Act 1980 s 11(5) it is three years from (a) the date of death; or (b) the date of the personal representative's knowledge.

41 [1938] 2 KB 203.

42 *Cobb v Williams* [1973] RTR 113; *Pratt v Patrick* [1924] 1 KB 488.

43 As *Sahin v Havard* [2017] Lloyd's Rep IR 110 illustrated, the person who permitted uninsured use may not always be the owner.

44 The RTA 1988 s 151(2)(b) and 151(8).

6.20 Under Article 13(1) of the Consolidated Directive an exclusion from the cover towards a third party victim with respect to "persons who do not have express or implied authorisation" to use the vehicle is void. If that is the true interpretation of the law, where the insurance contract in relation to that vehicle insures the person who permitted the uninsured use but then excludes use when it might cover that person but not the uninsured user, that exclusion may not be argued against the third party victim.

6.21 In *Sahin v Havard*, however, the Court of Appeal enforced the exclusion. In this case S's car collided with a motor car which was owned by L, a car hire company. L had hired the car to H who permitted X to drive the vehicle. Although H was a permitted driver under the car hire company's insurance, that insurance did not cover anyone whom she herself permitted to drive; indeed it expressly excluded any liability for loss or damage incurred while the motor vehicle was being driven by any person not permitted to drive. S obtained a default judgment against L, but L had gone into liquidation. S then began proceedings against H. As referred to in Chapter 8, instead of referring to the interpretation of the RTA 1988 s 151(2)(b), in *Sahin*, the Court identified s 145 of the RTA 1988 as a central provision in the case namely, whether H's liability to S was a liability "incurred . . . in respect of . . . damage to property caused by, or arising out of the use of the vehicle on a road or other public place." That then led to the discussion of whether the *Monk v Warbey* liability, the ground for an action against H, is to be covered by H's insurer under section 145 of the RTA 1988.

6.22 The Court ruled the *Monk v Warbey* liability did not fall under the insurance requirement as identified by section 145. Subsequently, H's liability as argued in this case was not such that the insurer was obliged to satisfy under section 151 of the RTA 1988.[45] Longmore LJ was of the view that permitting someone to drive a motor vehicle is not using that vehicle on a road.[46] His Lordship said, "Section 143 of the 1988 Act draws a clear distinction between the two [permitting the use of a vehicle and using the vehicle] and . . . section 143(1)(b) would scarcely be necessary if 'causing or permitting use' were the same as 'use'."[47]

6.23 Despite a reference to the relevant restriction that derives from Art 13 of the Consolidated Directive, Longmore LJ applied *Bristol Alliance Ltd Partnership v Williams*[48] Bristol and found that the exclusion from the insurance covered H was enforceable. *Sahin v Havard*[49] is also examined in Chapter 8 and a detailed discussion of *Bristol* can be found in Chapter 7 of this book. The analysis that presented in those chapters supports the submission in this chapter that the main issue in *Sahin*, with respect to the Court of Appeal, was section 151(2)(b) of the RTA 1988. The outcome therefore should have been that H's insurer was to cover the victim's loss with a right of recourse against H. Nevertheless, as examined in Chapter 8, the Supreme Court in *Cameron v Liverpool Victoria Insurance Co Ltd*[50] once again seems to have undermined section 151(2)(b).

---

45 [2017] Lloyd's Rep IR 110, [20].
46 Ibid.
47 Ibid.
48 [2013] RTR 9.
49 Also see *Allen v Mohammed* [2017] Lloyd's Rep IR 73 discussed in Chapter 8.
50 [2019] UKSC 6.

CIVIL LIABILITY

The user must be impecunious

6.24 If the uninsured user of the motor vehicle who negligently caused damage to the claimant is able to satisfy the judgment awarded against him and in favour of the claimant, can the victim still bring an action to the person who permitted uninsured use under *Monk v Warbey*? It was once held that if the driver was able to satisfy a judgment against him only in part, the person who permitted the uninsured use might be liable for the unsatisfied amount.[51]

This question should not be confused with a case where the owner who permitted uninsured use is also a user of the vehicle as highlighted in paragraph 6.18 above.

6.25 The owner (who is not a user of the vehicle but only permitted uninsured use)'s liability is quantified when the actual user who caused the accident is unable to pay the victim. It was therefore held that the person who permitted an uninsured use of the vehicle (second defendant) is also a defendant in an action brought against the user (first defendant); nominal damages would be awarded against the second defendant if the first defendant can satisfy the victim's claim.[52] Damages are awarded to recognise the breach and liability but because there is no damage to claim, it is a nominal amount awarded against the guilty party. This is in line with *Corfield v Groves*[53] referred to above. The victim's right of action against the owner arises as soon the user becomes uninsured, but the claim is assessed when the impecuniosity is established.

6.26 Irrespective of the loss suffered by a third party victim it is still the case that the owner of the vehicle permitted an uninsured driver to use the vehicle and contravened the relevant principle that the RTA section 143 tried to establish. This would be met by a criminal sanction.

Interpretation of "permit" and "cause"

6.27 As discussed in Chapter 3, permission within the meaning of the RTA 1988 s 143 may be given by a person who is in a position to forbid the use of the vehicle. However, one should not lose sight of the fact that each case may turn in its own facts. For instance, in *Goodbarne v Buck*,[54] which should be read on its own facts, the emphasis was put on the "owning" the vehicle that gave the power or control to forbid the other person to use the motor vehicle. This case should not be interpreted as setting a general rule to the effect limiting the persons who can forbid or permit another to use the vehicle to "owners" only.

6.28 In *Goodbarne v Buck*[55] the driver, W, became uninsured when the insurers successfully set aside the policy due to a number of fraudulent misrepresentations made at the pre-contractual stage. The claim against W's brother H under the *Monk v Warbey* liability was rejected. H stood by while, to his knowledge, W was putting forward some grossly

---

51 *Martin v Dean* [1971] 2 QB 208.
52 *Martin v Dean* [1971] 2 QB 208. C was knocked down by a motorcycle driven by D. The motorcycle belonged to P who had lent it to D. Both D and P erroneously thought that P's insurance policy covered the motorcycle whilst being driven by D. D would have been able to satisfy the judgment against him but could only afford a small instalment each week not promptly. A judgment was given against P as well as D; the loss against P was because of the claimant's loss for being deprived of a prompt payment.
53 [1950] 1 All ER 488.
54 [1940] 1 KB 771.
55 Ibid.

misleading and inaccurate statements to the insurer. Those statements included H being inserted in the proposal form as the proposer and owner of the vehicle, whereas it was W who owned it; the proposal showed that it was signed by "H" but was in fact signed by W. Trade or business was stated "Fruiterer or greengrocer," but H was a butcher; it was W who was the greengrocer. The Court carried out a careful analysis of the wording of section 35(1) of the RTA 1930 (now the RTA 1988 s 143(1)(b)). The wording of the relevant section was "to cause or permit any other person to use." The Court found that the word "permit" was much more easy of construction and interpretation than "cause." It was held that in order to permit another person to use a motor vehicle, he must be in a position to forbid the other person to use the motor vehicle. H did not own the vehicle and was not in such a position. Neither did H cause W to use the motor vehicle on a road. H's action best could be described as having assisted his brother while his brother was completing the proposal in a way which subsequently led the insurer to accept the insurance proposal.

On the facts, Mackinnon LJ used the word "owner" to justify that H was not in a position to forbid W to use the vehicle. As mentioned before, the case turned on its own facts and did not establish a generally applicable principle that only the owner of a vehicle may permit another to use it.

6.29 In *Lloyd v Singleton* the Divisional Court held that the judgment in *Goodbarne* went beyond what was necessary. Disagreeing with what had been held at first instance, the Divisional Court[56] stated that Mackinnon LJ had not thought, in giving an extemporary judgment, of all the various alternatives which could arise. In *Lloyd v Singleton* O was charged for unlawfully permitting his brother C to use a motor vehicle without having third party liability insurance as required by section 35 of the RTA 1930. The vehicle was owned by company A, of which J was managing director. O was A's assistant general manager, to whom the vehicle was entrusted for carrying out the duties of A and who had full discretion as to its use for the company's business. C was not an employee of the company. O and his brother were at a club in Southport with the lorry when O, who was ill, asked his brother to drive the lorry to the place where it was normally kept. In the course of that journey he was stopped by a police officer. There was in force a policy of insurance in the name of R, as director of A, covering the vehicle when driven with the policy holder's permission. R had not given C permission to drive the vehicle on that day. Disagreeing with what was decided in *Goodbarne* the Divisional Court found it clear that O here was in a position to forbid his brother to drive, but, instead, he requested him to do so.

The effect of avoidance of the insurance contract

6.30 Avoidance is a self-help remedy that the person who is avoiding a contract must communicate his intention to this effect to the other party of the contract.[57] Unlike a void contract, a contract that is avoidable is in force and, until it is avoided effectively,

---

56 [1953] 1 QB 357.

57 Insurers have a very limited availability to avoid the insurance contract and argue it against a third party victim. See Chapter 8.

it remains in force. Hence, if the *Monk v Warbey* liability is argued, and the insurer has not yet avoided the contract, the alleged offence would be rejected.[58]

6.31 Moreover, when an insurer successfully avoids the insurance contract by satisfying the conditions under section 152 of the RTA 1988, the victim may still have a right to claim against the MIB. The MIB may have right of recourse against the person who was using the vehicle and the person who permitted such use. Moreover, as discussed in Chapter 10, the MIB, under Article 75 of its Articles of Association, may nevertheless appoint the insurer to satisfy the victim's claim so long as the policy had not been avoided before the accident.

No extension to section 143(1)(a)

6.32 The *Monk v Warbey* liability applies when the defendant is the owner or another person who may permit the use, but not the user of the vehicle. If the owner is also the user together with the driver section 143(1)(a) applies.[59] In *Bretton v Hancock*[60] Rix LJ clearly distinguished subsections 1(a) and 1(b) of section 143 that whilst the former is concerned with personal use of a motor vehicle, the latter is concerned with causing or permitting another's use of a motor vehicle.[61] The *Monk v Warbey* jurisprudence considered above all concerns cases of causing or permitting, ie section 143(1)(b), but it does not extend to breach of section 143(1)(a).[62]

6.33 In *Bretton v Hancock*, as discussed in Chapter 5, M was involved in an accident for which he was partially to blame and he was killed. At the time of the accident M was driving the vehicle owned by H, H was also in the vehicle, H was insured for her relevant liability, but M did not have insurance to drive H's vehicle. The other vehicle that was involved in the accident in question was driven by J who also suffered personal injuries. The responsibility for the accident was shared between J and M, 75% and 25%, respectively. H claimed damages against J. J did not make any claim for his own personal injuries, but he argued that H was liable under *Monk v Warbey*, hence, H must contribute to the loss that H suffered and now claimed against J. In other words, J was seeking contribution by H to the loss that M caused by his fault of 25%.

6.34 It was argued that H was also using the vehicle and the trial judge accepted, and the Court of Appeal did not disturb the finding, that H was the user of the car. The breach argued against H was not contravention of section 143(1)(b) because H was found to have had reasonable grounds that M had the required insurance to drive H's vehicle. Here, the point to highlight is that since H was one of the users, J's claim against H was for contribution to the compensation of her own loss to the extent caused by M based on section 143(1)(a) of the RTA 1988. J's claim was rejected as section 143 of the 1988 Act is concerned only with insurance against statutory risks, death, personal injury and property damage, suffered by a third party, whereas the loss suffered by J was pure economic loss. It was held that a user was not bound to insure against the liability of one

---

58 *Goodbarne v Buck* [1940] 1 KB 107; *Durrant v MacLaren* [1956] 2 Lloyd's Rep 70; *Adams v Dunne* [1978] RTR 281.
59 See above paragraph 6.18 and Chapter 5.
60 [2005] RTR 22.
61 Ibid, [48].
62 Ibid.

tortfeasor to contribute with another tortfeasor in respect of their joint liability to the user. This issue will be explored further below.

Monk v Warbey liability and the MIB

6.35 Using a motor vehicle without insurance is a criminal offence under section 143(1)(a) of the RTA 1988. Where the person who was using the vehicle at the time of the accident was not insured but for instance the owner of that vehicle was insured, under section 151(2)(b), the insurer will be obliged to compensate the victim's loss as if the user was insured. The insurer then may recoup against the user and the owner of the vehicle. Where, for instance, neither the owner nor the user was insured, or the owner was insured but the insurer either avoided the insurance contract before the accident, or is permitted to rely on a contractual exclusion, the victim's loss was caused by an uninsured driver. The use of the vehicle, however, was required to be insured under section 145; therefore, the liability is relevant liability which would enable the victim to address his claim against the MIB. The significance of the *Monk v Warbey* liability is therefore in the context of the MIB's right of recourse against the person who permitted the uninsured use.

6.36 As mentioned above the *Monk v Warbey* liability is to be distinguished from the liability of the user which is required to be insured under section 145 of the RTA 1988. The *Monk v Warbey* liability is a common law civil liability that is attached to the person who allows an uninsured person to drive the vehicle in contravention of section 143(1)(b) of the RTA 1988 which expressly provides a criminal sanction for such contravention of the Act. If the Court of Appeal's ruling in *Sahin v Havard* is correct, the position is that whilst the victim's damage was caused by a negligent use of the vehicle which has to be insured and satisfied by the insurer, it is nevertheless not to be satisfied by the insurer. The reason is that the liability in question under *Monk v Warbey* is not a relevant liability that is to be insured, it is a liability that arises out of section 143(1)(b). Therefore the insurer's obligation under section 151(2)(b) does not arise. It would follow that under the *Monk v Warbey* principle, the MIB is not liable alongside the person who permitted the uninsured use of the vehicle either. This is because his liability does not arise out of the use of the vehicle and therefore is not a relevant liability. It is submitted that such an outcome which neither permits a recovery against the insurer nor the MIB, is not that of wither envisaged or desired by the compulsory MTPL insurance regime.

6.37 Where the owner who permits the uninsured use of the vehicle is also a user of the vehicle, the MIB will not meet or contribute to any judgment which another tortfeasor is liable for and is able to satisfy. Where the owner is not a joint user,[63] he is not a tortfeasor. The basis of his liability is not on the ground that he is also user but he permitted the uninsured person to drive the vehicle.

6.38 In *Corfield v Groves*[64] Hilberry J found no practical difficulties where the MIB would satisfy the judgment against the driver (MIB said in that case that it would), and the owner was also found liable under the *Monk v Warbey* claim, because the principles

---

63 See Chapter 5 where "user" is analysed.
64 [1950] 1 All ER 488.

of insurance law would not allow the claimant to recover twice.[65] This matter would not be discussed in the same scale today because when the MIB compensates the loss caused by an uninsured driver, it may recoup against the user and the owner.

Economic loss

6.39 The person primarily liable for the victim's loss is the tortfeasor. But the compulsory MTPL insurance regime allows the victim to address the claim against the user's insurer, the insurer's representative in a Member State of the EU, or the MIB as the case may be. Furthermore, the common law has recognised a tort action for contravention of section 143(1)(b) of the RTA 1988.

6.40 What the victim is permitted to claim under the *Monk v Warbey* liability is in respect of economic loss, but that is not to be extended to "pure economic loss."[66] Greer LJ stated in *Monk v Warbey* that "the cause of action is that the statute has been broken and that damage has been caused to the plaintiff."[67] The judge said,

> All that has to be shown is that the person primarily liable is in such a financial position that nothing is obtainable from him, and that nothing can be effected by bankruptcy proceedings against him, as, being an uninsured person, there can be no recourse against an insurance company.

6.41 This, however, should be read as that the civil action under *Monk v Warbey* is in respect of a third party's loss within the meaning of the statute.[68] Under the compulsory MTPL insurance scheme a user or one who causes or permits the use of a motor vehicle fails to insure that use is himself put in the position of being required directly to compensate the third party loss.[69]

6.42 In *Bretton v Hancock*, the facts of which were given above, the Court of Appeal discussed whether or not M's liability to J can be met other than from his own impecunious pocket. The *Monk v Warbey* claim only protects a claimant who has himself suffered personal injury or death, or property damage. This scheme has never been extended to pure economic loss as suggested by J in *Bretton*.

6.43 There is an essential difference between the claim of the primary victim and the joint tortfeasor, like J, who claims not in respect of his own injuries but only in respect of his tortfeasor's right of indemnity or contribution.[70] J's counterclaim attempted to charge H only with her own use of the vehicle, not with causing or permitting M's use. The breach argued against H was not contravention of section 143(1)(b) because H was found to have had reasonable grounds that M had the required insurance to drive H's vehicle.

6.44 J was a third party vis-à-vis H (with regards to the *Monk v Warbey* liability) as well as vis-à-vis M (whose negligent driving was established). However, even though he was injured in the accident, J's counterclaim was not premised on those injuries but

---

65 [1950] 1 All ER 488.

66 *Bretton v Hancock* [2005] RTR 22, Rix LJ, [45]; see the observation of Stuart-Smith L.J. in *Richardson v Pitt-Stanley* [1995] QB 123.

67 [1935] 1 KB 75, 83.

68 *Norman v Aziz* [2000] RTR 107.

69 *Bretton v Hancock* [2005] RTR 22, Rix LJ, [45].

70 Ibid, [43].

upon a claim for a contribution from M in respect of his own liability to H. That was a pure economic loss, namely the impossibility of recovering an indemnity or contribution from any insurer.

6.45 The only loss that falls within the RTA 1988 s 145 was the personal injury suffered by H, but hers was not a third party loss. S owed a duty to insure her use of the vehicle and her duty was owed to the public as a whole, but not to herself.

If H had sued either M or J separately in respect of her injuries, each of them would have been liable to indemnify her in full. It was counter-intuitive therefore to suppose that her recovery should be reduced because M was bound to contribute to J's liability. Rix LJ said it would be undesirable

> if a wife who could in some sense be said to be the user of the household car could lose 90 per cent of her recovery because her husband, who told her he was insured, was not insured and was found 90 per cent responsible for a collision involving another driver and tortfeasor.[71]

Limitation period

6.46 Section 2 of the Limitation Act 1980 provides, "An action founded on tort shall not be brought after the expiration of six years from the date on which the cause of action accrued."

6.47 Under section 11 of the Limitation Act 1980 the limitation period is three years where "any action for damages for negligence, nuisance or breach of duty...where the damages claimed by the [claimant] . . . consist of or include damages in respect of personal injuries to the [claimant]."

6.48 Whether the liability recognised by *Monk v Warbey* is subject to a three-year or six-year limitation period depends on the legal classification of that liability.

6.49 As referred to above a contravention of the breach of the statutory duty is a continuing breach operative at the time of the accident.[72] The person who permits the use of the vehicle is breaking section 143(1)(b) at the moment that the user becomes uninsured. An accident causes a personal injury, death or property damage to the victim. The victim's primary claim is against the driver who caused the loss. The *Monk v Warbey* claim is made against the person who permits the use of the vehicle when the uninsured driver is impecunious and the victim is unable to claim against an insurer. Hilberry J held in *Corfield v Groves*[73] that at the date of the victim's death and his wife ever issued her writ, there immediately accrued to the widow a right to claim under the then enforceable Fatal Accidents Acts against the tortfeasor for negligently causing her husband's death. Her claim was enforceable against the owner of the vehicle under the decision in *Monk v Warbey* for any damages which she then sustained by reason of the breach by the owner of her statutory duty. That breach existed at the time of the tortious act, to fulfil the requirements of the RTA 1930. The damage had, in fact, accrued to her inasmuch as at the time of the tortious act the driver was an uninsured person and in such a financial position that nothing was obtained from him.

---

71 Ibid, [47].
72 *Corfield v Groves* [1950] 1 All ER 488, 489.
73 Ibid.

6.50 As referred to above, it is possible to address the claim both against the driver and the person who permitted the uninsured use, but the damages against the latter would be nominal if the former has the means to compensate the victim's loss.

All of the above indicates that the limitation period under the *Monk v Warbey* claim accrues at the time of the traffic accident.

6.51 A question may arise whether a distinction here should be made in respect of a claim for damages in relation to personal injury and an action for damages in respect of the loss of the opportunity to be paid by the insurers. Is the former to be brought against the driver of the vehicle, and does the latter represent the ground of the claim against the person who permitted the uninsured use? Again, as discussed above the *Monk v Warbey* claim is not for a pure economic loss. It is an economic loss in the sense that it derives from a personal injury or damage to property which was caused by the driver. Giving permission for the vehicle to be used by an uninsured person did not cause the personal injury or damage to property – that was caused by the negligent driving. The permission here caused the injured party to be deprived of the value of an insurance policy when it came to enforcement of any judgment against the user. *Daniels v Vaux*[74] may raise doubts here. However, it should be borne in mind that in *Daniels* the claim had not been brought against the driver within the limitation period, hence, the liability was never established by a Court decision. When the liability is established against the driver, the liability of the person who permitted uninsured use is also established, and it materialises on the impecuniosity of the driver who caused the loss.

6.52 A claim under *Monk v Warbey* was brought in *Norman v Ali*,[75] and the proceedings were commenced within six years of the accident but not within three years of it. One of the questions for the Court of Appeal was whether the limitation period for the victim's right of action against the owner was three years, expiring on 9 October 1995, or six years, expiring on 9 October 1998. The Court of Appeal held that the *Monk v Warbey* claim for the breach of duty by the owner towards the person injured arises only when the person is in fact injured, ie when the accident takes place. It was an "action for damages for . . . breach of duty . . . where the damages claimed by the claimant for . . . breach of duty . . . include damages in respect of personal injuries to the claimant" and thus falls within section 11 of the Limitation Act 1980.

6.53 In a Scottish case of *Fleming v M'Gillivray*[76] Lord Mackintosh in the Outer House concluded that an action under *Monk v Warbey* was not competent against the owner of the car until it was known that the wrongdoer cannot pay and there was no

---

74 [1938] 2 KB 203.

75 [2000] RTR 107. N suffered personal injuries in a road traffic accident on 9 October 1992. On 2 April 1993 he claimed damages for personal injury against A, who was driving a car owned by Z. It had not been resolved even seven years after the accident whether A was insured to drive Z's motor car. The MIB was notified on 10 March 1993 of a claim under the UDA 1988. On 8 June 1993 N obtained judgment in default against A with damages to be assessed. However, the default judgment against A was set aside on 17 February 1995 with directions that proceedings be transferred to the High Court. In October 1995 Z was joined as second defendant, and on 9 January 1996 the claimant entered a default judgment, with damages to be assessed, against both A and Z. On 1 March 1996 the claimant issued a summons to join the MIB as third defendant. On 20 June 1996 the default judgment was set aside on the ground that Z had not been properly served, and the claimant commenced a new action against him. On 10 June 1997 the claimant issued a summons to determine as a preliminary issue whether the limitation period for her claim against Z had expired.

76 1945 SLT 301.

effective policy. In *Norman* the Court of Appeal found this decision was not binding for them.[77] The correct analysis was that the owner and driver are separate tortfeasors liable in respect of the same damage and their rights between themselves were governed by the Civil Liability (Contribution) Act 1978.[78] Hence, whether or not the impecuniosity of the driver was a necessary ingredient of the cause of action against the owner was yet to be decided by the English Court authoritatively.[79]

6.54 As explained above, impecuniosity of the driver is not a necessary ingredient of the cause of action against the owner. The loss claimed against the driver or the person who permitted uninsured use derives from the same accident. The cause of action arises against both of the defendants when the victim suffered the injury, ie usually when the accident occurs. From that time an action can be brought against both, but the liability against the defendant under *Monk v Warbey* is quantified when the driver is not able to fully compensate the victim's loss.

6.55 Greers LJ noted in *Monk v Warbey*,[80]

> All that has to be shown is that the person primarily liable is in such a financial position that nothing is obtainable from him, and that nothing can be effected by bankruptcy proceedings against him, as, being an uninsured person, there can be no recourse against an insurance company.

This statement does not address the timing of liability owed by the person who permitted the uninsured use, but it addresses when that person's liability materialises. The claimant has to prove loss and the loss is not being able to claim the damages from the driver, this loss was accrued at the time of the accident. If the driver compensates it, as *Martin v Dean*[81] established, the owner would not be liable at all or would be liable for the amount that is not satisfied by the driver.

---

77 [2000] RTR 107, 117–118.

78 Ibid, 118.

79 The Court of Appeal found it not necessary for the purpose of the disposal of this appeal for this Court to determine it [2000] RTR 107, 118.

80 [1935] 1 KB 75, 83.

81 [1971] 2 QB 208.

CHAPTER 7

Control of policy terms

Insurer v third party victim

7.1 With regards to the enforceability of policy conditions that aim to either restrict or limit the coverage provided by the insurance contract, first of all, the focus should be on the claimant who is making a claim against the insurer. The compulsory MTPL insurance scheme does not permit a number of terms to be contended against the third party victim where those terms aim either to exclude or limit the insurer's liability. On the other hand, such restrictions may be effective in the contractual relationship between the assured and the insurer so that the latter, after compensating the third party victim's loss, may recoup against the former. This would mean that towards the third party the insurance cover is provided although the insurer has a contractual defence, and that defence would be the basis of the claim against the assured. The insurer had compensated the third party because the compulsory MTPL insurance scheme requires the insurer to do so, so that the third party victim is not prejudiced because of such clauses in the insurance contract. On the other hand, since the insurer would have been entitled to argue those clauses towards the assured, now, the insurer can rely on them in a claim for reimbursement from the assured.

Domestic law

7.2 The Road Traffic Act 1988 section 148 contains provisions on "Avoidance of certain exceptions to policies or securities." This section has the effect of nullifying provisions in a certificate of insurance that purport to restrict the insurance of the person(s) insured by the policy in respect of eight identified conditions relating to the vehicle or its condition, which are set out in section 148(2). If an insurer has to pay out a sum in respect of any person by virtue of the fact that section 148(1) renders ineffective certain exclusions in the policy (as set out in section 148(2)), then, by virtue of section 148(4) the insurer can recover that sum from the person who would have been insured but for the exclusion.

7.3 Similarly, section 148(5) renders ineffective (so far as liabilities covered by section 145 are concerned) conditions in a policy entitling an insurer to avoid or cancel a policy upon the event of certain specified things being done or not being done. Again, under section 148(6) the insurer's contractual right (if any) to recover back from an insured any sums which the insurer has become liable to pay under the policy (because the avoidance or cancellation provision has been made ineffective by the Act) is preserved.

Conditions identified under section 148(2)

7.4 An insurer is not permitted to argue the following policy defences towards a third party victim of a traffic accident for whose injury the user of the vehicle is liable.[1]

(a) the age or physical or mental condition of persons driving the vehicle,

(b) the condition of the vehicle,

(c) the number of persons that the vehicle carries,

(d) the weight or physical characteristics of the goods that the vehicle carries,

(e) the time at which or the areas within which the vehicle is used,

(f) the horsepower or cylinder capacity or value of the vehicle,

(g) the carrying on the vehicle of any particular apparatus or

(h) the carrying on the vehicle of any particular means of identification other than any means of identification required to be carried by or under the [Vehicle Excise and Registration Act 1994].

7.5 Since exclusions in relation to the above conditions may not be argued against the third party victim, the insurer will have to meet the claim. However, the insurer's right of recourse against the person who is liable for the loss is retained under subsection (4).

7.6 At first sight it is arguable that the inference to be drawn from section 148 was that exceptions other than those listed under subsection 2 remain operative.[2] Whether this statement still stands after the most recent CJEU decisions on the MTPL insurance scheme will be explored later in this chapter.

Passengers

7.7 The RTA 1988 s 149 invalidates any restriction of liability to or acceptance of the risk of negligence on the part of a passenger. For the purpose of section 149 the agreement between the user and the passenger must be entered before the liability arises. This follows a question of whether an agreement to this effect and entered into after the liability arose is enforceable.

7.8 The CJEU ruled that the EU law governing compulsory motor vehicle insurance liability insurance may not exclude "personal injuries to persons travelling in a part of a motor vehicle which has not been designed and constructed with seating accommodation for passengers."[3]

7.9 The question remains whether that provision may be relied on against a body such as the MIB.

7.10 The Directives do not permit a derogation on the basis of the family relationship between the driver or the insured person and the persons injured as a result of the accident. The family members, in other words, are not to be treated any differently to any other

---

1 This person may be insured by the insurance policy or may be regarded as insured because of the compulsory insurance regime required. Who is insured and whose liability is to be insured is discussed throughout this book and especially in Chapter 8 – "Direct action against insurers." Hence, that is not repeated here.

2 *Bristol Alliance Ltd Partnership v Williams* [2013] RTR 9 [42].

3 *Farrell v Whitty* (C-356/05) [2007] Lloyd's Rep IR 525.

third party victim.[4] Further, whether or not passengers were being carried free of charge is irrelevant for the purposes of the protection provided for the traffic accident victims.[5]

Passenger's contribution to the accident

7.11 Where a national law disallows a claim against the insurer where passengers contributed to the accident the enforceability of this provision will be subject to the "proportionality" assessment. In *Candolin v Vahinkovakuutusosakeyhtiö Pohjola*[6] the CJEU ruled that a domestic legislation that disallowed passengers to seek compensation where they should have noticed the driver's drunken state prior to the accident was held to be incompatible with the Directives. In *Candolin* at the time of the accident the vehicle that R was driving was carrying four passengers. As a result of a road accident one of the passengers died and others were seriously injured. Paragraph 7(3) of the law on motor vehicle insurance as amended by Law 656/1994 in Finland disallowed the passengers to seek compensation because R and all the passengers were drunk at the time of the accident. The CJEU found that such a restriction allows the insurer to reject liability in a disproportionate manner on the basis of the passenger's contribution to the injury or loss he has suffered.

Insurers' liability to the assured where policy contains s 148 limitations

7.12 Traditionally English law permitted insurers to deny or limit liability under the insurance contract on the basis of the form of the relevant policy terms. Before the Insurance Act 2015 (IA 2015) came into force, remedy for breach of a contractual term used to be determined on the basis of the classification of the relevant term. If the term breached was a warranty the insurer was discharged from liability automatically at the time of the breach and the risk terminated at that moment.[7] If the term was a condition precedent to policy the policy never came into existence until the condition was satisfied, and if the term was a condition precedent to the attachment of the risk, the risk did not attach until the condition was satisfied.[8] If a contractual term was classified as a condition precedent to insurer's liability, the insurer was discharged from liability from the moment of the breach but only with regards to the claim that was tainted by the breach.[9] Breach of a mere condition did not permit the insurer to deny liability unless the breach created such serious circumstances that went to the root of the contract.[10] If the insurer was prejudiced as a result of the breach of mere condition the insurer was permitted to make a deduction from the insured indemnity.[11]

---

4 *Mendes Ferreira v Companhia de Seguros Mundial Confiança SA* (C-348/98) ECLI:EU:C:2000:442 [30], [31].

5 *Mendes Ferreira v Companhia de Seguros Mundial Confiança SA* (C-348/98) ECLI:EU:C:2000:442.

6 [2006] RTR 1.

7 *Bank of Nova Scotia v Hellenic Mutual War Risk Association (Bermuda) Ltd (The Good Luck)* [1992] 1 AC 233.

8 Colinvaux, [8–006]; *Zeus Tradition Marine Ltd v Bell (The Zeus V)* [2000] 2 Lloyd's Rep 587.

9 *MJ Harrington Syndicate 2000 v Axa Oyak Sigorta AS* [2007] Lloyd's Rep IR 60; *Aspen Insurance UK Ltd v Pectel Ltd* [2009] Lloyd's Rep IR 440; *Eagle Star Insurance Co Ltd v Cresswell* [2004] Lloyd's Rep IR 537.

10 *Friends Provident Life & Pensions Ltd v Sirius International Insurance Corp* [2005] 2 Lloyd's Rep 517.

11 *Milton Keynes BC v Nulty* [2013] Lloyd's Rep IR 243.

7.13 The IA 2015 reformed this area of law. With regards to warranties, by its section 10, the IA 2015 introduced a new type of remedy. Accordingly, if the warranty of a consumer or business insurance contract is breached, the insurer is not liable for the loss that occurs during the period that the assured's breach of warranty continues. Whilst at the pre-IA 2015 era the law did not allow the assured to reinstate the insurance cover by remedying the breach of a warranty, the IA 2015 enables the assured to remedy the breach so long as it is possible.[12] Hence, the insurer is not liable for the loss that occurs from the moment the assured breached the warranty until the breach is remedied. Once the assured complies with the warranty again, the cover that was suspended from the moment of the breach is lifted. Moreover, the IA 2015 s 10(2) provides that the insurer is not liable for any loss that is attributable to the happening of an event that occurs during the period that the cover is suspended because of the breach of a warranty.

7.14 With regards to conditions and conditions precedent, section 11 was introduced by the IA 2015. What has to be noted here is that the scope of section 11 is not limited to conditions or conditions precedent only, as section 11 applies to insurance contract terms irrespective of their technical classifications. Hence, with regards to remedies for breach of an insurance condition, references should be made to section 11 of the IA 2015 and the common law. In relation to breach of a warranty, references will be made to section 10 and section 11 of the IA 2015.[13]

7.15 The abovementioned rules are irrelevant so far as the third party victim's claim is concerned. However, whether the insurer may recoup against the person insured after compensating the third party victim, in other words, if the relevant restrictions may be argued against the assured[14] depends on the application of sections 10 and 11 of the IA 2015.

Terms that are not relevant to actual loss (IA 2015 s 11)

7.16 With regards to terms that do not define the risk as a whole but aim at reducing the risk of loss as identified under section 11, the Act introduced some novel law reforms with respect to insurers' ability to reject or limit liability on the basis of a breach of a contractual term. Sections 10 and 11 of the IA 2015 apply to consumer as well as business insurance policies. Moreover, these sections may not be contracted out to the detriment of a consumer assured.[15] If the transparency requirement under sections 16–17 of the IA 2015 is satisfied, sections 10 and 11 of the Act may be contracted out in favour of the insurer in respect of a business assured.

7.17 The traditional position mentioned above could operate stringently against the assured and might be described as disproportionate at times; however, the pre-IA 2015 connection between the classification of a particular term and the remedy attached to such categorisation used to provide clear-cut remedies. The IA 2015 did not abolish this firmness entirely. However, in certain defined circumstances set out in s 11, the IA 2015

---

12 IA 2015 s 10(2).
13 IA 2015 s 11(4) provides that section 11 may apply together with section 10.
14 Those restrictions would be the basis of no obligation to cover towards the assured.
15 IA 2015 s 15.

now restricts the insurer's power to deny liability against the assured in reliance only of the form of the relevant term of the insurance contract.

7.18 Section 11 of the IA 2015 entails an analysis that consists of several stages to find out whether or not the insurer can argue the express contractual defence against the assured. The very first step is to identify the purpose of the term in the policy and this will be done on the basis of two different criteria: Does the term define the risk as a whole; and if not, does the term tend to reduce the risk of loss under the categories enumerated by s 11(1)? Two initial, but very crucial, outcomes flow from this distinction. First, if the contractual clause in question is of a type that defines the risk as a whole, the s 11 assessments are not carried forward, as that category of terms falls outside the next stage of the application of section 11. In such a case, the insurer will return to the consequences of the breach of contract determined by s 10 of the IA 2015 or, by the common law, or by contract, as the case may be. Second, if the relevant clause is construed as risk-mitigating but not risk defining as a whole, the s 11 assessments continue, and the assured may take the opportunity of proving what s 11(3) entails, namely that the non-compliance with the term of the policy could not have increased the risk of loss in the way the risk has occurred. This exercise is fundamentally important: if the assured satisfies the burden of proof as set out under s 11(3), the insurer will be prevented from denying liability for the assured's non-compliance with the term in question.

7.19 The category of terms that are listed under s 11(1) as those that are subject to the s 11(3) assessments is clauses which, if complied with, would tend to reduce the risk of one or more of the following:

(a) loss of a particular kind;
(b) loss at a particular location;
(c) loss at a particular time.

7.20 The facts of *Dawsons v Bonnin*[16] would be a suitable analogy to explain how section 11 would operate under the circumstances that *Dawsons* was discussed. The assured declared in *Dawsons* that the insured lorry would be garaged at 46 Cadogan Street, but, in fact, it was garaged in the assured's premises on the outskirts of Glasgow. The application of strict technical rules created an outcome that was in favour of the insurer at the time. However, under the IA 2015 s 11, the Court would ask if the statement in relation to where the vehicle was to be garaged is a term that defines the risk as a whole. The answer is most likely to be that it is not. Following that the relevant term is to be classified as aiming to reduce the risk of loss as stipulated by s 11. The fact that the assured's premises on the outskirts of Glasgow was a safer place than Cadogan Street to keep the vehicle would lead to an outcome in favour of the assured. It would be because section 11(3) of the IA 2015 entitles the assured to claim under the insurance contract, if non-compliance with the risk mitigating term did not increase the risk of loss in the way that the loss has occurred. Consequently, the assured's non-compliance clearly cannot be argued against the third party, but, because of section 11(3), the insurer will not be able to recoup against the assured for the compensation for the third party victim's loss either.

---

16 [1922] 2 AC 413.

CONTROL OF POLICY TERMS

7.21 The technical classification of the restriction, whether as a warranty or condition, in the insurance contract is irrelevant so far as section 11(3) applies to the facts in question. If the relevant contractual term falls outside section 11(3) because the term defines the risk as whole, the remedy against the assured as available either under IA 2015 s 10, or, if the Act is contracted out, the remedy as determined either by the contract or by the common law will still be arguable. Consequently, the insurer may recoup against the assured for compensating the third party's loss.

Suspensory conditions

7.22 Some attempts by the judges to overcome the harsh consequences of the application of the pre-determined remedies to contractual breaches were observed in the pre-IA 2015 era.[17] One of the obvious illustrations of this was seen in *Farr v Motor Traders' Mutual Insurance Society*[18] where the assured insured his two taxicabs against accidental external damages by declaring as the basis of the contract that the two insured vehicles were to be used for public hire and that each vehicle would be used in one shift only. The two taxicabs had been in operation as declared, but one of the taxicabs was used for two shifts whilst the other was under repair. An accident occurred after the repair was completed, and the non-compliance with what had been declared pre-contractually had no relevance to the actual loss. The Court found that the insurance cover was suspended during the days that the taxi was used for two shifts but the suspension was lifted when the two cabs were again used for one shift each.[19]

7.23 In *Farr v Motor Traders' Mutual Insurance Society* the difficulties with the remedy applicable arose because the assured's declaration in the proposal form in respect of the number of shifts that each vehicle to be used at was made as the basis of the contract by the policy of insurance. The basis of the contract clauses was capable of rendering the statements made in the proposal form as warranties.[20] The clauses of that type were abolished in consumer[21] as well as in business[22] insurance contracts. Moreover, it is not possible to contract out of the statutory provisions that rendered the basis of the contract clauses unenforceable in insurance contracts.[23]

7.24 As well as abolishing the basis of the contract clauses, the IA 2015 ss 10 and 11 have overcome the difficulties such as those observed in *Farr*. However, it should always be remembered that the application of s 11, as discussed above, will largely be subject to the Courts' interpretation of what constitutes "a term that defines the risk as a whole." Whether a term defines the risk as a whole may be determined by asking if "what is intended by that term is to define the risk which the insurer is prepared to accept by way of the insurance contract." If the answer is in the positive, section 11(3) will not

---

17 July 2014 report [12.5].

18 [1920] 3 KB 669.

19 More recently, in *Bluebon Ltd v Ageas (UK) Ltd (Formerly Fortis Insurance Ltd)* [2017] EWHC 3301 (Comm), after a very lengthy discussion on identifying warranties in insurance contracts, the judge ruled that the clause expressly worded as a warranty was a suspensory condition.

20 [1922] 2 AC 413.

21 Consumer Insurance (Disclosure and Representations) Act 2012 (CIDRA), s 6.

22 IA 2015 s 9.

23 IA 2015, s 16(1), CIDRA, s 10.

intervene, and the remedy available under section 10 of the IA 2015 or by the common law will apply. The restriction discussed in *Farr v Motor Traders' Mutual Insurance Society*[24] would be of a risk defining type as the Court held in that case that the relevant restriction described and therefore limited the risk to be run. This, however, does not mean that the assured in *Farr* is in a worse position than he was before the IA 2015. What the IA 2015 provides now is, when a term defines the risk as a whole, the insurer may rely on either s 10 of the IA 2015 or, if the IA 2015 is contracted out, may seek the contractual or the common law remedy, as the case may be. Hence, under the IA 2015 the assured in *Farr* is entitled to have the same outcome but this time not by way of the Court's interpretation but under the statutory rules of the IA 2015.

7.25 Similarly, revisiting *Provincial Insurance Co Ltd v Morgan & Foxon*[25] would ensure that the above analysis is the correct interpretation of the law. In *Provincial* the assured stated in the proposal form that the vehicle would be used to carry coal. On the other hand, one day only, it was loaded of some timber as well as coal. After delivering timber and on the way to delivery of the coal the lorry was involved in a collision. The assured was held to recover under the policy but the focus was, due to the technical application of the remedy for the breach, on the parties' intention which, according to the Court, was not expressed as clearly as required.

7.26 Under the IA 2015, a case as such will be regarded as outside the scope of section 11(3) as the insurer defined the risk as a whole, as carriage of coal only. However, the assured would still succeed his claim against the insurer, because of the new remedy available under section 10 of the IA 2015. Accordingly, since section 11(3) is not available for the assured, the insurer, in theory, can rely on section 10. However, section 10 provides that the cover is suspended until the assured complies with the warranty again. The accident in *Provincial* occurred after the breach was remedied by the assured. Unless the insurer proves that the loss is attributable to something that happened during the time that the assured breached the warranty, the insurer is liable for the loss.

7.27 In this respect, for instance, a policy exclusion covering "any accident loss or damage caused or sustained while any motorcycle in respect of which indemnity is granted under this policy is carrying a passenger unless a sidecar is attached"[26] would be inoperative against a victim; however, with respect to assured against insurer, this term is to be interpreted as a term that defines the risk as a whole. This is because the insurer agreed to insure the risk only when a sidecar is attached. At the time the RTA 1930 was in force, in *Bright v Ashfold*[27] this clause was interpreted as circumscribing the operation of the policy from the beginning and leaving the claim uninsured. An accident occurred whilst a motorcycle was on a road with another person sitting behind him as a passenger on the pillion without a sidecar being attached to the motorcycle. Lord Hewart CJ held that there was no policy of insurance against third party risks at all in force in relation to the use of the motorcycle by the respondent, where a passenger was being carried otherwise than in a sidecar. The policy wording is unlikely to be interpreted today as affecting the policy from the outset rendering the user uninsured; however, in any case,

---

24 [1920] 3 KB 669.
25 [1933] AC 240.
26 *Bright v Ashfold* [1932] 2 KB 153.
27 [1932] 2 KB 153.

Conditions and conditions precedents after the IA 2015

7.28 As mentioned above, the IA 2015 section 11 applies to insurance contracts irrespective of the technical classification of the contractual terms. Therefore, breaches of conditions or conditions precedent, remedy of which used to be determined by the common law or by the contractual clauses, are now to be assessed by s 11 of the IA 2015.[28]

7.29 Claims provisions are of a different category than the terms that are addressed by section 11. The effect of breach of a claim provision will be discussed later in this chapter.

Restrictions referred to under the RTA 1988 s 148(2)

7.30 For each restriction it should be asked whether, by that term, the parties intended to define the risk that the insurer is prepared to accept by way of the insurance contract.

7.31 Under the abovementioned test, the age limitations (s 148(2)(a)), against the assured, would fall outside the scope of section 11 as that restriction tends to describe the risk as a whole rather than falling under the risk mitigation clauses listed under section 11(1) of the IA 2015.[29] On the other hand, again, under subsection 2(a), fitness of driver to use vehicle, clauses in relation to alcohol and drugs would be regarded as risk mitigating.[30]

7.32 The Law Commission's guidance in respect of the scope of section 11 of the IA 2015 was that (un)roadworthiness of the vehicle would not be of a type that describes the risk as a whole.[31] Therefore, s 148(2)(b)) would be subject to section 11(3) assessment in the relationship between the assured and the insurer.

7.33 Restrictions with regards to persons that the vehicle carries (s 148(2)(c) and (d) are likely to be assessed as risk mitigating.

7.34 A clause exempting the insurer from liability for damage caused or arising whilst the car was "conveying any load in excess of that for which it was constructed" was disputed in *Houghton v Trafalgar Insurance Co Ltd*[32] where the claimant was involved in an accident when there were six persons in the vehicle. The insurer argued that the load here was in excess of that for which the car was constructed, in that one passenger was seated on the knees of another and the seating accommodation was all occupied. The Court stated that if it was desired to exclude the insurance cover by reason of the fact that there was at the back one passenger more than the seating accommodation, that should have been stated more clearly so that the assured would have it drawn to his particular attention. The Court noted in *Houghton* that this clause was more apt to a situation where there was a weight load specified in respect of the motor vehicle, whether a lorry or van.

---

28 And sections 15–17 of the IA 2015 with regards to contracting out of section 11.

29 This is also in line with the list of examples that would describe the risk as whole by the Law Commission. See Stakeholder Note: Terms Not Relevant to the Actual Loss, at [.1.8, reproduced in HL Paper No.81, at p 47. See also Merkin/Gürses, *Insurance Contracts after the Insurance Act 2015* [2016] 132 *L.Q.R.*, 457.

30 Eg "The company shall not be liable . . . in respect of bodily injury . . . sustained whilst under the influence of drugs or intoxicating liquor." *Louden v British Merchants Insurance Co* [1961] 1 Lloyd's Rep 154.

31 Stakeholder Note: Terms Not Relevant to the Actual Loss, at [1.18(2)].

32 [1954] 1 QB 247.

7.35 It appears in *Houghton* that the Court held that the restriction did not apply to the facts in question, but it would have applied if the issue had focused on a weight load specified in respect of the motor vehicle. Under the IA 2015, whether with regards to the number of passengers or weight load specifications, the link between breach of a term similar to that in *Houghton* and the loss will be analysed under section 11(3) of the IA 2015.

7.36 The time at which or the areas within which the vehicle is used (s 148(2)(e)) may or may not be risk defining depending on the wording of the contract. The time restriction is likely to fall under section 11 and therefore subsection (3). However, the geographical limitation tends to describe the risk as whole.[33]

7.37 Terms in relation to the horsepower or cylinder capacity or value of the vehicle (s 148(2)(f)) would describe the risk as a whole.

7.38 Terms in relation to the carrying on the vehicle of any particular apparatus (s 148(2) (g)), and the carrying on the vehicle of any particular means of identification other than any means of identification required to be carried by or under the [Vehicle Excise and Registration Act 1994] (s 148(2)(h)), depending on their wording, are likely to be classified as a risk mitigating term.

Conditions in relation to driving license

7.39 Where injuries caused by a driver who does not hold a driving licence is excluded from the insurance cover, such an exclusion will be ineffective against the victim under section 151(3), but the insurer may, after having compensated the victim, recoup against the person who caused the injury.[34] This will be a term that defines the risk as a whole under section 11. It should nevertheless be noted that unless otherwise expressly stated, the condition that the driver is to hold a valid driving licence is complied with in the case the driver is holding a provisional licence.[35]

Claims provisions

7.40 It should be borne in mind that one area that the IA 2015 left unscathed is claims provisions. Claims provisions are not written as a warranty. Therefore, they are outside the scope of section 10 in any event. They are neither risk defining, nor risk mitigating for the purposes of section 11. Claims provisions, which appear either in the form of a claim co-operation or a claims control clause, tend to apply after the insured risk has occurred. They may be classified contractually either as a mere condition or condition precedent. Since they fall outside the scope of sections 10 and 11 of the IA 2015, the common law remedies as established for mere conditions and conditions precedent apply as mentioned above and the insurer may recoup against the assured after compensating the third party's loss.

7.41 Section 148(5) renders ineffective remedies for breach of claims provisions so far as liabilities covered by section 145 are concerned. This means that an insurer may not argue either the prejudice that the insurer suffered as a result of the breach of a claim

---

33 Stakeholder Note: Terms Not Relevant to the Actual Loss, at [1.8], reproduced in HL Paper No.81, p 47.
34 RTA 1988 s 151(7)(a).
35 *Rendlesham v Dunne* [1964] 1 Lloyd's Rep 192.

provision by the assured or may not claim that he was discharged from liability automatically for the loss that the third party claimed because the assured failed to comply with a claim provision. However, under subsection 6, section 148 reserves the insurer's right to enforce a policy term towards the assured to the effect that the insurer, after compensating the third party's loss, may seek the contractual remedy towards the assured by way of recoupment for the amount paid to the third party victim.

7.42 Rendering due observance of terms of an insurance contract to be a condition precedent to insurers' liability is not uncommon.[36] Whether or not a breach of a policy term will entitle the insurer to recoup against the assured depends on the function of the term in the insurance contract. If it is a risk defining warranty, section 10 of the IA 2015 will apply; if it is a risk defining condition precedent, the common law remedy or contractual remedy will apply; if it is a risk mitigating term, section 11(3) will be considered. The only area where this above-mentioned clause will be effective without considering the IA 2015 is if the term breach of which is disputed is a claim provision. As claims provisions are left intact by the IA 2015, the common law remedy will apply. This wording creates a condition precedent to insurer's liability, and the insurer will be discharged from liability automatically for the loss that is tainted by the breach.[37]

Notification provisions

7.43 A typical example of a claims provision may be in the following words:

> The insured or his legal personal representatives shall give notice in writing to . . . the company as soon as possible after the occurrence of any accident and/or loss and/or damage with full particulars thereof. Every letter claim writ summons and/or process shall be notified or forwarded to the company immediately on receipt. Notice shall also be given in writing to the company immediately. The insured or his legal personal representatives shall have knowledge of any impending prosecution or inquest in connection with any accident for which there may be liability under the policy.

Notice may be given to the insurer or to the broker who has been given the authority to receive notifications on behalf of the insurer. This authorisation may be expressed or might be inferred from the relationship between the insurer and the broker in the case in question.[38]

"As soon as possible"

7.44 Notification provisions are varied; they may require immediate notice has to be given or may set a fixed time for giving notice, or the assured may be required to give notice "as soon as possible." The interpretation of each clause is different. Further, whether the notification clause is complied with is a matter to be decided on the facts of each case. All existing circumstances are taken into account in determining whether a given notice was in time. *Verelst's Administratrix v Motor Union Insurance Co Ltd.*[39] was described as

---

36 For instance see the wording of the two policies discussed in *Gale v Motor Union Insurance Co Ltd* [1928] 1 KB 359; *Verelst's Administratrix v Motor Union Insurance Co Ltd.* [1925] 2 KB 137.

37 *Aspen Insurance UK Ltd v Pectel Ltd* [2009] Lloyd's Rep IR 440.

38 *Herbert v Railway Passengers Assurance Co* (1938) 60 Ll L Rep 143.

39 [1925] 2 KB 137.

an exceptional case where the insurance contract was for a payment of some amount to the assured's legal personal representatives upon her death as a result of a motor accident. The policy required notification of such accident, injury, damage or loss as soon as possible after it has come to the knowledge of the assured's representative. The assured was killed in a motor accident in January 1923. The assured's representatives found out about the existence of the policy of insurance in January 1924. Roche J held that the notice given to the insurance company as soon as possible thereafter complied with the notice provision. Further, the judge noted that the insurer suffered no prejudice as a result of the notification one year after the assured's death. In the somewhat exceptional circumstances of this case there was not any default or even extraordinary delay.

Claim co-operation clauses

7.45 A typical claim co-operation clause would require the assured not to admit liability or settle the claim with the third party before seeking the insurer's consent on this matter. One of the situations where claim co-operation clauses could be disputed was when the assured and the third party had entered into a knock-for-knock agreement which had been observed principally in relation to damage to vehicles caused by a collision.[40] If a collision occurred between two vehicles, each insured with different insurers, and damage resulted to one or both, each insurer bore its own loss (in respect of Own Damage) and waived any right of recovery one from the other on the ground of fault.[41] For instance, in *Bell Assurance Association v Licenses & General Insurance Corp & Guarantee Fund Ltd*[42] the agreement provided:

> On the occurrence of a collision between a vehicle insured with one of the above mentioned companies and a vehicle insured with the other above mentioned company, each company shall bear the cost of making good the damage (if any) actually caused by such collision to the vehicle insured with itself.

7.46 In *Tustin v Arnold*[43] the issue was admission of liability by an illiterate servant of the assured who signed a document which admits liability for a collision with another car as a result of which the assured paid the other party's losses. Under the policy the assured was required not to make any admission of liability to or otherwise negotiate with any person in respect of whom indemnity is or may be claimed under the policy. The Court rejected the insurer's reliance on breach of this clause as the driver did not have the defendant's authority to make the admission of liability, and the document signed by him did not amount to breach of contract by the assured.

7.47 As appears above, the term knock for knock was described as being coarse,[44] but it was expressive and had been generally adopted before and after the 1930 Act.[45] Nevertheless, they were abandoned in the 1990s.[46]

---

40 G.W. Gilbert, *Motor Insurance*, London, Sir Isaac Pitman & Sons, Ltd, 1933, p 98.
41 Gilbert, p 98.
42 (1923) 17 Ll L Rep 100.
43 (1915) 84 LJKB 2214 taken from Gilbert, p 153–154.
44 Gilbert, p 98.
45 See Gilbert, p 98.
46 Merkin/Hemsworth, [2–145].

What is insured under compulsory motor third party liability insurance?

7.48 Motor insurance policies include a schedule placed either at the head or foot thereof, containing particulars of the vehicle to be insured. The schedule include particulars of the car, the assured's name, address and occupation, the date when the proposal was made, the period of insurance, the amount of premium, renewal date and the date when the policy was signed.[47]

7.49 The term "insured vehicle" is a short form of expressing the insured person's interest in the vehicle.[48] One view expressed that so far as the compulsory third party liability is concerned, there is no such thing in law as an "insured vehicle";[49] insurance contract covers damage caused by the policyholder and by other persons expressly authorised in that policy to drive the vehicle.[50] On the other hand it has been also argued that it is probably more accurate today to describe policies as attaching to the vehicle rather than to its driver as a result of the changes in the law on compulsory cover introduced since 1987 by way of the implementation of the EU Motor Insurance Directives.[51] The Consolidated Directive Art 3[52] requires Member States to establish, in their domestic legal systems, a general obligation to insure vehicles.[53] Section 143 of the RTA 1988 complies with this.

7.50 Although the Attorney General in *Churchill Insurance Co Ltd v Wilkinson*[54] noted that, unlike in most of the other Member States of the European Union, in the UK what is insured is not the vehicle but the policyholder, it is submitted that, as discussed under the meaning of "use" and "user" of a vehicle in Chapter 5 and extension causes in Chapter 3, what is required to be insured is the use of the vehicle; in other words, for each user of a vehicle liability insurance is compulsory. Most recently Lord Sumption confirmed in *Cameron v Liverpool Victoria Insurance Co Ltd*[55] that "policies of motor insurance in the United Kingdom normally cover drivers rather than vehicles."

Permitted exclusions from cover

RTA 1988 section 145(4)

7.51 Under section 145(4) of the RTA 1988 a policy may exclude cover for

   (a)   liability in respect of the death, arising out of and in the course of his employment, of a person in the employment of a person insured by the policy or of bodily injury sustained by such a person arising out of and in the course of his employment,[56] or

---

47 Gilbert, p 9.

48 *Bell Assurance Association v Licenses & General Insurance Corp & Guarantee Fund Ltd* (1923) 17 Ll L Rep 100, p 101.

49 *Bell Assurance Association v Licenses & General Insurance Corp & Guarantee Fund Ltd* (1923) 17 Ll L Rep 100, p 101.

50 *Churchill Insurance Co Ltd v Wilkinson* (C-442/10) [2012] Lloyd's Rep IR 544, [1].

51 Merkin/Hemsworth, [3–42].

52 Previously, Art 3(1) of the First Directive, Council Directive 72/166/EEC.

53 *Csonka v Magyar Allam* (C-409/11) [2014] 1 CMLR 14 [24].

54 (C-442/10) [2012] Lloyd's Rep IR 544, [1].

55 [2019] UKSC 6 [5].

56 Employees position is analysed in detail in Chapter 3.

(b)　more than [£1,200,000]⁵⁷ in respect of all such liabilities as may be incurred in respect of damage to property caused by, or arising out of, any one accident involving the vehicle, or

(c)　to cover liability in respect of damage to the vehicle, or

(d)　to cover liability in respect of damage to goods carried for hire or reward in or on the vehicle or in or on any trailer (whether or not coupled) drawn by the vehicle, or

(e)　to cover any liability of a person in respect of damage to property in his custody or under his control, or

(f)　to cover any contractual liability.

7.52 The difference between sections 145(4) and 148(2) is that the former may be argued against the victim who claims the damage arose out of a traffic accident. Section 145(4) was interpreted as not being an exhaustive list of exclusions. Support was found from the wording of the statute which did not state that this is an exclusive list.[58] It follows that other forms of liability may be excluded by agreement between insurer and assured. The Cassel Committee on Compulsory Insurance, reporting in 1937, had recommended that a preferable approach would be to prohibit all policy terms other than those specifically identified in a list rather than to retain a list of unenforceable provisions contained in section 12 of the Road Traffic Act 1934, but that recommendation had not been accepted and section 12 had been retained in successive codifications of the legislation including section 148 of the 1988 Act. Ward LJ dismissed that the report would help the interpretation of section 145(4) as it was history of the section.[59]

7.53 It was confirmed in *Ul-Haq v CEVA logistics Ltd*[60] that EU law did not require policies to cover loss based on damage to the insured vehicle. A motor vehicle insurance policy may be in a comprehensive form that covers both third party as well as first party loss.[61] However, the owner is not obliged to purchase a first party cover.

Social, domestic, pleasure purposes

7.54 One of the obvious risk assessment features of a motor vehicle policy is the purpose of the use throughout the currency of the policy.[62] It is a common form of exclusion that insurers may limit the insurance cover to the use of the vehicle for "social, domestic or pleasure purpose" only.[63] Such a restriction historically was described as comprehensive and fairly easy to understand.[64] Where insurers received a premium for social, domestic and/or pleasure purposes, they do not wish to find themselves liable for a claim arising out of a business use, which the insurance market regard as a greater risk than the ordinary

---

57 The amount previously was "£1,000,000" which was substituted by Motor Vehicles (Compulsory Insurance) Regulations 2016/1193 Reg 2(2) (31 December 2016).

58 *Bristol Alliance Ltd Partnership v Williams* [2013] RTR 9, Ward LJ, [39].

59 *Bristol Alliance Ltd Partnership v Williams* [2013] RTR 9, [44], [50].

60 [2012] CLY 1903.

61 *Patel v London Transport Executive* [1981] RTR 29.

62 *Passmore v Vulcan Boiler & General Insurance Co Ltd* (1936) 54 Ll L Rep 92, 94.

63 *RoadPeace v Secretary of State for Transport* [2018] 1 WLR 1293.

64 Gilbert, p 24.

domestic risk.[65] If the policy covers for social, domestic and pleasure purposes and also covers the person who drives the vehicle with the assured's consent or permission and the person who drives it with the permission but for purposes other than social or domestic, the policy would not meet the accident.[66]

7.56 Section 148 does not expressly refer to the limitation to "social domestic or pleasure purpose" only, and the validity of this phrase has been subject to numerous challenges before the English Courts. Ward LJ said in *Bristol Alliance Ltd Partnership v Williams*[67] that section 145(4) was not an exhaustive list of permitted exclusions from cover. Moreover, his Lordship interpreted section 148(2) as an exhaustive list of exceptions which permit other exclusions to be effective.[68] Ward LJ noted that the validity of such time-honoured limitations on use had never been doubted.[69]

7.57 More recently, in *RoadPeace v Secretary of State for Transport*[70] Ouseley J rejected the argument that *Ruiz Bernaldez*[71] *Candolin v Vahinkovakuutusosakeyhtio Pohjola*[72] and Fideliade *Fidelidade-Companhia de Seguros SA v Caisse Suisse de Compensation* (C-287/16)[73] require nullifying the effect of this restriction.

7.58 A further development since *Bristol* was decided was *Vnuk v Zavarovalnica Triglav dd*[74] in which "normal function of the vehicle" was emphasised with regards to the scope of the compulsory insurance. Ouseley J found what the CJEU meant by normal function of the vehicle in *Vnuk* was unclear and many issues were left for debate. For instance, did the CJEU mean "the normal function of the type of vehicle" or "of the particular vehicle in question"? Further, if types, how are they broken down into different types? Hence, *Vnuk* did not support the argument, in Ouseley J's view that, that the Directives require that any use of a vehicle required compulsory insurance.

The essential character of the journey

7.59 The "essential character" of the journey may be described as the "primary purpose" of the journey.[75] This question indicates singularity: one essential character or one primary purpose of the journey. In each case it is a matter of fact to determine the purpose of the journey and the facts of particular cases will vary infinitely in their detail.[76] For instance, going home after work for a taxi driver who uses his own car as a cab will be

---

65 *Seddon v Binions* [1978] RTR 163, 169, Roskill LJ.

66 *Browning v Phoenix Assurance Co Ltd* [1960] 2 Lloyd's Rep 360; *Singh v Rathour* [1988] RTR 324. If such consent is given and relied upon under the terms of such a policy, it is important to consider what effect on the facts of the particular case the condition or limitation imposed upon the consent by the owner may have.

67 [2013] RTR 9 [45].

68 Ibid.

69 Ibid.

70 [2018] 1 WLR 1293.

71 (C-129/94) [1996] ECR I-1847.

72 (C-537/03) [2006] Lloyd's Rep IR 209.

73 [2017] RTR 26. *Churchill Insurance Co Ltd v Wilkinson* (C-442/10) [2012] Lloyd's Rep IR 544 was applied. Merkin/Hemsworth, [3–42].

74 *Vnuk v Zavarovalnica Triglav dd* (C-162/13) [2015] Lloyd's Rep IR 142.

75 *Seddon v Binions* [1978] RTR 163, 173, Megaw LJ.

76 *Seddon v Binions* [1978] RTR 163, 169, Roskill LJ; *Caple v Sewell* [2002] Lloyd's Rep IR 627, Rix LJ, [29].

for social and domestic purposes.[77] Further, if the essential character of the journey in question consists of use for a criminal purpose (as when a burglar takes his car out for a night of burgling other people's houses) then the car will not be being used for "social, domestic or pleasure purposes."[78]

7.60 The purpose has to be determined at the time when the incident occurred and not at the start of the journey as the essential character of the drive may change during the course of the journey.[79] In *AXN v Worboys*,[80] although the ride was for public hire from the victims' perspective, the primary character for the taxi driver changed by the time the claimants were sedated and assaulted.[81] On the other hand in *Keeley v Pashen*[82] the essential character of the journey remained unchanged when the driver, for 16 seconds, unwisely deviated and drove towards the claimants by 15 mph to frighten them. The Court held that the ride was for social and domestic purposes as the driver was, after working as a cab driver, driving home.

Borderline cases

7.61 Borderline cases are difficult as it is not possible to state any firm principle under which it can always be predicated which side of the line a particular case will fall.[83] Additionally, a finding may properly depend upon a wider context than the narrowest facts relating to the particular journey or use in question. In the words of Rix LJ, one "should not be blinkered" and should not neglect some wider considerations.[84]

7.62 In *Jones v Welsh Insurance Corp Ltd*[85] T, who worked for a motor omnibus company, bought five sheep to keep them, as he said, for a hobby. T hired the grazing on two acres so that he could pasture his sheep there till the weather was good enough to turn them out on the mountain. T had an accident when he was on the way to his father to bring two sheep and two lambs to their father's house to make some arrangement with his father to pasture them on his land. The intention was held to be the selling of the sheep to butchers or farmers to make a little extra money to supplement T's wages as a mechanic. It followed that at the time of the accident the insured vehicle was being used for the carriage of goods in connection with the business of sheep farming.

7.63 The objective is to determine a single essential character of the journey. Guidance is therefore needed to identify the primary purpose where seemingly there are more than one motivations of the journey.

Multiple characters of the journey

7.64 In some cases it may be clear that there are dual purposes and none of the purposes was more important or more essential than the other. In *Passmore v Vulcan Boiler*

---

77 *Keeley v Pashen* [2005] Lloyd's Rep IR 289.
78 Ibid, [19].
79 [2013] Lloyd's Rep IR 207.
80 Ibid.
81 Ibid.
82 [2005] Lloyd's Rep IR 289.
83 *Seddon v Binions* [1978] RTR 163, 169, Roskill LJ.
84 *Caple v Sewell* [2002] Lloyd's Rep IR 627, Rix LJ, [29].
85 (1937) 59 Ll L Rep 13.

CONTROL OF POLICY TERMS

& General Insurance Co Ltd[86] both C and P, representatives of the Realsilk Hosiery Company, were travelling to a place where they were planning to sell the products of the company. C was travelling also for her own business. An accident occurred due to P's fault whose insurance provided cover for "use for social domestic and pleasure purposes and use for the business of the insured," and it excluded cover in respect of any accident caused while the insured motor vehicle is being used other than in accordance with the "description of use." Due to the dual purpose of the use the accident fell outside the insurance cover.[87]

7.65 *Passmore* was applied in *McGoona v Motor Insurers' Bureau*[88] where the company who employed both M and K agreed to pay K £4.6 a day if K gave a lift to fellow employees. M was injured at an accident that occurred while K was taking M to work under this arrangement. K's insurance coverage was limited to "Use for Social, Domestic and Pleasure purposes and use by the Policyholder *in person* in connection with his business or profession as stated herein." Because of the fact that K agreed to accept payment to take fellow workmen down, he was acting not only for the purposes of his own business as a plumber but for the purposes of his employers' business, and the accident did not fall under the description of the policy cover.

7.66 *Passmore* is to be distinguished where the Court prefers to investigate a single essential motive of the journey. Megaw LJ said in *Seddon v Binions*,[89]

> If there be such a primary purpose, or essential character, then the Courts should not be meticulous to seek to find some possible secondary purpose, or some inessential character, the result of which could be suggested to be that the use of the car fell outside the proper use for the purposes to which cover was given by the insurance policy.[90]

In *Seddon v Binions* at the time of the accident the father was driving his son's car from his son's business to his home for lunch. An employee of the son was also in the vehicle to be taken to dentist. The son's vehicle was fully insured, and the father's own liability insurance covered him when he was driving a motor vehicle other than his own for social domestic and pleasure purposes and for purposes of his own business. The son's insurers sought contribution from the father's liability insurers. Whilst the trial judge found double elements (domestic purpose: going home for lunch; and the element of business user: taking the employee back home early) and held that the excluded element prevails; the Court of Appeal approached it differently but reached the same conclusion. The father's insurers were not to contribute to the insured loss as he was using the son's car for the son's business purpose.

7.67 A single essential motive was also identified in *Caple v Sewell*[91] where an accident occurred in Poole Harbour, when a powerboat, in the course of a demonstration with two other powerboats, collided with a Sea-Doo Explorer.[92] C, a photographer working for a local newspaper was injured in that collision. The essential character of the use

---

86 (1936) 54 Ll L Rep 92.
87 (1936) 54 Ll L Rep 92, 94, du Parcq J.
88 [1969] 2 Lloyd's Rep 34.
89 [1978] RTR 163, 174.
90 Ibid.
91 [2002] Lloyd's Rep IR 627.
92 A rigid inflatable boat.

of the boat at the time of the accident was demonstration purposes rather than those of commercial.[93] A press pre-view, during which the accident took place, was designed to generate pre-publicity for a public boat show due on the following date.

Motive to determine the essential character of the journey

7.68 As also appears, the critical factor primarily is the driver's intention at the time of the incident.[94] However, this rule is not absolute and may vary depending on the facts. In *Seddon* (1) the car belonged to the son, and (2) it was being taken on a journey by his father (3) at his son's request to take his son's employee home. The Court of Appeal in that case looked to the son's purposes in applying its test. It was not a case of the father using his own car, but a case of his using his son's car at his son's request to take his son's employee home. In *Caple* the Court of Appeal was concerned with only the Sea Do owner's boat and owner's insurance. One looks very much to the purpose of Sea-Doo's owner rather than to those of the photographer.[95] In *Jones v Welsh* the Court did not question the assured's brother (driver of the vehicle) but questioned the assured T's intention on the particular journey in question.[96]

Incidental deviations

7.69 The essential character of the journey is of a particular kind and does not change for incidental deviations such as in the way of giving a lift to a friend as an act of courtesy or charity.[97] Where the assured, as a matter of kindness, courtesy or charity, "gives a lift" to a friend or a colleague or even a stranger who is assisted in carrying on his business by the facilities which are given to him by the assured, the character of the journey remains unaltered. In the last mentioned example the essential character of this journey, from the assured's perspective, is not business. The assured was driving the vehicle for a social purpose, and it would not the less be used for a social purpose because the person benefiting by the courtesy was on business.[98] The outcome does not differ depending on the assured's knowledge on the passenger's business, which the assured may or may not know; the primary purpose of the journey remains as social and pleasure.

Hire and reward

7.70 The words "hire and reward" were said, at the time that the 1930 Act applied, to imply that if any consideration, direct or indirect, proceeds from the passenger or anyone on his behalf to the owner of the vehicle, then the latter must see to it that his policy includes an indemnity in respect of liability to such passenger.[99] The word

---

93 *Caple v Sewell* [2002] Lloyd's Rep IR 627, Rix LJ, [31].
94 [2013] Lloyd's Rep IR 207.
95 *Caple v Sewell* [2002] Lloyd's Rep IR 627, Rix LJ, [28].
96 The assured asked his brother to carry some sheep to his father's premises.
97 [1978] RTR 163, 170–171, Roskill LJ.
98 *Passmore v Vulcan Boiler & General Insurance Co Ltd* (1936) 54 Ll L Rep 92; approved in *Seddon v Binions* [1978] RTR 163, 170, 174.
99 Gilbert, 105.

"hiring" is interpreted broadly that it applies to the carrying of a person for reward.[100] Private motor car policies may cover only "use for social domestic and pleasure purposes" and exclude "use for hiring." In such a case if the assured carries a person in the motor vehicle for a reward, liability arising out of an accident during that journey will fall outside the insurance cover.[101] The reward is the consideration that takes this voyage out of "use for social domestic and pleasure purposes."[102] However, in any case, the RTA 1988 s 150 which is explored below should be borne in mind.

7.71 Further, if a person uses his motor vehicle as a cab and keeps his car at home, drives it from home at the beginning of his day's shift as a mini-cab driver; he then drives it for hire or reward while he was conveying passengers in it for that purpose; and he drives it back home at the end of his shift, his journey back home at the end of a days' shift is not used for hire or reward so long as his last fare-paying passengers of the day had left the car. In a case in which the cab driver unwisely deviates from his route by reversing down towards the men in order to frighten them this incidental deviation is not to be classified as a quite separate journey.[103] Neither does his visit to the controller at the mini-cab office on his way home change the character of the journey, again, so long as there is no evidence showing that somehow or other the period during which he used his car for hire or reward began and ended at the mini-cab office.

Car-sharing arrangements

7.72 The RTA 1988 section 150 makes a special provision for car sharing arrangements so that despite if a payment is made by the passengers the carriage is still regarded as being for social and domestic purposes. According to s 150(1), where a policy

    (a) restricts the insurance of the persons insured by the policy or the operation of the security (as the case may be) to use of the vehicle for specified purposes (for example, social, domestic and pleasure purposes) of a non-commercial character, or

    (b) excludes from that insurance or the operation of the security (as the case may be) –
        (i) use of the vehicle for hire or reward, or
        (ii) business or commercial use of the vehicle, or
        (iii) use of the vehicle for specified purposes of a business or commercial character,

then, for the purposes of the compulsory insurance requirement under RTA 1988 s 145, the use of a vehicle on a journey in the course of which one or more passengers are carried at separate fares shall, if the conditions specified in subsection (2) below are satisfied, be treated as falling within that restriction or as not falling within that exclusion (as the case may be).

7.73 The conditions listed under s 150(2) are

---

100 *Wyatt v Guildhall Insurance Company* [1937] 1 KB 653.
101 Ibid.
102 Ibid.
103 *Keeley v Pashen* [2005] Lloyd's Rep IR 289.

(a) The vehicle is not adapted to carry more than eight passengers and is not a motorcycle.

(b) The fare or aggregate of the fares paid in respect of the journey does not exceed the amount of the running costs of the vehicle for the journey (which for the purposes of this paragraph shall be taken to include an appropriate amount in respect of depreciation and general wear).

(c) The arrangements for the payment of fares by the passenger or passengers carried at separate fares were made before the journey began.

7.74 The above applies irrespective of however the restrictions or exclusions are framed or worded. Accordingly, *McGoona v Motor Insurers' Bureau*[104] could have fallen under section 150 if what was arranged was a car sharing between employees and satisfies the conditions of section 150.

Definition of assured

7.75 The policy cover may be restricted to some identified users only. This restriction will be insignificant so far as the victim is concerned: RTA 1988 s 151 requires an insurer to satisfy a judgment obtained by the victim of the user of the vehicle against the user whether or not the user is covered by the policy but, towards the assured, the insurer may recoup against him after compensating the victim. The policy may identify specifically the name of the assured who is insured as eg Mr B and Mrs B,[105] or "member of the assured's household,"[106] or the policyholder company's employee or in the case of a policy taken out by a company in a group, any person employed by an associated company.[107]

7.76 The common law position with regards to extension clauses was discussed in Chapter 3. It should be reiterated here that section 148(7) of the RTA 1988 provides:

> Notwithstanding anything in any enactment, a person issuing a policy of insurance under section 145 of this Act shall be liable to indemnify the persons or classes of persons specified in the policy in respect of any liability which the policy purports to cover in the case of those persons or classes of persons.

The EU dimension

7.77 As the CJEU decisions made it clear, derogations from a general rule are to be strictly construed.[108]

It is clear from the Directives that there cannot be any blanket derogation based on geography, intent or type of vehicle.[109] Article 3(1) of the First Directive (now Art 3(1) of the Consolidated Directive) precludes an insurer from being able to rely on statutory

---

104 [1969] 2 Lloyd's Rep 34.
105 *GFP Units v Monksfield* [1972] 2 Lloyd's Rep 79.
106 *English v Western* [1940] 2 KB 156.
107 *Biddle v Johnston* [1965] 2 Lloyd's Rep 121.
108 *Delaney v Secretary of State for Transport* [2015] Lloyd's Rep IR 441.
109 *Lewington v Motor Insurers' Bureau* [2018] Lloyd's Rep IR 562, [41].

provisions or contractual clauses to refuse to compensate third party victims of an accident caused by the insured vehicle.[110]

7.78 In view of the aim of ensuring protection, reiterated continuously by the Directives, Article 3(1) of the First Directive, as developed and supplemented by the Second and Third Directives, must be interpreted as meaning that compulsory motor insurance must enable third party victims of accidents caused by vehicles to be compensated for all the damage to property and injuries sustained by them, up to the amounts fixed in Article 1(2) of the Second Directive.[111] The CJEU's concern is that any other interpretation would have the effect of allowing Member States to limit payment of compensation to third party victims of a road-traffic accident to certain types of damage, thus bringing about disparities in the treatment of victims depending on where the accident occurred. Such an outcome is precisely what the Directives are intended to avoid.[112]

7.79 Article 13(1) of the Consolidated Directive renders void against a third party victim of a traffic accident the clauses that exclude insurer's liability in respect of the use of vehicles by

(a) persons who do not have express or implied authorisation to do so;

(b) persons who do not hold a licence permitting them to drive the vehicle concerned; and

(c) persons who are in breach of the statutory technical requirements concerning the condition and safety of the vehicle concerned.

The abovementioned exclusions may be invoked if and in so far as the victim may obtain compensation for the damage suffered from a social security body.[113]

7.80 The exclusion under Art 13(1)(a), however, may be invoked against persons who voluntarily entered the vehicle which caused the damage or injury, when the insurer can prove that they knew the vehicle was stolen.[114] This is a circumstance which victims themselves brought about.[115] In the case of vehicles stolen or obtained by violence, Member States may provide that the body specified in Article 10(1) is to pay compensation instead of the insurer under the conditions set out in paragraph 1 of this Article.[116] In such cases, in respect of damage to property, the compensation body may apply an excess of not more than EUR 250 to be borne by the victim.[117] The general rule otherwise is that insurers are not permitted to argue the deductible under the insurance contract against the third party victim. Article 17 of the Consolidated Directive provides:

> Insurance undertakings shall not require any party injured as a result of an accident to bear any excess as far as the insurance referred to in Article 3 is concerned.

---

110 *Ruiz Bernaldez* (C-129/94) [1996] All ER (EC) 741 [20].

111 Article 9 of Consolidated Directive.

112 *Ruiz Bernaldez* (C-129/94) [1996] All ER (EC) 741 [19].

113 Art 13(1), sub-para 3, Consolidated Directive.

114 Art 13(1), sub-para 2, Consolidated Directive; Art 2(1) Directive 84/5/EEC.

115 *Ruiz Bernaldez* (C-129/94) [1996] All ER (EC) 741 [21].

116 Art 13(2), Consolidated Directive. Where the vehicle is normally based in another Member State, that body can make no claim against any body in that Member State.

117 Art 13(2), Consolidated Directive.

7.81 Art 13(3) of the Consolidated Directive also disallows exclusions from the insurance cover for claims on the basis that a passenger knew or should have known that the driver of the vehicle was under the influence of alcohol or of any other intoxicating agent at the time of an accident. A clause to this effect in an insurance contract will be void in respect of the claims of such passenger but permissible against the driver or for a right of recourse to be given. This is a codification of a CJEU decision in *Ruiz Bernaldez*[118] in which the Court decided that a contractual clause excluding insurer's liability to pay compensation for the damage to property and personal injuries caused to third parties by the insured vehicle where the driver of the vehicle was intoxicated was incompatible with the Directives.

7.82 Consolidated Directive Art 13(1)(a) is codified under section 151(2)(b), and s 151(3) of the RTA 1988 is in parallel with Art 13(1)(b). Art 13(1)(c) appears under section 148(2) of the RTA 1988. Section 148 is analysed in this chapter.

Minimum coverage

7.83 The EU Directives do not attempt to harmonise the civil law principles that determine liability for losses that arise out of traffic accidents. The user's liability under the domestic law, whether fault based or strict, may therefore be determined without intervention of the Directives. By way of example, a national legislation may exclude the right of a motor vehicle driver, who caused the traffic accident by his own fault, to receive compensation for the material harm that he had suffered as a result of the death of his spouse who was a passenger in the vehicle that he was driving.[119]

7.84 The Directives' main concern is, once liability is established under national law, the Member States must ensure that such liability is covered by insurance. Further, the minimum levels of cover laid down in Article 9 of the Consolidated Directive must be provided, regardless of the type of liability applicable. Consequently, in the case of accidents to which that type of civil liability attaches, the Member State's domestic law may not lay down maximum limits for compensation which are lower than the said minimum amounts.[120] Moreover, where liability is established under national law, derogation and setting a lower limitation than that provided by Art 9 is not permitted on the basis that the driver responsible was not at fault.

The victim is the owner of the vehicle

7.85 Exclusion clauses that covered claims by the owner of the vehicle, the use of which was either insured or uninsured, have been disputed in a number of cases. In this context the words "the owner of the vehicle" should be read to include someone who is insured to drive the vehicle.[121] As those cases illustrate an owner may be injured

(1)   as the result of their own negligent driving;

(2)   as a passenger where the driver is a person covered by the owner's insurance;

---

118   (C-129/94) [1996] ECR I-1847.
119   *Neto de Sousa v Portugal* (C-506/16) EU:C:2017:642; [2018] Lloyd's Rep IR 118.
120   *Mendes Ferreira v Companhia de Seguros Mundial Confiança SA* (C-348/98) ECLI:EU:C:2000:442.
121   *Churchill Insurance Co Ltd v Fitzgerald* [2013] Lloyd's Rep IR 137, Aikens LJ, [28].

(3) as a passenger where the driver is not covered by the owner's insurance;

(4) as a pedestrian by a driver covered by the insurance, and also

(5) as a pedestrian by a driver not covered by the insurance; and

(6) as a pedestrian by a driver not covered by the insurance but he has caused or permitted uninsured use.

(1) Owner is the driver injured by their own negligence

7.86 This was discussed with regards to the scope of the compulsory insurance in Chapter 1. As was ruled by *Cooper v Motor Insurers' Bureau*[122] "any person" in section 145(3)(a) which expresses the scope of the compulsory insurance requirement does not include the driver of the vehicle at the time of the imagined risk. The loss is first party rather than third party, and there is coverage only if the policy itself contains the relevant extension. Further, Art 12(1) of the Consolidate Directive requires compulsory insurance to cover liability for personal injuries to all passengers, other than the driver, arising out of the use of a vehicle.

(2) Owner is a passenger and the driver is a person covered by the owner's insurance

7.87 The owner of a vehicle can recover. Article 12 of the Consolidated Directive provides that all passengers are entitled to the benefit of compulsory insurance.

As held by CJEU, under the EU law, compulsory motor vehicle insurance against civil liability in respect of the use of motor vehicles allows all passengers who are victims of an accident caused by a motor vehicle to be compensated for the injury or loss they have suffered.[123] The fact that the passenger concerned is the owner of the vehicle the driver of which caused the accident is irrelevant.[124] It follows that the legal position of the owner of the vehicle, present in the vehicle at the time of the accident as a passenger, is the same as that of any other passenger who is a victim of the accident.

(3) Owner is a passenger and the driver is not covered by the owner's insurance

7.88 The owner of a vehicle can recover. The rulings mentioned above under (2) are equally applicable to this situation. Article 12 of the Consolidated Directive provides that all passengers are entitled to the benefit of compulsory insurance.

7.89 The controversy arises here in respect of the insurer's right of recourse against the owner where he has caused or permitted uninsured use.[125]

---

122 [1985] QB 575.

123 *Churchill Insurance Co Ltd v Wilkinson* (C-442/10) [2012] Lloyd's Rep IR 544, [29].

124 *Candolin v Vahinkovakuutusosakeyhtio Pohjola* (C-537/03) [2006] Lloyd's Rep IR 209.

125 RTA 1988 s 151(8).

7.90 In *Churchill Insurance Co Ltd v Wilkinson*[126] the Court referred to the CJEU with regards to a common matter that arose in two different cases[127] in which the owners were injured as a result of accidents that took place when an uninsured driver was driving each vehicle. In the case of *Wilkinson* the owner and named insured knew that the driver was uninsured and in the *Evans* case the judge held that the owner/passenger gave no thought to the question as to whether or not her friend was insured. The insurers accepted liability to the passenger who was the owner; however, by relying on section 151(8) of the RTA 1988 they claimed a right of recourse against the passenger owner. The matter at the heart of the dispute was whether it was permitted to exclude from the benefit of insurance a victim of a road traffic accident when that accident was caused by an uninsured driver and when the victim, a passenger in the vehicle at the time of the accident, was insured to drive the vehicle himself and had given permission to the driver to drive it. The CJEU reiterated what was ruled by the Court before[128] that the legal position of the owner of the vehicle, present in the vehicle at the time of the accident as a passenger, to be the same as that of any other passenger who is a victim of the accident. The CJEU held that the Directive was to be interpreted as precluding national rules whose effect was to "omit[129] automatically" the requirement that the insurer should compensate a passenger who was a victim of a road traffic accident when that accident was caused by the driver who was not insured under the insurance policy and when the victim, who was a passenger in the vehicle at the time of the accident, was insured to drive the vehicle himself but who had given permission to the driver to drive it.

(4–6) Owner is a pedestrian

7.91 The owner of a vehicle can recover if he is injured as a pedestrian by a driver covered by the insurance, and also where he is injured as a pedestrian by a driver not covered by the insurance. Article 12(3) of the Consolidated Directive provides,

> The insurance referred to in Article 3 shall cover personal injuries and damage to property suffered by pedestrians, cyclists and other non-motorised users of the roads who, as a consequence of an accident in which a motor vehicle is involved, are entitled to compensation in accordance with national civil law.

7.92 Where the contractual exclusion relies solely on the fact that the victim is the owner of the vehicle which caused the loss, the CJEU ruled that the EU legislation does not permit such an exclusion from the compulsory insurance cover. In other words, the victim of an accident caused by the vehicle that is also owned by the victim falls under "third parties who have been victims" within the meaning of Article 13(1) of the Consolidated Directive. The illustration of this situation is seen in *Delgado Mendes v Credito*

---

126 (C-442/10) [2012] Lloyd's Rep IR 544.

127 Conjoined appeals of *Churchill Insurance Company Ltd v Benjamin Wilkinson* and *Tracey Evans v Equity Claims Ltd* [2010] Lloyd's Rep IR 591.

128 *Candolin v Vahinkovakuutusosakeyhtio Pohjola* (C-537/03) [2006] Lloyd's Rep IR 209.

129 Alternatively the word "exclude" may be used. In *Churchill Insurance Co Ltd v Fitzgerald* [2013] Lloyd's Rep IR 137, [31] Aikens LJ did not regard as important in this context the use of these different verbs (*"omit/ exclude"*).

Agricola Seguros – Companhia de Seguros de Ramos Reais SA (C-503/16)[130] where the relevant Portuguese law[131] provided, "In cases of theft, robbery or misappropriation of motor vehicles and motor vehicle accidents caused intentionally, the insurance shall not cover compensation payable by the perpetrators of such acts and their accomplices to the owner of the vehicle." The CJEU held that in the context that the owner was a victim of the accident when he was a pedestrian, on the sole ground of that he was the owner, insured person and the victim of the accident was not a permitted exclusion from the insurance cover. In *Delgado Mendes v Credito* whilst D and his wife parked the vehicles that each owned at a farm that they also owned, an attempted theft took place. D and his wife were in pursuit of the thief and D got out of the vehicle when the thief stopped at a junction. However, the thief reversed the vehicle towards D and injured him. In the question of whether the exclusion clause mentioned above was enforceable, the CJEU placed an emphasis on the continuing development of the EU law to protect the traffic accident victims' interest and in particular the extension of the compulsory insurance requirement to "personal injuries and damage to property suffered by pedestrians, cyclists and other non-motorised users of the roads."[132] D was a pedestrian at the time of the accident and he was entitled to compensation under the insurance contract. The exclusion whose sole ground was that D was the insurance policy holder and the owner of the vehicle that caused those injuries and that damage was not enforceable under the EU law. In *Delgado Mendes* the CJEU applied *Churchill Insurance Co Ltd v Wilkinson*[133] which will be referred to in the following paragraphs.

7.93 However, there remains a question as to whether the owner is required to reimburse the insurers where he is injured as a pedestrian by a driver not covered by the insurance but he has caused or permitted uninsured use. It is submitted that the insurer's right of recourse under section 151(8) is not to be omitted. Clearly, the Consolidated Directive includes injury suffered by pedestrians within the compulsory MTPL insurance. However, reading Art 12(3) together with section 151(8) concludes that, when the owner permitted the uninsured use of the vehicle and he was injured by the uninsured driver of his own vehicle, the insurer has a right of recourse against the user and the owner.

Single premium

7.94 Member States are required to take necessary measures that single premium is charged by the insurance bodies to insure vehicles in the entire territory of the Community.[134]

7.95 The single premium and the territorial scope of the insurance cover are aimed not exclusively at the relationship between the insurer and victim but also at the one between the insurer and the party insured.[135] Under Art 14, an insurance provision that enables the insurer to charge additional premium in case of the use of the vehicle in other Member States than the Member State where the vehicle is based, is unenforceable. The insurance

---

130 [2018] Lloyd's Rep IR 16.
131 Article 15(3) of that Decree-Law No 291/2007.
132 Directive 2005/14/EC, Art 4(2); Directive 2009/103/EC Art 12(3).
133 (C-442/10) [2012] Lloyd's Rep IR 544.
134 Art 14. Previously, Art 2 of the Third Directive.
135 *Litaksa Uab v Bta Insurance Co Se* (C-556/13) [2015] RTR 21, [29].

contract that was disputed in *Litaksa Uab v Bta Insurance Co Se*[136] stipulated that the vehicles would be used only for transporting passengers or goods in Lithuanian territory. The assured was contractually obliged, in the event that it intended to use the vehicles beyond a 28-day period in another Member State, or to transport persons or goods there, first to inform the insurer and to pay a premium supplement. Having emphasised the objectives of the Directives, the CJEU ruled that the insurer's commitment was to assume the risk of compensating the victims of any accident involving the insured vehicle, regardless of the EU Member State in whose territory that vehicle was used or the accident took place. Consequently a premium rate that varies according to the Member States in which the vehicle is used was contrary to the Directives.[137]

Exclusions for assured's deliberate act

7.96 This matter was discussed in a number of different contexts elsewhere in this book.[138] It is to be reiterated here briefly that *Hardy v Motor Insurers' Bureau*[139] interpreted the word "any" under section 145 of the RTA 1988 as including criminal use of the vehicle. It is worth noting that the Court separated two different circumstances: (1) taking out an insurance policy with an intention at the outset to use the vehicle for criminal purposes – the policy is illegal; (2) taking out the policy for legitimate uses at the outset but during the currency of the policy using the vehicle for criminal purposes – the policy is required to provide cover under section 145.

7.97 A question then follows whether an insurer may exclude liability for deliberate damage caused by the assured. In *Bristol Alliance Ltd Partnership v Williams*[140] Ward LJ, who gave the only reasoned judgment of the case, dismissed the proposition that a third party has to be compensated so long as the liability is of the kind which ought to have been covered by a policy complying with the RTA 1988 section 145 although the policy does not cover that particular liability.[141] Ward LJ was of the view that *Ruiz Bernaldez*[142] was not to be read to compel a *Marleasing*[143] meaning to be given to section 151(2)(a) read with section 145 of the RTA 1988.

7.98 Party autonomy, according to Ward LJ, was still retained by the Directives.[144] In order to support this statement the judge referred to domestic policies that often restrict the insurance cover to social and domestic purposes only (as discussed above).[145] When a policy stipulates such a restriction from the insurance cover, using the vehicle for hire in contravention of the limitation on use for social, domestic or pleasure purposes meant that there was no insurance within the terms of the RTA 1988 and the criminal offence

---

136 (C-556/13) [2015] RTR 21.
137 *Litaksa Uab v Bta Insurance Co Se* (C-556/13) [2015] RTR 21, [30].
138 See Chapter 12, reference to *Hardy v Motor Insurers' Bureau* and *ex turpi causa* discussions.
139 [1964] 2 QB 745.
140 [2013] RTR 9.
141 [2013] RTR 9, [51], [65].
142 (C-129/94) [1996] ECR I-1847.
143 *Marleasing SA v La Comercial Internacional de Alimentación SA* (C-106/89) [1990] ECR I-4135. See Chapter 1.
144 [2013] RTR 9, [65]; Approving *AXA Insurance UK Plc v Norwich Union Insurance Ltd* [2008] Lloyd's Rep IR 122.
145 Approving *Singh v Solihull Metropolitan Borough Council* [2007] 2 CMLR 1279.

was made out. The fact that the victim of any accident will be compensated either by the insurer concerned under section 151 or by the MIB does not affect the existence of such criminal liability.

7.99 In *Bristol* J, who was suffering from serious depression, deliberately swerved into a low wall which launched his car spinning into the air, bouncing off the roof of a car and smashing into the plate glass windows of the House of Fraser store causing over £200,000 of damage to that property. He was convicted of dangerous driving and of causing criminal damage. The damage to the shop windows was covered by its policy of property insurance, and a claim was brought against J by the property insurer by subrogation in the name of the claimant, the owner of the property. J's motor insurance cover excluded damage arising out of his deliberate acts. This particular use of the vehicle was, therefore, uninsured. Further, the MIB Agreement did not extend to compensating those who suffer property damage where such damage was insured by the victim's own insurer who brings a subrogated claim for recovery. In the battle between the property insurer and the motor insurer, the motor insurer won. Ward LJ held that the proper interpretation of the RTA 1988 s 151, under the domestic law interpretation or the EU law dimension, did not require the motor insurer to cover the damage claimed. It was not the insurer's but the driver's statutory duty to insure liability as required under the RTA 1988 s 145. If "any" liability is not insured, the driver commits the criminal offence under the RTA 1988 s 143. Ward LJ found that "if the Directives preclude the insurer being able to rely on that limitation to refuse to compensate the victim, and if the victim must be compensated, then section 143 loses its teeth."[146]

7.100 With respect, a number of difficulties are observed in Ward LJ's judgment especially in the light of some of the most recent developments in the EU compulsory MTPL insurance regime. In *Ruiz Bernaldez*[147] the compulsory insurance regime was held to be interpreted "as meaning that compulsory motor insurance must enable third-party victims of accidents caused by vehicles to be compensated for all the damage to property and injuries sustained by the victim, up to the amounts fixed in Article 1(2) of the Second Directive."[148] The Court's concern was the objectives of the Directives of ensuring third party victims would be compensated without any discrepancies amongst the Member States in the treatment of victims depending on where the accident occurred.[149]

7.101 It does not seem easy to reconcile Ward LJ's decision with the approach of the CJEU. For the same objective, also, Directives preclude an insurer from being able to rely on statutory provisions or contractual clauses to refuse to compensate third party victims of an accident caused by the insured vehicle.[150]

7.102 As Ward LJ also accepted, it is clear that "any" damage under the RTA 1988 s 145(3) covers "deliberate" damage.[151] Ward LJ's judgment did not separate the right of the third party victim for compensation from the right of the insured person against the insurer. Where the insurer has to compensate the loss which is not actually insured by

---

146 [2013] RTR 9, [65].
147 (C-129/94) [1996] All ER (EC) 741 [18].
148 Now Art 9 of Consolidated Directive.
149 [1996] All ER (EC) 741 [19].
150 [1996] All ER (EC) 741 [20].
151 *Bristol Alliance Ltd Partnership v Williams* [2013] RTR 9, [37]; *Gardner v Moore* [1984] AC 548.

the insurance contract, the insurer may recoup against the assured.[152] The assured's statutory duty is to insure against any liability under section 145, and failing to do so is the driver's criminal responsibility. However, this is independent of the third party victim's entitlement to compensation from the insurer for the loss caused by the driver. Unlike Ward LJ's comment stated above, when the insurer compensates the third party in the case that the liability is excluded under the contract section 143 does not lose its teeth, the criminal offence was still committed and the driver would be convicted. When the third party victim is compensated, the contractual autonomy between the insurer and the insured person is not jeopardized. So far as third party's claim is concerned, the statute requires the insurer to compensate the loss. The interpretation of the compulsory MTPL insurance requires a broader overview than considering the RTA 1988 s 148 in isolation.

7.103 The continuing development of the compulsory insurance regime has consistently revealed that securing the compensation for the loss suffered by the third party victim is to be taken into account in interpreting the MTPL insurance. It is submitted that there is hardly any support for Ward LJ's judgment in reading the compulsory MTPL insurance especially at the EU level. Further, as was recently noted in *Lewington v Motor Insurers' Bureau* by Bryan J, subject only to the specified derogations, Member States cannot create their own derogations.[153] With respect, it is not possible to agree with Ward LJ where his Lordship contended that there was no suggestion that the United Kingdom has failed to implement the Directive.

Arbitration clauses

7.104 At one time motor policies invariably contained an arbitration condition in a form familiarly known as the "*Scott v Avery*" clause.[154] In *Scott v Avery*[155] the insurance contract provided that no right of action shall arise until all disputes are settled by arbitration. The clause postponed but did not annihilate the right of access to the Court,[156] that no action could be brought until the award was made.[157] This embraced the liability of the insurers, the assessment of damage and the amount to be paid. When the insurer avoided the contract, the insurer was regarded as having waived the "*Scot v Avery*" clause.[158] If there was no contract, there was no clause to enforce to ask the assured to obtain an arbitration award before any action in the Courts against the insurer. On the other hand, if the contract was terminated, a clause providing arbitration "if any question shall arise touching this policy or the liability of the company thereunder" would require matters to be referred to arbitration.[159] A statement by the insurer in the following words therefore was a statement which urged a reference to the arbitrator rather than avoiding the contract or waiving the arbitration clause.[160]

---

152 *Hardy v Motor Insurers' Bureau* [1964] 2 QB 745. Eg see RTA 1988 s 148 and 151.
153 [2018] Lloyd's Rep IR 562, [41].
154 *Stebbing v Liverpool & London & Globe Insurance Co* [1917] 2 KB 433.
155 (1856) 5 H.L. Cas 811.
156 *Freshwater v Western Australian Assurance Co Ltd* [1933] 1 KB 515.
157 Ibid.
158 *Jureidini v National British & Irish Millers Insurance Co Ltd* [1915] AC 499.
159 *Woodall v Pearl Assurance Co Ltd* [1919] 1 KB 593.
160 *Golding v London & Edinburgh Insurance Co Ltd* (1932) 43 Ll L Rep 487.

CONTROL OF POLICY TERMS

> By reason of a term of the contract which you have broken, we are not liable under the contract, and if you dispute our contention that we are not liable there is an arbitration clause, and you cannot go to law with us about it, because there is an arbitration clause.

Moreover, the arbitration clause was binding for a third party victim who brought a direct claim against the negligent driver's insurer under the Third Parties Rights Against Insurers Act 1930.[161]

7.105 The arbitration was not to take the place of an action at law, but was a necessary step towards an action at law.[162] As a result, the limitation period did not start running until the making of the award.[163] The issue is rather historical because today arbitration clauses are rarely used in domestic insurance policies. Further, an arbitration agreement is unfair where[164] "so far as it relates to a claim for a pecuniary remedy which does not exceed the amount specified by order for the purposes of section 91 of the Arbitration Act 1996."[165]

Void or voidable contracts

7.106 The relevant EU Directives do not govern the legal conditions of validity of insurance contracts. It is a matter to be determined by the laws of the Member States.[166] Whether or not invalidity of an insurance contract may be argued against a victim of a traffic accident is, however, determined by the interpretation of the EU Directives and the compulsory MTPL insurance regime.

7.107 In *Fidelidade-Companhia de Seguros SA v Caisse Suisse de Compensation*[167] the CJEU discussed the enforceability of insurance policy defences in the context of a pre-contractual misrepresentation by the assured. The CJEU ruled that the matter should be considered together with the protection aimed by the Directives. The Member States must exercise their powers in setting the rules about enforceability of insurance contracts in a way consistent with EU law. Accordingly, avoiding an insurance contract should not be effective towards the third party victim. The availability of compensation by the national compensation body[168] does not enable the insurer to avoid the contract to deny the third party victim's claim. As mentioned in Chapter 10 the payment of compensation by the relevant body is designed to be a measure of last resort. It operates only when there is no insurance covering the accident in question. If there is insurance, although it can be avoided, such avoidance might not be argued against the third party. So long as the third party is concerned, there is insurance cover and the insurer will be liable to him.

7.108 In the light of the clear wordings that the CJEU used in *Fideliade*, it appears that there is no basis for enforcing section 151(2) under the RTA 1988. The CJEU said:

---

161 *Freshwater v Western Australian Assurance Co Ltd* [1933] 1 KB 515.

162 *Board Of Trade v Cayzer, Irvine And Co, Ltd* [1927] AC 610 at 629.

163 *Board Of Trade v Cayzer, Irvine And Co, Ltd* [1927] AC 610, at 626, Lord Atkinson.

164 Arbitration Act 1996 s 91.

165 The amount if the claim is for less than £5,000 under the Unfair Arbitration Agreements (Specified Amount) Order 1999 (SI 1999/2617).

166 *Fidelidade-Companhia de Seguros SA v Caisse Suisse de Compensation* (C-287/16) [2017] RTR 26, [31].

167 (C-287/16) [2017] RTR 26; *Churchill Insurance Co Ltd v Wilkinson* (C-442/10) [2012] Lloyd's Rep IR 544 was applied.

168 In the UK this body is MIB. See Chapter 10.

The fact that the insurance company has concluded that contract on the basis of omissions or false statements on the part of the policyholder does not enable the company to rely on statutory provisions regarding the nullity of the contract or to invoke that nullity against a third-party victim so as to be released from its obligation . . . to compensate that victim for an accident caused by the insured vehicle.

Unfair terms

7.109 In addition to the express provisions of the RTA 1988, policy terms are subject to the Consumer Rights Act 2015 that may affect the reliance by insurers on terms falling outside the RTA 1988 s 148. *Newbury v Davies*[169] was discussed in Chapter 3. It was followed in *Pearl Assurance Plc v Kavanagh*[170] where the assured K permitted H to drive her vehicle only if H arranged his own insurance cover. H, who drove the vehicle without insurance, was involved in an accident. The third party's loss was compensated by K's insurer. The insurers then sought recoupment from K by relying on either the RTA 1988 s 151(8) or the policy terms which provided, "If we are obliged by the laws of any country in which this policy operates to make a payment for which we would not otherwise be liable you must repay the amount to us within 21 days of a formal demand." The section 151(8) claim failed because K's permission, which was subject to a condition which was not fulfilled, was not a permission at all. The relevant policy term was unenforceable under the Unfair Terms in Consumer Contract Regulations 1994 Reg 6 and Sch 2 of the Regulations. The term was unfair as it was not individually negotiated, had not been drawn to K's attention and sought to impose an unlimited liability on K, removing her protection under the RTA 1988 s 151(8). The 1994 regulations were re-enacted with modifications by the Unfair Terms in Consumer Contracts Regulations 1999 (SI 1999/2083) (1999 Regulations). The 1999 Regulations were repealed[171] and replaced[172] by the Consumer Rights Act 2015.

---

169 [1974] RTR 367.
170 [2001] CLY 3832.
171 Consumer Rights Act 2015 Sch 4 para 34.
172 Consumer Rights Act 2015 Part 2 and Schedule 2 to the Act.

CHAPTER 8

Third party victim's right of direct action against insurers

8.1 The RTA 1988 controls not only the terms of the contract to be entered into between the assured and the insurers but also the statutory rights of the third party against the insurers. There is no contract between the insurer who insures liability as required by the RTA and the third party victim the protection of whose interest is the main concern of the relevant statutory provisions. The statutory compulsory liability insurance regime grants a direct right of action by the victim against the motorist's insurer. Currently there are two parallel sets of rules with regards to such direct right of action. The current section 151 of the RTA 1988 represents the approach that had been first adopted by the 1934 Act and retained until today. The RTA 1988 has no effect on the direct enforcement action under the Third Parties (Rights Against Insurers) Act 2010[1] (TPA 2010) that under the RTA 1988 s 153 the right of the third party to proceed against the assured despite the assured's insolvency is preserved. As will be examined below, similar to the regime under the TPA 2010, section 151 of the RTA 1988 demands the third party to satisfy some requirements as set out by the section before a right of direct action is available for him.

8.2 By the Consolidated Directive[2] Member States are required to ensure that where insurance is provided as required by the Directive, an injured third party victim should have a right of direct action against insurers.

8.3 The European Communities (Rights against Insurers) Regulations 2002/3061 adopts a system that also stipulates a right of direct action against the insurer by the third party victim with no pre-condition of a judgment awarding damages in favour of the claimant and against the assured motorist. The conditions of section 151 and the 2002 Regulations will be discussed separately in this chapter.

The regime under section 151 of the RTA 1988

8.4 Section 151 of the RTA 1988 provides the victim with a right of direct action against the insurers to meet a judgment left unsatisfied by the user. The basis of the third parties' claim is the judgment against the user rather than a claim under a policy at all. As a result, if the policy provides defence against the assured they cannot be enforced against the third party. Section 151 therefore represents a very different position to the TPA 2010 which provides for the transfer from an insured person of his right against his insurers to a third party in circumstances where the

---

1 RTA s 153(3).
2 Art 18.

insured person is insured against third party risks and becomes bankrupt with an outstanding liability to the third party.

8.5 The Courts have acknowledged that the interpretation of section 151 is "not easy."[3] It is an enforcement mechanism only and to trigger such tool the third party victim has to satisfy three requirements[4]:

(1)   a judgment to which this subsection applies is obtained (s 151(1));
(2)   the judgment relates "to a liability with respect to any matter where liability with respect to that matter is required to be covered by a policy of insurance under section 145," (s 151(2)); and
(3)   the liability is "covered by the terms of the policy . . . to which the certificate relates," (s 151(2)(a)).

Delivery of certificate

8.6 As referred to in Chapter 4, before it was amended by the Deregulation Act 2015, section 147(1) of the RTA 1988 used to provide, "A policy of insurance shall be of no effect for the purposes of this Part of this Act unless and until there is delivered by the insurer." It followed that the RTA 1988 s 151(1) used to require a certificate of insurance has been delivered under section 147 before a third party victim has a right of direct action against the insurer.

8.7 Before the implementation of the Deregulation Act 2015 the requirement about the delivery of the certificate could be satisfied after the accident took place but before the judgment against the assured was given. The Privy Council held in *Motor & General Insurance Co. Ltd. v Cox*[5] that section 151[6] did not compel that the policy that covered the required liability should have been in existence at the moment when liability was incurred. All that was required was that a policy had been effected prior to judgment which covered the liability in question. Accordingly, if a policy retrospectively effected for such liability, it satisfied the requirements of section 151(1). There followed a discussion on whether section 147 had any influence on section 151. The Privy Council answered in the negative as their Lordships read section 147 as providing neither that a policy cannot have effect at common law without the issue of a certificate nor that, having become effective, it cannot operate retrospectively. As a result, if the certificate had not been delivered to the assured, it would have seemed that he had the right to demand such delivery from the insurer, on the basis that the contract with the insurer was for a policy complying with the RTA 1988.[7] After the amendment of s 151(1) by the Deregulation Act 2015 the point is no longer of significance. One point, however, which still is important in respect of the link between the certificate and the policy is that in *R&S Pilling (t/a Phoenix Engineering) v UK Insurance Ltd*[8] Lord Hodge confirmed that, with

---

3   *Allen v Mohammed* [2017] Lloyd's Rep IR 73, [28].
4   *Bristol Alliance Ltd Partnership v Williams* [2013] RTR 9, Ward LJ, [34].
5   [1990] 1 WLR 1443.
6   The relevant legislation was that of counter in Barbados.
7   Colinvaux, [23–074].
8   [2019] UKSC 16 [30].

respect to coverage, exclusions, avoidance or cancellation, the focus of section 151 of the RTA 1988 is on the policy but not on the certificate.

Liability covered by section 151(2)

8.8 Two different forms of recovery for the third party victim are available under the RTA 1988 s 151(2), and they will be explored in the following paragraphs.

Section 151(2)(a)

8.9 Where the policy itself covers the loss, then if the victim obtains a judgment against the insured driver the insurers are required to satisfy the judgment. What triggers section 151(2)(a) is liability and not the identity of the driver: there has to be liability actually covered by the policy.[9]

One illustration of a situation that falls outside the scope of section 151(2)(a) is seen in *Stych v Dibble*[10] where A, who did part-time work at a garage, was driving a vehicle that he took from the garage. The vehicle belonged to a customer of the garage, and A did not have a permission to take it. The vehicle was covered by a valid road traffic policy insurance with T, but A clearly was not insured under this policy; he was not authorised by the owner to drive their vehicle at the time of the accident. It follows that the default judgment obtained against A was not a judgment obtained against the person who was insured by T as required by s 151(2)(a).

Section 151(2)(b)

8.10 Second, if the user was not insured but ought to have been insured in accordance with the requirements of the RTA 1988, then the victim is again entitled to enforce against the insurers any judgment against the user. It will be seen that section 151(2)(b) contemplates that the insurer may be liable to satisfy a judgment even though the person driving the vehicle is not covered by the policy. It is the motorist's liability to the third parties that is required to be covered by a policy of insurance.[11]

8.11 Art 13(1)(a)[12] of the Consolidated Directive disallows the insurer to argue an exclusion towards the third party victim on the basis that the user is a person who does not "have express or implied authorisation to do so." Hence, s 151(2)(b) implements Art 13(1)(a).

8.12 There are two obvious situations where s 151(2)(b) might apply. The first is where the assured has loaned the vehicle to an uninsured person. A typical example would be where the person driving was a partner or friend who was not actually a named driver on the policy. Second, where the vehicle has been stolen, section 151 would extend to driving by a thief.[13]

---

9 *Bristol Alliance Ltd Partnership v Williams* [2013] Lloyd's Rep IR 351.
10 [2013] Lloyd's Rep IR 80.
11 *McMinn v McMinn* [2006] RTR 33, [9].
12 Art 2 of the Second Motor Insurance Directive 1984.
13 *Farah v Abdullahi* [2018] EWHC 738 (QB), [8].

8.13 Before the adoption of this provision, in compliance with the EU law, the liability would have been faced by the MIB, but the effect of section 151(2)(b) is to transfer that liability back to the insurer. In *Wake v Wylie*[14] the claimant was injured by an accident that took place when he was a back seat passenger in a vehicle being driven by the defendant, who turned into the path of an oncoming car and thereby caused a collision. The defendant driver was not himself an insured driver under the terms of the policy that was taken out by his mother and insured her. It was apparent that any compensation would have to be provided by the defendant's mother's insurers under their statutory obligation in section 151 to meet judgments in respect of liabilities which would have been covered had the vehicle been properly insured.

8.14 In *Churchill Insurance Co Ltd v Wilkinson*[15] Waller LJ divided the potential insurers providing the guarantee into three: (1) contractual insurers, which cover the vast majority of cases (s 151(2)(a)); (2) statutory (sometimes called the RTA) insurers whose liability arises under the RTA, though there would be no contractual liability (s 151(2)(b) and s 151(3)); and (3) the Motor Insurers' Bureau (MIB).

8.15 The facts in *Stych v Dibble*[16] as mentioned above would fall under section 151(2)(b) as A's liability to the passenger was, for the purpose of the subsection, a liability which would be covered by the T policy if it insured all persons. The passenger obtained a judgment against A as that of against a person other than one who was insured by the policy. However, this matter must not be concluded without considering the RTA 1988 section 151(4).

Unlicensed driver exclusion – section 151(3)

8.16 It is to be noted here that, where section 151(2) is disputed, and the insurance policy excludes coverage for injuries caused by a driver who does not hold a driving licence, such an exclusion will be ineffective against the victim under section 151(3). The insurer, however, after having compensated the victim, may recoup against the person who caused the injury or the insured person under the contract.[17]

Excluded liability – section 151(4)

8.17 The RTA 1988 s 151(2)(b) covers "a liability, other than an excluded liability." The "excluded liability" in this context is then described in s 151(4) which provides:

a liability in respect of the death of, or bodily injury to, or damage to the property of any person who, at the time of the use which gave rise to liability, was allowing himself to be carried in or upon the vehicle and knew or had reason to believe that the vehicle had been stolen or unlawfully taken, not being a person who:
(1)   did not know and had no reason to believe that the vehicle had been stolen or unlawfully taken until after the commencement of their journey; and
(2)   could not reasonably have been expected to have alighted from the vehicle.

---

14 [2001] RTR 20.
15 [2010] Lloyd's Rep IR 591.
16 [2013] Lloyd's Rep IR 80.
17 RTA 1988 s 151(7)–(8).

8.18 Art 13(1) of the Consolidated Directive contains a similar exclusion in the following words:

> The provision or clause referred to in point (a) of the first subparagraph may be invoked against persons who voluntarily entered the vehicle which caused the damage or injury, when the insurer can prove that they knew the vehicle was stolen.

8.19 There are two main differences between section 151(4) of the 1988 Act, and Art 13 of the Consolidated Directive. The latter uses the phrase "stolen," whereas s 151(4) refers to "stolen or unlawfully taken"; and the Directive requires proof that the victim "knew" of the theft whereas s 151(4) lays down the wider test which removes coverage where the victim "knew or had reason to believe" that the vehicle had been stolen.

8.20 Additionally, both s 151(4) and Art 13(1) impose the burden on the insurer to prove that the victim knew that the vehicle was stolen or unlawfully taken as the case may be.[18] These issues are a matter of fact to be proven on the balance of probabilities.[19]

Stolen or unlawfully taken

8.21 It is accepted that the word stolen refers to the corresponding criminal offences in the Theft Act 1968; however, there is no unanimous view on the interpretation of the words "unlawfully taken." Whilst in *McMinn v McMinn*[20] Keith J stated that the words unlawfully taken were to be interpreted with the equivalent reference to the Theft Act 1968,[21] Stadlen J in *Stych v Dibble*[22] expressed doubts on the correctness of this interpretation which did not include some more broader considerations that might be derived from the relevant EU Directives.

8.22 It should be noted that in *Stych v Dibble* the parties did not dispute the interpretation of "unlawfully taken," but they accepted that the interpretation in *McMinn v McMinn* was correct. Therefore, Stadlen J's statement on the interpretation of unlawfully taken was obiter.[23]

8.23 In *McMinn v McMinn* an accident occurred when I, who was 17 at the time and did not hold a driving licence, was driving a van and his older brother A and R were passengers in it. The van belonged to R's employers, M, and R was allocated to drive it. The insurance coverage for the van was subject to the conditions that the van should be driven by someone who (a) had attained the age of 25, (b) held a driving licence and (c) had been permitted by M to drive it. A was seriously injured and made a claim against I. A was allowing himself to be carried in the van at the relevant time. The van was not stolen as I was given permission to drive it by R, but it was, as held by Keith J, unlawfully taken.

---

18 *McMinn v McMinn* [2006] RTR 33, [11]; *Stych v Dibble* [2013] Lloyd's Rep IR 80.

19 Ibid.

20 [2006] RTR 33.

21 *McMinn v McMinn* [2006] RTR 33, [18].

22 [2013] Lloyd's Rep IR 80.

23 The learned judge noted that if the matter had been fully argued, he would not have considered it to be *acte clair* that the word "stolen" in the Second Directive is to be interpreted so as to include unlawful taking or taking without permission. The concerns raised by the judge were that exceptions are to be construed strictly and here a stricter narrow interpretation and the proportionality that he referred to in the analysis of the meaning of "knew or had reason to believe." [2013] Lloyd's Rep IR 80, [67].

8.24 Applying the Theft Act 1968 s 12 Keith J found on the facts that R had known that his employer would not have permitted I to drive the van. Two different situations may be considered.

8.25 The first group of these examples is that a person who had originally been authorised to drive a vehicle has taken it by using it for a purpose for which he had not been authorised. For instance, L asks M to borrow M's car and M permits L to use the vehicle on the condition that the car would be returned by the end of midnight on the same day. However, L keeps using the car and does not return it by the time agreed.[24]

A further example would be an employee lorry driver uses the lorry one day after work to a public house to have a drink and then to drive some of the customers of the public house to their homes at different places.[25]

8.26 The second group of these situations is, a person who had originally been authorised to drive a vehicle has taken it by letting someone else, B, drive it, by knowing that the owner would not have permitted B to drive the vehicle. To decide whether the vehicle has been unlawfully taken the same test applies in both of these circumstances,[26] namely whether

> he appropriate[d] it to his own use in a manner which repudiates the rights of the true owner, and shows that he has assumed control of the vehicle for his own purposes.[27]

Not every brief, unauthorised diversion from his proper route by an employed driver in the course of his working day will necessarily involve a "taking" of the vehicle for his own use.[28]

In the second group of example above in paragraph 8.25, however, it was not in itself an answer that B was lawfully put in control of the vehicle by his employers;[29] at the time B took the vehicle when he left the first public house he assumed control for his own purposes in a manner which was inconsistent with his duty to his employer to finish his round and drive the vehicle to the depot.

8.27 The test was also satisfied in *McMinn* that R went through an induction process on his first day at work and he had been informed at least on two occasions that R would be driving on a fleet insurance policy, that all drivers had to be named and that they had to have the permission of the managers of M to drive any vehicle in the fleet. Keith J held that R did not believe that M would have permitted I to drive the van and the vehicle was unlawfully taken.

The state of mind under section 151(4)

Knew

8.28 The word "knew" in section 151(4) means actual knowledge or such knowledge as the law regards as equivalent to it, eg "turning a blind eye."[30] When the driver expressly

---

24 *R. v Phipps (Owen Roger)* [1970] RTR 209.
25 *McKnight v Davies* [1974] RTR 4.
26 *McMinn v McMinn* [2006] RTR 33.
27 *McMinn v McMinn* [2006] RTR 33, [20]; *McKnight v Davies* [1974] RTR 4, 8.
28 *McKnight v Davies* [1974] RTR 4, 8.
29 *McKnight v Davies* [1974] RTR 4.
30 *McMinn v McMinn* [2006] RTR 33; *Stych v Dibble* [2013] Lloyd's Rep IR 80, [36].

tells the victim passenger that he had taken the vehicle without the owner's permission, it clearly proves the actual knowledge on the claimant that the vehicle was either stolen or unlawfully taken.[31]

8.29 "Turning a blind eye" may be described as "suspicion accompanied by a deliberate refraining from asking questions."[32] This type of knowledge is treated as though the passenger had received the information which he deliberately sought to avoid. Therefore, both in the cases of actual knowledge and this latter type the passenger falls within the exception.

Had reason to believe

8.30 It should be first noted here that Article 2(1) of the Second Directive was consolidated under Article 13(1) of the Consolidated Directive. Further, Article 1(4) of the Second Directive now appears under Article 10(2) of the Consolidated Directive.

Second Directive Article 2(1) and Consolidated Directive Article 13(1) correspond with section 151(4) of the RTA 1988. Articles 1(4) of the Second and 10(2) of the Consolidated Directive are in relation to an exclusion from the compensation body's obligation to compensate the third party victim's loss. Compensation by a national body, who is the MIB in the UK, is covered under Chapter 10 of this book.

8.31 Ascertaining the meaning of "had reason to believe" is not easy. Previously, the House of Lords discussed in *White v White*,[33] in the context of an exception from the MIB Agreements, the meaning of "an injured passenger who *knew or ought to have known* that the driver was uninsured."[34] The majority reasoning in *White* focused mainly on two points. First, the Second Directive's objective was to improve guarantees of compensation for victims of motor accidents by insuring the minimum level of protection for them throughout the Community, and the purpose of the 1988 MIB Agreement was to give effect to the terms of the Second Directive. Second, some limited exclusions were permitted by the Directive, but such exclusions must be interpreted strictly and by requiring a high degree of personal fault on the injured passenger who might be deprived of compensation. Within the context of clause 6 of the MIB Agreements applicable at the relevant time, the House of Lords in *White v White* confirmed that knowledge included the blind eye knowledge as described above.

The House of Lords held that the phrase "knew or ought to have known" in the MIB Agreement was intended to be co-extensive with the exception permitted by Article 1(4) of the Directive.[35] In other words, it was intended to bear the same meaning as "knew" in the Directive.[36]

8.32 In the context of the wording of s 151(4) of the RTA 1988, whilst in *McMinn v McMinn* Keith J[37] held that s 151(4) of the RTA 1988 did not fall to be construed in the light of the Second Directive, in *Stych v Dibble* Stadlen J held that section 151(4) must

---

31 *Andersen v Hameed* [2010] CSOH 99.
32 *Stych v Dibble* [2013] Lloyd's Rep IR 80, [19].
33 [2001] RTR 25.
34 The 1988 MIB Agreements, clause 6(1)(e)(ii).
35 Now Article 10 of the Consolidated Directive. See *White v White* [2001] RTR 25, [23].
36 [2001] RTR 25, [23].
37 [2006] RTR 33, [16].

be interpreted so far as possible to fulfil its obligations in the exception in Article 2(1) of the Second Directive.[38] Stadlen J held that Lord Nicholls's interpretation in *White v White* of the word "knew" in Article 1(4) should apply equally to the word as it appears in Article 2(1).[39] Stadlen J acknowledged that s 151, along with other provisions of the RTA 1988, was brought in to force to seek to give effect to the United Kingdom's obligations under motor insurance Directives. According to Stadlen J, the English Courts are under an obligation to interpret s 151, as far as possible, in a way which gives effect to the Directive.[40] This was necessitated by the purposive interpretation of the domestic rules in the areas which also are regulated by the Directives, and also the rulings in *Churchill Insurance Co Ltd v Wilkinson*[41] and *Marleasing SA v La Comercial Internacional de Alimentación S.A.*[42]

8.33 The differences in views between Keith J and Stadlen J created the following outcome. If Keith J is to be followed, "had reason to believe" in section 151(4) is to be interpreted independently of the word "knew." The word "knew" in the Second Directive is not co-extensive with "knew or had reason to believe" in s 151(4).[43] In order to prove "had reason to believe" in s 151(4), which is to be construed independently of "knew," insurers do not have to prove that the injured passenger actually believed that the vehicle had been stolen or unlawfully taken.[44] The insurer has to establish that

> the injured passenger had the information[45] . . . which would have afforded him good reasons for believing that the vehicle had been stolen or unlawfully taken had he applied his mind to the topic. Shutting one's eyes to the obvious is therefore enough, provided that it would indeed have been obvious to the injured passenger if he had thought about it.[46]

Keith J found in *McMinn v McMinn* that this test was satisfied on its facts. With regards to A's state of knowledge or belief the judge held that A, I's brother, knew that I did not have a full driving licence and that he had never driven a vehicle on a public road. If he had thought about it, A would have had every reason to believe that I was not permitted to drive the van. A knew that the van belonged to R's employers, and although he would have had no reason to know that it could only be driven by someone who had reached the age of 25, he would have realised, had he thought about it for a moment, that it could have been driven only by someone who had been permitted by R's employers to drive the van, not by someone who is 17 and did not have a driving licence. A had reason to believe that the van had been unlawfully taken by R and I.

The facts would have justified a finding of blind-eye knowledge,[47] but the acceptance of the constructive knowledge test is not easy to reconcile. In *Stych v Dibble* Stadlen J

---

38 *Stych v Dibble* [2013] Lloyd's Rep IR 80, [35]. Although the case refers to Art 2(4) of the Second Directive, there is no paragraph 4 under Art 2. Article 2(1) corresponds with s 151(4) of the RTA 1988.

39 *Stych v Dibble* [2013] Lloyd's Rep IR 80, [34]. Although the case refers to Art 2(4) of the Second Directive, there is no paragraph 4 under Art 2. Article 2(1) corresponds with s 151(4) of the RTA 1988.

40 [2013] Lloyd's Rep IR 80, [16].

41 [2010] Lloyd's Rep IR 591.

42 (C-106/89) [1990] ECR I-4135.

43 [2006] RTR 33, [16].

44 *McMinn v McMinn* [2006] RTR 33, [17].

45 What is also called "the building blocks."

46 *McMinn v McMinn* [2006] RTR 33, [17].

47 Merkin/Hemsworth, [5–146].

said that Keith J's conclusions that (1) section 151(4) does not fall to be construed in the light of the Second Directive and that (2) "knew or had reason to believe" could be proved in the absence of proof that the uninsured passenger applied his mind to the topic of whether the vehicle had been stolen or unlawfully taken were both wrong.[48]

8.34 Stadlen J's contrary ruling was that "knew" and "knew and had reason to believe" were co-extensive, and hence, in the light of the ruling in *White v White*, the words "had reason to believe" should be construed narrowly. It meant that "the passenger had turned a blind eye to the truth" had to be proven.

"Turning a blind eye" could not be proven without the relevant mind has been applied to the question whether the fact exists or is true or not.[49] Further, a failure to ask questions was not sufficient to establish such knowledge.[50] The passenger must suspect that the relevant fact exists or must draw an actual conclusion that it might well exist and he must deliberately refrain from asking questions which might confirm his suspicions.[51] The derogation is aimed at any situation which the injured person has himself brought about.[52]

8.35 In *Stych v Dibble* the actual knowledge of the passenger on whether the vehicle had been stolen or unlawfully taken was not argued. The focus of the dispute was whether the passenger "had reason to believe that the vehicle had been stolen or unlawfully taken" within the meaning of s 151(4). Stadlen J was persuaded that the victim knew that the driver was living in the garage, had keys for the garage and saw him drive some other cars in the garage before. He, however, did not know that the vehicle was unlawfully taken by A, nor, he deliberately refrained from asking questions to avoid to find out the truth about the permission to drive the vehicle – according to the blind eye test set out by Lord Nicholls in *White v White*. The passenger's claim did not fall within s 151(4).

8.36 It appears that the authorities mentioned above unanimously accept that the state of mind required to be proved by the insurer under s 151(4) is actual knowledge or blind eye knowledge.[53] The latter expresses the state of mind of the passenger as described by Lord Nicholls as "I will not ask, because I would rather not know."[54] Putting in the context, the passenger

> had information from which he either actually drew the conclusion that the prescribed fact was in fact the case or actually drew the conclusion that it might well be the case and, suspecting that it was, deliberately refrained from asking questions so as to avoid confirmation that it was.[55]

8.37 According to *White v White* these are the only types of knowledge that prove the exception "knew or ought to have known," and the same test applies in the case of "knew or had reason to believe." The difference appears on the standards of proving

---

48 [2013] Lloyd's Rep IR 80, [45–46].
49 *Stych v Dibble* [2013] Lloyd's Rep IR 80, [46].
50 Ibid.
51 *Stych v Dibble* [2013] Lloyd's Rep IR 80, [46]; Stadlen J referred to Lord Scott in *White v White* at [53] and Lord Nicholls at [16].
52 *Stych v Dibble* [2013] Lloyd's Rep IR 80, [65].
53 *Stych v Dibble* [2013] Lloyd's Rep IR 80, [36].
54 *White v White* [2001] RTR 25, [16].
55 *Stych v Dibble* [2013] Lloyd's Rep IR 80, [36].

"had reason to believe" whether the same deliberate state of mind on the passenger is required or whether the passenger's negligence in not raising the questions he should have will be sufficient. At first sight reading literally "had reason to believe" may sound a looser expression than "knew." However, if a passenger had reason to believe that the vehicle had been stolen or unlawfully taken, objectively, the passenger was expected to ask questions about his suspicion. The disagreement between *McMinn* and *Stych* arose with regards to the degree of the passenger's omission in not asking the necessary questions. Does carelessness suffice or whether to exclude the insurer's liability it must be proven that the passenger deliberately refrained from asking about such questions? Whilst *McMinn v McMinn* found for the former, *Stych* adopted the latter approach.

It should be remembered that *McMinn* was decided by Queen's Bench Division and *Stych* is a decision by Queen's Bench Division District Registry (Birmingham). *Stych* therefore did not overrule *McMinn*. Currently, therefore, there are two conflicting interpretations of the knowledge requirement under s 151(4).

8.38 It should also be remembered that proving knowledge is a matter of fact and every case will depend on its own merit and what the parties proved in terms of the knowledge with the factual evidence. Further, the witnesses' reliability will also take into its part as seen in *Stych*. In *McMinn* the fact that the victim was the older brother of the driver and the progression of the events were not similar to the background information and how the events occurred on the day of the accident in *Stych*. Additionally, in *Stych* the reliability of the witness statements, the inconsistency of the statements by the driver to explain the course of the events in the police custody and in Courts all played some important roles in the analysis of the facts by the judge.

8.39 It is submitted that the interpretation of "ought to have known" together with the word "knew" as delivered by the majority of the House of Lords in *White v White*, the fact that the RTA 1988 and the MIB Agreements were interpreted in a number of occasions in line with the Directives, and the differences in clarity between *McMinn* and *Stych* render *Stych* a more persuasive authority as to the interpretation of "had reason to believe."

Ex turpi causa

8.40 The effect of a joint criminal enterprise between the user of the vehicle and a passenger to the latter's claim against the former in the case of a traffic accident is explored in detail in Chapter 12. Here it suffices to note that under the Theft Act 1968 section 12 it is a criminal offence to drive a vehicle without the owner's consent. A person who allows himself to be carried in such a vehicle will also commit the offence.[56] For a passenger who was being driven in a vehicle which was either stolen or unlawfully taken, with the state of mind as identified under s 151(4), coincides with the criminal offence under section 12 of the Theft Act 1968.

8.41 It was held in *Andersen v Hameed*[57] the claimant victim knew that the driver was using his parents' vehicle without their permission; he was 16 years old and did not hold either a driving licence or insurance at the time of the accident. The claimant was held to be participating in a joint criminal activity with the driver, and he was not entitled to

---

56 Theft Act 1968, section 12(1).
57 *Andersen v Hameed* [2010] CSOH 99.

recover damages from the driver for loss and injury sustained as a consequence of his negligent driving.

8.42 Where the liability is not excluded under s 151(4), if the assured loses the claim against the insurer, say for manslaughter, this does not affect the victim's recovery from the insurer.[58]

Policy restrictions and section 151

8.43 The RTA section 145, which is described as a neutral provision,[59] specifies what the requirements in respect of policies of insurance are. Further, it was clarified by the common law that it is the user's obligation to comply with the compulsory insurance requirement under section 143.[60] Therefore, if the policy does not cover the liability that falls within the relevant provisions of the RTA 1988, it is the assured but not the insurer who commits the criminal offence under section 143(2). If, therefore, the policy excludes cover for losses caused by deliberate acts, and the assured deliberately causes a loss to a third party, the assured is in breach of the requirement in the legislation to be covered by a liability policy.[61] In such a case, whether the insurer can rely on the contractual exclusion in a claim made by the third party victim of the accident is analysed differently as discussed in Chapter 7. The fact that the victim of any accident will be compensated either by the insurer concerned under s 151 or by the MIB does not affect the existence of the criminal liability.[62] With regards to the insurance claim, clearly, the compulsory MTPL insurance regime treats a claim against the insurer by the assured and a claim by the third party against either the insurer or the MIB separately.[63]

8.44 Section 145(3)(a) of the RTA 1988 provides that a policy

> must insure such person, persons or classes of persons as may be specified in the policy in respect of any liability which may be incurred by him or them in respect of the death of or bodily injury to any person or damage to property caused by, or arising out of, the use of the vehicle on a road or other public place in Great Britain.

8.45 The common law's interpretation of this subsection is that the statutory compulsory insurance requires the user to insure him in relation to whatever use of his motor vehicle on the road in respect of third party risks.[64] *Hardy v Motor Insurers' Bureau*[65] is not directly relevant to section 151 as the motorist was not insured, but the Court of Appeal's description of the scope of section 145(3)(a) of the RTA 1988 is significant for the references to liability to be covered by the policy under section 151.

---

58 *Keeley v Pashen* [2005] Lloyd's Rep IR 289.

59 It does not stipulate that the user must take out a policy of insurance complying with the Act nor does it say that the "authorised insurer" has to issue a policy which complies with the Act. *Bristol Alliance Ltd Partnership v Williams* [2013] RTR 9, Ward LJ, [37].

60 *Charlton v Fisher* [2002] QB 578, [63] Rix LJ; *Bristol Alliance Ltd Partnership v Williams* [2013] RTR 9, Ward LJ, [45].

61 *Bristol Alliance Ltd Partnership v Williams* [2013] RTR 9.

62 *Bristol Alliance Ltd Partnership v Williams* [2013] RTR 9, Ward LJ, [65].

63 *Charlton v Fisher* [2002] QB 578, [63] Rix LJ.

64 Ibid.

65 [1964] 2 QB 745.

8.46 In *Hardy v Motor Insurers' Bureau* the claim was against the MIB. The MIB is liable in case the victim's claim is in relation to "relevant liability" that is the liability required to be insured under the RTA 1988.[66] That liability is, in the wording of 145(3)(a) of the RTA 1988, "any" liability. In *Hardy v Motor Insurers' Bureau* the Court of Appeal held that the word "any" in this context includes the motorist's criminal conduct.[67] The assured's statutory obligation is to insure "any" liability. However, the Courts stated that it is not apparent that there is a similar obligation on his insurer to cover him in respect of any and every use to which the user may put his car.[68]

8.47 Between the assured and insurers the word "any" is not interpreted literally. Section 151 applies under two separate cases as mentioned above: when there is actual insurance and when there is no such insurance but should have been as required by the statute. Between the assured and the insurer, the proper construction of the policy affects the rights of the parties to the contract.[69] On the other hand, whatever rights a third party has and to be compensated by the insurer under both s 151(2)(a) and 151(2)(b) depends not upon the proper construction of the contract of insurance but upon the proper construction of the statutory provision that confers that right upon him.[70] If this is the true analysis of the statutory insurance obligation, towards the assured the insurer may include policy restrictions where normal contractual autonomy operates between assured and insurer, but such restrictions cannot be argued towards the third party victim. As between the third party and the insurer, the third party is protected as if the assured had been covered. It follows that the insurer, who has had to compensate the third party's loss that was caused by the assured, is entitled to recover payment from his insured.[71] Section 151 duty creates a separate statutory cause of action in favour of the third party, which may operate in circumstances where the insurer would be under no liability to indemnify the insured, for instance where the insurer is entitled to avoid or cancel the policy.[72]

A claim through the assured or through section 151

8.48 The enforceability of the policy restrictions must be analysed separately when the claimant is the assured and when the claimant is a third party victim. Additionally, when the claimant is a third party victim, a further distinction is to be made whether the third party's claim against the insurer is under s 151 of the RTA 1988 or under the TPA 2010. In the former, the third party's cause of action against the insurer is independent to that of the assured and it may go beyond the assured's rights against the insurer.[73] As appears in *Hardy v Motor Insurers' Bureau*[74] and *Gardner v Moore*,[75] the word "any"

---

66 With respect to section 203(3)(a) of the RTA 1960 which contained the wording of "must insure such person, persons or classes of persons as may be specified in the policy in respect of any liability which may be incurred by him or them." The same words appear in section 145(3)(a) of the RTA 1988.

67 *Gardner v Moore* [1984] AC 548 confirmed that *Hardy v Motor Insurers' Bureau* was correctly decided.

68 *Charlton v Fisher* [2002] QB 578, [63] Rix LJ.

69 *Bristol Alliance Ltd Partnership v Williams* [2013] RTR 9.

70 *Bristol Alliance Ltd Partnership v Williams* [2013] RTR 9.

71 RTA 1988 s 148(4), s 151(7), s 151(8).

72 RTA 1988 s 151(5).

73 *Charlton v Fisher* [2002] QB 578, [83] Rix LJ.

74 [1964] 2 QB 745.

75 [1984] AC 548.

is interpreted broadly in line with the principles lying behind the adoption of the compulsory liability insurance regime for motorists. In both of these cases the *ex turpi causa* doctrine which could have been arguable against the user did not preclude the third party's claim because the basis of the claim under the MIB Agreement was the judgment against the assured, rather than a claim under the insurance policy.[76] As a result, the claimants in those cases were successful because the driver's liability was one in respect of which he was required by statute to be covered, and that triggered the MIB's separate liability. In any event, in *Hardy* and *Gardner* there were no discussions of an insurance contract because the motorists were uninsured. Similarly, where such a claim is made under section 151 of the RTA 1988 the victim's right of action against the insurer is independent of that of the insured person. The victim's claim under s 151 of the RTA 1988 is not a claim "through the assured." Hence, the contractual restrictions that could be arguable in a claim by the assured are not permitted to be raised against the third party victim whose claim is not regarded as "through that of the wrongdoer."[77]

8.49 On the other hand, the third party's claim under the TPA 2010 is a derivative claim founded on the assured's claim against the insurer.[78] In other words, when the TPA 2010 operates, the assured steps into the assured's shoes with respect to the claim against the insurer under the insurance contract. As a result, where a contractual defence is available for the insurer, it is arguable equally towards the assured or the third party claimant under the TPA 2010. In *Charlton v Fisher*,[79] where the claim fell outside the scope of the compulsory MTPL insurance regime, the contractual restriction to the insurance cover was arguable against the third party victim whose claim was under the TPA 1930 (now TPA 2010). The assured had no right under the insurance policy for the damage he caused deliberately. Having acquired no better rights than the assured would have had against the insurer, the third party's claim under the TPA 2010 was equally met by this contractual restriction to the insurance cover.

Permitted exclusions

8.50 Although this matter is discussed in Chapter 7, it is going to be revisited below in respect of the effect of policy restrictions to rights of direct action against insurers under section 151 of the RTA 1988.

8.51 In *Bristol Alliance Ltd Partnership v Williams*[80] J, who was suffering from depression and in an apparent attempt to commit suicide, deliberately drove his car into a wall. The car bounced off and smashed into the windows of a House of Fraser store, causing damage of some £200,000. The property insurer of the premises where the store was located indemnified the property owner and brought a subrogation action against J's motor insurers. However, the motor insurance policy excluded from cover damages arising out of J's deliberate acts. Hence, with respect to this particular use of the vehicle J was clearly uninsured. Normally, victims of uninsured drivers may make a claim against the

---

76 *Charlton v Fisher* [2002] QB 578, [90] Rix LJ.
77 *Gardner v Moore* [1984] AC 548, 560.
78 *Charlton v Fisher* [2002] QB 578, [97] Rix LJ.
79 [2002] QB 578.
80 [2013] RTR 9.

MIB. However, the relevant MIB Agreement provided that the scheme did not extend to compensating those who suffer property damage where such damage was insured by the victim's own insurer who brings a subrogated claim for recovery. The claim therefore was against the motor insurers under section 151 of the RTA 1988 and the main question was whether the liability was covered by the insurance contract as required by section 151 of the RTA 1988.

If the policy exclusion was to be disregarded, because this was a claim under section 151, J's motor insurer would have been liable to compensate the third party's loss with a right of recourse against J. If the exclusion was enforceable, J would have been uninsured at the time of the accident and would have committed the offence under the RTA 1988 s 143(2); the MIB would have been expected to cover the loss, but the loss would have fallen within the exception to the MIB Agreements.

8.52 Since the damage to the shop windows was not covered by the terms of the policy, this claim fell outside the scope of s 151(2)(a). Ward LJ who gave the only reasoned judgment at the Court of Appeal acknowledged the previous cases such as *Hardy*, *Gardner* and *Charlton v Fisher* referred to in this chapter. Nevertheless, with a slightly different focus, Ward LJ decided for J's motor insurers. Seemingly, Ward LJ preferred to follow that route because the claim disputed in *Bristol Alliance Ltd Partnership v Williams*[81] was for damage to property for which the statutory compulsory MTPL insurance regime allows some defined exclusions. Such exclusions for instance include a maximum limit of £1.2m and any damage exceeding this amount is not subject to the compulsory insurance requirement.[82]

Ward LJ discussed whether the statute provides an exhaustive list of exclusions, and his Lordship concluded that it does not; that meant other exclusions were effective. Having acknowledged a long established exclusion in typical motor vehicle insurance for uses other than for social, domestic or pleasure purposes that has never been doubted, Ward LJ stated that if the list had been exhaustive the statute would have clearly stated it.

8.53 With respect, Ward LJ's assessment undermined the nature of section 151 claims which is a right of action against the insurer by the third party victim of a traffic accident as separate to that of the assured.[83] Whereas, Ward LJ analysed the third party's claim as if the third party stepped in to the assured's shoes as is the case under the TPA 2010 which was analysed above.

Ward LJ disagreed that "the purpose of s 151 is to secure the third party's right to recovery whatever the terms of the policy may dictate as between policy holder and insurer." In his Lordship's view this "cannot be correct."[84] On the other hand, this interpretation was at the heart of the analysis of the previous cases mentioned in this chapter on the construction of section 151 and the MIB Agreements. Ward LJ's statement therefore undermines the earlier comments about the function of section 151 in the compulsory MTPL insurance regime.

8.54 It is submitted that section 151(2)(b) of the RTA 1988 supports the broad interpretation of section 151 rather than a restricted interpretation as adopted by Ward LJ in

---

81 [2013] RTR 9.
82 See Chapter 4 and the RTA 1988 s 145(4).
83 See *Charlton v Fisher* [2002] QB 578.
84 [2013] RTR 9, [51].

Bristol v Williams. Further, the right of action is available despite any right of the insurer to avoid or cancel the policy (section 151(5)), and any term removing cover where the driver is unlicensed is similarly not enforceable (section 151(3)) and also strengthens the argument that the scope of section 151 is broader than that of suggested by Ward LJ. Moreover, the excluded liability permitted under section 152 is clearly set out by section 151(2)(b) and 151(4).

8.55 Seemingly Ward LJ's analysis was also influenced by the fact that the policy provided an express exclusion covering the claim in question. Further, Ward LJ's assessment of the claim relies on the principle that, under ordinary circumstances, the MIB would pick up the loss when the motorist was uninsured. The dispute arose in *Bristol*, however, because the relevant MIB Agreement excluded the claim for property loss which was indemnified by the claimant's insurer. Ward LJ also analysed whether, with regards to policy exclusions, the statutory compensation scheme failed to comply with the EU Directives. This is discussed in Chapter 7 where policy restrictions are examined.

8.56 Ward LJ did not differ from the cases such as *Hardy v Motor Insurers' Bureau*[85] and *Gardner v Moore*[86] where the Courts adopted broad interpretations of the word "any" in section 145(3)(a) of the RTA 1988. Moreover, his Lordship agreed that it is the assured's not the insurer's duty to comply with the insurance obligation under the RTA 1988 s 143. However, Ward LJ differed with respect to the power of a policy restriction towards a section 151 claimant. Since the duty to comply with the statutory insurance cover is on the assured but not the insurer, the insurer could not be expected to cover any liability where the policy provides restrictions to the cover. In other words, Ward LJ did not treat the third party as being placed in any better position than the assured. With respect, this is not in line with the principles either adopted by the previous authorities discussed in this chapter or the general view adopted in the interpretation of the statutory provisions with respect to compensating the losses suffered by the traffic accident victims.

Monk v Warbey liability and section 145 of the RTA 1988

8.57 This issue is mentioned here because in two different occasions the English Courts resolved the matter of whether the victim of a traffic accident could have a claim under section 151(2) of the RTA 1988 when the driver was unidentified-untraced and the insured person was guilty of section 143(1)(b), otherwise known as the *Monk v Warbey* liability,[87] and the insurance policy excluded cover when a person other than the assured used the vehicle. Under these circumstances a question could arise as to whether the victim's claim against the insurer still falls under s 151(2)(b) despite the express exclusion from the insurance cover.

8.58 The answer varies according to a narrow or broad reading of section 151(2)(b). In *Allen v Mohammed*[88] the victim was knocked off his bike by a motorist who was driving the vehicle with the permission of its owner. The owner was insured, but the insurance did not extend its cover to a third party who drove the vehicle with the owner's

---

85 [1964] 2 QB 745.
86 [1984] AC 548.
87 See Chapter 6.
88 [2017] Lloyd's Rep IR 73.

permission. The owner committed the offence under s 143(2) by permitting an uninsured person to drive the vehicle and was liable under s 143(1)(b).

No claim was made against the MIB. During the course of the proceedings the victim applied to join the MIB to the proceedings in the event that he was found to be unable to enforce the claim against the insurer. HHJ Tindal merely noted that on the face of things the MIB did face liability although there was an issue whether any claim against the MIB was time barred.

8.59 The claim fell outside the scope of s 151(2)(a) as the insured person was not the user of the vehicle who caused the accident. The question was whether the insured person may fall under section 151(2)(b) because the policy excluded liability in the case of the vehicle being driven by another person. In this respect the insured person is uninsured but that was a circumstance which was to be insured under the MTPL insurance so that the insurer would face liability because s 151(2)(b) is to cover losses caused by users who were not insured but were to be insured. The claimant argued that the judgment "relating to the liability" for his injury was obtained against the insured owner and that she was a person "other than the one who is insured by the policy" because she was not covered for that particular liability even though she was insured against other liabilities. On that reasoning, section 151(2)(b) applied to any case where judgment was given against the assured in circumstances where the policy did not respond.

8.60 A distinction had been drawn in section 151(2)(b) between security and policy. Under the provision as it applied to a security, the insurer was to be liable for a judgment relating to liability to be covered by a policy of insurance if the liability is one which would have been covered if the security covered the liability of all persons and judgment is obtained against any person other than the one whose liability is covered by the security. Had the present case involved a security rather than a policy, the insured person's liability was not one covered by the security but the assured was a person whose liability "is covered by the security." Accordingly, section 151(2)(b) would have applied. Given that the concepts of policy and security were interchangeable in the legislation, it made no sense to hold that section 151(2)(b) applied to a person who had given security but not to the holder of a policy.

8.61 HHJ Tindal proposed a three-step exercise[89]: the first step was identifying if the judgment related to section 145 of the RTA 1988. The second step was if the judgment was against a person who was not insured (section 151(2)(b)), and finally section 151(2)(b) applied to judgments against any person but only to liabilities that would be covered if the policy insured all persons.

8.62 HHJ Tindal gave section 151(2)(b) such a wide meaning that the uninsured driver, although uninsured, would have been insured if the policy had extended the cover to the driver who drove it with the assured's permission. In other words, excluding liability for the drivers whose use is permitted by the assured person is not enforceable when it comes to the interpretation of section 151(2)(b).

As a result, section 151(2)(b) was extended to *Monk v Warbey* liability. Had the MIB been involved, the insurer would have been the Art 75 insurer.[90] The interpretation adopted by HHJ Tindal had two advantages. First, it overcame the extra layer of complexity that

---

89 *Allen v Mohammed* [2017] Lloyd's Rep IR 73, [28].
90 See paragraph 8.125.

would have been created by involving the MIB who would have otherwise been the middleman. The insurer would have been nominated as the insurer required to pay under Article 75 of the MIB's Articles of Association, and in *Allen*, imposing direct liability upon the insurer "cut out the middleman."[91] Second, this interpretation confirms that the MIB is the insurer of last resort.[92]

8.63 However, this interpretation was undermined by the Court of Appeal in *Sahin v Havard*,[93] the facts of which were very close to those of *Allen v Mohammed*: S's car collided with a motor car which was owned by L, a car hire company. L had hired the car to H who permitted X to drive the vehicle. Although H was a permitted driver under the car hire company's insurance, that insurance did not cover anyone whom she herself permitted to drive; indeed it expressly excluded any liability for loss or damage incurred while the motor vehicle was being driven by any person not permitted to drive. S obtained a default judgment against L, but L had gone into liquidation. S then began proceedings against H. Similar to *Allen*, the permission which H gave to X to drive the motor vehicle led to the *Monk v Warbey* liability under s 143(1)(b) of the RTA 1988.

8.64 Whilst HHJ Tindal in *Allen* focussed on the interpretation of s 151(2)(b), in *Sahin*, the central provision was taken as s 145 of the RTA 1988: whether H's liability to S was a liability "incurred . . . in respect of . . . damage to property caused by, or arising out of the use of the vehicle on a road or other public place."

8.65 In *Sahin* the Court of Appeal was not referred to *Allen*.

The question in *Sahin* was identified as whether "permitting someone to drive a motor vehicle" was "using" that vehicle on a road. The Court of Appeal distinguished these two concepts under s 143 and held that otherwise s 143(1)(b) would scarcely be necessary if "causing or permitting use" were the same as "use." The natural consequence of this distinction was that the liability of someone who permits another to use a vehicle without an insurance policy is not a liability which is itself required to be insured under s 145 and is not therefore a liability which an insurer is obliged to satisfy under s 151.

The cause of the different interpretations in *Sahin* and *Allen* appears to have derived from the identification of the claim that was at the heart of the cases. It is true that the owner contravened s 143(1)(b) of the RTA 1988 which resulted in a criminal offence under s 143(2) and in theory, civil liability under *Monk v Warbey*. As discussed in Chapter 6 the *Monk v Warbey* liability arises at the time of contravening s 143(1)(b); however, the owner is not obliged to pay any more than nominal damages unless neither the insurer nor the MIB does compensate the loss and the driver is impecunious. Both in *Sahin* and *Allen* the owners contravened s 143(1)(b). One of the differences in facts was that in *Allen* no actual compensation under *Monk v Warbey* was awarded against the insured owner – the insurer was to bear the loss; in Sahin damages under *Monk v Warbey* were awarded in favour of the victim and against the person who permitted the uninsured use. In *Allen* the focus was, although closely linked with the permission for an uninsured use, not on the insured owner's liability under s 143(1) but the user's liability to the victim. In other words, the actual use by the uninsured driver which was excluded from the cover was disputed. The uninsured use was permitted by the owner and in theory this fell within

---

91 [2017] Lloyd's Rep IR 73, [31].
92 See Chapter 10.
93 [2017] Lloyd's Rep IR 110.

the *Monk v Warbey* liability, but the claim was not for damages awarded against the owner; the claim was for the use by uninsured use. If there had been no permission perhaps the use and therefore the accident would not have taken place. The exclusion from the cover for use by persons other than those expressly included in the insurance cover was not arguable against the third party victim. Under these circumstances, the use by the actual driver was a liability that was required to be insured and therefore it fell under s 151(2)(b). The insurer's right of recourse against the owner remains intact.

8.66 In *Sahin*, once again, the relevant use was excluded from the insurance cover. However, the Court's analysis did not reach to discussing the enforceability of the exclusion in a claim by the third party victim. The matter at stake was the claim which was for the damages awarded under *Monk v Warbey*. What was discussed therefore was not the actual user's liability but the liability of the person who permitted the uninsured use. This reveals the reason why the Court of Appeal found it necessary to distinguish the "use" under s 143(1)(a) and "cause or permit to use" under s 143(1)(b).

8.67 The issue in both cases derives from the exclusion from the insurance cover in respect of users of the vehicle other than the insured person. So far as s 151(2)(b) is concerned, what is required to be insured is the "use" not the actual "user." The core aim of the compulsory MTPL insurance regime is to ensure that there is insurer to compensate the traffic accident victims' claims. Hence, under s 151(2) not only the use of the vehicle by an insured person but also by any other person whose use is to be insured under the MTPL insurance regime is to be covered.

8.68 In the light of the above the problem appears to be on the enforceability of the driver exclusion in an insurance contract in a claim by the third party traffic accident victim. This is a very controversial matter discussed in Chapter 7. These matters are to be resolved between the insured person and the insurer contractually, so as far as the third party victim is concerned the insurer's liability is to be adjudicated upon according to the wording of the statute rather than upon the scope of the contract of insurance.[94] It follows that the exclusions as included by the insurance contracts disputed both in *Sahin* and *Allen* should not be available for the insurer in a claim by the third party victim. The insurer may recoup against the person who used the vehicle and against the insured owner. That is the systematic that is available under the RTA 1988 and the relevant EU Directives. HHJ Tindal's conclusion is apt to the facts in *Sahin* in the sense that the policy did not cover that liability but that the insurers were nevertheless required to meet a judgment because the policy was required to cover all persons.

Right of recourse

8.69 The insurer's liability under section 151 is to some extent mitigated by sections 151(7) and 151(8). By section 151(7), where an insurer faces liability under section 151 to satisfy a judgment despite otherwise not facing liability under the policy, there is a right of recourse against the assured. Under section 151(7)(a) and (b) the amount that the insurer may recoup is different depending on the ground of insurer's payment. If the insurer has to satisfy the judgment because the policy condition was rendered of no effect

---

94 *Wastell v Woodward and Chaucer Syndicates Ltd* [2017] Lloyd's Rep IR 474, [17].

by section 151(3), the insurer can recover the full amount. On the other hand, if the insurer would have been liable but the actual payment exceeded the amount insured by the contract, the insurer can claim the excess.

8.70 Further, under section 151(8), where there is liability for an uninsured driver, then the insurer has a right of recourse against the driver and also against the assured if the assured caused or permitted the uninsured use of the vehicle.

Section 151(8) provides

> (8) Where an insurer becomes liable under this section to pay an amount in respect of a liability of a person who is not insured by a policy or whose liability is not covered by a security, he is entitled to recover the amount from that person or from any person who –
>
> (a) is insured by the policy, or whose liability is covered by the security, by the terms of which the liability would be covered if the policy insured all persons or, as the case may be, the security covered the liability of all persons, and
>
> (b) caused or permitted the use of the vehicle which gave rise to the liability.

8.71 Section 151(8) was described as "the other side of a bargain."[95] It is the benefit that the compulsory motor insurer obtains in return for having to pay out in circumstances where it might otherwise have been able to avoid or cancel the policy. It is linked into section 148(6) of the Act.

Insurer's right of recourse against the owner who was a passenger

8.72 Section 151(8) creates a conflict between recovery and recourse where the victim is the assured. As discussed in Chapter 7 the owner of a vehicle could be a passenger victim in his own car when the owner either caused or permitted the uninsured use of the vehicle. When the owner is insured, under section 151(2)(b) of the RTA 1988 the insurer is to compensate the loss caused by the uninsured use. Reading literally, section 151(8) then grants a right of recourse against the uninsured user as well as the insured owner who caused or permitted the uninsured use of the vehicle. The question then becomes whether section 151(8) could be argued against the owner who caused or permitted uninsured use and is also a passenger victim. The insurer would, on the one hand, be obliged to compensate the owner passenger's loss, but on the other hand, could recover this amount back from the owner.

8.73 If the owner is to be taken as using a vehicle when he is a passenger and allows another person to drive the vehicle,[96] the insurer's right of recourse under s 151(8) should be available towards the owner passenger who permitted the use of vehicle outside the scope of the insurance contract. On the other hand, the wording of Art 12(1) of the Consolidated Directive is that the compulsory MTPL insurance requires insurance to cover "all passengers, other than the driver, arising out of use of a vehicle." Since the Article uses the word "driver" but not "user" the fact that the owner who is a passenger in his own vehicle is also "user" of the vehicle should not affect the passenger owner's

---

95 *Churchill Insurance Co Ltd v Fitzgerald* [2013] Lloyd's Rep IR 137, [61], Aikens LJ found it likely that insurer's right to claim an indemnity under section 151(8) was the bargain struck by statutory motor insurers at the time that compulsory motor insurance was first introduced into the UK by the 1930 Road Traffic Act.

96 *Cobb v Williams* [1973] RTR 113; *Pratt v Patrick* [1924] 1 KB 488.

right to compensation under the insurance cover. This is supported by the CJEU who held that the legal position of the owner of the vehicle, present in the vehicle at the time of the accident as a passenger, is the same as that of any other passenger who is a victim of the accident.[97]

8.74 Two issues need to be separated with regards to the influence of the EU Directives to the compulsory MTPL insurance as regulated by the domestic rules. These two matters are:

(a)   national rules concerning civil liability for damage and injury resulting from road accidents;

(b)   community law regarding compulsory insurance for civil liability towards "third parties," including passengers, arising out of accidents involving motor vehicles.

The injured victim's right for compensation for a traffic accident, the circumstance under (a) above, is affected by a limitation of the user's liability under the applicable civil liability rules. The victim's right to compensation from the insurer, as identified in (b) above, is affected by a limitation of the cover against civil liability by the insurance provisions.[98] A further distinction to be made between (a) and (b) is that whilst the former is essentially governed by national law, the latter is defined and guaranteed by European Union legislation.[99]

8.75 It follows that if the relevant national provision is a rule governing civil liability then the only limitation on their applicability is that such provisions must not deprive the Directives of their effectiveness.[100] But if the national provision is one that concerns the extent to which a passenger can benefit from civil liability insurance cover, then that does directly concern the Directives and the national law must not conflict with their objectives and provisions.[101]

8.76 An illustration of a rule that will fall under (a) above is seen in *Neto de Sousa v Portugal*[102] where the relevant Portuguese domestic legislation provided that a person who causes an accident by his/her own fault may not seek compensation for non-pecuniary damages suffered as a result of the loss of a spouse because of the accident.[103] In *Neto De Sousa* the claimant was injured and his wife, C, a passenger, was killed. The claimant argued that the motor vehicle liability insurer should compensate him for the material harm which he had suffered as a result of that death. On a reference by the Portuguese Supreme Court, the CJEU clearly separated the relevant exclusion in the domestic legislation from those that govern the insurance cover for civil liability in motor vehicle

---

97 *Churchill Insurance Co Ltd v Wilkinson* (C-442/10) [2012] Lloyd's Rep IR 544; *Candolin v Vahinkovakuutusosakeyhtio Pohjola* (C-537/03) [2006] Lloyd's Rep IR 209.

98 *Ambrosio Lavrador v Companhia de Seguros Fidelidade-Mundial SA* (C-409/09) [2012] Lloyd's Rep IR 236.

99 *Neto de Sousa v Portugal* (C-506/16) [2018] Lloyd's Rep IR 118, [28].

100 *Churchill Insurance Co Ltd v Wilkinson* (C-442/10) [2012] Lloyd's Rep IR 544, [48].

101 *Churchill Insurance Co Ltd v Fitzgerald* [2013] Lloyd's Rep IR 137, [45].

102 (C-506/16) [2018] Lloyd's Rep IR 118.

103 Under Article 7(3) of Decree-Law No 522/85, in the event of death following an accident, in particular of the spouse of the driver of the vehicle and holder of the insurance policy, payment of any compensation for non-pecuniary damage to the person at fault responsible for the accident is excluded.

accidents. The claimant could not recover compensation for his own injuries, nor could he recover compensation for loss flowing from the death of his wife.

8.77 As explained in Chapter 7, in *Churchill Insurance Co Ltd v Wilkinson*[104] the Court referred to the CJEU with regards to a common matter that arose in two different cases[105] in which the owners were injured as a result of accidents that took place when an uninsured driver was driving each vehicle. What is relevant to the present chapter is that in *Churchill Insurance Co Ltd v Wilkinson*[106] the CJEU refused to discuss the interpretation of section 151(8) as it was for the national Court to decide. Upon the remission of the case, in *Churchill Insurance Co Ltd v Fitzgerald*[107] the Court of Appeal discussed the conflict under section 151(8) of the RTA 1988 between recovery and recourse where the victim is the assured.

8.78 Aikens LJ[108] described the effect of section 151(8) as "to grant the insurer the right to claim a civil indemnity in circumstances where the insured has caused or permitted an uninsured driver to use the vehicle which gave rise to the liability."

Section 151(8) of RTA 1988 is, therefore, a right based on the insured passenger victim's "contribution" to the "occurrence of the loss."[109] For contribution it has to be shown that the assured caused or permitted the use of the vehicle and that the use of the vehicle gave rise to the liability. These features of section 151(8) are key to interpret the section in the light of the rulings of the CJEU in similar cases.

In view of Aikens LJ in *Churchill Insurance Co Ltd v Fitzgerald*, the RTA 1988 s 151(8) is a rule which related both to civil liability (a) and to the restriction of an insurance recovery (b).[110] Where the victim is not the assured the section purely concerns civil liability. It does not affect a passenger victim's right to compensation through compulsory motor insurance. It further retains the ability of an insurer to utilise its right to obtain an indemnity from an insured person. Where the insured person is the passenger victim who also caused or permitted the uninsured use of the vehicle which gave rise to the liability, the section operates to remove from the passenger owner the right to retain compensation payable for his injuries. In this respect, the section falls under category (b) above and it has to be tested against the Directive.

8.79 The Court of Appeal held in *Churchill v Fitzgerald* that section 151(8) has to be interpreted in a manner which is consistent with the interpretation of Articles 12(1) and 13(1) of the Consolidated Directive by the CJEU. Namely those provisions preclude national rules

> the effect of which is to omit automatically the requirement that the insurer should compensate a passenger, the victim of a road traffic accident, on the ground that the passenger was insured to drive the vehicle which caused the accident but that the driver was not.[111]

---

104 (C-442/10) [2012] Lloyd's Rep IR 544.

105 Conjoined appeals of *Churchill Insurance Company Ltd v Benjamin Wilkinson* and *Tracey Evans v Equity Claims Ltd* [2010] Lloyd's Rep IR 591.

106 (C-442/10) [2012] Lloyd's Rep IR 544, [22].

107 [2013] Lloyd's Rep IR 137.

108 Ibid, [73].

109 Ibid, [73].

110 [2013] Lloyd's Rep IR 137, [62], Etherton and Maurice Kay LJ agreed.

111 *Churchill Insurance Co Ltd v Wilkinson* (C-442/10) [2012] Lloyd's Rep IR 544; *Candolin v Vahinkovakuutusosakeyhtio Pohjola* (C-537/03) [2006] Lloyd's Rep IR 209.

The Court of Appeal in *Churchill v Fitzgerald*[112] therefore proposed that the RTA 1988 s 151(8) should be read as notionally including the words added in italics:

> Where an insurer becomes liable under this section to pay an amount in respect of a liability of a person who is not insured in a policy . . . he is entitled to recover the amount from . . . any person who –
>
> . . .
>
> (b)   caused or permitted the use of the vehicle which gave rise to the liability, *save that where the person insured by the policy may be entitled to the benefit of any judgment to which this section refers, any recovery by the insurer in respect of that judgment must be proportionate and determined on the basis of the circumstances of the case.*

8.80 Whether what is claimed from the owner passenger who permitted the uninsured use of the vehicle is proportionate is to be determined in every case on its own facts. It appears that the wording notionally added to s 151(8) by *Churchill v Fitzgerald*[113] takes into account contributory negligence on the owner of the vehicle. Whether or not contributory negligence applies in determining civil liability in motor vehicle accidents is a matter for national law and clearly Directives do not aim to harmonise this area of law. However, as also referred to by Aikens LJ, the national civil liability rules must not deprive the Directives of their effectiveness.[114] The proposed notional amendment to s 151(8) recognises the contributory negligence defence in the principles of tort law and permits the insurer to recoup against the owner where to do so is not disproportionate so that it does not go against the compulsory MTPL insurance regime.

A judgment against an untraced driver and a section 151 claim

8.81 After *Sahin v Havard*,[115] in a similar situation, one could question if it is possible to obtain a judgment against an untraced driver and enforce such judgment against the insurer of the person who permitted the untraced driver to drive the vehicle. This issue was discussed in *Cameron v Liverpool Victoria Insurance Co Ltd*[116] in which Lord Sumption (with whom Lord Reed, Lord Carnwath, Lord Hodge and Lady Black agree) denied that it was open to the claimant victim.

8.82 In *Cameron v Liverpool Victoria Insurance Co Ltd* a collision occurred between a Ford Fiesta and a Nissan Micra. The vehicle registration number of the Nissan was taken down by a passing taxi driver. It was discovered through the policy as registered to N and it was insured by L. Proceedings were issued against N in the belief that he was the driver of the vehicle, but at a later stage it was understood that N was not driving the vehicle at the time of the accident. The three-month time limit under section 152(2) as explained above to seek a declaration for the insurer to avoid the policy expired in this case. The victim then amended the proceeding to add a claim against Liverpool Victoria Insurance for a declaration that it would be liable to meet any judgment obtained against N under section 151 of the RTA 1988. L argued that its insured was B, a person whom

---

112 [2013] Lloyd's Rep IR 137, [76].
113 Ibid.
114 [2013] Lloyd's Rep IR 137, [45].
115 [2017] Lloyd's Rep IR 110.
116 [2019] UKSC 6.

it now believes to be fictitious, such that the policy was obtained by fraud. The claimant did not attempt to obtain a judgment against N for breach of section 143 as *Sahin v Havard* established, and L was not obliged to satisfy the *Monk v Warbey* liability under the circumstances.[117] Instead, the claimant made an application to amend the claim form to substitute for N "the person unknown driving vehicle registration number Y598 SPS who collided with vehicle registration number KG03 ZJZ on 26 May 2013." The question for the Supreme Court was whether the Court should exercise its power under the CPR to permit the proposed amendment to the claim form to substitute the unnamed defendant identified by the proposed description. It was by the Court of Appeal that the policy had not been shown to the Court and no argument was directed in relation to its terms.

8.83 The matter at stake was procedural that whether, when the registered keeper of the vehicle involved in an accident was not the driver of the vehicle and the identity of the driver was unknown, the inability of the claimant victim to name the driver is a bar to bringing proceedings against the unnamed driver.

8.84 The majority of the Court of Appeal permitted the amendment. Gloster J noted that if the claimant obtained a judgment for damages against the unnamed defendant by the relevant description, such a judgment would relate to a liability with respect to a matter that was required to be covered by a policy of insurance under section 145 and that such a liability would have been covered by the terms of the policy if the policy had insured "all persons" (section 151(2)(b).

There was no dispute that although the insurer would have been entitled to have avoided the policy under section 151(2)(a) on the ground of the fraudulent misrepresentation, the insurer had not sought a declaration to this effect within the relevant time limit, hence the insurer was bound by the terms of the policy.

Having adopted a broad interpretation of the objective of the RTA 1988, the majority's view was that a motor vehicle insurer agrees to take the risk insured by the compulsory insurance policy that insured persons may allow uninsured persons to drive the vehicle, the vehicle may be driven unlawfully by person without the consent of the insured and the existence or non-existence of the insured or named drivers. The insurer is in a position to assess the risk and make a business decision as to whether to accept the risk. More importantly, Gloster LJ noted that an insurer insuring motor vehicle compulsory insurance enters in the market by knowing that it may be held liable to satisfy judgments against third party tortfeasors who have driven the insured vehicle negligently, notwithstanding that the driver may not be insured under the terms of the policy.[118] In other words, the insurers, under the 1988 Act, may be obliged to compensate the victims' claim although, contractually, the insurer was not obliged to do so. Section 151(8) grants a right of recourse against the assured and whether that is a useful tool for the insurer falls on the insurer.

Having considered the regime and the dynamics of the insurance markets Gloster LJ concluded that an identified insurer's liability under section 151 should not depend on whether, as at the date of issue of the proceedings, the claimant can identify the tortfeasor by name. The majority of the Court of Appeal did not find it just to reject the application

---

117 Gloster LJ noted that such an argument might nevertheless have resulted in the registered keeper identifying the actual driver (on pain of punishment for contempt) [2017] EWCA Civ 366, [38].

118 [2017] Lloyd's Rep IR 487, [42].

in this case simply because an alternative remedy against the MIB was available. Sir Ross Cranston[119] disagreed, but his reasons, it is submitted with respect, are not persuasive. To exercise the relevant discretion, in view of Sir Ross Cranston, the reasons must be more compelling than they are in *Cameron*. The MIB could satisfy the claim in this case; moreover, to obtain a judgment a claimant must satisfy the requirements of both procedural and substantive law, whereas in *Cameron* the defendant could not be named and the procedural requirements were not met.

8.85 Lord Sumption, who gave the only reasoned judgment, agreed that the liability clearly falls on the MIB in this case. After a very detailed analysis and references to precedent cases, his Lordship ruled that there was nothing in the CPR that allowed or prohibited an action against an unidentified driver. CPR 6.3 required service of the claim form by the Court unless the claimant effected service himself, and CPR 6.15 provided for alternative service where there appeared to the Court to be good reason to authorise it. However, in all cases the method used had to put the recipient in a position to ascertain its contents. That was not possible by effecting service on the insurers. There was no evidence that the unidentified driver was trying to evade service, and so there was no basis for the Court giving permission under CPR 6.16 to dispense with service.

8.86 At first sight, the case seems to be purely procedural and its significance for motor vehicle third party liability insurance may not be obvious. However, Lord Sumption made some limited, but nevertheless significant, comments on the nature of the right of direct action against insurers under the domestic as well as the EU rules. Although Lord Sumption had no doubts that it was the MIB who should bear the obligation to compensate the victim, it is submitted with respect that the statutory provisions and the precedent case law references that are analysed throughout this book indicate that the obligation to compensate the victim's loss was on N's insurer. The reasons for this submission are as follows.

8.87 Lord Sumption's starting point in *Cameron* was that the Road Traffic Act scheme is expressly based on the principle that as a general rule there is no direct liability on the insurer, except for its liability to meet a judgment against the motorist once it has been obtained.[120] The assured can only make a claim under the policy when his liability to the third party is established.[121] Doubtless these are the general principles of liability insurance that also are applicable in respect of the compulsory motor third party liability insurance. However, Lord Sumption noted that the UTDA assumes that judgment cannot be obtained against the driver if he cannot be identified, and therefore that no liability will attach to the insurer in that case.[122] According to his Lordship, this was the reason for passing the liability on to the Motor Insurers' Bureau.[123] His Lordship explained that the victim was challenging this and such a challenge was unnecessary: it was cheaper and quicker to claim against the MIB.

8.88 However, the scheme under section 151 as highlighted in this chapter and the status and the role of the MIB as examined in Chapter 10 point otherwise.

---

119 [2017] EWCA Civ 366, [104], [105], [115].
120 [2019] UKSC 6 [5], [22].
121 [2019] UKSC 6 [5].
122 Ibid.
123 Ibid.

So far as s 151(2)(b) is concerned, what is required to be insured is the "use" not the actual "user." The core aim of the compulsory motor third party liability insurance regime is to ensure that there is insurer to compensate the traffic accident victims' claims. Hence, under s 151(2) not only the use of the vehicle by an insured person but also by any other person whose use is to be insured under the compulsory insurance regime is to be covered. In return, the insurer is granted rights of recourse under sections 151(7) and 151(8).

8.89 It is true that as Lord Sumption noted the insurer's liability under section 151 is contingent, and indeed the insurer has a sufficient interest to have itself joined to the proceedings in its own right, if it wishes to be. That is the reason, as referred to below, for the notification obligation under section 152 so that the insurer may seek either to cancel the policy with mutual consent or to seek a declaration that the policy is avoidable for breach of the duty of fair presentation of the risk by the assured.

8.90 Lord Sumption expressed that Parliament's intention that the victims of negligent motorists should be compensated by the insurer is qualified[124]: Parliament assumed that other arrangements would be made which would fill the compensation gap, as indeed they have been. It is true that it has been the intention of Parliament to fill gaps in respect of compensation of third party victim's loss but only where there is no way to hold the insurer liable for the loss. However, unlike what Lord Sumption stated, the UTDA assumes that there is no insurer to identify. Insurers may, as analysed again in this chapter, deny liability either under s 151(4) or, as examined in Chapter 7, because of permitted exclusions, for instance, where the insurer agreed to insure only for social, domestic and pleasure purposes and the vehicle was used for purposes other than that.[125] Except those circumstances, the RTA 1988 assumes that where an insurer is identified, it falls on the insurer to compensate the victim's loss with a right of recourse as mentioned above.

8.91 Notably, Lord Sumption added that the insurer should not be permitted to join in the proceedings as it is not to be assumed that the insurer had the authority to conduct the defence on the driver's behalf.[126] Lord Sumption's judgment seems to assume that the MIB compensates the victim's loss without investigating the claim. However, as examined in Chapter 10 the MIB also investigates the claim as set out under the relevant applicable Agreement and determines under the standards that the Court would apply in evaluating the user's liability.

Notifying the insurer of the action against the assured

8.92 Under section 151(5) of the Road Traffic Act 1988, notwithstanding that an insurer issuing a compulsory motor insurance policy may be entitled to avoid or cancel the policy, he must pay to the persons entitled to the benefit of a judgment against the driver any sum payable under the judgment.[127] Since insurers have to satisfy such a judgment, the 1988 Act provides them with a right to be informed of the proceedings against the

---

124 [2019] UKSC 6 [22].

125 *RoadPeace v Secretary of State for Transport* [2018] 1 WLR 1293; *Bristol Alliance Ltd Partnership v Williams* [2013] RTR 9 [45].

126 [2019] UKSC 6 [23].

127 The objective of this section is not to protect the drivers whether fraudulent or not, but to protect the people who may be injured. *Durrant v MacLaren* [1956] 2 Lloyd's Rep 70.

negligent driver, so that they can, if they choose, participate and defend the claim. For this reason, it is necessary for any claimant to comply with section 152(1)(a) of the 1988 Act, which provides that no sum is payable by insurers

> in respect of a judgment unless, before or within seven days after the commencement of the proceedings in which the judgment was given, the insurer had notice of the bringing of the proceedings.

8.93 The notice requirement was first introduced in the RTA 1934. It was then reproduced by the subsequent legislation, namely, the RTA 1962, the RTA 1972 and the RTA 1988.

8.94 The notice is a condition precedent to insurers' liability. This was explained by Porter J in *Herbert v Railway Passengers Assurance Co*[128] that

> where an Act of Parliament stipulates that recovery shall not take place except in certain events, those events must take place before the plaintiff can recover.

8.95 The nature of the notice requirement has been discussed in a number of cases by which the Courts adopted a strict[129] and purposive approach to its interpretation. The objective of the relevant notice is to avoid insurers being asked to satisfy a judgment against their insured in respect of a claim of which they knew nothing, obtained in proceedings of which they had no notice or warning.[130] A judgment may be given in default[131] of the defendant motorist assured which is a concern for the insurer.[132] Moreover, insurers may have repudiated liability as against their assured, or the insurers may wish to seek a declaration as to the right to avoid the policy under section 152 of the RTA 1988. Parliament intended the insurer to be informed at a stage that is early enough for the insurer to discover the details of the proceedings against their assured[133] so that they are in a position to intervene.[134]

Timing

8.96 The requirement is that the insurers have notice of "the bringing of the proceedings."[135] "Proceedings" mean the beginning of legal proceedings.[136] "The commencement of proceedings" is a different concept to the "bringing of the proceedings."[137] Both of these situations appear in section 152(1), and the notice of the bringing of the

---

128 (1938) 60 Ll L Rep 143, 146.

129 Where there is a statutory requirement of this kind, it must be pretty strictly fulfilled. *Weldrick v Essex & Suffolk Equitable Insurance Society Ltd*, (1949–50) 83 Ll L Rep 91, p 102, Birkett J.

130 *Desouza v Waterlow* [1999] RTR 71; *Wake v Wylie* [2001] RTR 20; *Nawaz v Crowe Insurance Group* [2003] RTR 29.

131 As discussed below, the insurer may seek to set aside a default judgment.

132 *McGoona v Motor Insurers' Bureau* [1969] 2 Lloyd's Rep 34; *Harrington v Link Motor Policies At Lloyd's* [1989] RTR 345.

133 *Desouza v Waterlow* [1999] RTR 71.

134 *McGoona v Motor Insurers' Bureau* [1969] 2 Lloyd's Rep 34; *Harrington v Link Motor Policies At Lloyd's* [1989] RTR 345.

135 *Desouza v Waterlow* [1999] RTR 71.

136 *McGoona v Motor Insurers' Bureau* [1969] 2 Lloyd's Rep 34, 46, Lawton J, obiter; *Harrington v Link Motor Policies At Lloyd's* [1989] RTR 345.

137 *Desouza v Waterlow* [1999] RTR 71.

proceedings can be given either before or within seven days after the commencement of proceedings.

8.97 Notice of the bringing of proceedings can be given even at a time when the proceedings have not been brought yet. What is required is not notice of the claim but notice of the bringing of the proceedings.[138] What the insurers should be made aware of is that the third party intends to commence an action against the insurers' assured.

8.98 Once such information reaches the insurers, they bear the burden of finding out the precise details of the proceedings.[139]

8.99 There is no time restriction for notifications of the bringing of the proceedings before their commencement. Some guidance is seen in *Stinton v Stinton*[140] where Beldam LJ said, "It must nevertheless, in my view, be a notice which indicates that proceedings . . . are about to be, brought." The approach of the Court of Appeal was interpreted by Colinvaux as an indication that the greater the gap between the notification and the commencement of proceedings the easier it will be for the Court to find that the notification did not fulfil the requirements for statutory notice.[141] In *Stinton v Stinton* the proceedings were brought 18 months after the letter, which in fact did not amount to sufficient notification, was sent to the insurers.

8.100 If the notice is to be given after the commencement of proceedings, it is necessary to ascertain when the seven-day period starts from. Under the Civil Procedure Rules proceedings are started when the Court issues a claim form at the request of the claimant.[142] When a cross action is brought within an action which has already commenced, the seven-day period starts running from the date of the cross action.

This was discussed in *Cross v British Oak Insurance Company, Ltd*[143] in which B and C were injured as a result of a motor vehicle accident. B brought an action alleging that he had been injured by negligence for which F was responsible. F denied liability and alleged that the accident was due to the fault of C against whom B claimed indemnity or contribution. A notice was given to the insurance company on the day F was granted a leave to serve a third party notice on C. A claim against C was decided on C's favour, but the judgment remained unsatisfied. F's insurer denied liability as they argued that no notice was given to them as required by the RTA. The Court held that the proceedings in which this judgment was given were commenced when C was made a third party.

Formality and the content of the notice

8.101 The RTA 1988 does not specify its form; hence a section 151(2) notice may be given either orally or in writing.[144] It had been previously stated that it must really be a notice in the sense that it is given formally as a notice; however, such degree of formality

---

138 *Harrington v Link Motor Policies At Lloyd's* [1989] RTR 345.

139 *Desouza v Waterlow* [1999] RTR 71. See on the other hand *McBlain v Dolan* 1998 SLT 512, where Lord Johnston at the Court of Session (Outer House) found it a little odd that "the authorities suggest that neither the Court in which the action is to be raised nor the date on which it is raised need be brought to the attention of the insurer, the two things I would have thought most essential to avoiding a decree in absence."

140 [1995] RTR 167, 174.

141 Colinvaux, [23–081].

142 CPR r.7.2(1).

143 [1938] 2 KB 167.

144 *Desouza v Waterlow* [1999] RTR 71.

was disapproved by Kennedy LJ (Rix and Laws LJJ agreed) in *Wake v Wylie*[145] and subsequently once more by the Court of Appeal in *Nawaz v Crowe Insurance Group*.[146] There must be more than evidence of a casual comment to someone who at times acted as an agent for the insurers notice.[147] Similarly, unless the broker is acting as an agent for the insurer in this respect, a notice to the insurance broker is not sufficient.

Bringing of the proceedings

8.102 As noted above, what is required is not notice of the claim but notice of the bringing of the proceedings.[148] Hence notification that a claim may be made is not notification of the commencement of proceedings.[149] The section contemplates something containing less than a precise specification of the action as it affords the possibility of giving notice before the action is filed.[150] Consequently, the name of the Court could no doubt be given, but the section does not require that this should be done and naturally, before the commencement of the proceedings, their number cannot be given either.[151]

8.103 What constitutes notice is a question of fact and degree.[152] In *Stinton v Stinton*[153] the letter stating the following was not a sufficient notification:

> our client has now been granted legal aid to take proceedings against [S] for damages for personal injury and loss arising out of the motor accident under review and accordingly we are now in a position to obtain medical evidence.

8.104 Whether the notice requirement is satisfied is determined on the extent to which the insurer has been made aware of the background circumstances and of the position of the claimant in regard to the taking of proceedings.[154] In *Weldrick v Essex & Suffolk Equitable Insurance Society Ltd,*[155] the relevant letter to the insurers stated

> We understand your Society has repudiated liability, and we shall be grateful to have your confirmation thereof in writing, because you will appreciate, we shall have to take proceedings as against M . . ., and as against the owner of the other vehicle, and at the same time give notice to the Motor Insurers Bureau of your repudiation of liability.

The insurers, in reply, confirmed that they had repudiated the liability under the insurance policy. Having adopted a strict approach and having followed *Herbert v Railway Passengers Assurance Company*[156] Birkett J held that what they did have was an intimation that in certain circumstances proceedings might be brought, but not necessarily that they

---

145 [2001] RTR 20, [12].

146 [2003] RTR 29. See following paragraphs for details.

147 *Herbert v Railway Passengers Assurance Co* (1938) 60 Ll L Rep 143, 146; *Wake v Wylie* [2001] RTR 20.

148 *Harrington v Link Motor Policies At Lloyd's* [1989] RTR 345.

149 *McGoona v Motor Insurers' Bureau* [1969] 2 Lloyd's Rep 34, 46–47, Lawton J, obiter; *Harrington v Link Motor Policies At Lloyd's* [1989] RTR 345.

150 *Ceylon Motor Insurance Association Ltd v Thambugala* [1953] AC 584.

151 Ibid.

152 *McBlain v Dolan* 1998 SLT 512; *Harrington v Link Motor Policies At Lloyd's* [1989] RTR 345.

153 [1995] RTR 167.

154 *Desouza v Waterlow* [1999] RTR 71; *Wake v Wylie* [2001] RTR 20.

155 (1949–50) 83 Ll L Rep 91.

156 (1938) 60 Ll L Rep 143.

would be brought.[157] That means that a warning that in certain circumstances proceedings might be brought, but not necessarily that they would be brought, is not sufficient.[158] This should be read with caution after *Wake v Wylie* where Kennedy LJ expressed his doubt if *Weldrick* can stand in the light of the later decisions and added that *Weldrick* certainly should be regarded as peculiar to its own facts.[159] Instead, Kennedy LJ proposed a modified rule which is stated below.

8.105 In *Ceylon Motor Insurance Association Ltd v Thambugala*[160] the Privy Council found the following letter sufficient to meet the requirements of such notification: "Our client is still under treatment and unless our client's claim is settled on or before the 31st instant, we are instructed to file action against the owner of the car." On the other hand, in *Harrington v Link Motor Policies At Lloyd's*[161] the letter in question was found to be very close to being the form of notice as required; nevertheless, it fell on the wrong side of the line.

8.106 In *Harrington* a traffic accident occurred on 24 October 1985. The claimant consulted solicitors promptly after the accident, and they communicated with the insurers. A series of correspondences took place and on 2 January 1986 the vital letter which was at the heart of the matter was written in the following words:

> We thank you for your letter of 19 December, the contents of which we note. It seems to us that liability cannot be in issue in this matter and unless, therefore, you are able to confirm to us within the next 14 days that an accident report has been received and that you will be dealing with the matter on a full liability basis, we will advise our client to institute proceedings against your insured without further reference to you.

The proceedings were issued against the assured on 3 June 1986 in the Worksop County Court, and a judgment in default was entered. The Court of Appeal adopted some rulings in the *Ceylon* case such as that the Court does not need to be specified in the notification. However, although it was highly persuasive, the Court of Appeal found *Ceylon* to be distinguished in *Harrington* which held that the letter of 2 January 1986 did not meet the requirement of the notice that was required by the RTA. It was merely stating that the claimant's solicitors would advise their clients to institute proceedings against the assured, not that the proceedings were to be instituted. The Court of Appeal acknowledged that it was likely that the proceedings would be instituted; nevertheless the letter did not amount to what is required by the section.

8.107 As a result, whilst an intention to serve was deemed to be sufficient if brought to the attention of the potential defenders (*Ceylon*), notice that the client would be advised to sue was held insufficient (*Harrington*). In *McBlain v Dolan*[162] Lord Johnston said,

---

157 As mentioned, above, Kennedy LJ stated that this finding must be regarded as peculiar to the facts in *Weldrick*.

158 *Weldrick v Essex and Suffolk Equitable Insurance Society Ltd* (1950) 83 Ll L Rep 91, obiter statement of Birkett J.

159 [2001] RTR 20, [16].

160 [1953] AC 584. The Privy Council were dealing with an Ordinance which was in force in Ceylon at the relevant time. The Ordinance was in virtually identical language to the provisions now contained in the Road Traffic Act 1972, but, instead of referring to notice having to be given of the proceedings, it referred to notice of the action.

161 [1989] RTR 345.

162 1998 SLT 512, 514.

THIRD PARTY VICTIM'S RIGHT OF DIRECT ACTION

I have the distinct impression that Woolf LJ was very unhappy with the *Ceylon* case which, as I have indicated, sits uneasily with *Harrington* and that the proper view might have been that in order for notice to be given the Court in which the action is raised and its date of raising must be brought to the attention of the insurer.

The distinction between these authorities is technical rather than substantive.[163]

8.108 *Harrington* may be compared with *Desouza v Waterlow*[164] where the claimant and B were involved in a road traffic accident in August 1990. Shortly after the accident the claimant wrote to B's insurers, giving full details of the accident, the names of the witnesses and two estimates for the repairs to his car. The insurers replied directly to the claimant authorising repairs, having received a report from their own engineer. In January 1991 the claimant informed the insurers of his intention to sue B if his claim was not met and he repeated his intention by a letter in April 1991 addressed to the insurers. In May 1991 he issued a writ against B and obtained a judgment in October 1993. The Court of Appeal held that the claimant had done enough to satisfy section 152(1)(a) as the course which was being proposed was made clear.

8.109 In *Wake v Wylie*[165] Kennedy LJ denied that *Desouza* and *Harrington* were in conflict. According to Kennedy LJ, in *Harrington* the notice was plainly conditional. The insurers had no means of knowing whether or not the solicitors' advice would be accepted. In *Desouza* the claimant, acting in person, told the insurers that he intended to commence legal proceedings and was encouraged to do so.[166] The guidance rule that Kennedy LJ derived from *Harrington*, *Weldrick* and *Ceylon* is that

> Any notification relied upon must not be subject to a condition which may or may not be fulfilled: see *Weldrick*, 83 Ll.L.R. 91 and *Harrington* [1989] R.T.R. 345; but if the only condition is one which requires action from the recipients which they choose not to take then by making that choice they render the notice unconditional and thus effective: see the *Ceylon Motor Insurance Association case* [1953] A.C. 584.[167]

8.110 In *Wake v Wylie* the claimant was seriously injured in an accident that occurred on 29 December 1993. He was a back seat passenger in a vehicle being driven by the defendant. A letter of claim was sent to the insurers in June 1995 to which the insurers responded by seeking further information. In November 1995 the insurers asked for medical evidence which was sent to them on 11 April 1996. A writ was issued against the defendant in November 1996, before the three-year limitation period under section 11 of the Limitation Act expired. Up to this point there had been no formal warning to the insurers that a claim was going to be made. On 3 February 1997 the claimant's solicitors wrote to the insurers confirming that a writ had been issued against the defendant. The insurers nominated solicitors in response to this letter without raising section 152(1)(a) of the RTA, and matters proceeded towards trial: in April 1997 the insurers' solicitors agreed to extend time to the claimant for the service of a statement of claim, and those themselves sought and obtained in May 1997 an extension of time for the service of a defence. It was only in June 1999 the issue of section 152(1)(a) was noticed by the

---

163 Colinvaux, [23–082].
164 [1999] RTR 71.
165 [2001] RTR 20.
166 Ibid, [30].
167 Ibid, [29].

insurers upon instructing a counsel for the trial. The letter of June 1995 did not amount to notice of the commencement of judicial proceedings as such, but rather notice that a claim was being pressed against insurers.

8.111 The need for notice of proceedings, as opposed to notice of a claim, was clear from *Harrington*. Kennedy LJ, although with reluctance, reached the conclusion that the notice requirement was not satisfied although the object of section 152(1) was satisfied given that the insurers were kept in the picture from the start, and were never in danger of being faced with a judgment which they had to satisfy without having had an opportunity to take part in the proceedings. However, this did not suffice to fulfil the wording of section 152(1) that "before or within 7 days after the commencement of the proceedings . . . the insurer had notice of the bringing of the proceedings." Kennedy LJ was ready to find, although noting that all would depend on the facts of the case, even an informal contact, shortly before the commencement of proceedings would put the insurer in the position of having notice of the bringing of the proceedings. However, in the light of the facts in this case there was no room for argument.[168] A prudent solicitor would be well advised to ensure that the insurer received written notice within seven days after the commencement of proceedings.[169]

Is mere contact sufficient?

8.112 Later, *Nawaz v Crowe Insurance Group*[170] confirmed the "contact" that Kennedy LJ referred to in this last mentioned paragraph. In *Nawaz* the correspondences that were questioned within the meaning of section 152(1)(a) took place between the secretary of a partner of the law firm that insurers instructed and a trainee solicitor of the firm representing the claimant. The trainee solicitor telephoned the insurer's solicitors and talked to the secretary of the partner who dealt with the claim in question. On the first of these telephone conversations the trainee solicitor asked for the defendant's address. The secretary said that she would get back to the trainee solicitor. When the secretary did not do so the trainee solicitor telephoned her again the next day, obtained the address and informed her that this was required as it was intended to issue proceedings against him. The secretary did not make the record she normally would, as a result of which this issue arose. What was said by the trainee solicitor was sufficient for the notice required. The Court held this was so although the trainee solicitor's intention was not to give such a notice and it lacked the formality that Porter J had in mind when he said in *Herbert v Railway Passengers Assurance Co.* that a degree of formality was required.

8.113 Hence, *Nawaz* confirmed Kennedy LJ's comment on *Herbert* that it does not stand in terms of the formality of the notice. Further, although all depends on the circumstances, in this case, the legal secretary who had seven years of experience as a legal secretary at the time of the event was an appropriate person to whom to give notice. Moreover, it was well within her authority and reasonable for her to receive that notice.

---

168 Ibid, [32].
169 Ibid, [32].
170 [2003] RTR 29.

Waiver

8.114 Waiver is established when insurers indicate that although he is entitled to claim otherwise, which is in his favour, he intends to give up on that option available to him but chooses another option which is in favour of the assured. Insurers may prompt this by express words or by conduct. A waiver by insurers' conduct was discussed in *McBlain v Dolan*[171] in which the accident in question occurred on 20 September 1990. The insurers were notified of a claim on 5 April 1991 and, by a letter dated 18 November 1991, they stated that they considered the policy to be void. Thereafter, however, correspondence was maintained between the victim of the accident and the insurers for almost two years, during which time the insurers gave every indication that they regarded themselves on risk. In particular, they made an offer on a without prejudice basis on 5 March 1993. An action was brought against the assured motorist in September 1993. The insurers were not notified of the proceedings until November 1993, and they sought avoiding the insurance contract in the spring of 1994. The Court found that for more than two years the insurers had had the opportunity to seek a declaration if they were intending to rely upon section 152, and it was highly artificial for them to rely upon the notice provision in section 152(1)(a) and to complain that the three-month period in section 152(2) had been struck down to their prejudice because of want of notice of the present proceedings. It was apparent from the correspondence that the insurers had continued to act as though they were on risk, and there was a strong indication to the pursuer's advisors that the claim would be dealt with. Accordingly, it was appropriate to allow to go to trial the issue whether the insurers, having been aware of the proceedings but not having received the proper statutory notice, were able to rely upon the absence of notice.

8.115 The facts of *Wake v Wylie* were stated above. It was argued that the insurers had been given notice of the proceedings by the letter of 3 February 1997. The wording of the letter was, "We confirm that a Writ has been issued against Mr P . . . on 28th November 1996. No doubt you will be wishing to nominate solicitors to accept service and we shall be grateful to hear from you in that regard." The assertion was that it must have been clear to the insurer on its receipt that section 152(1)(a) was not satisfied; the proceedings had been commenced more than seven days before the date of the letter. Nevertheless, they chose not to take the point until June 1999, and by that time they were taken to have waived the defence, or alternatively were estopped from relying upon it. Kennedy LJ, Laws and Rix LJJ agreed, however, found on the facts of the case no room for an argument of waiver by estoppel.[172] His Lordship defined section 152(1)(a) as a condition precedent to liability which Kennedy LJ described as more important than mere procedure. His Lordship held that the insurers had simply overlooked the defence until it had been drawn to their attention by counsel in June 1999. In the words of Kennedy LJ section 152(1)(a) is not a statutory defence.[173] A proof of an unequivocal representation was required under this subsection, but the insurer's responses to the claims in this case did not amount to such a representation that the insurer would not rely on section 152(1)(a).

---

171 1998 SLT 512.
172 [2001] RTR 20, [42].
173 Ibid, [34].

Kennedy LJ acknowledged *McBlain* and found the case of limited assistance.[174] However unattractive the solution that his Lordship reached, Kennedy LJ noted that it would be legal, and that was how in *McBlain*'s case it seems to have been envisaged that the action might proceed.[175]

8.116 Kennedy LJ's reasons are not immune from doubt, but the conclusion reached is in line with the waiver principles as established. Waiver may be proved by virtue of affirming the breach and electing between two inconsistent options available for the party who holds those preferences. A typical example of a remedy which may be waived by virtue of affirmation is avoidance of the insurance contract. The innocent party may elect either to avoid or not to avoid it because avoidance is a self-help remedy that requires a positive action by the party who wishes to do so. Election may be communicated by express words or by some conduct which is inconsistent with treating the contract avoided, for instance, the insurer relies upon a policy term whereas he is expected to treat the contract avoided,[176] as if it never existed, and as if there are no contractual terms governing the relationship with the assured.

8.117 Waiver by affirmation is available only when affirming the breach of contract is available for the innocent party. Where, for instance, the remedy has its effects automatically by law and there is no option to either elect or affirm for the innocent party, waiver may not be proved by affirmation and the only possible means of waiver becomes promissory estoppel.[177]

8.118 Condition precedent under section 152(1)(a) means that without a positive action by the insurer, unless the third party satisfies the notice requirements, the right granted by the statute would not arise. Such a requirement therefore may only be waived by promissory estoppel that the insurer unequivocally represents that they do not intend to force the lack of notification as required under section 151(2)(a). Nothing prevents the insurer from paying to the third party even though the necessary notice was not given. However, if the insurer rejects payment because of the lack of notice, arguing that the insurers waived their rights requires an unequivocal representation by the insurer to that effect which is a matter of fact to be proven.

8.119 Kennedy LJ was right that *McBlain* was of limited assistance as the facts of these two cases are not similar. In *McBlain* the insurers' dealings for two years that was referred to in the judgment took place before the proceedings were commenced. Moreover, the insurers, at that period falling before the commencement of the proceedings against the assured, declared to the third party that the policy was void but then it carried on and offered a without prejudice settlement. During this period, having been aware that proceedings might be brought in the future, the insurers might seek a declaration to avoid the contract. When they attempted to do so after the proceedings were brought, it was found inappropriate on the facts but the decision was not final on the estoppel view, and it was sent back for a trial. On the other hand, in *Wake*, although the insurers were aware of the action through the letter of 3 February, on the facts, their conduct did not

---

174 Ibid, [41].
175 Ibid, [42].
176 *WISE Underwriting Agency Ltd v Grupo Nacional Provincial SA* [2004] Lloyd's Rep IR 764.
177 *Motor Oil Hellas (Corinth) Refineries SA v Shipping Corp of India (The Kanchenjunga)* [1990] 1 Lloyd's Rep 391; *Kosmar Villa Holidays Plc v Trustees of Syndicate 1243* [2008] Lloyd's Rep IR 489.

indicate that they would accept liability under the insurance. Having been silent about the lack of notice within the period of time permitted under section 152(1) did not amount to an unequivocal representation. A number of years of inaction after discovering the breach which entitles the insurer to elect to avoid the contract may prove a waiver by affirmation,[178] but such a silence does not equally amount to an unequivocal representation to establish promissory estoppel. Therefore, it is submitted that the result in *Wake* is in line with the established principles of waiver by estoppel.

Cancellation of the policy

8.120 Before its amendment by the Deregulation Act 2015, the insurer's liability could be extended beyond the cancellation of the policy where a policy had been cancelled but the assured remained in possession of the certificate of insurance. Only an action for surrender of the certificate within some certain period of time could avail the insurer to avoid that liability. As noted in Chapter 4, the Deregulation Act 2015 repealed the necessity of surrendering certificate after the cancellation of the policy or security under section 152 of the RTA 1988. It now suffices for the insurer to escape from liability if, amongst other things, "before the happening of the event which was the cause of the death or bodily injury or damage to property giving rise to the liability, the policy or security was cancelled by mutual consent or by virtue of any provision contained in it."[179] Hence, mere cancellation is enough to terminate the risk and the retention of the certificate by the assured cannot affect the liability of the insurer after cancellation.[180]

Stay of execution

8.121 Under section 152(1)(b) of the RTA 1988 an insurer is not required to pay any sum under the RTA 1988 s 151 in respect of any judgment so long as execution on the judgment is stayed pending an appeal.

Seeking declaration to avoid the insurance contract

8.122 The Road Traffic Acts have tried to compromise between the two desirable but conflicting objectives. The most emphasised of those two is clearly protecting the public from the danger of impecunious tortfeasors on the roads. However, the legislation should take into account of the need for avoiding the injustice of putting on a wholly innocent and misled insurer the whole pecuniary burden of a policy which, neither in law nor equity, is his policy.[181] As a result, the mere fact that the insurer can escape his liability vis-à-vis the assured, by reason of something which entitles the insurer to avoid or cancel the policy, does not prevent the victim of the negligent driving of the insured person from

---

178 *Argo Systems FZE v Liberty Insurance Pte Ltd* [2011] 2 Lloyd's Rep 61. The case was appealed, but the waiver of avoidance argument was given up and the appeal discussed the breach of warranty. [2012] 1 Lloyd's Rep 129.

179 The RTA s 152(1)(c).

180 This confirms the effect of *Re Drake Insurance Plc* [2001] Lloyd's Rep IR 643.

181 *Merchants & Manufacturers Insurance Co Ltd v Hunt (Charles & John (An Infant))* [1941] 1 KB 295, 308, Scott LJ.

recovering against the insurers, but the insurers can take steps which will protect themselves. They may obtain a declaration that they are entitled to avoid the policy in certain cases where it was obtained by the "non-disclosure of a material fact, or by a representation of fact which was false in some material particular," but if that declaration is to avail the insurer, he must obtain it "in an action commenced before, or within three months after, the commencement of the proceedings in which the judgment was given."[182]

8.123 Obtaining such a declaration is an essential precondition to avoiding the terms of section 151.[183] A clause to the effect that nothing in the policy is to affect third party rights under the legislation does not affect the insurer's right to a declaration under the RTA 1988 s 152.[184] If insurance cover is avoided the claim would then fall to be dealt with by the Motor Insurers' Bureau.[185]

For instance, in *Ageas Insurance Ltd v Stoodley*[186] the insurer successfully sought avoidance of the contract as permitted under s 152(2). In *Ageas* the assured misrepresented the fact that before the insurance policy was renewed in 2014 and again in 2015, she was involved in a road traffic accident in 2013. The answer to the question: "Have you or any person who will drive the motorhome had any accidents, claims, damage, theft or loss involving any motor vehicle (including motorhome, car, motorcycle or van) during the past five years, whether or not a claim was made, and regardless of blame?" was in the negative. On the facts the judge held that the assured had not acted with reasonable care in failing to answer truthfully a straightforward, clear and specific question. The breach was committed either deliberately or recklessly, and the insurer had shown that but for the misrepresentation, it would not have entered into the contract. The insurers were also successful in *Delaney v Pickett*[187] where the assured failed to disclose that he suffered from diabetes and depression and was a habitual user of cannabis.

8.124 It should be noted that Gloster LJ stated in *Cameron v Hussain*,[188] as a matter of practice insurers, on occasion, in high value cases, bring proceedings for a declaration under section 152(2), but they almost never do so in small value cases. The precedent cases do confirm that this statement is accurate.[189]

As noted in the Preface, the Motor Vehicles (Compulsory Insurance) (Miscellaneous Amendments) Regulations 2019[190] come into force on 1 November 2019. These Regulations repeal the availability for the insurer to seek a declaration to avoid the insurance policy after the accident that caused the victim's loss has occurred. Readers should be aware of the 2019 Regulations and, for accidents occurring after1 November 2019, Chapter 8 should be read together with these Regulations.

---

182 RTA 1988 s 152(2); *Croxford v Universal Insurance Co Ltd* [1936] 2 KB 253.

183 *McBlain v Dolan* 1998 SLT 512; *National Farmers Union Mutual Insurance Society Ltd v Tully* 1935 SLT 574.

184 *Merchants & Manufacturers Insurance Co Ltd v Hunt (Charles & John (An Infant))* [1941] 1 KB 295.

185 *McBlain v Dolan* 1998 SLT 512.

186 [2018] 4 WLUK 40.

187 [2013] Lloyd's Rep IR 24.

188 [2017] EWCA Civ 366 [38].

189 *Merchants & Manufacturers Insurance Co Ltd v Hunt (Charles & John (An Infant))* [1941] 1 KB 295; *National Farmers Union Mutual Insurance Society Ltd v Tully* 1935 SLT 574; *Guardian Assurance Co Ltd v Sutherland* (1939) 63 Ll L Rep 220; *Croxford v Universal Insurance Co Ltd* [1936] 2 KB 253; *Zurich General Accident & Liability Insurance Co Ltd v Morrison* [1942] 2 KB 53; *Contingency Insurance Co Ltd v Lyons* (1939) 65 Ll L Rep 53.

190 SI 2019/1047.

Motor Insurers' Bureau Articles of Association, Article 75

8.125 The Motor Insurers' Bureau (MIB) is analysed in detail in Chapter 10. What is referred to here is the role of the insurer to compensate third party victim's loss when the insurer is appointed by the MIB as an Article 75 insurer.

8.126 Article 75 of the MIB Articles of Association provides that an insurer that insures[191] a risk as required to be insured under the Road Traffic Act 1988 may be appointed by the MIB as an Article 75 insurer. An insurer may be an Article 75 insurer although the insurance has been obtained by fraud, misrepresentation, non-disclosure of material facts or mistake; or, the cover has been back-dated, or the use of the vehicle is other than that permitted under the policy.[192] The significance of policies that are avoidable or cancelled is that, where, before the accident, the insurer obtains a judgment that the policy is void or unenforceable, the insurer ceases to be an Article 75 insurer.[193] However, if the policy is cancelled or a declaration that the policy is avoidable is obtained after the accident, the insurer remains as Article 75 insurer with no right of recourse against the MIB.[194]

8.127 Under Article 75(2)(a)(2) a Member only ceases to be the Article 75 insurer:

(i) if a renewal notice is issued, incorporating a temporary cover note extending cover, conditionally or otherwise, beyond the date of expiry of the policy, as of the expiry date of that extension of cover;

(ii) from the expiry date specified in the policy if, by provision in the policy or by notice in writing by either party to the policy, the policy is not intended to be renewed;

(iii) when the policy has been cancelled by mutual consent or by virtue of any provision contained in it before the date on which the Road Traffic Act liability was incurred and, in addition, before that date, either

    (1) in respect of policies cancelled on or after 30 June 2015: any record on the MID for the policy in question has been updated to show that policy has been cancelled; for this purposes, any update of the MID record must be in accordance with the guidance issued by MIB from time to time; or

    (2) In respect of policies cancelled before 30 June 2015: one of the following has occurred, namely:

        (a) the certificate of insurance has been surrendered to the insurer by the policyholder, or (in the case of a certificate which is not in electronic form) the policyholder has made a Statutory Declaration stating that the certificate has been lost or destroyed; or

        (b) the insurer has commenced proceedings under the Road Traffic Act 1988 in respect of the failure to surrender the certificate.

        For the purpose of (a) and (b), the references to "surrender," "surrendered" and "Statutory Declaration" bear the same meaning as under the Road Traffic act 1988 and for the purpose of (iii) "cancelled" means cancellation by specific request of the insured, or strictly in accordance

---

191 MIB Articles of Association, Art 75(2)(a).
192 MIB Articles of Association, Art 75(2)(a)(1).
193 See below Art 75(2)(a)(2)(iii) and (iv).
194 MIB Articles of Association, Art 75(3)(b).

with the power of cancellation contained in the Member's contract for the risk, notwithstanding that such contract may not have been issued.[195]

(iv) when, before the date on which the Road Traffic Act Liability was incurred, the Member has obtained a declaration from a Court of competent jurisdiction that the insurance is void or unenforceable;

(v) when the insurance has ceased to operate by reason of a transfer of interest in the vehicle involved in the accident, which the insurance purports to cover, and which transfer is proved by evidence;

(vi) when the theft of the certificate of insurance was reported to the police (provided that the report was made within 30 days of the date of discovery of the theft);

(vii) if the certificate of insurance has been forged by someone other than the Member or an intermediary acting on behalf of the Member or an officer, employee or agent of the Member or of an intermediary acting on behalf of the Member; or

(viii) if the event giving rise to the Road Traffic Act Liability occurred on or after 1 January 2019 and that liability has been caused by or arises out of an act of terrorism within the meaning of section 1 of the Terrorism Act 2000.

8.128 Where an insurer argues that it is not the Article 75 insurer the burden of proving such contention, on the balance of probabilities, is on the insurer.[196]

8.129 Double insurance cases are referred to in Chapter 3. If there is more than one Article 75 insurer in respect of a particular vehicle then the handling of any claims will be by agreement between the Article 75 insurers. In default of agreement it is determined by the Technical Committee. The costs of handling and settling the claims shall be shared between those Article 75 insurers proportionate to the number of policies issued.[197] Further, any right of an Article 75 insurer to indemnity or contribution from another insurer whether such right arises at common law, by statute, from a claims sharing or other agreement, by subrogation or by assignment of the original judgment creditor's judgment is preserved under Article 75(3)(c).

8.130 If a Road Traffic Act judgment is obtained the Article 75 insurer will satisfy the original judgment creditor if and to the extent that the judgment has not within seven days of the execution date been satisfied by the judgment debtor.[198]

8.131 Where expedient, the MIB may decide to pay the victim's claim with a right of recourse against the Article 75 insurer. As the obligation to satisfy a judgment against an uninsured/untraced driver is, so far as the third party is concerned, one imposed on the MIB, the MIB has an obligation to satisfy the judgment, subject to the terms of the Uninsured and Untraced Drivers Agreements. With regards to the claims received on or after 1 May 2017, where the MIB compensated a claim for a policy excess under the terms of the Untraced Drivers Agreement dated 7 February 2003 ("the 2003 Agreement")

---

195 Provided that where an intermediary cancels the policy and the certificate of insurance has been surrendered to the intermediary, either as agent for the Member or under the terms of any separate agreement between the intermediary and the insured, cancellation of the policy must be exercised strictly in accordance with the Member's standard form of contract for the risk and there must be clear evidence that the intermediary is empowered to do so by the policy wording.

196 MIB Articles of Association, Art 75(2)(a)(4).

197 MIB Articles of Association, Art 75(2)(a)(3).

198 MIB Articles of Association, Art 75(3)(a).

(as amended) or the Untraced Drivers Agreement dated 28 February 2017 ("the 2017 Agreement") the Member who issued the policy under which the policy excess operated shall reimburse the MIB the amount it has paid including any contribution towards legal costs applicable under the 2003 or 2017 Agreements.[199] Similarly, in a claim received by the bureau on or after 1 August 2017, the bureau has paid a claim for a policy excess under the terms of the Uninsured Drivers Agreement dated 13 August 1999 (as amended) or the Uninsured Drivers Agreement dated 3 July 2015 (as amended), the Member who issued the policy under which the policy excess operated shall reimburse the bureau the amount it has paid including any associated legal costs.[200]

8.132 The MIB Articles of Association Article 75(5) provides a procedure to follow when a dispute arises between the Article 75 insurers and the MIB in relation to the interpretation, application or implementation of Article 75 or any other matters falling within the powers of the Technical Committee as defined in Article 74. A right of appeal of a Technical Committee decision and the procedure to follow are provided under Article 75(6) which was a matter of dispute recently before the Court of Appeal. Article 75(6)(a) provides for a member of the MIB to appeal to an arbitrator within 30 days of "being notified of the decision of the Technical Committee." In *Haven Insurance Co Ltd v EUI Ltd (t/a Elephant Insurance)*[201] a dispute arose between two insurers, Haven and EUI, as to liability, and at a meeting on 13 February 2015 it was decided that EUI faced liability. The minutes of the Technical Committee containing the decision were released on 31 March 2015 and EUI gave written notice of appeal on 30 April 2015. Haven contended that Elephant's appeal was out of time because Elephant had been notified of the decision of the Technical Committee in accordance with Article 75 more than 30 days before service of its written notice of appeal, either (a) by being physically present at the 13 February 2015 meeting, or (b) as the result of a 24 February 2015 email from MIB's secretariat to Elephant confirming in writing the decisions taken on that earlier date. Elephant contended that its appeal was in time because time for an appeal only ran from 31 March 2015, being the date at which the final draft minutes of the meeting were released to members of the Technical Committee by MIB's secretariat. The arbitrator rejected Haven's argument and an appeal to the High Court was made on two different bases: by Haven, on jurisdictional grounds under section 67 of the Arbitration Act 1996, and by EUI, for an extension of time under section 12 of the 1996 Act. Under section 12 of the 1996 Act the court may extend time if it is of the view "that the circumstances are such as were outside the reasonable contemplation of the parties when they agreed the provision in question, and that it would be just to extend the time." Knowles J held and the Court of Appeal approved that Elephant believed *"reasonably if wrongly "* that it had 30 days after receipt of the final minutes of the Technical Committee to lodge an appeal. Elephant's belief was described as in line with *"widely accepted"* interpretation of Article 75 shared by MIB itself who had confirmed it has been the Technical Committee's custom and practice to allow 30 days from the date of final minutes.

8.133 The point to be reiterated with regards to the insurer's liability is that if, before the relevant traffic accident takes place, the insurer cancels the insurance contract or

---

199 MIB Articles of Association, Art 75(4)(b).
200 MIB Articles of Association, Art 75(4)(c).
201 [2018] EWCA Civ 2494.

obtains a declaration from a Court that the policy is void or unenforceable, the victim's claim will be against an uninsured driver. On the other hand, if the policy is cancelled or the declaration referred to here is obtained after the accident has occurred, despite the cancellation or the declaration obtained from the Court, the insurer remains as Article 75 insurer and has to handle the claim without a right of recourse against the MIB.

Notification of the third party claimant

8.134 The insurer has to notify the victim of the accident who could claim against the assured, either before, or within seven days after, the commencement of the action specifying the non-disclosure or false representation on which he proposes to rely.[202] The insurer bears the burden of proving, as a matter of fact, that notice has actually been given under section 152(3).[203] A person to whom notice of such an action is so given is entitled, if he thinks fit, to be made a party to it.[204] It is essential that he should have notice of any such action by the insurer, and also be given the right to appear in it and there defend his rights. The third party victim must not be deprived of the pecuniary safeguard provided by the RTA 1988 s 151 through the possibility of the policy being avoided in proceedings under section 152 without his knowledge, and even by collusion between the insurer and the assured.[205]

8.135 What the insurer identifies in his notification under section 152(3) is important. If the insurer discovers further facts that could be relied on to avoid the insurance contract for failing to comply with the duty of fair presentation of the risk, he could not argue such further facts against the victim claimant if the insurer did not identify them earlier in his notice. If an insurer was intending to avoid a policy, it was only fair that the third party victim should know the grounds on which avoidance was sought before he went to the expense of endeavouring to establish his claim against the assured, who, if not entitled to indemnity, might be unable to satisfy a judgment.[206] The insurer can still argue that against the assured but not against the third party victim under these circumstances.[207] Lord Greene MR stated in *Zurich General Accident & Liability Insurance Co Ltd v Morrison*,[208] "If the insurer could as against the third party, bring forward matters not specified in the notice the protection which the proviso gives could be rendered completely abortive." In *Zurich General Accident & Liability Insurance Co Ltd v Morrison* the accident occurred on 30 September 1939. The insurers sought a declaration against the assured for non-disclosure of a material fact on 1 March 1940, and on 28 February 1940 the insurer notified the victim of the traffic accident the matters on which they intended to rely to avoid the insurance policy. On 29 August 1940

---

202 RTA 1988 s 152(3).

203 *Colonial Fire and General Insurance Company Ltd v Sarana Harry* [2008] Lloyd's Rep IR 382.

204 RTA 1988 s 152(4); *Merchants & Manufacturers Insurance Co Ltd v Hunt (Charles & John (An Infant))* [1941] 1 KB 295.

205 *Merchants & Manufacturers Insurance Co Ltd v Hunt (Charles & John (An Infant))* [1941] 1 KB 295, 308, Scott LJ.

206 *Zurich General Accident & Liability Insurance Co Ltd v Morrison* [1942] 2 KB 53.

207 Ibid.

208 [1942] 2 KB 53, 57.

the third party victim obtained a judgment against the assured. In 1941 the insurer discovered further facts which they wanted to include in their seeking the declaration by adding some further grounds to avoid the policy. The Court of Appeal held that whilst against the assured there is no limitation as to the grounds on which the policy can be disputed, newly discovered facts that had not been to the insurer's knowledge prior to the notice, an amendment should be granted, the same is not the case against the third party. Holding otherwise would render the right given to the third party victim nugatory. Indeed the relevant sections of the RTA 1934 (also the RTA 1988) do not contain words expressly precluding the insurer from setting up any grounds not mentioned in his notice, that is its effect.

Section 152 and EU law

8.136 It has become necessary to read section 152 together with *Fidelidade-Companhia de Seguros SA v Caisse Suisse de Compensation*.[209] This case came before the CJEU in relation to an accident that occurred in Portugal and caused the death of a Swiss motorcyclist. The car involved in the accident was being used by TP, a family member of CP. Whilst the latter was insured, the driver was not. The Swiss compensation body paid compensation and sought to recover it from the Portuguese compensation body. The defence was that the claim had to be brought against CP's liability insurers. The CJEU ruled that the insurers, having faced with a third party claim, had no right to rely upon an avoidance defence, and that was the case even though the person driving the car was not authorised to do so.

8.137 In *Farah v Abdullahi*,[210] although no legislative change had been effected in the UK yet, Master Davidson's judgment seemingly was influenced heavily by *Fidelidade-Companhia de Seguros SA v Caisse Suisse de Compensation*[211] mentioned above.

In *Farah* the claimant was a pedestrian together with a group of people. He was injured when he was pushed by D's Ford Focus into the path of a Mercedes driven by an unidentified driver and then run over by D's Ford Focus. The insurers of the Mercedes were identified, and they obtained a declaration under the RTA 1988 s 152 and avoided the policy for material non-disclosure. The question was whether the claimant could commence proceedings against the unidentified driver. The effect was that any judgment obtained against the unidentified driver would have to be satisfied by the insurers under section 151 of the 1988 Act. It was argued by the insurers of the Mercedes that the existence of a non-avoided insurance policy was critical to the exercise of discretion to permit the claimant to join an unnamed defendant as held in *Cameron v Hussain*.[212] The difference between *Cameron* and *Farah*, as asserted, was that in the latter the insurers

---

209 (C-287/16) EU:C:2017:57.

210 [2018] EWHC 738 (QB).

211 (C-287/16) [2017] RTR 26; *Churchill Insurance Co Ltd v Wilkinson* (C-442/10) [2012] Lloyd's Rep IR 544 was applied.

212 [2017] EWCA Civ 366 [38]. Appeal to the Supreme Court was upheld. *Cameron v Liverpool Victoria Insurance Co Ltd* [2019] UKSC 6. See above paragraph 8.82 et seq.

of the untraced driver had avoided the policy, and it was contended that there still remained doubts as to whether they stayed liable under section 151.

8.138 Master Davidson rejected the insurer's argument. Master Davidson noted that after *Fidelidade-Companhia de Seguros SA v Caisse Suisse de Compensation*[213] there is an issue of compatibility of the RTA 1988 s 152(2) with the Consolidated Directive. Moreover, according to Master Davidson, *Cameron* did not rest on the existence of a section 151 liability, but it was decided in the way it was because a judgment for damages against an unknown person may confer a real benefit on the claimant.

8.139 In *Farah v Abdullahi*[214] Master Davidson found that the claim against the unnamed driver was capable of conferring a real benefit on the claimant. Such benefits were that the claimant might seek to challenge the declaration made by the Court that the policy of insurance was avoidable ab ibinitio. The decision of *Fidelidade-Companhia*, in the view of Master Davidson, has strengthened the claimant's position in this respect. Moreover, even if the insurer were to be held to be entitled to avoid the policy after the claimant's challenge, under the MIB rules, Article 75, it would still need to compensate the victim's claim.[215] As discussed above in paragraph 8.125 et seq and in Chapter 10, this is indeed the case where the insurer successfully avoids the insurance contract after the accident has occurred.

8.140 Although the majority of the Court of Appeal in *Cameron* emphasised repeatedly that an insurer agrees to insure a risk after assessing the risk at the pre-contractual stage, the Supreme Court upheld the insurer's appeal. This matter is discussed at paragraph 8.82 et seq.

8.141 Further, avoidance of the contract is treating the contract as if it never existed. That may explain why the RTA 1988 permitted the declaration under s 152. On the other hand, after *Fidelidade-Companhia* the compatibility of the RTA 1988 s 152 will be questioned. To this extent Master Davidson's judgment is not surprising. Moreover, because of Article 75 of the MIB's Articles of Association, it will ultimately be the insurer to compensate the victim's claim with a right of recourse against the assured or the person who caused the loss. The situation that falls outside the scope of Article 75, which is that where the insurer avoids the contract before the accident occurs, is still to be reviewed in the light of the ruling in *Fideliade*. More recently, in *Colley v Shuker*[216] O'Farrell J approved that the claimant motor accident victim had a real prospect of success in its claim that s 152(2) is incompatible with the Consolidated Directive. Moreover, the judge stated that the clear wording of s 152, unlike the insurer argued, does not allow any incompatibility between s 152 and EU law to be resolved by any permissible purposive interpretation. As referred to in para 8.124, after 1 November 2019 please note the Motor Vehicles (Compulsory Insurance) (Miscellaneous Amendments) Regulations 2019 whilst reading the above.[217]

---

213 (C-287/16) [2017] RTR 26; *Churchill Insurance Co Ltd v Wilkinson* (C-442/10) [2012] Lloyd's Rep IR 544 was applied.
214 [2018] EWHC 738 (QB).
215 See Chapter 10.
216 [2019] EWHC 781 (QB), [34].
217 SI 2019/1047.

Discretion on the court to set aside a default judgment

8.142 The common law position is that a stranger to an action, who is affected through any judgment suffered by a defendant by default, can set that judgment aside.[218] An insurer, although not parties to the action between the third party and the assured motorist, is affected by the judgment against the nominal defendant assured where, under the RTA 1988 the insurer is asked to satisfy the judgment.[219] An insurer therefore has an interest to be entitled to an order setting aside the judgment and giving it leave to enter an appearance in the action in the name of the defendant or in its own name, and to deliver a defence.[220] Where the insurer is given a notice either before or within seven days after the proceedings have been brought, the insurer will have the opportunity to follow the action by himself. Where the assured fails to give the notice the insurer's liability cannot be argued under section 151 as the notice is a condition precedent for a right of direct action against the insurer for the judgment obtained. If the notice is provided but the insurer chooses not to involve in defending the claim, it should not be able to seek the judgment in default of the assured set aside. Lord Woolf noted in *Nawaz v Crowe Insurance Group*[221] that the Civil Procedure Rules conferred discretion upon the court to avoid insurers suffering undue hardship because of their failure to appreciate in time that a notice had been given.[222] It was apposite in this case to apply the options permitted under the relevant Civil Procedure Rules because insurers, rightly or wrongly, had reason to suspect that the claim there had been collusion between those involved to put forward a claim when there was no justification for it. The insurers should be entitled to investigate whether that was the position or not. The Court of Appeal thus indicated in *Nawaz* that, had the insurers sought to have the judgment set aside so that allegations of collusion could properly be investigated, such an application, through which justice would be enabled, would have almost certainly been granted by the Court.[223]

Primary direct actions against insurers under the EU law

8.143 The relevant provisions are now found in the Consolidated Motor Insurance Directive 2009 which stipulates a procedure whereby a victim of a motor accident in a Member State other than that of his residence can, in the first instance, in the Member State of his domicile seek indemnification from the insurers.

8.144 Article 18 of the Consolidated Directives provides,

> Member States shall ensure that any party injured as a result of an accident caused by a vehicle covered by insurance as referred to in Article 3 enjoys a direct right of action against the insurance undertaking covering the person responsible against civil liability.

---

218 -*Jacques v Harrison* (1884) 12 QBD. 165.

219 *Windsor v Chalcraft* [1939] 1 KB 279.

220 Ibid.

221 [2003] RTR 29.

222 Additionally, as addressed in *Nawaz*, the court can make an order the result of which will be that the insurers become second defendants in those proceedings. Woolf LJ would have made that order had the insurers requested that. With regards to the orders mentioned in this case references were made to Pt 13, Pt 19, Pt 20, together with Pt 40 of the Civil Procedure Rules.

223 [2003] RTR 29 [22].

In the UK such direct right of action against insurers is regulated by the European Communities (Rights Against Insurers) Regulations 2002.[224] Regulation 3(2) stipulates that the victim of a motor accident who is a resident[225] of an EU or EEA Member State may, without prejudice to his right to issue proceedings against the insured person, issue proceedings against the insurer which issued the policy of insurance relating to the insured vehicle.

Accident means an accident on a road or other public place in the United Kingdom caused by, or arising out of, the use of any insured vehicle.[226] Regulation 2(1) defines vehicle as "any motor vehicle intended for travel on land and propelled by mechanical power, but not running on rails, and any trailer whether or not coupled, which is normally based (within the meaning of paragraph 2 of this regulation) in the United Kingdom."

8.145 As a result the residents of the EU and EEA states may bring a direct action against the insurer for an accident that took place in the UK and the driver is liable in tort to the victim. The entitled party may be a visitor from another EU or an EEA Member State or may be a resident of the UK. Once these conditions are satisfied the insurer shall be directly liable to the entitled party to the extent that he is liable to the insured person.[227] The "insured person" is defined by Reg 2(1) and 2(3) of the 2002 Regulations as a person insured under a policy of insurance (including a covering note) which is in force in relation to the use of that vehicle on a road or other public place in the UK by the insured person and which fulfils the requirements of s 145 of the RTA 1988.

8.146 The direct right of action under the 2002 Regulations is an alternative to the victim's right of claim under section 151. Whilst the latter is an enforcement mechanism only and a judgment must be obtained against the assured in favour of the third party as a pre-condition of the claim, under the 2002 Regulations the victim steps into the assured's shoes. In other words, the 2002 Regulations put the victim in exactly the same position as the assured towards the insurer.

8.147 The Regulations thus do not give the third party any better rights than the assured would have, so if the insurers have a policy defence then the third party will not have a claim. As discussed at paragraph 8.48 et seq and further explored below the English Courts held that under the 2002 Regulations the victim's entitlement cannot be any better than what the assured would be entitled if the claim was made by the latter rather than the former.[228]

8.148 However, one distinction is to be made between acting contrary to the policy provisions either before or after the insured loss has occurred. In *Bayraz v Acromas Insurance Co*[229] the insurers submitted that they had been discharged from any liability to the driver under the policy by his breach of their policy terms and that, under Reg 3(2), they were directly liable to the claimants only to the extent that they were liable to the insured person so that they were not liable to the claimants. The Court held that clauses removing the liability of an insurer for any post-loss breach of contract by the assured

---

224 SI 2002/3061.
225 Entitled party under the 2002 Regulations, Reg 2(1).
226 2002 Regulations, Reg 2(1).
227 2002 Regulations, Reg 2 and 3.
228 *RoadPeace v Secretary of State for Transport* [2018] Lloyd's Rep IR 478; *Allen v Mohammed* [2017] Lloyd's Rep IR 73; *Bayraz v Acromas Insurance Co* County Court (Central London), 6 February 2014.
229 County Court (Central London), 6 February 2014.

are, by section 148(5), unenforceable in third party claims. Accordingly, if the only reason why the insurer was not liable to the insured driver under the policy was because of post-accident procedural failures by the driver to communicate with the insurer who refused indemnity, then the Reg 3 claimant could recover from the insurer.

8.149 Where the driver is not covered by the insurance of the vehicle, either because the driver was a thief or any other person uninsured, the claim has to rely on section 151 after a judgment is obtained against the negligent motorist. Under the 2002 Regulations, the third party victim does have a direct right of action only "to the extent that he is liable to the insured person" so that the liability should be caused by an insured driver. The Regulations do not extend to liabilities of insurers in respect of the uninsured use of the vehicle. Moreover, in section 148 nothing prevents reliance by an insurer on driver exclusions. In *Allen v Mohammed*[230] the insurance contract covered only the owner of the vehicle, Mrs A Mohammed. The unidentified and untraced driver was not insured by the insurer for the liability in question. It followed that the wording of Regulation 3(2) prevented reliance by the victim on the 2002 Regulations.

8.150 The outcome of Reg 3(2) that specifies the insurer's liability towards the third party victim "to the extent that he is liable to the insured person" is that, where the insurer relies upon policy defences to defeat the claim by the victim, the victim will have to resort to the MIB.

8.151 In *RoadPeace v Secretary of State for Transport*[231] Ouseley J held that Reg 3 of the 2002 Regulations was compatible with the Consolidated Directive.

---

230 [2017] Lloyd's Rep IR 73.
231 [2018] Lloyd's Rep IR 478.

CHAPTER 9

Credit hire agreements

General principles of claiming damages when a vehicle is damaged

Cost of repair

9.1 When a property is damaged by the negligence of another, the diminution in value that the property has suffered represents the direct loss that is measured as a result of such wrongdoing.[1] This is also expressed as "a capital account loss."[2] This loss is suffered as soon as the motor vehicle is damaged.[3] The claimant is not obliged to, but he is entitled to, where the property can be economically repaired, have it repaired at the cost of the wrongdoer.

9.2 The measure of loss is assessed as a matter of fact that the expenditure required to put the vehicle back into the same state as it was in before the accident.[4] Where a vehicle is damaged beyond economic repair the claim is properly made for the money equivalent of its pre-accident value which can be assessed on the basis of tables and guides to the second-hand value of vehicles.[5]

9.3 In calculating the diminution in value, events occurring after the infliction of the damage are irrelevant.[6] If the property is subsequently destroyed or the repairs were carried out under an unenforceable credit agreement, the claimant is not prevented from recovering the diminution in value from the wrongdoer.[7] Moreover, in respect of a loss that is covered by insurance, the benefits obtained under the insurance are irrelevant in assessing the correct measure of damages recoverable.[8] The assured has bought the benefits by paying the premium demanded which the tortfeasor should not inure.[9]

9.4 If the claimant's insurer has arranged the repair, the reasonableness of the repair charge is to be judged by reference to what a person in the position of the claimant could

---

1 *Livingstone v Rawyards Coal Co* (1880) 5 App. Cas. 25; *Dimond v Lovell* [2002] 1 AC 384; *Coles v Hetherton* [2015] RTR 7.

2 *Dimond v Lovell* [2002] 1 AC 384, at 406, per Lord Hoffman; *Coles v Hetherton* [2015] RTR 7.

3 *Dimond v Lovell* [2002] 1 AC 384, at 406; *Coles v Hetherton* [2015] RTR 7.

4 Ibid.

5 Merkin/Hemsworth, [4–26].

6 *Burdis v Livsey* [2003] RTR 3; *Coles v Hetherton* [2015] RTR 7.

7 *Burdis v Livsey* [2003] RTR 3; *The Glenfinlas (Note)* [1918] P 363; *The London Corporation* [1935] P 70.

8 *Bradburn v Great Western Railway Co* (1874–75) L.R. 10 Ex. 1; *Bee v Jenson (No 2)* [2008] Lloyd's Rep IR 221; *Copley v Lawn* [2009] Lloyd's Rep IR 496, [12], Longmore LJ.

9 *Parry v Cleaver* [1970] AC 1.

obtain on the open market.[10] An insurer may itself have a repair scheme which the assured may choose. In such cases the question to consider is whether the actual sum claimed against the defendant is equal to or less than the notional sum the assured would have paid, by way of a reasonable cost of repair, if he had gone into the open market to have those repairs done. Furthermore, the insurer may have included some ancillary expenses such as "administrative charges" or "sundry service charges." Such charges are not automatically rejected from the reasonable cost of repair so long as the total charge by the insurer who carried out the repairs does not exceed the notional sum referred to above.[11]

9.5 Damages for non-pecuniary losses such as for worry and for the nuisance caused by having to deal with the consequences of an accident are not recoverable.[12]

Cost of hire

9.6 A victim whose vehicle was damaged by a negligent driver is entitled to recover the cost of repair and the damages for the loss of use of his vehicle.[13] The cost of hiring a replacement vehicle substitutes the claimant's claim for loss of use by way of general damages.[14] Diminution in value of the property, which is a direct loss, is not regarded as subject to the duty to mitigate.[15] However, the loss of use of the vehicle is regarded as a consequential loss the recovery of which is subject to the duty to mitigate.[16] Similar to contract law principles, in tort also, this is not a duty in the sense breach of which does not render the claimant liable for non-compliance with the duty; however, the claimant cannot recover damages for any part of his loss consequent upon the defendant's breach of duty of care where the claimant could have avoided such losses by taking reasonable steps.[17] What was reasonable for a person to do in mitigation of damage is a question of fact to decide in the circumstances of each particular case.[18]

9.7 The reason for the defendant's liability for the loss of use of the damaged vehicle is that his wrongdoing deprived the claimant from the use of the vehicle. The claimant's loss crystallises in the form of the cost of hiring a more or less equivalent[19] replacement vehicle while his own car is off the road.[20] The burden of proof of need for a replacement vehicle is on the claimant motorist.[21] The defendant bears the burden of proof that the hire charge paid was unreasonable.[22]

---

10 *Coles v Hetherton* [2015] RTR 7. What the insurer can obtain on the open market by way of a "reasonable repair charge" is irrelevant, because the position of the insurer is, as a matter of law, irrelevant.

11 *Coles v Hetherton* [2015] RTR 7.

12 *Dimond v Lovell* [2002] 1 AC 384; *Alexander v Rolls Royce Motor Cars Ltd* [1996] RTR 95.

13 *Lagden v O'Connor* [2004] 1 AC 1067.

14 Ibid, 1077–1078.

15 *Coles v Hetherton* [2015] RTR 7, [29].

16 *Coles v Hetherton* [2015] RTR 7; *Bee v Jenson (No.2); Mattocks v Mann* [1993] RTR 13.

17 *Clerk & Lindsell on Torts*, 22nd ed, 2018, Sweet & Maxwell [28–09]; H. Beale, *Chitty on Contracts*, 33rd ed, 2018, Sweet & Maxwell [26–089].

18 See generally in contract: *Chitty on Contracts*, 33rd ed, 2018, Sweet & Maxwell [26–090].

19 *Ryan Brain v Yorkshire Rider Ltd* [2007] Lloyd's Rep IR 564; *Watson Norie v Shaw* [1967] 1 Lloyd's Rep 515.

20 *Lagden v O'Connor* [2004] 1 AC 1067.

21 *Giles v Thompson* [1994] 1 AC 142; *Singh v Yaqubi* [2013] Lloyd's Rep IR 398; *Ryan Brain v Yorkshire Rider Ltd* [2007] Lloyd's Rep IR 564.

22 *Perehenic v Deboa Structuring* County Court (Banbury), 7 July 1998 [1998] CLY 1467.

Car hire

9.8 A claimant may hire a vehicle from a car hirer or he may enter into a credit hire agreement. A claimant may choose the latter option especially when the loss of use is not recoverable under a comprehensive policy.[23] In some other cases the policy may provide cover but the assured motorist may not wish to jeopardise his own no claims discount on his own policy.[24] Additionally, where there is no personal injury claim and where the damage to the motorist's vehicle is dealt with as between insurers there are few motorists who would have the time, energy and resources to go to law solely to recover the cost of a substitute vehicle. Furthermore, under an ordinary car hiring arrangement, the hirer has to produce the hire charge up front. Credit hire companies on the other hand do not require an upfront payment and undertake to seek the cost from the defendant motorist in the name of the hirer motorist. Also, the motorist does not need to claim the loss of the use of the car against the party who caused the damage; the company does it at its own expense, in the name of the motorist. The nature of accident hire is, therefore, to provide the victim with the use of a vehicle, and also to relieve him from the concern that the costs of hire will have to be met by him if they prove to be irrecoverable from the negligent driver (in practice, the negligent driver's motor vehicle liability insurers). The hiring company is, therefore, providing not just a car but also the security of the cost being met. In Lord Nicholls' words,[25] "Accident car hire companies are fulfilling a real need."

9.9 When a motorist seeks a replacement car for the period while his own car is off the road, the credit hire company checks whether the motorist seems to have an answerable claim against the other driver. Having satisfied itself on this score, the company provides the car sought and then seeks to recover its charges from the negligent driver's insurers. In this claim the company's aim is to recover the charges for the loan of the replacement car. Given the risk that there may be no recovery, and also the costs of operating the business, it is scarcely surprising that the rates charged by accident hire companies are somewhat greater than the rates on offer from ordinary hire car operators who seek payment from the victim himself and have no concern with the success or otherwise of any action against the wrongdoing driver and his insurers. The credit hire company's gain then is seen here that such charges include not only the actual cost of the replacement car but also the profit that the company is expecting to gain. When there is a recovery from the party who caused the loss the company receives the charges for the hire of the vehicle.

9.10 The general principles demand that where there is an available market in which the innocent party can obtain what he has been deprived of, he is normally expected to go into that market to obtain it.[26] As a result, the fact that there are two different ways of hiring a replacement vehicle, an ordinary hire and hire through credit, leads the two different variations of cost of hire to compete in respect of the quantum of damages for loss of use: the claim may be based on the spot hire charge[27] for a comparable vehicle

---

23 *Sobrany v UAB Transtira* [2016] Lloyd's Rep IR 266.

24 *Stevens v Equity Syndicate Management Ltd* [2015] RTR 24.

25 *Dimond v Lovell* [2002] 1 AC 384, 390.

26 *Golden Strait Corp v Nippon Yusen Kubishika Kaisha (The Golden Victory)* [2007] 2 AC 353; *Maple Leaf Macro Volatility Master Fund v Rouvroy* [2009] 1 Lloyd's Rep 475.

27 As will be mentioned below spot charge was later replaced with BHR – basic hire rate.

or the cost of hire charged by a credit hire company.[28] Whilst the former is not controversial, the latter has been challenged numerous times before the Courts.

Legal statutes of credit hire agreements

Champerty and public policy considerations

9.11 As appears, the credit hire agreements are costly businesses. This is to a disadvantage of both the insurers and the defendants who caused the loss. The insurers' argument that such hiring agreements are champertous and accordingly unlawful, or otherwise contrary to public policy, were rejected by the House of Lords in *Giles v Thompson*.[29] The House of Lords explained that champerty, which had been treated as both criminal and tortious, had allowed the exploitation of worthless claims which the defendant lacked the resources and influence to withstand. The purchase of a share in litigation presented an obvious temptation to the suborning of justices. As the centuries passed the Courts' mechanisms became more consistent, their participants more self-reliant and abuses could be more easily detected. Parliament abolished the crimes and torts of maintenance and champerty when it was believed that litigations were more easily determined in accordance with the demands of justice.[30]

9.12 Maintenance involves wanton and officious intermeddling with the disputes of others when the maintainer has no interest and where the assistance he renders to the one or the other party is without justification or excuse.[31] A division of the spoils is added to maintenance to describe champerty. In other words, champerty has been defined as "an aggravated form of maintenance"[32]

9.13 Comparing all of these elements with the operation of the credit hire agreements the House of Lords held that there is no element of maintenance or champerty in the latter.[33] Their Lordships found that the company does not meddle but allows the motorist to get on with the claim, and merely awaits a favourable result. It is true that the company incurs such activities for a profit, but the important point is that the profit comes from the hiring, not from the litigation.[34] Further, the House of Lords explained that credit hire agreements do not create a charge over the proceeds of the claim, either as regards the hiring charges, or the damages for personal injuries, or any other item. Motorists are asked to co-operate with the company to pursue the claim against the defendant. There is usually no assignment of the proceeds of the action or of the cause of action itself. It is no more than a mechanism designed to ensure that, once the motorist was put in funds by the successful actions, the appropriate part of them reached the company. As a result, their Lordships found such agreements not against public policy.

---

28 *Lagden v O'Connor* [2004] 1 AC 1067; *Ben v Jenson (No.2)* [2008] Lloyd's Rep IR 221, *Kelly v Mackle* [2009] NIQB 39.

29 [1994] 1 AC 142.

30 Section 14 of the Criminal Law Act 1967. Section 14(2) of the 1967 Act which stipulated that the abolition of civil and criminal liability "shall not affect any rule of [the law of England and Wales] as to the cases in which a contract is to be treated as contrary to public policy or otherwise illegal."

31 *Chitty on Contracts*, 33rd ed, [16–078].

32 Ibid, [16–083].

33 *Giles v Thompson* [1994] 1 AC 142.

34 Ibid.

Contingent liability

9.14 It was further questioned whether a claimant can recover credit hire charges against a defendant even when the claimant has been assured by the credit hire company that they will never have to pay the outstanding sums out of her own pocket. The Courts accepted that "a liability owing from A to B can exist notwithstanding that B has agreed not to enforce it directly against A. A non-recourse loan is a good example of that."[35] This is described as contingent liability; liability to pay charges to a third party is contingent on the success of the claim against the defendant. It was further held recently that neither an overcompensation nor a double recovery is in question in credit hire arrangements.[36]

Mitigation point

9.15 Is the cost of hiring a vehicle itself the cost of mitigating the claimant motorist's loss or is it the loss which is itself subject to the duty to mitigate? Lord Hope said in *Lagden v O'Connor*[37] that hiring a replacement car is the means for the claimant motorist to avoid or mitigate the loss of deprivation of the use of the vehicle and the expense of doing so will then become the measure of the loss which he has sustained under this head of his claim.[38]

9.16 With respect, this point of Lord Hope is not immune from doubts.[39] The starting point is the accident. If the victim's vehicle can be repaired, as explained above, the cost of repair is the direct loss that can be claimed from the defendant motorist. The cost of hire appears as a consequence of the need for the repair. The object of the awarding damages is to put the injured party into the same position as he was before the accident. The loss is the deprivation and it materialises in the form of the cost of hiring a replacement vehicle to remedy the inconvenience that such deprivation might otherwise cause. Identifying such costs as "mitigation" therefore becomes a misdescription.[40]

9.17 As expressed by Dillon LJ in *McAll v Brooks*,[41]

> The plaintiff . . . has suffered an injury which deprived him of his car for several weeks and put him in a position in which it was reasonably necessary that he should have the use of a hired car while his own was not there. That is the injury for which he is compensated by the award of damages and it is an injury to him.

It hence appears that the cost of hire is not the mitigation cost, but it is the loss subject to the duty of mitigation. The claimant motorist's claim for the cost of hire therefore is subject to limitations that are assessed by the application of the rules to mitigate the

---

35 *Wakeling v Harrington* [2007] EWCH 1184 (Ch); *Irving v Morgan Sindall PLC* [2018] EWHC 1147 (QB).
36 *Irving v Morgan Sindall PLC* [2018] EWHC 1147 (QB).
37 [2004] 1 AC 1067 [27].
38 Applied in *Umerji v Khan* [2014] RTR 23, [37] Underhill LJ said: "A claim for the cost of hire of a replacement vehicle is, strictly, a claim for expenditure incurred in mitigation of the primary loss, namely the loss of use of the damaged vehicle."
39 See Lord Scott in *Lagden v O'Connor* [2004] 1 AC 1067.
40 *Lagden v O'Connor* [2004] 1 AC 1067, Lord Scott, [78].
41 [1984] RTR 99, 105.

loss.[42] He is under the duty to mitigate the loss by acting reasonable in terms of his need, rate and duration.[43]

9.18 The claimant does not have to prove that he would have suffered financial loss as a result of being unable to use his car during this period, as inconvenience is another form of loss for which, in principle, damages are recoverable.[44] It may be the case that a claimant never hired a replacement car for instance because he did not need it as he already had a spare,[45] or he was in hospital or on holiday and did not seem to need the replacement vehicle for the period that he argued that he had needed.[46] In such cases compensation may be awarded for the inconvenience caused for example, that the owner has had to use public transport, or walk or that a family have been deprived of the advantage of a family car where otherwise they would have used the car which had been damaged.[47] It was mentioned in *Lagden v O'Connor*[48] that where a claimant has not hired a replacement car, the County Court routinely awards general damages at the rate of about £10 a day for loss of the use of the car.

9.19 Where the claimant is a corporation damages have sometimes been calculated upon the maintenance costs or the interest on the capital value of the property damaged.[49] In *West Midlands Travel Ltd v Aviva Insurance UK Ltd*[50] the claimant's bus was off the road for 31 days undergoing repairs. During the time that this bus was being repaired, the cost of which was not challenged, the company covered the loss of the use from its existing resources by using a spare vehicle available. The general damages for loss of use were nevertheless raised. The claimant used a formula produced by the Confederation of Passenger Transport UK (CPT), which ascribed to each bus in the operator's fleet a proportion of the total overheads incurred in operating the whole fleet. On that "standing charge" approach, the claim for loss of use was £106.80 a day, totalling £3,310.80. The lack of profit loss meant that the operator's loss was to be assessed by reference to interest on the average capital value of the buses employed by the claimant, together with expenses thrown away, as representing the marginal cost of being forced to use another bus from the fleet in place of the one that had been damaged.

9.20 The methodology in assessing general damages for the cost of hiring a replacement vehicle entails asking the following questions[51]:

(1) Did the claimant need a replacement vehicle?

---

42 *Everson v Flurry* [1999] CLY 3411. This is a claim for tort but the same principles apply in tort and contract to mitigate the claimant's loss. See *British Westinghouse Electric and Manufacturing Co Ltd. v Underground Electric Railways Co of London Ltd* [1912] AC 673, *Payzu Ltd v Saunders* [1919] 2 KB 581 and *Sotiros Shipping Inc and Aeco Maritime SA v Sameiet Solholt (The "Solholt")* [1983] 1 Ll. Rep. 605.

43 *Umerji v Khan* [2014] RTR 23; In *Beechwood Birmingham Ltd v Hoyer Group UK Ltd* [2011] QB 357 at [28] Sir Mark Potter P said, "The principle that a claimant must take reasonable steps to mitigate his loss applies across the piece."

44 *Lagden v O'Connor* [2004] 1 AC 1067.

45 *Alexander v Rolls Royce Motor Cars Ltd* [1996] RTR 95.

46 *Singh v Yaqubi* [2013] Lloyd's Rep IR 398; *Kelly v Mackle* [2009] NIQB 39.

47 *Alexander v Rolls Royce Motor Cars Ltd* [1996] RTR 95, 102; *Bee v Jenson (No.2)* [2008] Lloyd's Rep IR 221.

48 [2004] 1 AC 1067, [101].

49 *West Midlands Travel Ltd v Aviva Insurance UK Ltd* [2014] Lloyd's Rep IR 66.

50 [2014] Lloyd's Rep IR 66.

51 *Pattni v First Leicester Buses Ltd* [2012] Lloyd's Rep IR 577; *Stevens v Equity Syndicate Management Ltd* [2015] RTR 24; *Ryan Brain v Yorkshire Rider Ltd* [2007] Lloyd's Rep IR 564.

(2) Was it reasonable, in all the circumstances, to hire the particular type of vehicle actually hired at the rate agreed?

(3) Did the claimant pay an excessive hire rate?

(4) Was the period of hire longer than necessary?

9.21 It is essential for the claimant to quantify his loss, and it would then be open to the defendant to challenge the reasonableness of incurring hire charges in the circumstances.[52] It is a matter of fact to be proven in each case whether the claimant was acting reasonably.[53] This will include the assessment of the claimant's actions in deciding to hire a vehicle, in selecting the vehicle to hire and from where to hire and on what price to hire. In line with the general principles applicable in mitigating losses, if the claimant motorist was not acting reasonably, he would not lose his entire claim but he would be able to claim the amount in case he had acted reasonably.[54] For instance if the claimant hires a vehicle for a period longer than he needs it, he should recover only to the extent of the time that he needed reflecting again his actual loss, not mitigation. Similarly, if the claimant enters into a credit hire agreement, whereas he could hire a vehicle from a hirer with paying for the cost of hire in the conventional way, the amount that exceeds the cost of hire and is charged by the hirer is not compensatable.[55] However, where the credit hire charge exceeds the actual value of the vehicle itself does not mean that entering into a credit hire agreement was unreasonable.[56] Further, the victim motorist is entitled to an equivalent vehicle even if the vehicle is an expensive type.[57] It should however be noted that in cases of pecunious claimants the damages recoverable will be the sum attributable to the basic hire rate (BHR) of the replacement car.[58] All of these matters will be explored in detail below.

Calculating damages

9.22 As mentioned above, the cost of hire of a replacement vehicle whilst the damaged vehicle is being repaired can be claimed from the defendant motorist as general damages. Whether such damages is classified as the cost of mitigating the motorist's loss or whether that is described as the loss itself, two different amounts compete against each other in identifying the compensatable loss of the claimant: the basic hire rate (or spot rate)[59] available in the market and the actual credit hire rate charged by the company. Credit hire companies charge more because they offer more. In other words, the hirer pays and then claims against the defendant motorist not only for the actual cost of hiring the vehicle

---

52 *Everson v Flurry* [1999] CLY 3411.

53 *Ryan Brain v Yorkshire Rider Ltd* [2007] Lloyd's Rep IR 564.

54 See above *Beechwood Birmingham Ltd v Hoyer Group UK Ltd* [2011] QB 357.

55 *Dimond v Lovell* [2002] 1 AC 384.

56 See *W v Veolia Environmental Services (UK plc)* [2012] Lloyd's Rep IR 419 where the claimant hired a Bentley car to replace his damaged Bentley whilst it was under repair. His car was worth £16,000 and he claimed £138,000 as the cost of hiring the vehicle.

57 *Bent v Highways & Utilities Construction Ltd* [2010] EWCA Civ 292.

58 Ibid.

59 In *Pattni v First Leicester Buses Ltd* [2012] Lloyd's Rep IR 577 Aikens LJ stated that "spot rate" here is a misnomer as the term is more appropriately applied to rates of freight or charter hire, or the price of a commodity in open, often international markets, where the service or commodity is bought for delivery today, as opposed to some time in the future. Aikens LJ suggested that the term basic hire rate BHR should be used to express such expenses.

but also the price that he pays for the convenience that such agreements provide for the assured.

9.23 There are numerous examples illustrating the differences between the rate charged by credit hirers and the basic hire rate available from the ordinary hirer. For instance, in *Dimond v Lovell*[60] it cost D £41.37 per day to hire from the accident hire company; a similar car could have been gotten from an ordinary car hire company for under £24 per day. The justification for charging more than the actual cost of hire, £24, was that the company was bearing a commercial (though normally not the legal) risk that there might be a failure to make the recovery from the defendant. Moreover, it was bearing the cost of handling the claim and effecting the recovery. £17 was the margin of its profit.

9.24 Whether or not the claimant can recover the full cost of hire from a credit hire company is considered together with an element which is not directly linked with the loss itself, and has been added by the common law, that whether the claimant entered into the credit hire agreement, but not an ordinary car hire, because he was impecunious at the relevant time.[61] If the claimant was pecunious, the rule is that he is entitled to recover from the defendant motorist only the basic hire rate available on the market in the relevant geographical area at the relevant time.[62] If the claimant was impecunious, he is allowed to recover the charges paid for the additional benefits[63] which otherwise have to be stripped out in the case of a pecunious claimant.

Assessing the basic hire rate

9.25 Since cost of hiring a vehicle can be claimed as general damages it is assessed by asking what would have been a reasonable amount for the hire of a replacement vehicle.[64] BHR is the figure that is described as the lowest reasonable rate quoted by a mainstream car hire company or a reputable local company.[65] The practical difficulties that are experienced in calculating the BHR component of any particular credit hire rate was explained by Kitchin LJ in *Stevens v Equity Syndicate Management Ltd*:[66]

> The claims are generally for relatively small sums and often proceed in the fast track. Lawyers preparing them and judges trying them endeavour to do so at proportionate cost. ... breaking down the actual credit hire charge made by a credit hire company in any particular case so as to enable the unrecoverable element to be stripped out would require disclosure and analysis, the cost of which would far exceed the value of the claim.

9.26 The burden is on the defendant to demonstrate by evidence that the credit hire rate exceeds the BHR of an equivalent vehicle to that hired from the credit hire company.[67] Credit hire companies may quote and charge a single credit hire rate. Hence, any attempt to value the additional benefits at a later stage in a proportionate way must necessarily

---

60 [2002] 1 AC 384.
61 *McBride v UK Insurance Ltd* [2017] Lloyd's Rep IR 352.
62 *Dimond v Lovell* [2002] 1 AC 384.
63 *Lagden v O'Connor* [2004] 1 AC 1067.
64 *Kelly v Mackle* [2009] NIQB 39.
65 *McBride v UK Insurance Ltd* [2017] Lloyd's Rep IR 352.
66 [2015] RTR 24, [30].
67 *McBride v UK Insurance Ltd* [2017] Lloyd's Rep IR 352; *Clelland v Quinn Direct* 2011 G.W.D. 2–91.

involve a degree of imprecision. The claimant did not in fact hire a comparable car from a mainstream or reputable local car hire company. However, he could easily obtain through an internet search comparable prices in the relevant geographical area by a mainstream supplier or a reputable local supplier.[68] It follows that identifying BHR is an exercise to determine hypothetically[69] what the BHR would have been for a reasonable person in the position of the claimant to hire a car of the kind actually hired on credit.[70] This method will provide a figure which approximates what the claimant motorist would have paid if he had followed the route of hiring a vehicle from an ordinary car hirer on the assumption that he would not have been willing to pay any higher than the lowest reasonable rate[71] found through this search.[72] The Court would take into account if the claimant would have incurred such expenses if he had had to pay for it himself.

9.27 The assessment of BHR may be difficult because both the vehicles damaged and then hired as a replacement may be very rarely available (eg because they are very expensive sports cars). However, such a difficulty is not an obstacle to calculate the BHR on the evidence presented by the parties.[73]

Impecuniosity

9.28 In principle, if the cost of hire claimed is the whole fee charged by a credit hire company, the figure that was charged for the benefits additional to hiring the vehicle only is to be stripped out in calculating the amount recoverable from the defendant. This was held obiter in *Dimond v Lovell* where the majority of the House of Lords explained that the value of the additional benefits is represented by the difference between what the motorist was willing to pay to the credit hire company and what she would have been willing to pay an ordinary car hire company for the use of a car.[74] The damages recoverable for loss of use are limited to the BHR quoted by hirers other than accident hire companies.[75] Only the BHR of hiring an alternative vehicle is recoverable, and not the higher rates charged by credit hire companies. The fact that the claimant motorist hiring a replacement car was reasonable does not necessarily mean that it was mitigating the loss.[76]

9.29 In *Lagden*, later, the majority of the House of Lords drew attention to the situations where the innocent motorist is unable to afford the cost of hiring a replacement car from a car hire company. Such a motorist will be unable to obtain a replacement car unless he can use the services of a credit hire company. In other words, in practice, he

---

68 *McBride v UK Insurance Ltd* [2017] Lloyd's Rep IR 352.

69 The basis for this calculation is hypothetical because the motorist did not hire the vehicle from an ordinary hirer. *McBride v UK Insurance Ltd* [2017] Lloyd's Rep IR 352; *Stevens v Equity Syndicate Management Ltd* [2015] RTR 24, [34]; *Greenlees v Allianz Insurance* [2011] CSOH Number 173.

70 *Stevens v Equity Syndicate Management Ltd* [2015] RTR 24, [34].

71 Ibid, [35].

72 *Dimond v Lovell*, [2002] 1 AC 384, 402, Lord Hoffman.

73 *Bent v Highways & Utilities Construction Ltd* [2010] EWCA Civ 292.

74 This was obiter given that the credit hire agreement was not enforceable in *Dimond v Lovell* [2002] 1 AC 384.

75 See *Kelly v Mackle* [2009] NIQB 39 where the claimant hired a vehicle for £175 per day whereas the reasonable cost of hire would have been £55 per day. The claimant was entitled to claim the latter for the period that his vehicle was being repaired.

76 *Lagden v O'Connor* [2004] 1 AC 1067, [79], Lord Scott.

will receive little or no recompense for the inconvenience involved. The majority view in *Lagden* held that the obiter view in *Dimond* does not apply to a claimant who had no alternative but to use the services of a credit hire company.[77] The majority found that the law would be seriously defective and therefore unacceptable if in such cases the cost of hiring a replacement vehicle, including the charges added by the credit hire company, is not permitted.

9.30 What *Lagden* did therefore is to convert what was described as not compensatable by *Dimond v Lovell* to a compensatable type of loss because of the claimant's impecunious position. This approach in *Lagden* brings a number of questions, the most obvious one of which is "How badly off does a claimant have to be to satisfy the test of impecuniosity?" The majority accepted that the term "impecuniosity" is incapable of precise definition. The minority in *Lagden* found the lack of clarity in the meaning of this term dangerously open-ended. The subsequent cases however attempted to find out whether the claimant was impecunious without questioning whether the test is vague.

9.31 Impecuniosity in this context signifies inability to pay car hire charges without making sacrifices that the claimant could not reasonably be expected to make. The question is "Would hiring a replacement vehicle at BHR be a significant financial challenge for the claimant?"[78] The answer depends in each case on the facts and degree. The Court would take into account the claimant's monthly income, current and saving accounts balance, whether the claimants' accounts are in credit and the credit card limits.

9.32 In *Lagden* the claimant was unemployed and in poor health, and the majority found it satisfactory on the facts that the claimant proved impecuniosity. It should be noted that impecuniosity need not amount to penury.[79] Clearly, each case has to be looked at carefully on its own facts to conclude whether the claimant had no other choice but entering into a credit hire agreement.[80] In *Irving v Morgan Sindall PLC*[81] the county Court judge held that the claimant, by depleting her bank accounts which were in credit and spending up to her credit card limit could have raised an amount sufficient to purchase a replacement car of the value of that written off by the accident. On appeal Turner J overturned the judgment by expressing that

> I cannot ignore the fact that by reducing her capital to the bare minimum and increasing her debt, the claimant would have been exposing herself to the risk of a serious financial challenge in the event that even a modest but unexpected financial reverse might have afflicted her before her claim was satisfied.[82]

9.33 A claimant who is in a financial position to hire a vehicle on the spot market is not impecunious. In *Clelland v Quinn Direct*[83] the Court found that at the time he entered into the credit hire agreement, the claimant had a choice as to whether to enter into that agreement or to obtain a comparable replacement vehicle on the BHR while his

---

77 *Lagden v O'Connor* [2004] 1 AC 1067.

78 *W v Veolia Environmental Services (UK plc)* [2012] Lloyd's Rep IR 419; *Clelland v Quinn Direct* 2011 G.W.D. 2–91.

79 *Irving v Morgan Sindall PLC* [2018] EWHC 1147 (QB), [36].

80 The majority referred to *The Gazelle* (1844) 2 W Rob 279 and *Harbutt's "Plasticine" Ltd v Wayne Tank and Pump Co Ltd* [1970] 1 QB 447 on this point.

81 [2018] EWHC 1147 (QB).

82 [2018] EWHC 1147 (QB), [36].

83 2011 G.W.D. 2–91.

own was repaired. He could hire a vehicle on the spot market through his credit card, hence the defendant met the burden of proof that the claimant failed to mitigate his loss. Again, the claimant was pecunious in *Bent v Highways & Utilities Construction Ltd*[84] and was only entitled to claim the BHR.

9.34 The object of the law of damages is to put the injured party into the same position as he was before the accident. However, as Lord Walker stated,[85] it would not be right to permit a claimant's impecuniosity, however much it may attract sympathy, to enable him to obtain compensation under a head which English law does not regard as part of his compensatable loss. Lord Scott said that the separation adopted by the majority would be a disservice to the development of the law.[86] For instance, if the credit hire company charges interest on the hire rate, that would be the additional benefit referred to in *Dimond v Lovell* and therefore would not be recoverable. However, its nature will change and become recoverable if the claimant is impecunious.[87] It is submitted that the majority in *Lagden* did not present a persuasive justification for converting a loss which was defined as not compensatable by *Dimond v Lovell* to compensatable. The most obvious reason in *Lagden* may be that the claimant had no other choice, but this solution, as noted by Lord Scott, ignores *Dimond* whereas in *Lagden* none of their Lordships suggested that *Dimond* was wrong. Looking at the matter technically, what caused the claimant's loss is his financial position, namely a special circumstance for which, normally, the defendant motorist is not liable. In *Lagden* Lord Nicholls[88] stated that *Dimond v Lovell* proceeded on the basis that the claimant motorist could have found the money needed to hire a replacement car until she was reimbursed by the defendant motorist or his insurers.

9.35 With respect, it is observed that the House of Lords hardly touched upon this matter in *Dimond*. The obiter view relied on the general principles rather than the claimant's facts and case specific position. *Dimond v Lovell* found the cost of extra benefits provided by the credit hire companies not compensatable. One solution could be, as Lord Scott touched upon in *Lagden*, considering the claimant's position of having had no other choice but hiring through credit hire agreement, from the reasonableness point of view. However, even this does not answer the issue raised by *Dimond* that such loss is not compensatable. This point exactly must be the reason that in *Lagden* the majority identified the cost of hire as mitigating the loss but not the loss itself, and so long as the expenses incurred to mitigate the loss are reasonable, it is recoverable. When the claimant is impecunious, a credit hire agreement was regarded as reasonable. This may justify awarding credit hire charge in favour of the claimant within the explanation of the majority in *Lagden* but it leaves out the decisions and general principles outside this case. There does not seem to be, at least technically, any persuasive justification for awarding the whole cost of credit hire in favour of the claimant, either considering it from general–special damages point of view, or reasonableness point of view. From the foreseeability point of view, the effect of *Lagden* is that the defendant must take the claimant as he finds him, not only with respect to his physical constitution but also with respect to his means.[89]

---

84 [2010] EWCA Civ 292.
85 *Lagden v O'Connor* [2004] 1 AC 1067, [104].
86 [2004] 1 AC 1067, [87], [88].
87 *Pattni v First Leicester Buses Ltd* [2012] Lloyd's Rep IR 577.
88 *Lagden v O'Connor* [2004] 1 AC 1067, [5].
89 *Clerk & Lindsell on Torts*, 22nd ed, [2–176].

9.36 It is submitted that having identified the cost of hire as the loss itself, the claimant is under the duty to mitigate the loss and reasonable expenses incurred for mitigation is permitted. However, the cost of mitigating the loss must not exceed the actual loss itself which is the cost of hire of the vehicle. The claimant can recover cost of hire if the cost is reasonable and where the claimant has no choice but enter into a credit hire agreement, the cost might be regarded as reasonable. As a matter of general principles, the claimant is under the duty to mitigate his loss only if the steps available to do so are reasonable. In the position of an impecunious claimant it can be regarded as not reasonable to try to hire the vehicle from a car hirer that would require an upfront payment. Therefore, when he pays some additional charges to the credit hire company he is not failing to mitigate his loss. His loss is cost of hire and that cost, inevitably, included some additional benefits and therefore costs.

Failure to mitigate the loss

9.37 Where the claimant fails to take steps to mitigate the loss of use of the vehicle, he would lose his right to recover the amount that would have been prevented by the steps taken to mitigate it and he can recover the remaining amount, if any, after such adjustment.

Failure to examine the insurance documents

9.38 It is the responsibility of the claimant to examine his policy documents to see if there are any steps can be taken to mitigate his loss. It may be the case that the insurers may provide a replacement vehicle free of charge for the assured motorist. In *Bucknall v Jepson*[90] the claim was for the cost of hire of a replacement vehicle for 53 days. The claimant, by an oversight, did not realise that his policy provided for a free replacement vehicle. He neither had examined his policy documents nor had he made any enquiries through his broker about the replacement car before hiring one for himself. The Court held that he should have considered the defendant's interests as well as his own and his oversight cost him his hire claim in full. Almost identically, in *Spence v United Taxis*[91] the Court rejected S's claim for credit hire charges for the hire of an alternative vehicle for 27 days whilst S's own vehicle was being repaired. Liability was admitted and there was no dispute as to the period or charges for the hire vehicle. However, although S's insurers operated an approved repairer scheme together with a courtesy car for their policy holders, none of the repairers proposed by S's insurance brokers were approved repairers. S failed to mitigate his loss by omitting to examine the policy documents.

Proof of a need for a replacement vehicle

9.39 As mentioned above the claimant bears the burden of proof that he needed to hire a replacement vehicle. In *Beechwood Birmingham Ltd v Hoyer Group UK Ltd*[92] the

---

90 County Court (Leigh), 9 September 1998 [1998] CLY 1456.
91 County Court (Newcastle upon Tyne), 20 May 1997 [1998] CLY 1465.
92 [2011] QB 357.

claimant, who held at any one time a large stock of vehicles for sale, failed to satisfy this burden. Nevertheless, its service manager entered into a credit hire agreement instead of choosing to reallocate to himself a similar car from the stock. The Court held that the claimant could recover only the general damages assessed based on the interest and capital employed and any depreciation sustained over the period of repairs.

9.40 The abovementioned cases illustrate persuasively that the cost of hire is the damage which is subject to the duty to mitigate. In *West Midlands Travel Ltd v Aviva Insurance UK Ltd*[93] such loss was mitigated by using a spare vehicle and the claimant was awarded the costs insured to mitigate its loss. In *Beechwood Birmingham Ltd v Hoyer Group UK Ltd*[94] the claimant could have mitigated the loss but chose not to and lost its claim which could have been prevented if he had taken reasonable steps to mitigate its loss. The general damages are assessed by asking what would have been a reasonable amount for the hire of a replacement vehicle. If the claimant did not need to hire a vehicle he can still claim damages as explained above.

Offer for a replacement vehicle by the defendant's insurer

9.41 In principle there is no obligation on the victim of a road traffic accident to accept the offer of a replacement vehicle from the defendant rather than obtain a vehicle himself.[95] However, the claimant's decision to reject such an offer should satisfy the test of whether the claimant acted reasonably in doing so. This is a question of fact, which requires an evaluation of the primary facts, and inevitably includes an element of judgment.[96] A claimant does not act unreasonably for the purposes of mitigation in rejecting an offer from the defendant unless he is aware that by doing so he will increase the ultimate burden on the defendant, regardless of the effect on his own position.[97] This was established by *Copley v Lawn*,[98] a joint appeal from *Copley v Lawn* and *Maden v Haller*. In the former C was an estate agent who needed a replacement car immediately after her own car was damaged by an accident caused by the negligence of L. After she signed a credit hire agreement, on the same day, she received a telephone call from L's insurers K, offering her a replacement car. K later repeated the offer by a letter. C sought advice from solicitors upon receiving the letter but no response was delivered from them before the repair of C's car was completed. Similarly, in *Maden v Haller*, K offered a replacement car to M, who, unlike C, ignored the offer. M also signed a credit hire agreement. The relevant hire agreements required both C and M to sign (1) a Mitigation Questionnaire which informed them of their duty to mitigate their loss and asked if they had had any offer of a replacement from the defendants, (2) a hire agreement with Helphire and (3) a combined credit agreement which enabled the claimants to cancel the hire agreement up to 14 days after its receipt. On the facts, both C and M were held to have acted reasonably. C consulted a solicitor as soon as she received K's letter. The fact that

---

93 [2014] Lloyd's Rep IR 66.
94 [2011] QB 357.
95 *Sayce v TNT (UK) Ltd* [2012] Lloyd's Rep IR 183.
96 *Sayce v TNT (UK) Ltd* [2012] Lloyd's Rep IR 183, Moore-Bick LJ, [18]. See generally on duty to mitigate loss: *Chitty on Contracts*, 33rd ed, [26–090].
97 *Copley v Lawn* [2009] Lloyd's Rep IR 496; *Sayce v TNT (UK) Ltd* [2012] Lloyd's Rep IR 183.
98 [2009] Lloyd's Rep IR 496.

the solicitor's advice never came was not the fault of C. It was also mentioned in the case that M sent K's letter to his own brokers or insurers,[99] although he ignored K's letter and also omitted to tick a box in the hire agreement in which he was specifically asked if he had been offered a replacement car by the defendant or his insurers.

9.42 A question may be raised here with regards to the reasonableness of especially M's conduct in this case. Longmore LJ explained that it should be first checked if the claimants and their advisers knew the true cost of providing a replacement vehicle to the defendant and his insurers. It might be the case that the cost of the defendant's insurers hiring the replacement car was actually the same as (or more than) the cost of hiring a replacement from the credit hire company. In any event, even if the defendant proves that he would have hired replacement cars more cheaply than the claimants did, so that having known the cost, the claimant acted unreasonably to mitigate his loss, he can still recover the actual reasonable cost of hire.

9.43 A similar ruling is seen in *Sayce v TNT (UK) Ltd*[100] in which the defendant offered a replacement vehicle and also noted that

> if you choose not to . . . take advantage of our offer (see below) this may affect your entitlement to recover hire or storage charges that you have incurred by using the services of a third party.

The Court of Appeal upheld the appeal and decided that HHJ Harris QC was wrong in refusing to follow *Copley*.

9.44 The claimant's action was held to be unreasonable in *Evans v TNT Logistics Ltd*[101] where the claimant's decision to hire a car himself was a significantly more costly alternative than accepting the defendant's offer of a suitable replacement vehicle. The basis of the ruling is that the duty to mitigate is to ensure that the wrongdoer does not pay out a sum greater than that which the innocent party reasonably needs to make good the loss he has suffered.[102] As a result, the claimant could recover only the BHR which was estimated in *Evans* as the cost that the defendant's insurer would have had to bear.[103]

Delay in arranging a repair

9.45 It may be argued that a claimant motorist fails to mitigate his loss when he delays in start to repair his damaged vehicle: any delay would mean an increase in the number of days that a replacement car is needed. Once again, it is a fact sensitive exercise judging if the claimant acted reasonably. For instance, if the claimant insists on awaiting the defendant's insurer's response and approval for the repair, such delay may be regarded as reasonable if the claimant's concern was the loss of "no claim" discount in case of a claim against his own insurer. In *Martindale v Duncan*[104] the impecunious claimant contacted the defendant's insurers to ask if they would approve the repair and noted that

---

99 This was described as SAGA.
100 [2012] Lloyd's Rep IR 183.
101 [2007] Lloyd's Rep IR 708.
102 *Evans v TNT Logistics Ltd* [2007] Lloyd's Rep IR 708.
103 Similarly, in *Heap-Hammond v TNT UK Ltd* County Court (Yeovil), 15 June 2007, the claimant was awarded a spot rate for an equivalent vehicle to his damaged car.
104 [1973] 1 Lloyd's Rep 558.

the repair would not start until they received a confirmation from them. The Court of Appeal found this case very different to the cases where it was held that impecuniosity was not an excuse for not mitigating the loss.[105] The claimant was seeking in the first instance to recover his damage from the defendant's insurer, and if anything went wrong with that claim, his recovery claim would be against his own insurers. Until he had had authorisation for doing the work he could not be at all certain that he would stand in a good position vis-à-vis the insurance company.

Claimant's no claim discount

9.46 *Martindale v Duncan*[106] as mentioned above confirmed that it is reasonable for an assured motorist who is a victim of a traffic accident to contact the defendant first before informing his own insurer of the loss he suffered. This case was applied in *Perehenic v Deboa Structuring*[107] where P's motor insurance cover included a courtesy car free of charge whilst his own vehicle was being repaired. P chose not to take advantage of the policy and instead arranged repairs through a credit hire company. P signed a credit agreement by which he hired a car at the full commercial rate for the period his car was being repaired. The Court imposed no obligation on the claimant to avail himself of a policy of insurance in order to mitigate his loss. P's action was held to be reasonable, because if he chose to claim from his own insurer he would have incurred a substantial policy excess up front and he would have lost his no claims bonus for several months.

Where the claimant did not pay for the cost of hire himself

Fruit of the claimant's own insurance and insurer's subrogation

9.47 There is no obligation on the victim motorist to take advantage of the fruit of his own policy which may provide a replacement car hire service for the assured. As noted above, this rule is subject to the claimant's choice being reasonable under the circumstances. A few other points are to be noted here that where the assured motorist chooses to follow to take advantage of his own insurance cover, the fact that the claimant's insurer has incurred the hire charges does not relieve the defendant from liability for it. It was held that it is not a pre-requisite of a cost of hire claim that the claimant motorist should himself have incurred the liability to pay the hire charges.[108] The loss is the claimant's for deprivation of the use of his vehicle which does not disappear because the claimant's insurer provided a replacement car for him.[109]

9.48 Nor is it the case that the fact that the claim is made by the insurer in the name of the assured renders the claim invalid simply because the assured exercised his contractual right and was provided with a vehicle by his insurer.[110] The amount that the defendant

---

105 *The Liesbosch* [1933] AC 449 was distinguished.
106 [1973] 1 Lloyd's Rep 558.
107 County Court (Banbury), 7 July 1998 [1998] CLY 1467.
108 *Ben v Jenson (No.2)* [2008] Lloyd's Rep IR 221.
109 *Parry v Cleaver* [1970] AC 1; *Coles v Hetherton* [2015] RTR 7.
110 *Coles v Hetherton* [2015] RTR 7.

CREDIT HIRE AGREEMENTS

is liable in such circumstances is the reasonable cost of hire, namely the basic hire rate for a comparable vehicle.[111] In *Bee v Jenson (No.2)*[112] the assured motorist was entitled under his insurance cover to the cost of hiring a replacement car. He was provided with a car for 21 days pending repairs to his own vehicle. The total cost was £610.46, although the assured was not required to pay any of this sum. Not surprisingly, the Court held that the cost of hire is still recoverable even though it has been paid directly to the hire company by his insurers rather than by the assured himself.

Insuring the credit hire charge

9.49 It could be argued that the hirer suffers no loss where the hiring agreement is unenforceable: the hirer has obtained the use of a car for which he does not have to pay. If he is awarded damages for services which he has received but for which he has not had to pay it would mean that he recovered damages for a loss for which he had already been compensated by the provision of a free car. This would mean a form of double recovery. This was the analysis of the claimant's position in *Dimond v Lovell* where the credit hire agreement was unenforceable under the Consumer Credit Act 1974 because the information required by the Consumer Credit (Agreements) Regulations 1983, SI 1983 No 1553 (made under ss 60 and 61 of the 1974 Act), as to the amount of the credit, had not been supplied.[113] That rendered the agreement "improperly executed" under s 65 of the 1974 Act and thereby removed the discretion of the Court to make an order enforcing the agreement under s 127 of the 1974 Act. The agreement was improperly executed, which meant that the hirer, D, had been given the use of a car without any corresponding obligations on her part and therefore was not under any contractual obligation to the hirer. The hirer, consequently, had no right to proceed against the defendant in D's name.

9.50 The double recovery impediment is now avoided by the credit hire companies by offering a package to the motorists. The package includes a car hire the payment of which is not required by the motorist hirer but an insurer which is included in this package.[114] The motorist hence hires the replacement vehicle free of charge.

9.51 The English Courts allow this practice.[115] A payment by the insurers is treated as a payment by the claimant. The insurers step into the assured's shoes and make a claim for the damages suffered in the assured's name. This was permitted even where the credit hire agreement itself was not enforceable and the assured was not obliged to pay for the cost of hiring the vehicle. This is because the claimant received the service and did not fail to mitigate his loss of deprivation of the use of his vehicle.[116] In *W v*

---

111 *Bee v Jenson (No.2)* [2008] Lloyd's Rep IR 221.

112 [2008] Lloyd's Rep IR 221.

113 The general scheme under the 1974 Act is to regulate all *"personal credit agreements"* (s 8), of which various types are identified by ss 11 to 19. Also regulated is a *"consumer hire agreement"* as defined by s 15. Under the Consumer Credit Act 1974 any personal credit agreement (as defined by s 8 of the Act) is regulated, although a consumer hiring agreement is regulated only if it is capable of lasting for more than three months (s 15). In *Dimond v Lovell* [2002] 1 AC 384 the contract did not meet the requirements for regulation as a hiring agreement. However, "credit" had been provided so as to bring the agreement within s 8 since IAL had deferred its right to recover the hire charges.

114 See eg *Sobrany v UAB Transtira* [2016] Lloyd's Rep IR 266.

115 *W v Veolia Environmental Services (UK plc)* [2012] Lloyd's Rep IR 419.

116 Ibid.

Veolia Environmental Services (UK plc)[117] the agreement was defective because the notice requirement under the Cancellation of Contracts made in a Consumer's Home or Place of Work etc Regulations 2008 were not satisfied, but the actual payment by the insurer had been made and there was no chance of a double recovery by the claimant motorist.[118] The Court ruled that it was not unreasonable for a claimant to pay for services actually received even though he had not been legally obliged to do so, and accordingly the claimant had suffered a loss for which he could recover damages from the defendant. In *Sobrany v UAB Transtira*[119] the insurer who insured against non-payment of the credit hire brought a subrogation action against the defendant motorist. The Court of Appeal referred to *Veolia* and held that the prohibition based on double recovery did not apply where there had been actual payment by insurers in respect of the hire charges, because the action was then by way of subrogation and there was no question of double recovery. A subrogation claim is permitted in respect of the full payment so long as it falls below the maximum limit for which the policy provided cover. If the insurer makes an *ex gratia* payment, that cannot be recovered from the defendant motorist. The English Courts do not regard such *ex gratia* payment that exceeds the policy limit "as being a good faith payment of a claim made under the policy."[120]

Ex turpi causa

9.52 Claiming the cost of hiring a vehicle where the credit hire agreement is unenforceable because it did not meet some statutory requirements should be distinguished from the claimant's inability to make a claim because of the *ex turpi causa* element in it. The meaning of *ex turpi causa* is discussed in Chapter 12. Briefly, it suffices to mention here that public policy may prevent a claimant from recovering the whole of the damages which, but for the rule of public policy, he would otherwise have recovered. A typical example is the principle that a person who makes his living from burglary cannot have damages assessed on the basis of what he would have earned from burglary but for the defendant's negligence.[121]

9.53 In *Agheampong v Allied Manufacturing (London) Ltd*[122] HHJ Dean QC discussed the rule in the context of a claimant motorist who was using a vehicle without insurance in contravention to the RTA 1988 and therefore guilty of a criminal offence. The claimant's action was for the credit hire cost incurred as a result of an accident that the defendant caused. HHJ Dean QC held that the claimant's loss of deprivation was in relation to an uninsured vehicle which, without the accident, the claimant would have

---

117 [2012] Lloyd's Rep IR 419.

118 Under the Regulations, consumers who have made a contract for the supply of goods or services during a visit by a trader to their home or place of work have a right to cancel within a cancellation period. A trader who supplies goods or services is bound to give the consumer a written notice of his right to cancel when the contract is made. In *Veolia* Judge Mackie held that the failure to give the requisite notice rendered the hiring agreement unenforceable.

119 [2016] Lloyd's Rep IR 266.

120 *W v Veolia Environmental Services (UK plc)* [2012] Lloyd's Rep IR 419.

121 *Hewison v Meridian Shipping Services Pte Ltd* [2003] PIQR P17, [28].

122 [2009] Lloyd's Rep IR 379.

kept using without insurance. As a result, his claim that relied on his own wrongdoing had to be rejected.

Different forms of arrangement

9.54 A credit hire agreement may be entered into either before or after the accident in question,[123] and this does not make a difference with regards to the recoverability of cost.

9.55 *Prudential Insurance Co v Inland Revenue Commissioners*[124] established that by an insurance contract, in return for payment of premium, the assured secures to himself some benefit usually, but not necessarily, the payment of a sum of money, upon the happening of some event. It was further explained in *Prudential* that there must be either uncertainty whether the event will ever happen or not, or if the event is one which must happen at some time there must be uncertainty as to the time at which it will happen. The insurance is to provide for the payment of a sum of money to meet a loss or detriment which will or may be suffered upon the happening of the event.

9.56 It was held in *Department of Trade and Industry v St. Christopher Motorists' Association Ltd.*[125] a contract for the provision of assistance to motorists satisfied the requirements identified in *Prudential*. The agreement was between an association and its members who were provided with some benefits which had not been expressed in terms of money but could be quantified and were the equivalent of money. More precisely, the services provided were advertised as:

> Association protects you against being unable to drive your car. For as little as £10 a year the . . . Association will help keep you on the road, when you can't be behind the wheel. Whether disqualification or injury prevents you from driving, SCMA will provide you with a driver and, if necessary, a car and driver, for up to 40 hours a week, for a maximum of 12 months.

The Court interpreted the annual sum that a member would pay as resembling a premium. The justification for such resemblance is that the member is frightened of some uncertain disaster which may fall upon him and which will have adverse consequences to him. If such an uncertain event happens, the member is entitled to services and those services are to compensate him for the loss or disadvantage which has happened to him as a result of the happening of the uncertain event. The Court followed a similar approach in *Everson v Flurry*[126] where E entered into a legal protection policy with DAS under which, in return for a small premium, DAS agreed to provide a hire care to E in the event of an accident. All cars were provided by companies in the GG group by arrangement with DAS. E received a hire car for six days following an accident in which E's car was allegedly negligently damaged by F. Having paid the hire charges to GG, DAS claimed against F in E's name. The question was whether DAS's claim was sustainable. It could be, if the arrangement between DAS and E was insurance so that DAS, upon payment, subrogated into E's right against F. The essence of insurance was once more observed

---

123 *McAll v Brooks* [1984] RTR 99; *Everson v Flurry* [1999] CLY 3411.
124 [1904] 2 KB 658.
125 [1974] 1 WLR 99.
126 [1999] CLY 3411.

by Recorder Flather that a premium was payable; DAS's liability arose on the happening of an uncertain event (a motor accident requiring repair to the assured's car); and the event was contrary to the assured's interests. The fact that the policy did not result in a cash payment to the assured but instead the assured received services provided by a third party did not prevent the contract from being one of insurance. Similarly, a condition that the benefits under the policy were available only where the assured's car was road-worthy and the accident was not the assured's fault was similar to those seen in insurance policies.

CHAPTER 10

Motor Insurers' Bureau

The Motor Insurers' Bureau Agreements

10.1 The compulsory insurance regime under the Road Traffic Acts protects the innocent third party from the inability to pay of a driver who incurs liability by causing him death or personal injuries. The third party victim is protected by imposing an obligation on all drivers to insure against third party liability under sanction of the criminal law, and also by conferring on a third party victim a right of direct action against the driver's insurers. A motorist, however, may be uninsured because he never took out insurance but also the claim may be against an uninsured motorist if, for instance, the insurance contract is avoided by the insurer before the accident took place for misrepresentation of a material fact. There used to be a gap in the case of accidents the drivers of which were either uninsured or untraced. The RTA 1930 gave no protection to third parties injured in motor vehicle accidents where there was no insurance cover.[1] The lack of a fund to which the victims of uninsured drivers can apply had been drawn attention by judiciary.[2] The report that first discussed compensation for damages caused by uninsured and untraced drivers was produced in 1937.[3] In 1937 a committee under the chairmanship of Sir Felix Cassel recommended that, in cases of failure to insure as required, an injured third party who had obtained a judgment against the person responsible should be able to recover from a central fund.[4] The fund should be set up and financed by insurers licensed to transact compulsory motor vehicle insurance business.[5]

10.2 In order to fill the gap in providing compensation for injuries caused by uninsured motorists, the insurers transacting compulsory motor vehicle insurance business in Great Britain, acting in agreement with the Minister of Transport, formed

---

1 When the assured was insolvent, the third party could claim from the assured's insurer under the Third Parties (Rights Against Insurers) Act 1930, but this Act enabled such an action only where there was an insurance cover for the user of the vehicle. The 1930 Act was replaced by the Third Parties (Rights Against Insurers) Act 2010 which retains the same insurance requirement for a right of direct claim against the insurer.

2 *Peters v General Accident Fire & Life Assurance Corp Ltd* (1937) 59 Ll L Rep 148, Goddard J. *Jones v Welsh Insurance Corporation* (1937) 59 Ll L Rep 13.

3 The chairman was Sir Felix Cassel, K.C. See *Carswell v Secretary of State for Transport* [2011] Lloyd's Rep IR 644, [8]; Donald B. Williams, Chasing the Uninsured and Hit-and-Run Motorists, 59 A.B.A. J. 75 (1973).

4 Report of the Committee on Compulsory Insurance (Cmd 5528).

5 *White v White* [2001] RTR 25, Lord Nicholls, [5].

a company,[6] the Motor Insurers' Bureau (MIB), to assume liability to satisfy judgments of these kinds.[7]

10.3 The MIB's obligation applies only where either the motorist failed to comply with his statutory obligation to insure or the motorist is never traced. However, in these cases the role of the MIB under the relevant Agreements[8] is not to guarantee but to provide a safety net for innocent victims of identified but uninsured or untraced drivers. In other words the MIB's obligation to satisfy traffic accident victims' claims is not absolute but is subject to exceptions where the MIB has either no liability[9] or there is a limitation to its liability.[10] Additionally, there are pre-conditions to the MIB's liability which the claimant must first comply with.[11] The MIB will aim to compensate innocent victims of negligent unidentified drivers fairly and promptly and will be open and honest in dealing with all claimants. It may perform all or part of its obligations through agents appointed on its behalf.[12] The MIB is also responsible for operating the "Green Card" system in the UK.

10.4 Where an insurer becomes insolvent, any ongoing claim will typically be dealt with under the provisions of the Financial Services Compensation Scheme, but, if, for whatever reason, a judgment is not satisfied under that Scheme, the MIB will meet the judgment and then look to recover its outlay from the Scheme. The MIB will, however, expect that every reasonable effort must first be made to pursue the claim through the Scheme, this reflecting the MIB's status as a safety net.

10.5 Every insurer underwriting compulsory motor insurance is obliged, by virtue of the Road Traffic Act 1998, to be a member of the MIB[13] and to contribute to its funding. The MIB is funded by the levies paid by its members based on the premium that they received.[14]

10.6 Claims against the MIB for losses caused either by uninsured or untraced drivers are not uncommon. The MIB has revealed that thousands of people are breaking the law by driving other people's cars without insurance, resulting in over 3,000 vehicles being seized between July 2016 and June 2018.[15] In 2017 the MIB concluded 17,700 applications by victims of untraced drivers.[16]

---

6 RTA 1988, s 95(2). A company limited by guarantee and incorporated under the Companies Act 1929 on 14 June 1946; *Carswell v Secretary of State for Transport* [2011] Lloyd's Rep IR 644, [9].

7 The MIB is a company limited by Guarantee registered in England and Wales whose registered office is at Linford Wood House, 6–12 Capital Drive, Milton Keynes MK14 6XT.

8 These agreements are explained below.

9 See UTDA 2017 clause 4 to clause 9; UDA 2015 clause 4 to clause 10. Where only part of the claim is excluded, the remainder will be considered by the MIB.

10 See UTDA 2017, clause 11; UDA 2015 clause 11.

11 UTDA, clause 10; UDA 2015 clause 12 to clause 15.

12 See UDA 2015 clause 1(3).

13 The RTA 1988 ss 145(5) and 95.

14 www.mib.org.uk/media/423529/mib-articles-of-association-19-july-2018.pdf.

15 MIB news October 2018 www.mib.org.uk/media-centre/news/2018/october/thousands-of-people-unwittingly-breaking-the-law-by-driving-other-cars-without-insurance/.

16 Uninsured Drivers must have been referred to the insurers under Article 75 of the MIB Articles of Association. For Article 75 see below.

Uninsured Drivers Agreement

10.7 The obligations of the MIB are not to be found in an Act of Parliament but in the MIB Agreements with the appropriate minister.[17] The first Agreement was made on 17 June 1946, between the Minister of Transport and the MIB with the objective of satisfying judgments against uninsured motorists in respect of a liability which is the subject of a compulsory insurance obligation under the Road Traffic Acts. That Agreement was replaced by an Agreement which operated in respect of accidents occurring on or after 1 March 1971 which in turn was replaced by a new Agreement to operate in respect of accidents occurring on or after 1 December 1972. The Agreement was subject to further replacements in 1988 and 1999 with a Supplementary Agreement in 2008. The current Agreement was made in July 2015 and was brought into force on 1 August 2015. A Supplementary Agreement of January 2017 came into force on 1 March 2017 in relation to accidents occurring on or after that date.

Untraced Drivers Agreement

10.8 The MIB also paid compensation on an *ex gratia* basis to persons injured in motor accidents in cases where the driver could not be traced, a practice that was placed on a formal footing by the first Untraced Drivers Agreement dated 21 April 1969.[18] This Agreement was replaced by a new Agreement which operated in respect of accidents occurring on or after 1 December 1972. This Second Agreement was added to by a Supplemental Agreement dated 7 December 1977 which operated in respect of accidents occurring on or after 3 January 1978. The Agreement was subject to further replacements in 1996 and then in 2003 with Supplementary Agreements of 2008, 2011, 2013 and 2015. The current Untraced Drivers Agreement came into force on 1 March 2017 replacing the 2003 Agreement and applying in relation to accidents occurring on or after that date.

EU Directives

10.9 The influence of the European law on the MIB Agreements has been inevitable.[19] As referred to in Chapter 1 the main purpose of the Second Directive, Directive 84/5/EEC, was to improve guarantees of compensation for victims of motor accidents by ensuring a minimum level of protection for them throughout the Community. The intention was "to entitle victims of damage or injury caused by unidentified or insufficiently

---

17 *White v White* [2001] RTR 25, Lord Nicholls, [7].

18 See *Adams v Andrews* [1964] 2 Lloyd's Rep 347. The claimant was injured whilst being a passenger in the car which overturned while being driven by defendant. The judge accepted that the accident was as a result of the fault of a motorcycle which was driven on the opposite to the wrong direction. The defendant was not insured against claims by passengers. His insurer made payment of £750 being an *ex gratia*. The judge noted the information provided about the MIB's *ex gratia* payments (possibly for untraced drivers) and invited a legislative change to the effect victims of untraced drivers to be compensated. It was also stated that the MIB was obligated under the 1946 Agreement only to give sympathetic consideration to the claims as a result of which the MIB could make and in practice had been making *ex gratia* payment by way of compensation to victims. *American Bar Association Journal*, January 1973, at 76. See *Jacobs v Motor Insurers' Bureau* [2011] Lloyd's Rep IR 355, [7].

19 *Carswell v Secretary of State for Transport* [2011] Lloyd's Rep IR 644, [11].

insured vehicles to protection equivalent to, and as effective as, that available to persons injured by identified and insured vehicles."[20]

10.10 Second Directive therefore required Member States to put in place provisions for the protection of those injured by uninsured or untraced drivers of motor vehicles. The sixth recital to the Second Directive drew attention to the need for making provision for a body to guarantee that the victim will not remain without compensation where the vehicle which caused the accident is uninsured or unidentified. Article 1(4) of the Directive therefore imposed an obligation on Member States to set up or authorise a body with the task of providing compensation to the victims of unidentified or uninsured drivers, ie in the case of the insurance obligation not being satisfied. Article 1(4) of the Directive permitted the victim to make a direct claim against the relevant body. The compensation body's liability to provide compensation should at least be up to the limits of the insurance obligation for damage to property or personal injuries caused by an unidentified vehicle or a vehicle for which the insurance obligation provided for in paragraph 1 has not been satisfied.[21] However, Member States were allowed to limit or exclude the payment of compensation by that body in the event of damage to property by an unidentified vehicle.

10.11 The Third Directive also improved the position of a victim in the case of an uninsured driver in that the compensation body referred to in Art 1(4) of the Second Directive was not permitted to require that the victim, if he is to be compensated, should establish that the party liable (uninsured driver) is unable or refuses to pay.[22] Where a dispute arises as to whether the compensation body or the civil liability insurer is responsible to compensate the traffic accident victim's loss, the Third Directive required the Member States to take the appropriate measures so that one of these parties is designated to be responsible in the first instance for paying compensation to the victim without delay.[23] Article 4 retained the right of recourse by the body who paid for the loss to the other either for the whole (in case the other body should have paid) or part (in case the other body is responsible in part).

10.12 As referred to in Chapter 2, First Directive Article 4 allowed some derogations from compulsory insurance requirements with respect to certain vehicles belong to public or private persons and vehicles with certain plates. The Fifth Directive provided that the Member States shall ensure that for the former a compensation system is in operation and for the latter, with respect to vehicles with certain plates, that are treated in the same way as vehicles for which the insurance obligation provided for in Article 3(1) has not been satisfied.[24] The compensation body of the Member State in which the accident has taken place shall then have a claim against the guarantee fund provided for in Article 1(4) of Directive 84/5/EEC in the Member State where the vehicle is normally based.[25]

10.13 Article 2(4) of the Fifth Directive amended the Second Directive in respect of the property damage caused by an unidentified vehicle that each Member State shall set up or authorise a body with the task of providing compensation, at least up to the

---

20 *Evans v Secretary of State for the Environment, Transport and the Regions* (C-63/01) [2004] RTR 32, [27].
21 Second Directive, Art 1(4).
22 Third Directive, Art 3.
23 Third Directive, Art 4.
24 Fifth Directive, Art 1(3).
25 Fifth Directive, Art 1(3)(b).

limits of the insurance obligation for damage to property or personal injuries caused by an unidentified vehicle or a vehicle for which the insurance obligation provided for in paragraph 1 has not been satisfied. Member States may limit or exclude the payment of compensation by the body in the event of damage to property by an unidentified vehicle.[26] However, where the body has paid compensation for significant personal injuries to any victim of the same accident in which damage to property was caused by an unidentified vehicle, Member States may not exclude the payment of compensation for damage to property on the basis that the vehicle is not identified. Nevertheless, Member States may provide for an excess of not more than EUR 500 for which the victim of such damage to property may be responsible.[27]

10.14 The provisions with regards to the compensation body responsible for satisfying third party victims' claims in the case of uninsured or untraced drivers were carried to the Consolidated Directive Article 10 from the previous relevant Directives. Similar to the provisions available before, the compensation body should be responsible for covering at least up to the limits of the insurance obligation for damage to property or personal injuries caused by an unidentified or uninsured vehicle. The victim is permitted to apply directly to the body for compensation who is allowed to exclude liability in respect of persons who voluntarily entered the vehicle which caused the damage or injury when the body can prove that they knew it was uninsured. Moreover, Member States may limit or exclude the payment of compensation by the body in the event of damage to property by an unidentified vehicle. This is nevertheless subject to a case where compensation is paid for significant personal injuries and damage to property caused by an unidentified vehicle. In such circumstances Member States are allowed to provide for an excess not more than EUR 500 to be borne by the victim of such damage to property but they are not permitted to exclude the payment of compensation for damage to property on the basis that the vehicle is unidentified.

10.15 The Consolidated Directive also retained the rule that in the case of having a dispute between the insurer and the compensation body as to who is liable to meet the victim's claim the Member States shall take the appropriate measures so that one of those parties is designated to be responsible in the first instance for paying compensation to the victim without delay.[28] Once it is ultimately decided that the other party should have paid all or part of the compensation, that other party shall reimburse accordingly the party which has paid.

10.16 It is worth noting that under the schemes established by the Second and Fourth Directives (now Consolidated Directive) the duties imposed on the compensation body cannot be regarded as the implementation of a guarantee scheme in respect of insurance against civil liability relating to the use of motor vehicles.[29] The scheme was designed to be a measure of last resort, envisaged only for specific, clearly identified sets of circumstances in the Directives.[30] One important aspect of why this classification is significant is covered below under "Insurer's Insolvency."

---

26 Fifth Directive, Art 2(6).

27 Ibid.

28 Consolidated Directive, Art 11.

29 *Csonka v Magyar Allam* (C-409/11) [2014] 1 CMLR 14 [30]–[32].

30 *Fundo de Garantia Automovel v Juliana* (C-80/17) EU:C:2018:661, [45].

10.17 In the United Kingdom, the UK MIB acts both as the bureau or guarantee fund contemplated by Article 1(4) of the Second Directive (Article 10 of the Sixth Directive) and, under Regulation 10 of the Motor Vehicles (Compulsory Insurance) (Information Centre and Compensation Body) Regulations 2003,[31] as the compensation body required under Articles 6 and 7 of the Fourth Directive (now Articles 24(1) and 25(1) of the Sixth Directive).

The legal status of the MIB Agreements

10.18 The MIB is a mutual of profit-making insurance companies.[32] As explained above, the obligations of the MIB are not imposed by statute, as they could have been.[33] They derive from the Agreements reached between the MIB and the United Kingdom Government (through the relevant Minister of State), one relating to victims of uninsured drivers (the "Uninsured Drivers Agreement" – UDA) and the other concerned with the victims of hit and run or otherwise unidentified drivers (the "Untraced Drivers Agreement" – UTDA). Under each Agreement, the MIB is obliged to pay defined compensation in specific circumstances to the victims of motor vehicle accidents who, in fact, are not parties to these Agreements. These Agreements are, on their face, contracts between two parties for the benefit of a third person.[34] Under the traditional doctrine of privity of contract before the Contracts (Rights of Third Parties) Act 1999,[35] no person would have been entitled to sue the bureau on its contract with the Minister other than the Minister himself.[36] It might be argued that the 1999 Act fixed this matter; however, the problem with the operation of the MIB Agreements together with the 1999 Act is that the latter requires the third party beneficiary to be identified in the contract[37] whereas the UDA or UTDA practically cannot perform this: the claims are to be made by traffic accident victims who are not known at the time the Agreements are made.

10.19 The 2003 UTDA clause 31 (5) stated that the 2003 Agreement was intended by the parties to confer a benefit on applicants as non-parties. It was argued in *Carswell v Secretary of State for Transport*[38] and the judge approved that clause 31(5) makes expressly and abundantly clear that the 2003 Agreement is intended by the parties to confer a benefit on applicants as non-parties. Subsequently, clause 31(5) gives a clear signpost that non-party applicants are intended to have a right to sue on the contract where there is no right to appeal to an arbitrator.[39] The 2017 UTDA does not contain a similar wording to that of clause 31(5) of the 2003 Agreement, but[40] its clause 25 provides

---

31 SI 2003/37. See Chapter 1, footnote 53.

32 *Carswell v Secretary of State for Transport* [2011] Lloyd's Rep IR 644, [74].

33 Ibid, [10].

34 *Hardy v Motor Insurers' Bureau* [1964] 2 QB 745, 757, Lord Denning (for the 1946 agreement Lord Denning made this statement).

35 The 1999 Act hereinafter.

36 *Gurtner v Circuit* [1968] 2 QB 587, 606, Salmon LJ.

37 The 1999 Act s 1(3).

38 [2011] Lloyd's Rep IR 644, [62].

39 Ibid.

40 The UDA 2015 does not refer to this matter in the same manner, but clause 2(1) provides that the Agreement may be terminated by the Secretary of State or by the MIB giving to the other not less than 12 months' notice in writing but without prejudice to its continued operation in respect of accidents occurring before the date of termination.

that for the purposes of the 1999 Act the UTDA may be (a) varied or rescinded without the consent of any person other than the parties hereto, and (b) determined pursuant to clause 2(3) without the consent of any such person. This may be regarded as an attempt to give formal recognition to the practical position as it has existed since the MIB was established[41] that a third party can enforce the MIB Agreements.[42] In any event third party victim's claims had never been objected by the MIB for lack of contract between the MIB and the claimant.[43] The claims have been processed on the basis that the intention of the Agreements is to benefit the victims of uninsured and untraced drivers.[44] The method adopted by the Agreements was described as an oblique and extra-statutory way of imposing liability upon the MIB[45] and so far as they are permitted by the rules, to make it work with justice to the bureau as well as to the persons for whose benefit the Minister made the contract.[46]

10.20 The way that the UK implemented the Second Directive through a private agreement between a private body and the relevant Ministry was challenged in *Evans v Secretary of State for the Environment, Transport and the Regions*.[47] This was before the 2009 Directive consolidated the previous five Directives referred to in Chapter 1. The Court of Justice of the European Communities noted that the first subparagraph of Art 4(1) of Directive 84/5 (Second Directive) contained no provision concerning the legal status of the body or the detailed arrangements for its authorisation.[48] Further, what mattered was whether the relevant body was to provide victims with the compensation guaranteed to them by the Directive and it was enabled for victims to address themselves directly to the body for such compensation. The Court was of the view that so long as the body agreement satisfied these conditions the nature of the agreement was immaterial.[49]

Is the MIB an emanation of the state?

10.21 Emanation of the state may also be expressed as "organ of the state," "public authority" and "state authority" which are used as overlapping and synonymous terms.[50] The classification of the MIB is significant for the following reasons. If the MIB is not an emanation of the state and a victim of a traffic accident is unable to recover from the MIB in circumstances in which recovery is required by the Directives, the victim will have to resort to an action in damages against the UK Government for

---

41 Colinvaux, Chapter 23 section 3.
42 See *Hardy v Motor Insurers' Bureau* [1964] 2 QB 745, 757, Lord Denning; *Silverton v Goodall And Motor Insurers' Bureau* [1997] PIQR P451. In *Gurtner v Circuit* [1968] 2 QB 587 the Court of Appeal confirmed that the Minister of Transport can sue for specific performance of it and once an order for specific performance is obtained, the injured person can enforce it for his own benefit under *Beswick v Beswick*. [1968] AC 58.
43 *White v White* [2001] RTR 25, Lord Cooke, [39]; *Persson v London Country Buses* [1974] 1 Lloyd's Rep 415. In *Coward v Motor Insurers' Bureau* [1963] 1 QB 259, 265 Upjohn LJ noted: "As we understand other actions have been maintained in circumstances similar to this in the High Court, this Court has not thought it necessary to raise any such objection independently and the appeal has been entertained accordingly."
44 *Gurtner v Circuit* [1968] 2 QB 587.
45 *Gurtner v Circuit* [1968] 2 QB 587, 603, Diplock LJ.
46 Ibid.
47 (C-63/01) [2004] RTR 32.
48 [2004] RTR 32, [32].
49 [2004] RTR 32, [34].
50 *Foster v British Gas Plc* (C-188/89) [1991] 1 QB 405, [6].

failing in its duties to implement the Directives properly. The condition of the Member States' liability in this respect is discussed in Chapter 1. On the other hand, if the MIB is an emanation of the state, the victim may be able to recover from the MIB for that reason and therefore does not have to claim damages against the UK Government for failing to implement the Directive.

10.22 The legal form of the body is not determinative of whether or not it is an emanation of state. However the following matters should be taken into account, that[51]

    (i) the body has been made responsible, pursuant to a measure adopted by the State, for providing a public service;

    (ii) such public service is provided under the control of the State; and

    (iii) the body has for that purpose special powers beyond those which result from the normal rules applicable in relations between individuals is included among the bodies against which the provisions of a Directive capable of having direct effect may be relied upon.

10.23 Judiciary disagreed on the matter of whether the MIB's status matches with the abovementioned conditions. Those who disagreed that the MIB is an emanation of the State were of the view that, although the MIB performs a public service with regards to the protection and compensation for victims of accidents involving uninsured or untraced drivers, it is not under the control of the State. Further, the MIB acts on its own behalf in the commercial interest of its members, not on behalf of the State or as a delegate of the State. It enters into commercial private law contracts with inter alia the Secretary of State. When seeking to implement the Second Directive in relation to uninsured and untraced drivers, the Secretary of State chose to make an Agreement with the MIB. The only capacity in which the bureau has acted is as a private law entity and the only obligations it has assumed have been private law contractual obligations. This cannot be said to be a situation where any public law relationship has come into existence.[52]

10.24 On the other hand, some expressly held that the MIB is an emanation of the State.[53]

10.25 The dispute in *Farrell v Whitty*[54] was referred in paragraph 10.129 onwards. It suffices here to briefly mention that in *Farrell*, the Motor Insurers' Bureau of Ireland (MIBI) rejected a claim made by a victim of a traffic accident. The reason for rejecting the claim was that the domestic legislation of Ireland excluded from the benefit of the guarantee provided by compulsory insurance cover "persons travelling in any part of a vehicle which is not designed and constructed with seating accommodation for passengers." F, at the time of the accident, was seated on the floor in the rear of the van which was neither designed nor constructed to carry passengers in the rear. In reference to the CJEU the Court ruled that such an exclusion is not permitted under the Third Motor Insurance Directive which has a direct effect so that an individual can claim the benefit derives from the Directive before a national Court. Whether such a claim could be made

---

51 Ibid, [20].

52 *Byrne v Motor Insurers' Bureau* [2009] QB 66, [61–63] Arden LJ; *Mighell v Reading* [1999] Lloyd's Rep IR 30, [73] Hobhouse LJ; *RoadPeace v Secretary of State for Transport* [2018] Lloyd's Rep IR 478.

53 *NUT v St Mary's Church* [1996] T.L.R. 726. 16 December 1996; *C.A. Silverton v Goodall* [1997] PIQR P451, p 463; *Motor Insurers' Bureau v Lewis* [2019] EWCA Civ 909.

54 (C-356/05) [2007] Lloyd's Rep IR 525.

against the MIBI was not determined by the Court of Justice in *Farrell v Whitty*[55] who noted that the national (referring) Court did not provide sufficient information regarding the MIBI to enable them to make such a ruling. Consequently, the CJEU left it to the national Court to ascertain this matter.[56] On return, the High Court in Ireland decided that the MIBI was an emanation of the state and that, consequently, the claimant had a right to obtain compensation from it. The MIBI appealed on the ground that it was not an emanation of the state and that the provisions of a Directive, even those having direct effect, which had not been transposed into national law could not be relied on against it. In the meantime, following an agreement between the parties, the claimant received compensation for her injuries, but the parties disagreed on the question of who should bear the cost. By an order dated 12 May 2015, the Supreme Court of Ireland stayed the appeal proceedings and referred to the Court of Justice for a preliminary ruling on the issue of whether provisions of the Second Directive as amended by the Third Directive, which were capable of having direct effect, could be relied upon against a private law body on which a Member State had conferred the task which was the subject of Article 1(4) of the Second Directive.[57] In *Farrell v Whitty*[58] the CJEU held that the conditions were not conjunctive. This means that it is sufficient if (i) the Member State has delegated a task in the public interest and (ii) the delegate possesses "special powers" for that purpose.

10.26 In *Lewis v Tindale*[59] Soole J held, and the Court of Appeal approved[60] that for the purposes of this issue there is no relevant difference between the structure of the MIBI[61] and MIB.[62] The judge decided that the CJEU's ruling in *Farrell v Whitty*[63] is to supersede[64] the reasoning in *Byrne v Motor Insurers' Bureau*[65] and the observations of Hobhouse LJ in *Mighell v Reading*,[66] both of which were mentioned above.

Is the MIB independent of its members insurers?

10.27 A further angle of the discussion on the legal nature of the MIB and its obligations raises the question about its reliability as to the objective nature of its decisions.

10.28 It was argued in *Carswell v Secretary of State for Transport* that the MIB is not independent: it comprises all motor insurers (who are companies run for profit); it is commercially interested in the outcome of any claim; and it is both investigator and the body liable to pay any award. Hickinbottom J held that the fact that the body charged with being the investigator/inquisitor is not a public body, but a private commercial body,

---

55 Ibid.
56 [2007] Lloyd's Rep IR 525, [41].
57 See above EU Directives.
58 (C-413/15) [2018] Lloyd's Rep IR 103.
59 [2018] EWHC 2376 (QB).
60 *Motor Insurers' Bureau v Lewis* [2019] EWCA Civ 909.
61 The MIBI is a company limited by guarantee, but without a share capital, that is entirely funded by its members, who are the insurers operating in the motor vehicle insurance market in Ireland. The MIBI was established in November 1954, following an agreement between the Department of Local Government and the insurers writing motor insurance in Ireland.
62 [2018] EWHC 2376 (QB), [115], [127]; cf *Byrne v Motor Insurers' Bureau* [2009] QB 66.
63 (C-413/15) [2018] Lloyd's Rep IR 103.
64 [2018] EWHC 2376 (QB), [126].
65 [2009] QB 66.
66 [1999] Lloyd's Rep IR 30.

is not determinative in this respect.[67] Further matters that should be taken into account are that a United Kingdom motorist cannot insure but through an MIB insurer: there is no option to go outside of it.[68] Any increase in the levels of payout by the MIB is more likely to affect premium rates than profitability. Consequently, the extent to which the effects of payouts on the profitability of insurance companies would impact on those involved in settling MIB claims is very uncertain.[69] Hickinbottom J held that the measures built into the scheme adequately safeguard the rights of those who are the victims of untraced drivers against the MIB acting in a biased or unfair or self-serving way. The judge pointed out that the applicants are enabled to obtain legal advice in relation to both the application they make and any decision of the MIB, and at the MIB's cost. The existing appeal procedures enable an applicant to take a decision of the MIB to an arbitrator and thence, on a point of law, onwards to the Supreme Court if appropriate.[70]

Where the MIB is unnecessarily involved

10.29 Victims of traffic accidents and their solicitors should avoid involving the MIB unnecessarily in their claim for the injuries suffered as a result of the accident. Otherwise the Court may order that the bureau's costs be borne by the victim or his solicitors. The examples include where the MIB was involved by the victim's solicitor before making reasonable enquiries to identify the defendant motorist's insurers prior to notifying the MIB;[71] where the claim falls below the deductible permitted for property claims;[72] where the defendant motorist's insurer had confirmed they were the relevant insurer for the driver of the vehicle;[73] and where the MIB was notified without investigating properly whether the liability is that of falling within the MIB's obligation to compensate the victim.[74]

Untraced or Uninsured Drivers Agreement

10.30 As seen below, different procedures apply to UDA and UTDA mainly because whilst in the former either the driver or the vehicle and therefore the owner and the insurer may be chased, in the latter for one reason or another the identity of the driver is unknown and so are the vehicle's owner or insurer. The developments of the MIB Agreements over decades and the continuing expansion of the cover of the compulsory insurance regime rendered some issues which were discussed to a great extent in the past otiose. In other words, it is a more straightforward exercise today than it was in the past to determine whether the Uninsured or Untraced Drivers Agreement will apply to the victim's claim. Previously, where the vehicle was stolen and the owner's insurers repudiated liability, the claim was dealt with under the Untraced

---

67 [2011] Lloyd's Rep IR 644, [72].
68 RTA 1988 s 145(5).
69 [2011] Lloyd's Rep IR 644, [74].
70 *Carswell v Secretary of State for Transport* discussed the 2003 MIB Untraced Drivers Agreement. The 2017 Untraced Drivers Agreement contains similar provisions.
71 *Granada UK Rental & Retail v SPN Fareway* [1995] CLY 3728.
72 *Mastin v Blanchard* [1995] CLY 3727.
73 *Mills v Toner* [1995] CLY 3725.
74 *Severn Trent Water v Williams* [1995] CLY 3724.

Drivers Agreement.[75] Whereas today the insurer, when chased, has to cover even when the vehicle is stolen and therefore neither of the Agreements will apply.

10.31 Where the victim makes a direct claim against the insurer under section 151 of the RTA 1988 that will only be subject to the insurer's avoidance or cancellation of the policy as discussed in Chapter 8. However, it will be examined below that where the insurer avoids the contract after the accident has occurred, although sections 151 and 152[76] of the RTA 1988 read literally permit the insurer to reject the third party victim's claim, Article 75 of the Motor Insurers' Bureau Articles of Association will still require the insurer to compensate the third party victim with no rights of recourse against the MIB.

Uninsured Drivers Agreement

Scope

10.32 The latest form of UDA applies to accidents which occur on or after 1 August 2015.[77] Accidents occurring before this date will be dealt with under previous UDAs in accordance with their period of application. For example, the UDA dated 13 August 1999 continues to apply in respect of accidents occurring between 1 October 1999 and the date of operation of the 2015 Agreement, namely 1 August 2015. The RTA 1988 sections 143–145 apply to the use of a vehicle in Great Britain and the EEA, and the Uninsured Drivers Agreement is of corresponding scope. Where the owner or driver of a vehicle has not been identified (either because it is shown, on a balance of probabilities, that the named person does not exist or false particulars for the individual have been provided), the claim will be dealt with under the relevant UTDA.

Relevant liability

10.33 Relevant liability plays a crucial role in determining the scope of the claims that may be brought against the MIB. Under UDA 2015 a "relevant liability" means a liability in respect of which a contract of insurance must be in force to comply with Part VI of the 1988 Act. Namely, in order to constitute a "relevant liability" within the meaning of the UDA, the judgment which has been obtained against the defendant motorist must have been a judgment payable in respect of a liability incurred by him for damages for personal injury "caused by, or arising out of, the use of" the vehicle on the road or a public place.

10.34 It has also been confirmed by the CJEU that the scope of obligatory intervention of the compensation body referred to in Article 1(4) of the Second Directive is, as regards the damage or injuries caused by an identified vehicle, coextensive with the scope of the general insurance obligation laid down in Article 3(1) of the First Directive.[78] The obligatory intervention of that body in such a situation cannot therefore

---

75 *Clarke v Vedel* [1979] RTR 26.

76 See above paragraph 8.136 et seq for a discussion on the compatibility of s 152 and EU law.

77 See clause 2. As noted above, the 2015 Agreement was amended with the Supplementary Agreement dated 10 January 2017.

78 *Fundo de Garantia Automovel v Juliana* (C-80/17) EU:C:2018:661, [46].

extend to situations in which the vehicle involved in an accident was not covered by the insurance obligation.[79]

10.35 This liability does not include the loss suffered by the actual driver himself. In *Cooper v Motor Insurers' Bureau*,[80] which was also referred to in Chapter 4, with respect to section 143 of the RTA1972 (now section 143 of the RTA 1988), C claimed against the MIB because the defendant K was unable to satisfy the judgment against him. The relevant accident took place when C was road testing the motorcycle that belonged to K. During the course of that test the brakes failed and C collided with a motor car on the highway. Having suffered very severe injuries C claimed against the MIB to recover the judgment that was obtained against uninsured K, but the claim against the MIB was rejected because the obligation to insure and therefore obligation to be covered by the MIB in the absence of insurance excluded the losses suffered by the driver himself. As a result, in *Cooper* the only liability which fell to be covered under section 143(1) and sections 145(3)(a) was C's liability to others. Since K's liability to C was not that of which fell to be covered by the statute, the MIB was under no obligation to satisfy the judgment against K in this case.

10.36 As again referred to in Chapter 4, it appears in *Hardy v Motor Insurers' Bureau* that the relevant liability is interpreted broadly in conjunction with the wording of section 145 of the RTA 1988.

Unsatisfied judgment

10.37 The MIB's obligation under the UDA 2015 is strictly only to satisfy a judgment obtained by the claimant in respect of a "relevant liability" which is not met by the offending driver within seven days.[81] However, where it is appropriate to avoid unnecessary expense and delay, the MIB may seek to settle the claim before a formal judgment is obtained and ask the claimant to assign his rights to pursue the driver so that the MIB may attempt to recover its outlay.[82]

Authorities excluded

10.38 Local authorities, the National Health Service, the police and the Ministry of Defence are some of the public bodies that will meet claims arising from the use of vehicles in their ownership or possession and do not need to have insurance cover.[83] As such, the MIB is not liable for any judgment arising out of the use of such vehicles. However, if it can be shown that the vehicle in question is in fact covered by insurance the MIB's obligation arises if the insurer does not satisfy the judgment.[84]

---

79 Ibid.
80 [1985] QB 575.
81 UDA 2015, clause 1(4), 3(1).
82 UDA 2015, clause 15.
83 RTA 1988 s 144.
84 UDA 2015, clause 5.

Other sources of recovery

10.39 In circumstances where there is an insurer to cover the loss in place of the MIB, then that insurer should deal with the claim leaving the MIB to satisfy any uninsured losses.

10.40 Clause 6(1) stipulates that subject to paragraph 2, the MIB is not liable for any claim, or any part of a claim, in respect of which the claimant has received, or is entitled to receive or demand, payment or indemnity from any other person (including an insurer), not being the Criminal Injuries Compensation Authority or its successor. For instance, if the claimant has his own comprehensive policy cover which would meet the cost of repair, the claimant should address the claim to the insurer. If the insurer denies liability, for instance, because the claimant did not satisfy the policy conditions, the MIB will not be obliged to compensate the loss which was refused by the insurer for that reason. The same rule applies, for instance, where the claimant's loss is insured by a private medical insurer or any other insurance backed part of the claim or where some other person pays the claimant and seeks to recover in the claimant's name.

10.41 However, clause 6(2) provides that the MIB will remain liable in respect of claims for:

(1) the reimbursement of employers' payments to cover a claimant's absence from work unless the employer is insured for that loss, and

(2) legal costs where the claimant is backed by legal expenses insurance.

10.42 Clause 6 is not intended to be used to enable the MIB to deduct proceeds received or receivable from a personal accident or life policy taken out by the claimant prior to the accident to provide benefits in the event of injury or death occurring. That type of policy is designed to provide the claimant with an additional benefit, and the MIB will not take it into account when paying compensation following an accident.[85]

The 2017 Supplementary Agreement

10.43 The 2015 Agreement clause 7(1) used to exclude

> any claim, or any part of a claim, in respect of damage to a motor vehicle, or losses arising therefrom, where at the time when the damage to it was sustained- (a) there was no contract of insurance in force in relation to that use of the vehicle; and (b) the claimant either knew or had reason to believe that that was the case.

There is no basis for this exclusion in the Consolidated Motor Insurance Directive. Consequently, the 2017 Supplementary Agreement omitted the whole of clause 7 from the 2015 Agreement for accidents occurred after 1 March 2017.

10.44 Similarly, in the Consolidated Directive there is no basis for the terrorism exclusion which used to appear under clause 9 of the 2015 UDA. Before it was omitted by the 2017 Supplementary Agreement, clause 9 used to exclude claims where the death, bodily injury or damage to property was caused by, or in the course of, an act of terrorism within the meaning of section 1 of the Terrorism Act 2000. With the recent

---

85 https://www.mib.org.uk/media/352780/2015-uninsured-drivers-agreement-notes-for-guidance-v2-0.pdf

Passengers

10.45 Clause 8(1) excludes, subject to paragraph 2,

> any claim, or any part of a claim, in respect of a relevant liability by a claimant who, at the time of the use giving rise to that liability, was voluntarily allowing himself to be a passenger in the vehicle and, either before the start of the claimant's journey in the vehicle or after its start if the claimant could reasonably be expected to have alighted from it, knew or had reason to believe that –
>
> (a) the vehicle had been stolen or unlawfully taken; or
> (b) the vehicle was being used without there being in force in relation to its use a contract of insurance complying with Part VI of the 1988 Act.[86]

10.46 References to the claimant being a passenger in a vehicle include references to the claimant being carried upon or entering or getting on to or alighting from the vehicle.[87] This exception applies where the relevant liability is incurred by the owner[88] or registered keeper or a person using the vehicle in which the claimant was a passenger.[89]

10.47 This exclusion appears in the UDA because the passenger that falls within this clause is regarded to have accepted the risk of inability to recover compensation from the uninsured driver.[90]

10.48 The MIB bears the burden of proving that the claimant knew or had reason to believe any matter set out in clause 8(1).[91] Knowledge[92] which the claimant had, or had reason to have, includes knowledge of matters which the claimant could reasonably be expected to have been aware of had he not been under the self-induced influence of drink or drugs.[93] Where the passenger makes it clear to the driver that her car was not insured and that she required an insured driver, and the driver having volunteered to drive in those circumstances, the passenger was held to be entitled to rely on the assumption that he was an insured driver and the exception does not apply.[94]

10.49 The words "had reason to believe" replaced "ought to have known" from the previous Agreements. The meaning of "ought to have known" is discussed below.

10.50 In the absence of evidence to the contrary, proof by the MIB of any of the following matters is to be taken as proof of the claimant's knowledge as to the vehicle being used without there being in force in relation to its use a contract of insurance complying with Part VI of the 1988 Act:[95]

---

86 This exclusion reflects what the RTA 1988 s 151(4) and Consolidated Directive Article 13(1) each provides. See Chapters 7 and 8.

87 UDA clause 8(5)(a).

88 In the case of a vehicle which is the subject of a hiring agreement or a hire-purchase agreement, the "owner" means the person in possession of the vehicle under that agreement. UDA clause 8(5)(c).

89 UDA 2015 clause 8(2).

90 *Pickett v Roberts* [2004] RTR 28.

91 UDA clause 8(3).

92 See also Chapter 8.

93 UDA clause 8(5)(b).

94 *Porter v Addo* [1978] 2 Lloyd's Rep 463.

95 UDA clause 8(3).

(a) that the claimant was the owner or registered keeper of the vehicle or had caused or permitted its use;

(b) that the claimant knew the vehicle was being used by a person who was below the minimum age at which he could be granted a licence authorising the driving of a vehicle of that class; or

(c) that the claimant knew that the person driving the vehicle was disqualified from holding or obtaining a driving licence.

Withdrawn consent

10.51 It is inherent in this exception that once acquired that the vehicle is uninsured, it is presumed that the knowledge persists throughout the journey.[96] However, there is no presumption that consent, once given, cannot be withdrawn.[97] In other words, a passenger who at first agreed voluntarily to be carried in such a vehicle can revoke that consent during the course of the journey, thereby obtaining the benefit of cover under the MIB Agreement in the event of a later accident. That will be a matter of fact in each case,[98] and revoking such a consent was discussed in *Pickett v Roberts*[99] on its facts. In this case the claimant and the defendant driver were co-habiting and they bought a car which they could not afford to insure. The claimant who owned the car knew that her partner who was driving it did not have a driving licence. On a day they borrowed £100 they filled the car's tank with some petrol and went for a drive for some fun during which the driver began doing handbreak turns. The claimant asked him to stop, he slowed down, and she unclipped the seatbelt so, she said, she could help the dog to get out of the car as quickly as possible when stopped. The driver then unexpectedly did another handbreak turn, after which he lost the control of the car and had an accident. The matter at the heart of the case was whether, at the time of the use which gave rise to the driver's liability to the claimant, the claimant was allowing herself to be carried in the vehicle which he was driving so that she would be regarded to have accepted the risk of inability to recover compensation from the uninsured driver. Chadwick LJ[100] held and May LJ agreed that

> Voluntary acceptance of the risk that compensation will not be recoverable from the uninsured driver requires that, before the commencement of the relevant journey or (at the latest) no later than the last reasonable opportunity to alight, the person injured had knowledge that the vehicle in which he is allowing himself to be carried is not insured. A person who discovers, in the course of a journey which he cannot reasonably be expected to bring to an end by alighting from the vehicle, that the vehicle is not insured cannot sensibly be said to have accepted the risk of inability to recover compensation from the uninsured driver. But a person who has accepted that risk by entering the vehicle with the relevant knowledge – or by failing to alight when, having acquired that knowledge in the course of the journey, he could reasonably have been expected to do so – and who allows and continues to allow himself to be carried in the vehicle up to and including the time of the use which gave rise to the uninsured

---

96 [2004] RTR 28, [24].
97 Ibid.
98 Ibid.
99 [2004] RTR 28.
100 [2004] RTR 28, [23].

driver's liability, can sensibly be said to have accepted the risk of being driven in the vehicle, knowing it to be uninsured, at the time of that use.

Their Lordships held that the claimant's objection by voicing to the manner in which the vehicle was driven was not sufficient to express revoking the consent. Something more than that was required to the extent that the protest must amount to an unequivocal repudiation of the common venture to which consent was given when the protester entered the vehicle. May LJ[101] said, "In so far as she was asking him to stop making handbrake turns, this did not extend to a demand that she herself should be let out of the car." Pill LJ, dissenting, found that the demand to be let out was implicit in the demand to stop and the claimant's conduct was more than objecting to a bad piece of driving amounting to withdraw her consent to the use to which the vehicle was being put.[102]

RTA s 151(8)

10.52 The MIB is not liable for any claim, or any part of a claim, where the insurer is entitled to recover all or part of its outlay from the claimant under section 151(8) of the RTA 1988.[103] The insurers' right of recourse under section 151(8) where the passenger was the owner of the vehicle who permitted the uninsured person to drive the vehicle was discussed in Chapter 8. Clause 10 of the UDA approves that the MIB is not liable and the claim should be made against the insurer who is obliged to satisfy the claim as held in those cases cited in Chapter 8.

Where a claim is made by the dependants

10.53 Where a claim was made by the dependants, the question arose in the past as to whether the relevant knowledge was that of the deceased victim's or their dependants'? In *Phillips v Rafiq*[104] when R was driving P's car an accident occurred on M25 as a result of which the three passengers in the car were killed. R was not insured to drive P's car,[105] therefore, P's widow addressed her claim to the MIB. The issue arose out of clause 6(1)(e)[106] of the 1999 UDA which excluded a passenger's claim where the passenger, before agreeing to be a passenger in a car, had not asked the driver whether he had insurance cover to drive. P did not make any inquiries as such before allowing R to drive the car. Hence, had it been relevant, P knew or ought to have known that he was being carried in the vehicle when its use was uninsured. However, the claim by P's widow relied on section 1 of the Fatal Accidents Act 1976 that confers upon the deceased's

---

101 Ibid, [49].
102 Ibid, [63].
103 UDA clause 10.
104 [2007] 1 WLR 1351.
105 P had been insured, but at the time of the accident the insurance was expired. In any event, as discussed in Chapter 8, P's insurer would be obliged to satisfy third party victim's claims as if the user was insured (RTA s 151(2)(b)). However, when an insurer compensates traffic accident victims' loss under section 151(2)(b), the insurer can recoup against the owner who permitted the uninsured use (RTA s 151(8)). Where the victim is the owner who permitted uninsured use whether the insurer should be able to exercise his right of recourse under s 151(8) is not answered conclusively by the Courts yet but, as mentioned in Chapter 8, it is submitted that the insurer would have its right of recourse under s 151(8).
106 Clause 8(1) under the 2015 Agreement.

dependants their own independent cause of action if death is caused by a wrongful act which would have given rise to damages for the victim had he survived. The claim was for loss of income after the death of the deceased P. Had P's widow been a passenger in the vehicle at the time, and had she been aware of the fact that the driver was uninsured, her dependency claim under the 1976 Act would have been lost because she would have fallen squarely within the clause 6.1(e) exception. The Court of Appeal held that construing objectively, a reasonable man could not confidently say that the purpose of the 1999 Agreement is to exclude a dependant's claim. The literal meaning of the word "claimant" in clause 6.1(e) was clear and referred to the person who commenced the proceedings. The Court of Appeal held that where the victim had been killed and the claim was brought by a dependant under the Fatal Accidents Act 1976, the relevant knowledge was that of the dependant and not the victim.

10.54 Clause 8(4) of the UDA 2015 now provides,

> In the case of a claim brought by the dependants or estate of a deceased person who could otherwise have made a claim under this Agreement had they survived, it is the state of knowledge of the deceased which is determinative for the purpose of determining a claimant's state of knowledge under paragraph 8(1) where "dependant" has the same meaning as the term – (a) "dependant" in section 1(3) of the Fatal Accidents Act 1976 in England and Wales.

Duties of the claimant

10.55 The MIB requires a fully completed claim form to be submitted so as to gain the necessary background to enable it to start processing the claim. The claim form can be found online at www.mib.org.uk.

10.56 The claimant should take reasonable (but not exhaustive) steps to establish whether there is in fact any insurance covering the use of the vehicle which caused the injury or damage. This can be done by visiting www.askMID.com.

10.57 Immediately post-accident, if possible, the claimant should exchange names, addresses, insurance particulars and vehicle registration numbers with the other party. The claimant, if the vehicle registration number is known, should immediately interrogate the Motor Insurance Database at www.askMID.com.

10.58 If enquiries show that there is an insurer recorded against that vehicle registration number, then the claim should be pursued via that insurer. If enquiries disclose that there is no insurance covering the use of the vehicle concerned, or if the insurer cannot be identified or the insurer asserts that it is under no obligation to handle the claim or if for any reason it is clear that the insurer will not satisfy a judgment, the claim should be directed to the MIB in accordance with the terms of the 2015 UDA as soon as is reasonably practicable.

10.59 The MIB incurs no liability unless it is joined from the outset as an additional defendant to the relevant proceedings.[107] The previous forms of the UDA rendered it a condition precedent to the MIB's liability that notice in writing of the bringing of the

---

107 UDA clause 13(1).

proceedings is given within seven days[108] of the commencement of the proceedings.[109] The wording used by the previous MIB Agreements was, "MIB shall not incur any liability . . . unless" and the relevant conditions followed. In this context "shall" had been interpreted as being more than directory and of mandatory in nature.[110] The MIB would have had the notice that proceedings have been initiated but with official evidence that the proceedings have been issued, and of the date issued and the Court where they have been issued. This was discussed to a great detail in *Cambridge v Motor Insurers' Bureau*[111] where it was held that what the condition required was that the MIB should be served with official evidence of the initiation of the proceedings.[112]

10.60 However, the relevant condition precedent has now been removed from the latest of the MIB UDA clause 13(1) which instead provides:

> Subject to paragraph (2), MIB incurs no liability under MIB's obligation unless MIB is joined from the outset as an additional Defendant to the relevant proceedings.

10.61 The objective of this requirement is that, following effective service of the proceedings, the MIB should receive from the Court the appropriate notices of procedural matters in the action. The MIB is not a tortfeasor but, if a judgment for an injured person against a motorist is not satisfied in full within seven days, it will pay the amount of the judgment to the injured person. Such an undertaking renders the MIB interested in seeing that all proper defences in that action as respects liability are raised and that all relevant material which tends to reduce the quantum of damages recoverable is adduced to the Court.[113] Naturally, the MIB would desire to investigate the claim; being served with the proceedings, it should be treated in the same way as any other party. The MIB's liability only crystallises upon a final judgment not being satisfied for seven days after payment under the judgment falls due. Its liability is, therefore, contingent until there is a declaration that it is liable to meet an unsatisfied judgment. To reflect this status and to clarify the MIB's position for the benefit of the Court, the Particulars of Claim, when served, should include the following wording, namely:

> The second defendant (or whichever numbering is appropriate), "MIB," is a company limited by guarantee under the Companies' Acts. Pursuant to an Agreement with the Secretary of State dated day of 2015 (hereinafter the Agreement), MIB provides compensation in certain circumstances to persons suffering injury or damage as a result of the negligence of the uninsured motorist.
>
> The claimant has used all reasonable endeavours to ascertain the identity and liability of an insurer for the first defendant (or whichever numbering is appropriate) and, at the time of commencement of these proceedings, believes that the first defendant is not insured.

---

108 14 days under 1999 Agreement, clause (9(1). In *Horton v Sadler* [2007] 1 AC 307 the claimant missed the 14-day notification period but then issued duplicate proceedings against the defendant motorist and gave the necessary notice to the MIB. The latest form of UDA, as mentioned above, replaced this requirement with joining the MIB from the outset as an additional defendant to the relevant proceedings.

109 1972 Agreement, clause 5(1) (a), 1988 Agreement, clause 5(1)(a). The words "the commencement of the proceedings" in clause 5(1)(a) had their ordinary meaning, namely the point in time at which under the rules of the relevant Court the proceedings commenced. *Silverton v Goodall* [1997] PIQR P451.

110 *Cambridge v Motor Insurers' Bureau* [1998] RTR 365.

111 [1998] RTR 365.

112 That could be achieved by either supplying the MIB with a copy of the stamped writ or summons itself or with a copy of the notice of issue of default summons. [1998] RTR 365, 372.

113 *Gurtner v Circuit* [1968] 2 QB 587, 599–600, Diplock LJ.

The claimant accepts that, only if a final judgment is obtained against the first defendant (which judgment has not been satisfied in full within seven days from the date upon which the claimant became entitled to enforce it), can MIB be required to satisfy the judgment and then only if the conditions and terms set out in the Agreement are satisfied. Until that time, any liability of MIB is only contingent. To avoid MIB having later to apply separately to join itself in this action, the claimant includes MIB from the outset, recognising fully MIB's position as reflected above and the rights of MIB fully to participate in the action to protect its position as a separate party to the action. The claimant also acknowledges that such joinder of MIB does not alter in any way the requirement for the claimant to serve the first defendant by a method permitted under the Civil Procedure Rules (or in Scotland, the Court of Session or Sheriff Court Rules as the context requires).

With the above in mind, the claimant seeks a declaration of MIB's contingent liability for damages to the claimant in this action.

10.62 Clause 13(1) is a condition precedent to the MIB's liability as interpreted by reference to ordinary principles of construction, having due regard to the language used and to the purpose of the Agreement derived from the Agreement as a whole.[114] As a result, in order for the MIB to deny liability the MIB was not obliged to provide that it was prejudiced by the non-compliance with the condition precedent. Moreover, waiver of condition precedent can be proved by promissory estoppel, the first condition of which is an unequivocal representation by the waiving party as to not argue the non-compliance with it.[115] Silence is unlikely to be interpreted as amounting to such a representation.[116] If the MIB's response is, "The MIB may have no liability and we reserve our position," this statement is not an unequivocal representation indicating a waiver by estoppel.[117]

10.63 The MIB is free to waive the requirement, or not, according to its own judgment and is not required to justify a decision not to waive.[118] Under the 1988 UDA, in a case where the injured victim was represented by a solicitor from the outset and delayed in notifying the MIB of commencing the proceedings the MIB chose not to waive the condition precedent – possibly because there was no real difficulty for a competent solicitor who pays attention to the language of the Agreement and the notes attached to it, to comply with the relevant requirement.[119] The Court of Appeal noted the MIB might waive the notice requirements where the interests of the MIB do not require that a claimant be put to the trouble and expense of starting again so as to give due notice. On the other hand, where a solicitor for a claimant was responsible for the failure, that solicitor may have been required to pay any loss resulting from the failure.

10.64 Where the claimant initially and reasonably believes he is covered by a contract of insurance with an insurer whose identity can be ascertained but later discovers that that is not the case, if the requirements defined by cl 13(2) are satisfied, the MIB is not entitled to rely on paragraph 1 above. The requirements listed under clause 13(2) are:

---

114 *Silverton v Goodall* [1997] PIQR P451, p 461.

115 *Cooper v Motor Insurers' Bureau* [1985] QB 575; *Silverton v Goodall* [1997] PIQR P451.

116 *Cooper v Motor Insurers' Bureau* [1985] QB 575.

117 *Silverton v Goodall* [1997] PIQR P451.

118 Indeed, by a letter submitted as evidence in *Silverton v Goodall* [1997] PIQR P451 the MIB confirms that in some cases it chooses to waive the condition precedent.

119 *Silverton v Goodall* [1997] PIQR P451.

If the claimant:

(a) has given notice of commencement of the relevant proceedings complying with the requirements of the 1988 Act to that insurer;

(b) notifies MIB promptly after the claimant ceases to have a reasonable belief as to the involvement of the insurer;

(c) consents to MIB being joined to the relevant proceedings; and

(d) promptly sends to MIB a copy of any court proceedings, pleadings and documents, and any evidence and supporting documentation which has previously been sent to the defendant or the insurer.

10.65 The MIB may require the claimant to bring proceedings and attempt to secure a judgment against any other person or persons whom the MIB believes to be wholly or partly responsible for the loss or damage or who may be contracted to indemnify the claimant.

10.66 A further obligation on the claimant is that when required by the MIB and the costs are met by the MIB, the claimant is under the duty to take all reasonable steps to obtain judgment against every person who may be liable (including any person who may be vicariously liable) in respect of the injury or death or damage to property. Moreover, in such cases the claimant is required to allow the MIB to control the steps to be taken and act in accordance with the MIB's reasonable instructions. Failing these requirements will avail the MIB to refuse compensating the claimant.[120]

10.67 Additionally, the claimant is obliged to assign to the MIB the unsatisfied judgment, whether or not that judgment includes an amount in respect of a liability other than a relevant liability, and the benefit of any order for costs made in the relevant proceedings.[121] Where the MIB settles the claimant's claim prior to an unsatisfied judgment being obtained the claimant is required to agree to assign to the MIB the benefit of any future settlement or judgment (including costs) in respect of a relevant liability. The MIB, before making any payment to the claimant, requires the claimant to undertake that after the claimant received payment from the MIB if the judgment is subsequently set aside either as a whole or in respect of the part of the relevant liability to which that sum relates, the claimant must repay the amount to the MIB and initially he is required to undertake to do so. Further, he also has to repay the amount received from the MIB where he receives any payment by any other person, except the Criminal Injuries Compensation Authority or its successor, in respect of the same death, bodily injury or other damage to which the judgment or settlement relate. Unless such undertaking is received, the MIB is not obliged to compensate the claim.

10.68 Clause 12 requires the claimant to submit his claim in a specified form and he is under the duty to provide the information and documents required by the MIB. It further adds that the MIB incurs no liability under MIB's obligation, unless the claimant provides to MIB within a reasonable timeframe after being required to do so such further information and/or documentation in support of the claim as MIB may reasonably require.

As mentioned above, under clause 14, the claimant is under the duty to take reasonable steps to obtain a judgment against the person who might be liable for the injuries for

---

120 UDA clause 14.
121 UDA clause 15(a).

which the claimant seeks compensation. The standard of "reasonable" under clauses 12 and 14, if disputed, must be referred by the claimant or the MIB to an arbitrator appointed by the Secretary of State.[122]

MIB's response

10.69 The MIB is required to notify the claimant as soon as reasonably practicable in writing of its decision regarding the payment of the relevant sum, together with the reasons for that decision.[123]

10.70 If the claimant or his legal representative is not satisfied with the way in which his claim is dealt with in accordance with the Agreement, he may register a complaint with the MIB. The MIB's formal complaints procedure is set out in detail within the Customer Charter which can be found on the MIB's website at www.mib.org.uk. Alternatively, full details of the procedure can be requested from the MIB.

Untraced Drivers Agreement

Scope

10.71 Where the driver of a vehicle has not been identified (either because it is shown, on a balance of probabilities, that the named person does not exist or false particulars for the individual have been provided), the claim will be dealt with under the relevant UTDA. In circumstances where either the offending vehicle is unidentified or no one can be identified who can be held at fault for the use of an identified vehicle, there will be nobody to bring Court proceedings against and, hence, no judgment can be obtained. The MIB will effectively take the place of an insurer to provide compensation strictly in accordance with the framework provided by the UTDA, the latest form of which came into force on 1 March 2017[124] in relation to accidents occurring on or after that date. Unlike the UDA 2015, the UTDA 2017 is limited in its scope to accidents occurring in Great Britain.[125]

10.72 The trigger of the MIB's obligation to investigate a claim presented to it is regulated under clause 3 which defines the scope of the UTDA 2017. The Agreement applies when the person who is allegedly liable in respect of the death of or bodily injury to any individual or damage to property is an unidentified person. The liability should be a kind required to be covered by a contract of insurance under Part VI of the 1988 Act.[126] Even where the claim is in scope, it does not mean the claim will be accepted. It merely means that it will be investigated and the MIB will then reach a decision as to whether an award is appropriate.

10.73 The claim might fall within one of the exclusions under clauses 4 to 9, or the claimant might be found to have failed to comply with the obligations set out in clause 10.

---

122 UDA clause 17(1).
123 UDA clause 16.
124 The 2003 Agreement continues in force in relation to accidents occurring on or after 14 February 2003 but before 1 March 2017. UTDA clause 2.
125 UTDA clause 3(1)(a).
126 UTDA clause 3(1)(b).

There are also various procedural requirements and timeframes which must be followed.[127] Further, the limitation period that applies to tort claims under the Limitation Act 1980 (with regard to England and Wales) or in delict by the Prescription and Limitation (Scotland) Act 1973 (with regard to Scotland) applies to the claims under the UTDA 2017.[128]

Joint liability of identified and unidentified persons

10.74 If more than one person is alleged to have been responsible and some are identified, the MIB will reject the claim.[129] The MIB will only have any potential liability under the Agreement if all the persons claimed to be responsible are unidentified. The MIB may still be liable under the applicable UDA where the identified responsible person happens to be an uninsured user of the vehicle. If the identified person is liable in circumstances where he was not required to have motor insurance in place and he does not meet a judgment obtained by the claimant, the claimant may claim against the MIB to the extent that a judgment obtained against the identified person has not been satisfied after a period of three months from when it first fell due and then only to the extent of the unidentified person's share of responsibility for the accident.[130] On the other hand, where the claimant and the identified person settle the claim for less than the full amount claimed, and the latter satisfies the settled amount, no further sum can be sought from the MIB.[131]

Other sources of recovery

10.75 Similar to the UDA, where the claimant has received, or is entitled to receive or demand, payment or indemnity from any other person (including an insurer or the giver of a security),[132] the MIB will not be liable for that amount. Additionally, as seen in the UDA, if an insurance cover was available for the loss, the MIB will not be liable.[133] That includes the cases where the claimant is unable to claim against the insurer, for instance because the claimant did not comply with the policy conditions.

Damage to property

10.76 Damage to property caused by an untraced driver is excluded from the UTDA 2017 except for the situations where an award for significant personal injury has been paid to any claimant in respect of the same event, and the loss incurred in respect of damage to property exceeds the specified excess.[134] The UTDA defines significant personal injury as that of resulting death or two nights or more of hospital in-patient treatment,

---

127 UTDA Part 2.
128 UTDA clause 3(1)(d).
129 Where more than one person is alleged to be so liable, all such persons are unidentified persons, UTDA 2017 clause 3(1)(c).
130 UTDA clause 23.
131 UTDA clause 23(7).
132 Excluding the Criminal Injuries Compensation Authority or its successor.
133 UTDA clause 6(3).
134 UTDA clause 7(1).

or three sessions or more of hospital out-patient treatment.[135] It only applies to bar a property damage claim, not a claim for personal injury.

Passengers

10.77 What is mentioned about the passenger's claim under clause 8 of UDA applies for the claims for UTDA under clause 8.

Duties of the claimant

10.78 Clause 10(2) requires the claimant to notify the MIB by completion and submission of the MIB's claim form. The claim form can be completed online at www.mib.org. uk. Additionally, the claimant must, for example, respond to the MIB's reasonable requests for information and documentation to support the claim put forward and provide a statement by means of an interview with the MIB or its agent if this is required.[136]

10.79 Under clause 10(6) the UTDA 2017 stipulates,

> The claimant, if so required by MIB and having been granted an indemnity by MIB as to the reasonable costs incurred, must take all reasonable steps to obtain judgment against every person who may be liable (including any person who may be vicariously liable) in respect of the death, bodily injury or damage to property, allowing MIB to control the steps to be taken and only acting in accordance with MIB's reasonable instructions.

It was held in *White v London Transport*[137] that the MIB, standing behind the claimant, will be able to require the claimant to conduct it with diligence but it should not be joined as a party. In other words, the MIB can control the proceedings but cannot be made a party to them.

Compensation

10.80 The MIB will only pay compensation and interest where it decides, in the same way as a Court would decide, that the unidentified person was liable to the claimant.[138] If the MIB concludes that the unidentified person would have been liable, it will determine the extent to which the claimant should be allowed to recover having regard to his contributory negligence.

10.81 It is a matter of fact to determine how the accident occurred and whether on the facts the untraced driver was liable. In *Elizabeth v Motor Insurers' Bureau*[139] the Court allowed the appeal from the arbitrator's decision putting the burden of proof on

---

135 UTDA clause 7(2).

136 UTDA clause 10(3) and (4).

137 [1971] RTR 326.

138 UTDA clause 11(1). It was held in *Evans v Secretary of State for the Environment, Transport and the Regions* (C-63/01) [2004] RTR 32, [71] that compensation for loss is intended so far as possible to provide restitution for the victim of an accident. Accordingly, adequate compensation for the victims is provided by interpreting Art 1(4) of Directive 84/5 as meaning that the compensation awarded for damage or injuries caused by an unidentified or uninsured vehicle, paid by the body authorised for that purpose, must take account of the effluxion of time until actual payment of the sums awarded.

139 [1981] RTR 405.

the claimant to show that the untraced van driver put on his brakes without good reason. Whilst the claimant was driving along quite properly behind a van, the van suddenly braked, the claimant could not stop in time and ran into the back of the van. The claimant was injured, and the van driver drove off and could not be traced. The Court held the burden was on the driver of the van to prove that he had good reason for braking so suddenly. No one gave evidence that there was something in front of him which caused him to brake. It was held that in the absence of evidence from the van driver, the claimant's version of the accident should have been accepted. The appeal was allowed, and the award was remitted to another arbitrator for consideration.

10.82 The MIB may, in the same way as a Court, award: lump sum compensation; a combination of lump sum compensation and periodical payments; provisional compensation, to be supplemented on conditions laid down; and, where the amount of loss cannot be quantified, an interim payment. The decisions that the MIB may reach are listed under clause 11(2), and the claimant may appeal to an arbitrator against the MIB's decision.

10.83 The MIB's obligation to investigate claims and reach a determination appears under clause 12. The MIB's primary obligation is to carry out all reasonable enquiries in order to investigate each claim to the extent which it deems appropriate in order to make a decision on whether to make an award. Whatever decision the MIB reaches under clause 12, it must notify the claimant of that decision in writing, giving its reasons for the decision and setting out all the evidence obtained during its investigation. Such notification in writing will trigger the claimant's entitlement to appeal if he is not satisfied with the decision reached.

10.84 Clause 12 was clause 7 under the 2003 Agreement which similarly provided that the MIB shall investigate the claim at its own cost and reach a determination on the claim.[140] In *Carswell v Secretary of State for Transport*[141] the power of the MIB's investigation of the claim was challenged. It was argued that the MIB was both the investigator and the body liable to pay the award, and accordingly the scheme was flawed in that it gave the MIB a commercial interest in the outcome of any claim. That arrangement infringed the principles of equivalence and effectiveness as recognised by EU law. Further, the provisions relating to the recoverability of legal costs by an applicant were at the heart of the claim in *Carswell*.

10.85 In *Carswell v Secretary of State for Transport*[142] the issue arose when C was knocked down and killed by a car when he was crossing the road at the moment that the traffic lights governing the crossing showed red against him. The car that struck C was never traced. C's wife accepted an offer from the MIB of £250,000 (made on the basis of a reduction of 40% for contributory negligence), together with costs due under the 2003 Agreement, the MIB paid 2% of the sum awarded by way of the cost of obtaining legal advice, in accordance with clause 10 of, and the schedule to, the 2003 Agreement: those provisions fix the MIB's contribution to costs at 2% of any award exceeding £150,000

---

140 It was held in *Evans v Secretary of State for the Environment, Transport and the Regions* (C-63/01) [2004] RTR 32, [78] that compensation awarded for injuries suffered by victims of uninsured or untraced drivers, under Art 1(4) of Directive 84/5, should include some expenses to the extent "to which such reimbursement is necessary to safeguard the rights derived by victims from the Directive in conformity with the principles of equivalence and effectiveness."

141 [2011] Lloyd's Rep IR 644.

142 Ibid.

ie 2% of the award as a contribution towards solicitors' profit costs (£5,750 inclusive of VAT) and disbursements (£5,022.65 again inclusive of VAT). That aggregate sum had been paid. C's wife paid to the solicitors out of the substantive sum paid to her by the MIB. However, there was an outstanding solicitors' fee £14,977.31, as damages from the Secretary of State on the basis that he has failed properly to implement various European Motor Insurance Directives (but particularly Article 1(4) of EEC Council Directive 84/5/EEC) with the result that she has not been paid a sufficient sum for the legal costs she incurred in her application to the MIB.

10.86 The judge found clauses 7 and 11 complementary and eliminated the argument that the particular scheme set out in the 2003 Agreement was fatally flawed because the MIB is not independent but is commercially interested in the outcome of the investigation.[143] The learned judge also strongly rejected the suggestion that the inquisitorial approach was inherently bad or necessarily offended the principles of equivalence and effectiveness. It was necessary to adopt a different approach where the person whose liability was to be established could not by definition be identified, and it could be said that the judicial and the MIB systems were comparable given the nature of the inquiry. Further, the judge was not persuaded that the fact that the MIB is not a public body, but a private commercial body means that it cannot, as a matter of law, properly carry out its functions.[144] The judge held that scheme, in general, adequately safeguards the rights of those who are the victims of untraced drivers.[145]

10.87 Moreover, in *Evans v Secretary of State for the Environment, Transport and the Regions*,[146] the CJEU saw no objection in principle to the fact that the Agreement introduced a different, inquisitorial, system, as compared with the adversarial civil system[147] which applies in the United Kingdom in the case of identified and insured vehicles. The CJEU emphasised that it was for the national legal system of each Member State to lay down detailed procedural rules governing actions for safeguarding rights of individuals derived from European law. What matters is whether the private body is to provide victims with the compensation guaranteed to them by the Second Directive (now the Consolidated Directive). Further, in *Byrne v Motor Insurers' Bureau*[148] the UTDA was not regarded as inadequate for the purposes simply because the MIB is a private body.

10.88 Under the 2003 Agreement, where an applicant seeks legal advice in respect of making an application, the correctness of a decision of the MIB or the adequacy of an award offered by the MIB, the legal adviser is entitled to costs on a fixed scale. That assistance also covers advice upon responding to the proper requests from the MIB under clause 11. It is not surprising after *Carswell* that under the 2017 Agreement these issues were maintained.

Costs

10.89 The MIB's contribution towards legal costs is found in clause 21. The MIB is required to make a contribution to costs, consisting of legal fees plus reasonable

---

143 Ibid, [85].
144 Ibid, [72].
145 Ibid, [76].
146 (C-63/01) [2004] RTR 32.
147 The awarding body (ie the MIB) is placed in the same position as a defendant tortfeasor in civil liability.
148 [2009] QB 66.

disbursements on the making of a final award, where it is satisfied that the claimant actually incurred such costs. Clause 21(7)(a) stipulates that the contribution shall be the total of the fee calculated in accordance with paragraph 8. Clause 21 paragraph 8 provides the following table:

Amount of the award	Fee entitlement
not more than £10,000	£450;
more than £10,000 but not more than £25,000	£700;
more than £25,000 but not more than £50,000	£700 plus 10% of the damages over £25,000;
more than £50,000 but not more than £100,000	£3,200 plus 10% of the damages over £50,000;
more than £100,000 but not more than £175,000	£8,200 plus 7% of the damages over £100,000;
More than £175,000 but not more than £250,000	£13,450 plus 7% of the damages over £175,000
more than £250,000	£18,700 plus 7% of the damages over £250,000 but not exceeding a total of £250,000

Dispute resolution

10.90 The UTDA 2017 specifies a six-week period during which an appeal to an arbitrator can be made.[149] Clause 16(3) permits the claimant to apply to the MIB for an extension of time, and if refused the matter can be determined by the arbitrator.

Under clause 16(4) the MIB agrees to abide by the final decision of the arbitrator made under this Agreement. The MIB has the right to appeal to the Court only for want of jurisdiction or serious irregularity in the award, respectively under sections 67 and 68 of the Arbitration Act 1996. Thus, clause 16(4) does not reserve to the MIB the right to appeal on the ground of error of law, under s 69 of the Arbitration Act 1996. There is no such restriction on the claimant who can, however, only appeal on a question of law. There is no possibility of the grant of permission for an appeal on a question of fact[150] for instance when the arbitrator found that there was no evidence that the untraced motorist involved had been driving negligently.

10.91 If arbitration is held, the hearing is to be in private.[151] A single arbitral process applies for all disputes. The range of decisions open to an arbitrator is listed by clause 20. For instance, the arbitrator may determine whether the UTDA 2017 applies, may remit the claim to the MIB or may determine what the award should be. In *Carswell* the claimant also argued the scheme of the 2003 Agreement was flawed because there was no clear

---

149 Clause 16(1).

150 *Harvey v Motor Insurers' Bureau* Queen's Bench Division (Mercantile Court) (Manchester), 21 December 2011.

151 Clause 19(12)(a).

and effective way for an applicant to enforce the MIB's obligation under clause 7 to investigate a claim. Hickinbottom J rejected the submission and held that an applicant had the right to enforce the MIB's clause 7 obligation. According to the judge it was common ground that if the MIB made a decision or determination during the course of its investigation into a claim, then such decision or determination was appealable to an arbitrator under clause 18 or clause 28 (now clauses 15–20 under the UTDA 2017). If the MIB took no steps to investigate a claim, that might amount to a decision not to take any steps, which would be appealable under clause 28. Alternatively, the judge held the Contract (Rights of Third Parties) Act 1999 (with or without the aid of clause 31(5)) gave an applicant the right to sue the MIB in contract in Court proceedings to enforce the obligation to investigate.

10.92 In *Evans v Secretary of State for the Environment, Transport and the Regions*[152] one of the issues[153] that was challenged by the victim of a motor traffic accident was the arbitration procedure under the MIB Agreements. The victim argued that the procedure did not grant the victim an oral hearing, he could appeal against the arbitrator's award only on the ground of serious irregularity affecting the arbitration or on a question of law, and in the latter case leave to appeal must be obtained. The CJEU held that the arbitration procedure for appeals from the MIB awards was broadly fair.[154] The Court took into consideration that the MIB is required to determine the amount of the compensation as the Court would do so; the victim has a right of appeal to an arbitrator; the arbitrator is appointed under conditions which ensure that he is independent; the right of appeal is automatically available to a victim who alleges a serious irregularity affecting the arbitration; and finally a victim may, subject to obtaining leave from the competent Court, subsequently appeal to the Court of Appeal and then to the House of Lords.[155] The CJEU found that the MIB Agreement gives the victim the advantages of speed and economy of legal costs rather than being practically impossible or excessively difficult to exercise the right to compensation conferred on victims of damage or injury caused by unidentified or uninsured drivers.

Set-off

10.93 Clause 25 and its relationship with the 1999 Agreement was referred to above. It should be noted here that under clause 25(3) the MIB has the right to set off against a claim under the UTDA any liability which the claimant may have to the MIB. For example, the claimant might be a defendant in a separate claim under the UDA. The MIB would have been entitled to recover its payment in that claim from the claimant and, hence, can offset that amount from the claimant's claim under this Agreement.

---

152 (C-63/01) [2004] RTR 32.

153 The claimant also challenged the MIB Agreement in terms of failing to provide for payment of legal costs and interest on the award.

154 [2004] RTR 32, [48]–[54]

155 Whereas under the 1969 UTDA it was held in *Persson v London Country Buses* [1974] 1 WLR 569 that the MIB's decisions to reject the application was in performance of the terms of the agreement and not a repudiation of the agreement. If an applicant was dissatisfied with that decision he had the right of appeal provided by the agreement but he could not bring an action alleging a breach of the agreement on a basis of fact which is reserved by the agreement for the decision of the bureau in accordance with the terms of the contract.

Enforcement of payment

10.94 Under clause 26 if the MIB fails to pay compensation in accordance with an award or the final decision of an arbitrator pursuant to the provisions of the UTDA, the claimant is entitled to enforce payment through the Courts.

The nature of claim against the MIB

10.95 The method adopted by the Minister of Transport in the MIB Agreements to fill a gap in the protection of third parties injured by negligent driving of motor vehicles provided by the Road Traffic Acts often has been subject to criticisms with respect to the legal anomalies inherent in the Agreements.[156] The Agreements therefore were described as being not the most appropriate way of compensation to achieve the legislative purpose.[157]

10.96 The third party's right to claim against the MIB derives from the MIB Agreements. The motorists' insolvency or bankruptcy is not required for the third party victim to address his claim against the MIB. The Third Parties (Rights Against Insurers) Act 2010 regulates cases as such that in the liability insurance context, when the assured's position falls in one of those circumstances that are defined by the 2010 Act, the third party victim steps into the assured's shoes and can raise a claim against the insurer. The claim against the MIB is different in nature than that already mentioned above, the motorist is either not insured or not traced and hence the MIB undertakes to compensate the injured victim as a result of the accident caused by the uninsured or untraced motorist. The victim does not stand in the shoes of the motorist.[158]

10.97 In *Charlton v Fisher*[159] Rix LJ, although with diffidence, stated that the basis of the third parties' claim against the MIB is a judgment against the driver rather than a claim under a policy at all. At first sight it seems a number of principles that apply to third party claims confirm what Rix LJ proposed here, that, for instance, in the case of an untraced driver there is no hint of the driver let alone the insurance policy. In the case of uninsured drivers, if the driver was not insured because he never had taken insurance, the same is the case. If the insurance was taken but the loss falls outside the insurance cover again the claim is not under the insurance policy. The "relevant liability" point which will be referred to above should also be considered here. The MIB's liability has to be with respect to the events that are required to be insured under the Road Traffic Act. As mentioned throughout this book the objective of the Road Traffic Acts has been repeatedly confirmed as being protecting the third party victims of road traffic accidents. In *Hardy v Motor Insurers' Bureau*[160] the reason for judgment in favour of the claimant was that if there had been insurance, it would have been required to cover the deliberate action of the assured. Hence, the availability of a claim against the MIB derives from the agreements which complement the Road Traffic Acts and respect the objective of the protecting the innocent victims of road traffic accidents.

---

156 See for instance *Gurtner v Circuit* [1968] 2 QB 587.
157 Ibid.
158 *Charlton v Fisher* [2002] QB 578 [92].
159 [2002] QB 578.
160 [1964] 2 QB 745.

10.98 As mentioned above, the system provided by the national body referred to in Art 1(4) of the Second Directive[161] is not a guarantee scheme.[162] The payment of compensation under that arrangement is designed to be a measure of last resort, envisaged only for cases in which the vehicle that caused the injury or damage is uninsured or unidentified or has not satisfied the insurance requirements referred to in Art 3(1) of the First Directive.[163] The national bodies referred to here therefore are, in essence, intended to provide a safety net which will be called upon only in rare cases where the tortfeasor is unidentified or uninsured or where for some reason the insurer fails to respond to a claim within the prescribed time.[164]

Defences available to the MIB

Stolen vehicles

10.99 The Motor Insurers' Bureau excludes liability in some certain cases. Such exclusions have been subject to a number of modifications due to the influence of the relevant EU Directives and the interpretation of such Directives by the CJEU. Article 5 of the EC Treaty obliges Member States to take all appropriate measures to ensure fulfilment of their obligations arising out of the Treaty. Under the *Marleasing* principle, if the subject matter of the interpretation is embodied in legislation, the purposive interpretation is to be adopted and the English Court would have been under an obligation to interpret its provisions, as far as possible, in a way which gives effect to the Directive[165]:

10.100 The objective of the Second Directive which has been consolidated by the 2009 Directive was to improve guarantees of compensation for victims of motor accidents by ensuring a minimum level of protection for them throughout the Community.

> Each Member State shall set up or authorise a body with the task of providing compensation, at least up to the limits of the insurance obligation, for damage to property or personal injuries caused by an unidentified vehicle or a vehicle for which the insurance obligation provided for in paragraph 1 has not been satisfied.[166]

10.101 Member states are permitted to exclude[167]

> the payment of compensation by that body in respect of persons who voluntarily entered the vehicle which caused the damage or injury when the body can prove that they knew it was uninsured.

---

161 Article 10 of the Consolidated Directive.

162 *Delaney v Secretary of State for Transport* [2015] Lloyd's Rep IR 441, [33] Richards LJ.

163 Also Article 3(1) of the Consolidated Directive. *Fidelidade-Companhia de Seguros SA v Caisse Suisse de Compensation* (C-287/16) [2017] RTR 26, [35]; *Churchill Insurance Co Ltd v Wilkinson* (C-442/10) [2012] RTR 10, [41].

164 *Jacobs v Motor Insurers' Bureau* [2011] Lloyd's Rep IR 355, [21], Moore-Bick LJ.

165 *Marleasing SA v La Comercial Internacional de Alimentación SA* (C-106/89) [1990] ECR I-4135. As Lord Oliver of Aylmerton observed in *Litster v Forth Dry Dock & Engineering Co. Ltd* [1990] 1 AC 546, 559.

166 Consolidated Directive Article 10(1).

167 Consolidated Directive Article 10(2).

10.102 The 1988 UDA phrased the exception in the following words: Clause 6(1):

MIB shall not incur any liability under clause 2 of this agreement in a case where – . . . (e) at the time of the use which gave rise to the liability the person suffering death or bodily injury . . . was allowing himself to be carried in or upon the vehicle and . . . before the commencement of his journey in the vehicle . . . he – (i) knew or ought to have known that the vehicle had been stolen or unlawfully taken, or (ii) knew or ought to have known that the vehicle was being used without there being in force in relation to its use such a contract of insurance as would comply with Part VI of the Road Traffic Act 1972 .

10.103 The crucial phrase for the purposes of this case is "knew or ought to have known." The exception permitted by the Directives[168] uses the word "knew" without any adornment. The 1988 UDA was to implement the Second Directive. The question arose as to the interpretation of the phrase "knew or ought to have known" and to what extent the interpretation was to be independent of or in line with the interpretation of the Directive.

The meaning of "knew" in the context of the Directives

10.104 The interpretation of the Directives is a matter governed by Community law under which exceptions are to be construed strictly.[169] The general rule is that victims of accidents should have the benefit of protection up to specified minimum amounts, whether or not the vehicle which caused the damage was insured. When applying an exception to this rule and disallowing a victim to claim compensation for injury suffered, a high degree of personal fault must exist.[170] The phrase "must have entered the vehicle voluntarily" reflects this and adds to this interpretation that the exception is aimed at persons who were consciously colluding in the use of an uninsured vehicle.[171] Furthermore, the institution responsible for paying compensation will carry the burden of proving knowledge on the party who seeks to invoke the exception.[172]

10.105 In many ways a passenger may possess actual knowledge that a driver is uninsured. The obvious example is that the driver told the passenger that he had no insurance cover. Another instance would be when the passenger was aware, from his family or other connections with the driver, that the driver had taken but not passed the driving test.[173]

10.106 "Ought to have known" is a commonly used expression in English law.[174] It is described as a person, although lacking actual knowledge, is nevertheless treated by the law as having knowledge of the relevant information. This phrase normally includes negligence that is measured by the standard of the reasonable person. It is explained as "he ought to have known, because he ought to have made sure."[175] This occurs where it is found that a passenger had information from which he drew the conclusion that the driver might well not be insured but deliberately refrained from asking questions lest his

---

168 Article 1(4) of the Second Directive and Article 10(2) of the Consolidated Directive.
169 *White v White* [2001] RTR 25, Lord Nicholls, [13]–[14].
170 Ibid, [14].
171 Ibid.
172 Ibid.
173 Ibid, [15].
174 *White v White* [2001] RTR 25, Lord Scott, [55].
175 *White v White* [2001] RTR 25, Lord Cooke, [42], confirming the trial judge's definition.

suspicions should be confirmed.[176] Lord Nicholls stated in *White v White* that the principle of equal treatment requires that these two persons (knew or ought to have known) shall be treated alike and the Directives were to be construed accordingly.[177] However, the House of Lords in *White v White* was divided in the view of the standards to apply to measure if the passenger ought to have known in the context of motor vehicle insurance. The majority adopted a narrow interpretation that a passenger who was careless in not knowing the driver was not insured did not collude in the use of an uninsured vehicle.[178] "Carelessness" may be established when a passenger, as an ordinary prudent passenger, ought to have made inquiries but gave no thought to the question of insurance.

10.107 In *White v White* an accident occurred when B was a front seat passenger in a Ford Capri driven by his brother S, going to a late-night party. The car crashed and rolled over violently. B was very seriously injured. No other vehicle was involved. S had not passed a driving test. Moreover, he was disqualified from driving. At the time of the accident B did not know his brother was unlicensed and, hence, uninsured, but he had known that his brother was driving without a licence in the past. As found by the trial judge, both brothers had been accustomed to drive while uninsured. Three years before the accident, however, they had agreed that it would be better to put themselves in a position where they could drive cars legally. The trial judge held it sufficient for the MIB to reject payment on the ground that B ought not to have gotten into a car driven by his brother without making sure his brother "had carried out the good resolution and really had made himself a legal driver."

10.108 The House of Lords, by majority, disagreed and decided for the claimant. Lord Nicholls described the findings of the trial judge as no more than of carelessness which was assessed by the standard of the ordinary prudent passenger having the knowledge possessed by this particular passenger.[179] On the other hand, "ought to have known" in the present context required more than carelessness to find knowledge to apply the exception to the obligation of the MIB.

10.109 Had the MIB Agreement been embodied in legislation, whether primary or secondary, the English Court would have been under an obligation to interpret its provisions, as far as possible, in a way which gave effect to the Directive.[180] However, the present case did not involve legislation and the principle did not apply to contracts made between citizens, and that was so even in the case of a contract where one of the parties was an emanation of government.[181] Therefore the *Marleasing* principle must be put on one side[182] but in any case the MIB Agreement was entered into with the specific intention of giving effect to the Directive. The relevant Directive must be at least an aid to the interpretation of contracts entered into by the United Kingdom Government which are manifestly intended to give effect to Community Directive section 2(4) of the European

---

176 *White v White* [2001] RTR 25, Lord Nicholls, [16].
177 Ibid.
178 *White v White* [2001] RTR 25 Lord Nicholls, [17], referred to as Lord Denning M.R. in *Compania Maritima San Basilio SA v Oceanus Mutual Underwriting Association (Bermuda) Ltd* [1977] QB 49, 68, negligence in not knowing the truth is not equivalent to knowledge of it.
179 *White v White* [2001] RTR 25, [19].
180 Ibid, [21].
181 Ibid, [22].
182 Ibid, [23].

Communities Act 1972[183] under the principle of European compatibility. As a result, the MIB Agreement intended to carry through the provisions of the Second Directive that the phrase "knew or ought to have known" in the Agreement was intended to be co-extensive with the exception permitted by Article 1. Therefore the meaning of "ought to have known" should be interpreted as the word "knew" as interpreted under the Second Directive. The former phrase, under its narrow and restrictive interpretation, is apt to include the case of a passenger who deliberately refrains from asking questions but it is not apt to include mere carelessness or negligence. A wilful blindness of an honest person who enters the vehicle voluntarily would be covered by "ought to have known," but a mere failure to act with reasonable prudence falls outside its scope.[184]

10.110 Lord Scott dissented. His Lordship referred to his definition of "blind-eye" knowledge in *The Star Sea*[185] as

> a suspicion that the relevant facts do exist and a deliberate decision to avoid confirming that they exist. . . . The deliberate decision must be a decision to avoid obtaining confirmation of facts in whose existence the individual has good reason to believe.

The word "knew" in Article 1(4) of the Second Directive, on its correct construction, must surely comprehend blind-eye knowledge as described.

10.111 As appears, both the majority and the dissenting views in *White v White* were in agreement with the general principle that the MIB Agreement should be read together with the Second Directive. They also unanimously expressed that the interpretation of the word "knew" in Article 1(4) includes the blind eye knowledge in the words of Lord Scott and wilful blindness in the words of Lord Nicholls. They also unanimously accepted that "knew" does not cover inadvertence. However, their Lordships departed in the point of whether the expression "ought to have known" should be construed so as to exclude negligence. For Lord Scott the contrast between "knew" and "ought to have known" was conclusive:[186] knew and ought to have known is opposing actual knowledge on the one hand, with a state of mind involving the absence of actual knowledge on the other hand. According to Lord Scott, "knew" in the Directive did not include negligence and the parties to the MIB Agreement, either under a misapprehension as to the meaning to be attributed to "knew" in Article 1(4) or without properly directing their minds to the point, intended to include negligence by adding "ought to have known" to clause 6 of the Agreement.[187]

The law subsequent

10.112 The majority view in *White v White* that clarified the interpretation of the meaning of "knew or ought to have known" has been applied consistently since then. In *Akers v*

---

183 Ibid, [32].

184 *White v White* [2001] RTR 25, Lord Cooke, [34]. It means if he had information from which he realised that the driver might well not be insured but he deliberately refrained from asking questions lest his suspicions be confirmed.

185 *Manifest Shipping Co Ltd v Uni-Polaris Insurance Co Ltd (The Star Sea)* [2003] 1 AC 469, [116].

186 *White v White* [2001] RTR 25, Lord Scott [55].

187 Ibid.

Motor Insurers' Bureau[188] G was killed in a traffic accident on 14 June 1997. He was 16 years old at the time and was one of a number of passengers in a Toyota car being driven by R, who was subsequently convicted of causing death by dangerous driving. R was uninsured, hence the claim was against the MIB who denied liability under the exception in clause 6(1)(e) of the 1988 Agreement. Guildford County Court judge held that there had been contributory negligence, both in not wearing a seat-belt and in accepting a lift from somebody whom he knew had been drinking and had taken cannabis.

10.113 In *Akers v Motor Insurers' Bureau* G and M were stranded in the Margate area to where they arrived in a car driven by another young man who had then been arrested by the police. They wanted a lift back to London and M pressed R to give them a lift. R, although later he agreed to do so, initially informed M in the presence of G that R did not have a licence and that the car was not insured. Two important pieces of evidence were that R, in the presence of G, said that he did not have a licence and that the car was not insured. But R was not sure, or clear, that G heard that. In the car there was a discussion about R not being insured. The evidence was that everyone was aware that something was wrong with the insurance. Keene LJ was very reluctant to interfere with the judge's conclusion reached after having heard oral evidence at a trial, but Keene LJ had the benefit of the transcripts of the oral evidence, as well as the witness statements. G was in this tight little group when the statement was made; he was anxious to know if R would drive them home and it would seem likely that he was concentrating, therefore, on what was being said. Keene LJ found it difficult to see how it could properly be concluded that, on the balance of probabilities, G did not hear that being said. It would follow that G knew that there was no insurance but, nonetheless, decided to accept the lift. Putting it at its lowest, one is forced to conclude that G must have been aware that there was a problem about insurance, and in those circumstances he ought to have known, in the sense established in *White v White*, that there was no insurance. At the very least, he was deliberately avoiding specifically inquiring further about that topic.

10.114 The differences in the outcome of applying the standard of "negligence" and a higher standard applied by the majority in *White v White* can clearly be seen in *Whyatt v Powell*[189] in which, ultimately, the County Court judge HHJ John's decision was remitted on appeal to be re-heard and re-determined. In this case P and the three claimants – J (aged 23), G (aged 16) and A (celebrating his 15th birthday) – had been at the house of another man. At about 22:00 on 15 April 2013 the four left in a car driven by P. There was an accident, and the three claimants suffered injuries. P was subsequently convicted of a road traffic offence and disqualified from driving. Since P was not insured as required by the RTA 1988, the claims were made against the MIB who relied upon the exception in clause 6(1)(e)(ii) of the UDA 1999.

10.115 At the County Court the three claimants gave evidence. J confirmed that he knew that P had been in trouble with the police before but did not know what for. He said that he did not know that P had been previously disqualified from driving and that he believed that P had some penalty points for speeding. J said that he had heard that P had been in trouble for burglaries and he had been in prison. J said that P had told him that the car was "legit." A said he did not ask P if he had insurance but just assumed

---

188 [2003] Lloyd's Rep IR 427.
189 [2017] Lloyd's Rep IR 478.

that he had. He said that he did not know that P had previous convictions for dishonesty offences nor that he had been previously disqualified from driving nor that he had convictions for driving offences. He also said that he did not know that P had been to prison. G stated that he knew P had been in trouble with the police and he believed it was to do with robbery and a driving offence but he did not know the details.

10.116 HHJ John found all of the evidence leads to the conclusion that the claimants knew more than enough to put them on inquiry within in the sense established by *White v White*: they ought to have known that there was no insurance because there was enough there to put them on inquiry and they did not ask. As stated above, this is an application of the test for negligence and it is not surprising that on appeal Lewis J remitted the case to the County Court to be re-heard on the basis of the application of the correct test. That was "deliberately refrained from asking questions" in *White v White* and "deliberate closing of the mind" in *Akers v Motor Insurers' Bureau*.

10.117 The MIB argued the constructive knowledge on the claimants of the fact that P was uninsured was established because of P's past offending, his ownership of numerous cars over a short period and the absence of any funds to pay for the cars or insurance for them. Lewis J held that that finding did not lead to the conclusion that the claimants ought to have known that P was uninsured. What mattered was the state of mind of each claimant when they got into the car to be driven by P. Lewis J applied *White v White* and *Akers v Motor Insurers' Bureau* in holding that turning a blind eye, or constructive knowledge is also knowledge within the meaning of the exception of the MIB cover. It includes the case of a passenger who deliberately refrains from asking questions. However, it does not cover a mere failure to act with reasonable prudence. Simply failing to make inquiries which a reasonable passenger might make, with knowledge of that information, would not be sufficient to bring the case within the exception. On the facts the three claimants did not know actually or constructively that P was uninsured.

10.118 It is worth noting that the County Court judge was particularly influenced by the consideration that each of the claimants had not told the truth in their evidence: all had lied about the amount of alcohol they had consumed that night; all lived in the same small Community and knew each other. However, Lewis J emphasised the importance of applying the test mentioned above in the light of the state of mind of each claimant when they got into the car to be driven by P. It appears that victims who undermine their credibility generally by making misstatements in their evidence are not thereby automatically to be treated as being aware of sufficient facts to put them on warning of uninsured driving.[190]

Insurer's insolvency

10.119 Compensation bodies that Article 10 of the Consolidated Directive requires the Member States to establish for compensation of the third party victim in various different circumstances that are highlighted in this chapter as well as Chapter 11 are not currently required to meet costs arising from claims where the motor insurer of the liable party is insolvent. The scheme established under the Directives is not a guarantee scheme but a

---

190 *Insurance Law Monthly*, August 2017.

scheme to ensure that civil liability for use of a motor vehicle is covered either by insurance or by the compensation body in the circumstances set out under the relevant Directives. This matter was referred to above at paragraphs 10.3, 10.16 and 10.98. The concern of the Directives was also explained in Chapter 1. On that basis, previously, it was held by the CJEU that the insolvency of an insurer does not fall within those identified circumstances because in such a situation, the insurance obligation has been satisfied.[191]

10.120 On the other hand, the evaluation that was carried out in order to assess the effectiveness and efficiency of the functioning of the Consolidated Directive[192] revealed that where national law does not provide for any specific protection scheme, victims of accidents caused by a vehicle insured with an insolvent insurer may be left without compensation. When the insurer is providing insurance cross-border via free provision of services, where the insurer is insolvent, victims of motor accidents caused by policyholders of the insolvent insurers may suffer delays in payment of compensation, while national legal procedures determined the responsibility for and the level of compensation.

10.121 In order to ensure compensation of the loss that traffic accident victims suffered without undue delay, the Proposed Amendment by the European Council that is referred to in Chapter 1 includes adding Article 10a to current Article 10. The proposed Article 10a(1) provides,

> Member States shall set up or authorise a body to compensate injured parties habitually residing within their territory, at least up to the limits of the insurance obligation referred to in Article 9(1) for personal injuries or material damage, caused by a vehicle insured by an insurance undertaking in any of the following situations:
>
> (a) the insurance undertaking is subject to bankruptcy proceedings;
> (b) the insurance undertaking is subject to a winding up procedure as defined in Article 268(d) of Directive 2009/138/EC of the European Parliament and of the Council***[193];
> (c) the insurance undertaking or its claims representative has not provided a reasoned reply to the points made in a claim for compensation within three months after the date on which the injured party presented his or her claim to that insurance undertaking.

Where injured parties have already presented a claim directly to or taken legal action directly against the insurance undertaking and such claim or legal action is still pending, no claim may be presented to the body referred to in paragraph 1 above.[194]

10.122 The body referred to in paragraph 1 is given two months to reply to the claim after the claim is made by the injured party.[195] Further, Member States are not permitted to allow the body referred to in paragraph 1 to make the payment of compensation subject to any requirements other than those laid down in this Directive and in particular not the requirement that the injured party should establish that the party liable is unable or refuses to pay.[196]

---

191 *Csonka v Magyar Allam* (C-409/11) [2014] 1 CMLR 14 [33].
192 https://ec.europa.eu/info/sites/info/files/2017-motor-insurance-consultation-document_en.pdf.
193 *** Directive 2009/138/EC of the European Parliament and of the Council of 25 November 2009 on the taking-up and pursuit of the business of Insurance and Reinsurance (Solvency II) (OJ L 335 17.12.2009, p 1).
194 Proposed amendment, Article 10a(2).
195 Proposed amendment, Article 10a(3).
196 Proposed amendment, Article 10a(6).

10.123 The international dimension of the claims made against the compensation bodies are discussed in Chapter 11. It should be noted here that the proposed Article 10a(4) reserves the compensation body's right of recourse against the compensation body of the Member State referred to in paragraph 1 and which has compensated that injured party in his or her Member State of residence, against the compensation body of the Member State in which the insurance undertaking referred to in paragraph 1 is established.

10.124 The current Directives do not provide an obligation on Member States to establish a body to ensure that compensation is provided to victims of road accidents in situations where, although the persons responsible for the damage had taken out insurance covering their civil liability in respect of the use of motor vehicles, the insurer has become insolvent. This matter was disputed in *Csonka v Magyar Allam*[197] in which the applicant brought proceedings for damages against Hungary for an alleged failure to implement fully the First Directive. The applicants argued that the obligation under Article 3(1) to ensure that civil liability in respect of the use of vehicles is covered by insurance was breached by a failure to establish a body to ensure that compensation was provided to victims of road accidents in situations where the insurer had become insolvent. In *Csonka* MÁV General Insurance Company's licence to engage in its activities had been withdrawn by the supervisory authority, and subsequently, MÁV was declared insolvent. The applicants in the main proceedings had taken out an insurance policy with MÁV against civil liability arising out of the use of their vehicles. They were assureds and caused damage with their vehicles. On account of its insolvency, MÁV was unable to discharge its obligations as an insurer. Accordingly, the applicants in the main proceedings themselves had to pay the compensation for the damage caused by their vehicles. After their unsuccessful attempt to claim damages from the Member State for failing to implement the Directives properly, the loss fell on the applicants.

10.125 *Csonka v Magyar Allam* was relied on by the Motor Insurers' Bureau in *Wigley-Foster v Wilson*[198] where the claimant was a passenger on 30 August 2008 in a Greek-registered jeep which the first defendant N, who is resident in England, had rented. N had consumed excessive alcohol and drove into a head-on collision with a taxi coming from the opposite direction causing the claimant serious physical and psychiatric injuries. The jeep was insured by Commercial Value Ins. Co. SA (the Greek insurer). On or about 27 May 2009 the claimant made a claim for compensation against the UK claims representative of the Greek insurer from whom the claimant heard only after the expiry of the three months after the claim was made. On 16 September 2009, the claims representative informed the claimant that since the car rental company had brought proceedings in Greece, the case will need to be put on hold until the Court case in Greece has been determined. In February 2010 the Greek insurer became insolvent. By reason of the insolvency of the Greek insurer, its policy holders were entitled to compensation under Greek law from the Greek Auxiliary Fund for the Insurance of Liability (GAF).[199] By a letter dated 1 March 2010, the claims representative informed the claimant of the Greek insurer's insolvency. The claimant then notified the MIB of the above events

---

197 (C-409/11) [2014] 1 CMLR 14. The Consolidated Directive was not in force, the First and Second Directives were the applicable references for the case.

198 [2016] Lloyd's Rep IR 622.

199 These arrangements are similar to those provided by the Financial Services Compensation Scheme in the case of an insolvent English insurer.

and requested assistance on 19 October 2010. The MIB advised that a claim should be addressed to the Greek Auxiliary Fund.

The Court emphasised that the initial claim was made in May 2009 and the claimant was entitled to notify a claim for compensation to the MIB from the beginning of September 2009, after the expiry of the three-month period without a reasoned reply from the Greek insurer's claims representative in the UK. Had there been a notification at the time the MIB would have been obliged to respond to the claim within two months of receiving it. The MIB argued that and relied on *Csonka* at this point, as a result of the intervening insolvency of the Greek insurer, the claimant's accrued right to notify and make a claim against it had by then ceased to exist. The MIB added that the compensation regime established by the Directives ". . . is not intended to be guarantee or compensation arrangements . . . " protecting policy holders and others against the insolvency of an insurer. The latter point was indeed correct. However, here, the MIB's obligation to deal with the claim and respond to the claimant was triggered.[200] The insolvency took place after that date. The Court held that the compensation regime is not a guarantee against the insolvency of the insurer does not mean that the obligation of the compensation body that had been triggered previously ceased later by reason of the subsequent insolvency of the insurer.

10.126 Clearly, *Wigley* and *Csonka* were different that in *Csonka* the claim was made by the insured persons who compensated the injured third parties' claims. Since the third party victims' losses had already been satisfied, there was also no need for the compulsory insurance or compensation regime to intervene. In *Wigley-Foster v Wilson*,[201] however, the claim was made by the third party injured person and moreover, the MIB's obligation to respond to the victim's claim was triggered under the circumstances. Hence, the objective of the compulsory liability insurance regime had already been satisfied by a third party victim.

10.127 That compensation body can then seek reimbursement from the compensation body of the Member State where the risk is insured by an insurer. *Csonka* is not overruled by the proposed amendment so far as the claim is raised by the assured, not by the third party victim. What the proposed amendment aims for is that in a case similar to *Csonka*, a third party victim should be able to seek compensation from the national body established as required by Article 10a. Since the proposed amendment forbids Member States to adopt a measure that demands the victim first to establish that the insured person is not able to compensate for the loss, the victim can make a claim without seeking first compensation from the insured person. The proposed amendment refers to the right of recoupment between the compensation bodies where the victim is compensated and where the insurance was taken out. It does not refer to this expressly; however, naturally, it is expected that the compensation body of the Member State where the insurance was established can recoup against the insured person for reimbursement. In *Csonka* it is understood that the insured person had the means to pay for the victim's loss and if the proposed amendment had applied at the time, the compensation body would have

---

200 Under the scheme established by the Fourth Directive the compensation body in the State where the injured person resides provides a person from whom he can recover if the driver's insurer fails to respond promptly to his claim or the driver is uninsured or a relevant insurer cannot be identified.

201 [2016] Lloyd's Rep IR 622.

compensated the third party victim's loss and it would have recouped against the insured person or the compensation body where the insurance was taken out. It would have been ultimately the insured person who was responsible for the victim's loss and that was the exact outcome achieved in *Csonka*. The proposed amendment adds here a right of claim by the victim against the compensation body rather than the insured person where the insurer is in one of the financial positions listed under proposed Article 10a.

Does the MIB protect the vehicle users?

10.128 As appears from the above introduction the intention of the MIB Agreements is not to "safeguard insureds" in their relationship with their insurers.[202] In reality what the MIB does is to compensate the victim for the loss which is in fact the user's responsibility. In the case of the uninsured motorist, the motorist will still be personally liable, but the MIB covers liability because the motorist is impecunious. Under the Consolidated Directive the compensation body that has paid compensation to an injured party has the right to obtain reimbursement from the corresponding body in the State where the insurer is established. The corresponding body in the place of accident in turn subrogates to the driver's rights against the insurer or the victim's rights against the driver in case the driver was uninsured.[203] The central concept behind the scheme, therefore, is to provide the claimant with easy access to a defendant in his own country while ensuring that the liability ultimately comes to rest with the person or body with whom it ought to reside. In theory the MIB can turn to the motorist to claim the amount compensated the third party victim, but the MIB's chance of recovery will depend on the financial means that the user has. It was hence argued that "in that sense it can be said that the MIB "protects" him, however unintentional that protection may have been."[204]

Relying on a Directive in a claim against the MIB?

10.129 Direct effect of the EU Directives is referred to in Chapter 1. Accordingly,[205] if a measure adopted by a Directive appears to be unconditional and sufficiently precise, those provisions may, in the absence of implementing measures adopted within the prescribed period, be relied upon as against any national provision which is incompatible with the Directive. It should be noted here that in *Farrell v Whitty* (C-356/05),[206] where the CJEU discussed the direct effect of the Third Directive, ruled that Article 1[207] which extended the compulsory insurance requirement to "liability for personal injuries to all passengers, other than the driver, arising out of the use of a vehicle" satisfies the conditions for having a direct effect. Ms Farrell was injured in a road accident in Ireland, when travelling as a passenger in the rear of Mr Whitty's van. As the vehicle was not fitted with seats in the rear, she was sitting on the floor. Mr Whitty had been uninsured, so Ms Farrell sought compensation from the Motor Insurers' Bureau of Ireland

---

202 R. W. Hodgin, "Protection of the Insured," 11 *Holdsworth L. Rev.* 43 (1986), p 69.

203 *Moreno v Motor Insurers' Bureau* [2017] Lloyd's Rep IR 99, [3].

204 R. W. Hodgin, "Protection of the Insured," 11 *Holdsworth L. Rev.* 43 (1986) p 70.

205 *Becker v Finanzamt Munster-Innenstadt* (8/81) [1982] 1 CMLR 499.

206 [2007] Lloyd's Rep IR 525.

207 Now Consolidated Directive Art 12(1).

(MIBI) pursuant to the terms of its Agreement with the Minister of the Environment (the MIBI Agreement) whereby it undertook to compensate victims of road accidents involving drivers who had not taken out the compulsory insurance required by Ireland's Road Traffic Act 1961 s 65(1)(a)(i) of which excluded from the benefit of the guarantee provided by compulsory insurance cover "persons travelling in any part of a vehicle which is not designed and constructed with seating accommodation for passengers." The MIBI refused to indemnify F as the injuries she had suffered when in the rear of this vehicle were not a liability in respect of which insurance was required under Irish law. In this context the CJEU ruled that the relevant Article confers rights upon which individuals may rely directly before the national Courts

> in order to set aside provisions of national law which exclude from the benefit of the guarantee provided by compulsory insurance cover persons travelling in any part of a vehicle which is not designed and constructed with seating accommodation for passengers.[208]

10.130 In *Lewis v Tindale*, which was also discussed in Chapter 3, the accident occurred on a private land which fell outside the scope of the compulsory insurance requirement under the RTA 1988. It normally follows that, as analysed below, this injury is not a "relevant liability" for which the MIB is under the obligation to compensate. On the other hand, a series of CJEU decisions established that the Directives do not provide a restriction as such and the scope of the compulsory insurance cover is not limited to some certain terrain.[209] It hence appears that whilst the UK has the limitation that the accident must occur either on a road or other public place, the interpretation of the Directives denies such a restriction. If the MIB is an emanation of the state, the Directives as interpreted by the CJEU would be binding for the MIB although the domestic legislation says it would not. Whether the Directives had a direct effect in this respect depends on the satisfaction of the test that "as far as its subject matter is concerned, to be unconditional and sufficiently precise."[210] Those provisions may, in the absence of implementing measures adopted within the prescribed period, be relied upon as against any national provision which is incompatible with the Directive or insofar as the provisions define rights which individuals are able to assert against the State.[211] The effectiveness of such a measure would be diminished if persons were prevented from relying upon it in proceedings before a Court and national Courts were prevented from taking it into consideration as an element of Community law.[212] As explained in Chapter 3, the CJEU has made it unequivocal that the obligation of compulsory insurance extends to the use of vehicles on private land. Having concluded that Article 3 satisfies that the obligation placed on the State is unconditional and sufficiently precise[213] Soole J held that Article 3 has direct effect to the extent of at least the minimum requirement of EUR 1m per victim (Article 9).

---

208 [2007] Lloyd's Rep IR 525, [38].

209 *Vnuk v Zavarovalnica Triglav dd* (C-162/13) [2015] Lloyd's Rep IR 142; *Rodrigues de Andrade v Proenca Salvador* (C-514/16) [2018] Lloyd's Rep IR 164; *Nunez Torreiro v AIG Europe Ltd* (C-334/16) [2018] Lloyd's Rep IR 418.

210 *Farrell v Whitty* (C-356/05) [2007] 2 CMLR 1250.

211 *Becker v Finanzamt Münster-Innenstadt (Case 8/81)* [1982] ECR 53 at [23–25].

212 Ibid.

213 [2018] EWHC 2376 (QB), [95]. The Court of Appeal approved in *Motor Insurers Bureau v Lewis* [2019] EWCA Civ 909.

10.131 In *Lewis v Tindale*[214] Soole J rejected to read down section 145(3) of the RTA 1988 to the effect as if it was applicable to accidents that occurred on a private land. The judge accepted the submission that such a reading down would clearly go against the grain and thrust of legislation which provides that limitation. The effect would be an amendment, not an interpretation, of section 145(3).[215] It raises policy ramifications which are not for the Court.[216]

10.132 A Directive cannot be relied on against individuals[217] but can it be relied on against MIB? The answer, once again, depends on the legal status of the MIB, whether it is regarded as an emanation of the state. It should be taken into account whether, pursuant to a measure adopted by the State, the body is responsible for providing a public service under the control of the State and whether it has for that purpose special powers beyond those which result from the normal rules applicable in relations between individuals.[218] With regards to the Motor Insurers' Bureau of Ireland, in *Farrell v Whitty*[219] the CJEU did not rule whether the MIBI's status satisfied these conditions by noting that the national (referring) Court did not provide sufficient information regarding the MIBI. The CJEU left it to the national Court to ascertain this matter.[220]

10.133 As discussed in Chapter 3 in *Lewis v Tindale*[221] Soole J was persuaded that the effect of European law is to treat the designated compensation body as if the obligation imposed on the State had been delegated to it in full.[222] The judge acknowledged the fact that the MIB is a private law body whose contract with the Secretary of State requires it only to meet an unsatisfied Part VI liability. However in the light of the developments of European law, Soole J held that the State's unimplemented obligation under the Directives must be met by its designated compensation body.[223] The judge noted that the combined effect of sections 95, 143 and 145 of the 1988 Act is that the compulsory policy of motor insurance must be issued by an insurer who is a member of the MIB. The Court of Appeal also approved that the insurers' obligation to fund the MIB is provided by the MIB Articles of Association, which include that an insurer ceases to be a member if it fails to pay the requisite annual levy.

---

214 [2018] EWHC 2376 (QB).

215 Ibid, [58].

216 Ibid, [58].

217 *Farrell v Whitty* (C-356/05) [2007] Lloyd's Rep IR 525, [40]; *Colley v Shuker* [2019] EWHC 781 (QB).

218 *Foster v British Gas Plc* (C-188/89) [1991] 1 QB 405; *Farrell v Whitty* (C-356/05) [2007] Lloyd's Rep IR 525, [40]; *Lewis v Tindale* [2018] EWHC 2376 (QB), cf *Byrne v Motor Insurers' Bureau* [2009] QB 66.

219 (C-356/05) [2007] Lloyd's Rep IR 525.

220 [2007] Lloyd's Rep IR 525, [41].

221 [2018] EWHC 2376 (QB).

222 Ibid, [131].

223 Ibid, [133].

CHAPTER 11

Injuries suffered in the EU

11.1 The developments in the motor third party liability insurance brought forward by the Directives are referred to throughout this book. This chapter focuses on the Fourth Directive, Directive 2000/26/EC of 16 May 2000, and its implementation in the UK. This chapter will also examine the Green Card System.

11.2 Most notably, the Fourth Directive aimed at giving victims of foreign motor accidents various possibilities of recourse in their home states of residence. The measures adopted by the Fourth Directive now appear in the Consolidated Directive in Articles 20–26[1] which provide rules governing compensation in respect of any loss or injury resulting from accidents occurring in a Member State other than the Member State of residence of the injured party which are caused by the use of vehicles insured and normally based in a Member State.

11.3 Accordingly, each Member State shall take all measures necessary to ensure that all insurers insuring compulsory motor vehicle third party insurance appoint a claims representative in each Member State other than that in which they have received their official authorisation.[2] Additionally, each Member State shall establish or approve a compensation body responsible for providing compensation to injured parties in the cases referred to in Article 20(1).[3] Art 20(1) covers compensation in respect of any loss or injury resulting from accidents occurring in a Member State other than the Member State of residence of the injured party which are caused by the use of vehicles insured and normally based in a Member State. In case an insurer has not appointed a claims representative or when the insurer or claims representative does not formulate a reasoned offer or reasoned reply within the required time limit, the victim can address a claim to a compensation body in his or her own Member State. The same body can be appealed to in case the victim has suffered an accident in another Member State, caused by an unidentified or uninsured vehicle. The compensation body which would meet the claims made by a motor traffic accident victim at the home state of residence rather than at the place of the accident can seek reimbursement from the compensation body where the accident took place.

11.4 In order to allow the victim to identify the right body to turn to, the Fourth Motor Insurance Directive required the EEA Member States to establish Information

---

1 "Special provisions concerning compensation for injured parties following an accident in a Member State other than that of their residence."

2 Consolidated Directive Art 21(1).

3 Consolidated Directive Art 24(1).

Centres.[4] The relevant obligations of the Member States are now set out under Art 23 of the Consolidated Directive. Such centres are responsible for keeping a register containing information in relation to where the vehicle is registered, insurance undertakings and the list of vehicles which, in each Member State, benefit from the derogation from the requirement for civil liability insurance cover in accordance with Article 5(1) and (2) as well as the relevant bodies that back up the compensation requirement in the case of such derogations. Where the injured party has a legitimate interest in obtaining it, the Information Centre shall provide the injured party with the name and address of the owner or usual driver or registered keeper of the vehicle.[5]

11.5 All of the measures mentioned here aim to enable a victim of a motor vehicle accident to make a claim for the injuries suffered to the compensation body in their Member State of residence.[6]

11.6 The Fourth Motor Insurance Directive also required insurers and claims representatives to provide a prompt settlement of claims. Procedural requirements are now set out in Article 22 of the Consolidated Directive. Briefly, the Member States are required to establish appropriate measures that the claims representatives provide either compensation or a reasoned response[7] to the claimant victim within three months of the date when the injured party presented his claim for compensation.

11.7 If an injured party has not taken legal action directly against the insurer, he may seek compensation from the body if within three months after he made a claim, he has not been provided with either compensation or reasoned response from either the insurer or the claims representative as the case may be. If an injured party has taken legal action directly against the insurer, he may not seek compensation from the body. The compensation body is required to take action within two months of the date when the injured party presents a claim for compensation to it. The compensation body shall immediately inform the insurer, the compensation body in the Member State in which the insurance undertaking which issued the policy is established and, if known, the person who caused the accident that it has received a claim from the injured party and that it will respond to that claim within two months of the presentation of that claim. The compensation body is required to terminate its action if the insurance undertaking, or its claims representative, subsequently makes a reasoned reply to the claim. The relevant body may not impose on the injured party's establishing in any way that the person liable is unable or refuses to pay. Article 24(2) provides that the compensation body which has compensated the injured party in his Member State of residence shall be entitled to claim reimbursement of the sum paid by way of compensation from the compensation body in the Member State in which the insurance undertaking which issued the policy is established. The latter body shall be subrogated to the injured party in his rights against the person who caused the accident or his insurance undertaking in so far as the compensation body in the Member State of residence of the injured party has provided compensation for the loss or injury suffered.

---

4 Fourth Directive Art 5.

5 Consolidated Directive Art 23 (4).

6 Art 24(1).

7 In cases where liability is denied or has not been clearly determined or the damages have not been fully quantified.

11.8 The injured party may also apply for compensation to the compensation body in the Member State that he resides if it is not possible to identify the vehicle that caused the accident or within two months of the date of the accident it is not possible to identify the insurer. The compensation body that responded to the claim is entitled to reimbursement, if the vehicle is identified, against the guarantee fund in the Member State where the vehicle is normally based and against the guarantee fund in the Member State in which the accident took place in the case of an unidentified vehicle. Where the accident was caused by a vehicle from a third-country vehicle, the right of recourse is against the guarantee fund in the Member State in which the accident took place.

11.9 Where an injured party is resident of a Member State and is injured in a third party country whose National Insurers' Bureau has joined the Green Card System, these provisions shall also apply to claims by such victims.

Implementation of the Fourth Directive

11.10 The compensation body's right of recourse under the Directives is referred to above. Here it is necessary to set the wording of the relevant Articles for the purposes of explaining the implementation procedure of the Directive.

Article 6(2) of the Fourth Directive[8] provided:

> The compensation body which has compensated the injured party in his member state of residence shall be entitled to claim reimbursement of the sum paid by way of compensation from the compensation body in the member state of the insurance undertaking's establishment which issued the policy.
>
> The latter body shall then be subrogated to the injured party in his rights against the person who caused the accident or his insurance undertaking in so far as the compensation body in the member state of residence of the injured party has provided compensation for the loss or injury suffered. Each member state is obliged to acknowledge this subrogation as provided for by any other member state.

11.11 Under Article 7(2) of the Fourth Directive[9] the compensation body referred to above in Art 6(2) shall have a claim, on the conditions laid down in Art 6(2) of this Directive:

(a) where the insurance undertaking cannot be identified: against the guarantee fund provided for in article 1(4) of [the Second] Directive 84/5/EEC in the member state where the vehicle is normally based;

(b) in the case of an unidentified vehicle: against the guarantee fund in the member state in which the accident took place;

(c) in the case of third-country vehicles: against the guarantee fund of the member state in which the accident took place.

11.12 The operation of both Articles 6 and 7 were to be suspended until an agreement has been concluded between the compensation bodies established or approved by the Member States relating to their functions and obligations and the procedures for

---

8 Subject to very minor linguistic differences, Article 24(2) of the Sixth Directive is identical.
9 Sixth Directive Art 25(1).

reimbursement.[10] An agreement between compensation bodies and guarantee funds was reached on 29 April 2002. Articles 6 and 7 took effect from 20 January 2003.

The Motor Vehicles (Compulsory Insurance) (Information Centre and Compensation Body) Regulations 2003 (SI 2003/37) ("Regulations 2003/37") were enacted to enable this arrangement. Regulations 2003/37 came into force on 19 January 2003.[11]

11.13 In the UK the MIB is the compensation body required under Articles 6 and 7 of the Fourth Directive (now Articles 24(1) and 25(1) of the Sixth Directive).[12] The effect of the 2003 Regulations is that the victim is entitled to pursue the MIB, rather than pursue the defendant outside the UK or search for some insurer of the defendant or pursue the foreign body responsible for providing compensation in respect of uninsured vehicles involved in the country outside the UK but within the cover of the Directive and Regulations.[13] In that capacity, the MIB is required to compensate a resident of the UK who is injured in a road traffic accident elsewhere in the European Economic Area and it has not been possible to identify either the driver or the driver's insurers. In that situation, under Regulation 13(2), the injured party may make a claim against the MIB and the MIB, under Regulation 13(2)(b), "shall compensate the injured party . . . as if . . . the accident had occurred in Great Britain."

11.14 The effect of the Consolidated Directive and the Regulations is as follows.

Entitlement to compensation where the insurer is identified

11.15 If an individual resident in the UK is injured in another EU Member State, a claim may be made against the insurer's claims representative in the UK, in line with the requirement under the regime whereby every insurer must appoint a claims representative in each EU Member State. Regulations 11 and 12 set out the relevant requirements that

- an injured party is resident in the United Kingdom;[14]
- that person claims to be entitled to compensation in respect of an accident occurring in an EEA State other than the United Kingdom or in a subscribing state;[15]
- the loss or injury to which the claim relates has been caused by or arises out of the use of a vehicle which is normally based in an EEA State other than the United Kingdom; and[16]
- that vehicle is insured through an establishment in an EEA State other than the United Kingdom.[17]

---

10 Fourth Directive, Art 6(3); Sixth Directive Art 24(3).

11 Reg 1.

12 Reg 10.

13 *Moreno v Motor Insurers' Bureau* [2017] Lloyd's Rep IR 99, Lord Mance, [3].

14 Residency requirement Reg 11(a).

15 Place of accident Reg 11(b). "Subscribing State" means a State other than an EEA State whose National Insurers' Bureau as defined in Article 1(3) of the first motor insurance Directive has joined the Green Card System. Reg 2(1).

16 Vehicle requirement Reg 11(c)(i).

17 Insurance requirement Reg 11(c)(ii).

Where the above conditions are satisfied the injured party may make a claim for compensation from the compensation body if[18]

(a) he has not commenced legal proceedings against the insurer of the vehicle the use of which caused the accident, and

(b) either of the conditions set out in paragraph 3 is fulfilled.

Reg 11 paragraph 3 sets out the following conditions:

(a) that the injured party has claimed compensation from the insurer of the vehicle or the insurer's claims representative, and neither the insurer nor the claims representative has provided a reasoned reply to the claim within the period of three months after the date it was made;

(b) that the insurer has failed to appoint a claims representative in the United Kingdom, and the injured party has not claimed compensation directly from that insurer.

Compensation body's response

11.16 The MIB, upon receipt of a claim under Reg 11, shall respond to a claim for compensation within two months of receiving the claim.[19] The MIB shall also immediately notify the insurer of the vehicle the use of which is alleged to have caused the accident, or that insurer's claims representative[20]; the foreign compensation body in the EEA State in which that insurer's establishment is situated[21] and, if known, the person who is alleged to have caused the accident.[22]

The MIB should inform the relevant persons identified above that it has received a claim from the injured party and that it will respond to that claim within two months from the date on which the claim was received.[23]

11.17 The MIB shall indemnify the injured party in respect of the loss and damage the amount of which, including interest, is properly recoverable in consequence of that accident by the injured party from that person under the laws applying in that part of the United Kingdom in which the injured party resided at the date of the accident.[24] Under Reg 12(4)(a) it is necessary that a person whose liability for the use of the vehicle is insured by the insurer referred to in Reg 11(1)(c) is liable to the injured party in respect of the accident which is the subject of the claim. The compensation body shall cease to act in respect of a claim as soon as it becomes aware that the insurer or its claim representative has made a reasoned response to the claim[25] or the injured party has commenced legal proceedings against the insurer.[26]

---

18 Reg 11(2).
19 Reg 12(2).
20 Reg 12(1)(a).
21 Reg 12(1)(b).
22 Reg 12(1)(c).
23 Reg 12(1).
24 Reg 12(3) and 12(4)(b).
25 Reg 12(5)(a).
26 Reg 12(5)(b).

Vehicle or insurer is not identified

11.18 Entitlement to compensation from the MIB where the vehicle or insurer is not identified is enabled under Reg 13 upon the satisfaction of the following:

- injured person's residency is in the UK;[27]
- an accident, caused by or arising out of the use of a vehicle which is normally based in an EEA State,[28] occurs on the territory of
  (i)   an EEA State other than the United Kingdom, or
  (ii)   a subscribing State.[29]

11.19 Reg 13(1) specifies that the injured party should have requested information under Reg 9(2) and it must be proved impossible to identify either the vehicle the use of which is alleged to have been responsible for the accident, or, within a period of two months after the date of the request, to identify an insurance undertaking which insures the use of the vehicle.

11.20 Upon the satisfaction of the abovementioned conditions, the compensation body shall compensate the injured party in accordance with the provisions of Article 1 of the Second Motor Insurance Directive[30] as if it were the body authorised under paragraph 4 of that Article[31] and the accident had occurred in Great Britain.[32]

11.21 As referred to in the following paragraphs several cases have discussed the proper interpretation and application of Reg 13. The issues discussed were varied to a great extent, but the outcome of those discussions may be summarised as: (1) with respect to the law that is applicable to the assessment of the damages claimed against the compensation body is the place where the motor accident occurred; (2) this also determines the limitation period that will apply to the claim against the motorist; and (3) the cap for the indemnity is also assessed by the law where the accident happened.

11.22 Regulation 14 sets out the right of recourse between compensation bodies and insurers where the latter is identified. Where the compensation body in a Member State where the victim resides compensates his loss under Reg 12(3) as identified above, and the accident in respect of which compensation has been paid was caused by, or arose out of, the use of a vehicle which is normally based in an EEA State other than the State in which the injured party resides, and the use of it is insured by an insurer established in the United Kingdom the MIB shall be liable to indemnify the foreign compensation body. The MIB then is subrogated to the rights of the injured party against the person who caused the accident or that person's insurer to the extent that it has indemnified the foreign compensation body.[33]

11.23 Where the abovementioned conditions with respect to the victim's residence and the place where the body who compensated the victim's loss is based are satisfied and the accident took place in the UK but either the vehicle was unidentified or was a

---

27 Reg 13(1).
28 Vehicle requirement.
29 For definition of Subscribing State see fn 15.
30 Consolidated Directive Article 3.
31 Consolidated Directive Article 6.
32 Reg 13(2)(b).
33 Reg 14(2).

vehicle normally based in a territory which is not an EEA State or a subscribing State or part of any such State, the MIB shall compensate the loss.[34] The MIB's obligation also extends to where the accident was caused by, or arose from the use of, a vehicle normally based in the United Kingdom but it has proved impossible to identify the insurer of that vehicle within two months from the date when the request for compensation was lodged with the foreign compensation body.[35]

Level of compensation – applicable law

11.24 As the case may be, the level of compensation under English law can be less or more favourable than that provided under the law of the State where the accident occurred. The issue then may arise whether the scope of the UK MIB's liability to the victim is to be measured according to English law or the law of the country where the accident took place. Two questions are central.[36] The first is do the Directives prescribe any particular approach to the scope or measure of recovery applicable in a claim against a compensation body under Article 7 of the Fourth Directive (Article 25(1) of the Sixth Directive)? If they do, the second question follows whether the Regulations 2003/37 Reg 13(2)(b) provides any particular approach by either reflecting what the Directive provides or mandating some different approach, whatever the Directives may have required.

11.25 So far as the UK is concerned, the right of an injured person to make a claim against the compensation body derives from the Regulations 2003/37 themselves.[37] The Regulations 2003/37 should be interpreted in a sense which is not in any way inconsistent with the Directives.[38] This principle was emphasised as being the starting point: not merely an add-on.[39]

11.26 The scheme appears to proceed on the assumption that the existence of the driver's liability and the determination of the amount of compensation payable to the injured party will be governed by the same principles at all stages of the process. The right to recover compensation is not wholly independent of the existence of liability on the part of the motorist defendant who caused the accident. However, the Directives do not harmonise the rules applicable to the civil liability of the driver. What the Directive obliges Member States is to put in place legislation to achieve the objective of the Directives that the third party victims will be compensated where there is liability under the national civil law principles. It is for Member States to decide how to achieve compensation through a compensation body and they are entitled, if they wish, to put in place legislation that goes beyond the minimum requirements, provided its effect does not conflict with the object of the Directive.

---

34 Reg 15(2)(a).

35 Reg 15(2)(b).

36 *Moreno v The Motor Insurers' Bureau* [2017] Lloyd's Rep IR 99, [29].

37 *Jacobs v Motor Insurers' Bureau* [2011] Lloyd's Rep IR 355, [23], Moore-Bick LJ; approved by Lord Mance in *Moreno v The Motor Insurers' Bureau* [2017] Lloyd's Rep IR 99, [19].

38 *Marleasing SA v La Comercial Internacional de Alimentación SA* (C-106/89) [1990] ECR I-4135. Lord Mance in *Moreno v The Motor Insurers' Bureau* [2017] Lloyd's Rep IR 99, [26].

39 *Moreno v The Motor Insurers' Bureau* [2017] Lloyd's Rep IR 99, [26]; *Howe v Motor Insurers' Bureau* [2017] Lloyd's Rep IR 576 Lewison LJ, [20].

11.27 The scheme established by the Directives provides that liabilities imposed on the compensation body in the State where the injured person resides will be passed back, usually to the driver's insurer by way of the compensation body in the State where the insurer is established, but in the case of an uninsured or unidentified vehicle to the relevant guarantee/compensation fund. The guarantee fund might have a right of recourse against the driver himself (in the case of an uninsured driver) under local law.

11.28 There is a related procedure where the driver or his insurers cannot be identified: in that situation the MIB must meet the claim and then has an action for indemnity against the compensation body of the Member State where the accident occurred.

11.29 Both of the questions raised above were discussed and answered by the UK Supreme Court in *Moreno v Motor Insurers' Bureau*.[40] In this case M, a United Kingdom resident, whilst on holiday in Greece was struck from behind by a vehicle registered in Greece driven by an uninsured driver, B. B, who admitted responsibility for the accident, did not have a driving licence. M suffered very serious injuries, which included loss of her right leg requiring her to use a wheelchair. M claimed against the MIB in the UK under the Regulations 2003/37. Under the Consolidated Directive the UK MIB will, once it has compensated M, be able to claim reimbursement from the Greek compensation body, which will in turn be subrogated to M's rights against B.

11.30 Prior to *Moreno v Motor Insurers' Bureau*, Moore-Bick LJ held in *Jacobs v Motor Insurers' Bureau*[41] that the Fourth Directive did not go so far as to provide that the motorist's liability and the amount of compensation are to be determined by reference to the law of the country in which the accident occurred. Moore-Bick LJ supported that where the mechanism by which the compensation body's obligation towards the injured person in accidents occurred abroad is treated as if the accident occurred in the UK, the damages may also be assessed under the same assumption in the absence of any provision limiting its scope. Whilst *Jacobs v Motor Insurers' Bureau* was followed in *Bloy v Motor Insurers' Bureau*,[42] both cases were overruled by *Moreno v The Motor Insurers' Bureau*[43] as far as Reg 13(2)(b) is concerned. Having acknowledged that it is open to the domestic legislator to introduce provisions more favourable to the injured party, in *Moreno* Lord Mance drew attention to cases where such provisions may operate less favourable to them. His Lordship held that ruling that the damages must be assessed according to the domestic law where the claim was first raised against the compensation body (at the injured person's home state of residence) may provide a higher compensation than that of would have been available under the law of the place where the accident occurred.

11.31 In *Moreno* the victim's concern was that Greek law (where the accident occurred) would yield a lesser measure of compensation than English law (where a claim against the compensation body was made). Nevertheless, Lord Mance acknowledged that in other contexts the reverse might be the case. For example, Irish personal injuries' damages can

---

40 [2017] Lloyd's Rep IR 99.
41 [2011] Lloyd's Rep IR 355, [21].
42 [2014] Lloyd's Rep IR 75.
43 [2017] Lloyd's Rep IR 99.

be significantly higher than English, and Italian law can in fatal accident cases award significantly more than English law.[44]

11.32 Lord Mance inferred from the scheme created and represented by the Directives that, whether the claim is addressed against the driver responsible, or their insurer, or the guarantee fund, the compensation to which the victim is entitled will be the same.[45] Lord Mance drew attention to the danger that may be faced in case the rule in *Jacobs* is adopted, namely that the measure of compensation could vary according to the happenchance of the route to recovery which the victim chose or was forced to pursue:[46] if the victim chose to pursue the driver in the place of accident, the measure would be that applicable in the State of the accident; whereas if the claim is addressed to the local compensation body, the domestic law of the compensation body would provide the measure of compensation. Lord Mance listed a number of reasons for adopting the rule that the law applicable where the accident occurred measures the amount of compensation. His Lordship interpreted the Second Directive as formalising and generalising at a Union level the requirement for a local guarantee fund which up to that point only existed under the international Green Card[47] scheme and the Agreement between EU insurers' bureaux contemplated by Article 2(2) of the First Directive. Green Card bureaux would handle claims in conformity with the legal provisions applicable in the country of accident relating to both liability and compensation.[48] Moreover, the Agreement reached between compensation bodies and guarantee funds dated April 2002 referred to above should be seen as part of a consistent scheme.[49] Clauses 7.2 and 8.2 of the Agreement expressly provide that the compensation body established to give effect to those Articles is to "apply, in evaluating liability and assessing compensation, the law of the country in which the accident occurred." The compensation body's right to reimbursement is referred to under paragraph 8 of the Agreement. The scope of the UK MIB's liability to M is to be determined in accordance with the law of Greece.

11.33 In answering the second question Lord Mance put emphasis on a consistent measure of compensation as one of the objectives of the Directives.[50] In this respect, Regulation 13(2)(b) should be read as having a purely mechanical or functional operation.[51] it is implicit under reg 13(2)(b), "the implicit proviso", that the injured party must be able to show that the driver is liable to him. it is wrong to draw a distinction between liability and heads of damage on the one hand and measure of compensation on the other.[52] Further, Lord Mance expressed doubts whether the legislator, when drafting Regulation 12(4)(b), was intending to draw a distinction between liability and heads of recovery (subject "implicitly" to the law of the State of the accident) and the measure of compensation.[53] Even if the legislator had been intending that, the distinction has with Rome II now been abolished.[54]

---

44 *Moreno v The Motor Insurers' Bureau* [2017] Lloyd's Rep IR 99, [26].
45 Ibid, [31].
46 Ibid.
47 For the Green Card scheme see below paragraph 11.42 et seq.
48 Ibid, [32].
49 Ibid, [33].
50 Ibid, [41].
51 Ibid.
52 Ibid.
53 Ibid, [42].
54 Ibid.

11.34 Lord Mance found it unnecessary to contemplate a reference to the Court of Justice given that the position as a matter of European Union law is in all these respects clear.[55] Lord Mance held that once it is concluded that the scheme of the Directives is to provide a consistent measure of compensation, whatever the route to recovery taken by the victim, there is certainly no need to regard Reg 13(2)(b) and Reg 12(4)(b) as having any further purpose or effect.[56]

11.35 Similarly, the English Courts held that in a case where a driver was injured in France because the lorry he was driving collided with a wheel that detached from a lorry in front of him and neither the other vehicle nor its driver has been traced, the victim's claim that is addressed to the UK MIB will be subject to the time bar that is determined under French limitation law.[57]

Jurisdiction matters

11.36 Where the defendant is domiciled in one of the 28 countries of the EU or one of the three members of the European Free Trade Association (EFTA) which is party to the European Economic Area Agreement (EEA) with the EU,[58] jurisdictional rules are laid down which govern the allocation of disputes between the courts of those countries. Those rules make special provision for insurance disputes. Jurisdictional conflicts between EU states are governed by the Brussels Regulation Recast, European Parliament and Council Regulation 1215/2012 (Brussels Recast Regulation), replacing with effect from 10 January 2015 the Brussels Regulation, European Parliament and Council Regulation 44/2001.[59]

11.37 Chapter II of the Brussels Recast Regulation, laying down the rules of jurisdiction, includes Section 1, entitled "General provisions," which consists of Articles 4 to 6. Accordingly,

> "persons domiciled in a Member State shall, whatever their nationality, be sued in the courts of that Member State."[60]

Additionally, persons domiciled in a Member State may be sued in the courts of another Member State only by virtue of the rules set out in Sections 2 to 7 of Chapter II of the Regulation.[61]

11.38 For the purposes of this chapter, the rules of the Brussels Recast Regulation are set out by Articles 10–16 in respect of "matters relating to insurance." Recital 18 of the Regulation Recast 1215/2012 provides, "In relation to insurance, consumer and

---

55 Ibid, [39].

56 Ibid, [41–42].

57 *Howe v Motor Insurers' Bureau* [2017] Lloyd's Rep IR 576.

58 Iceland and Norway: Switzerland is a member of EFTA but is not a party to the EEA.

59 Jurisdictional disputes between EU and EFTA states are governed by the Lugano Conventions. Jurisdiction between the constituent parts of the UK is governed by Sch 4 to the Civil Jurisdiction and Judgments Act 1982, which applies principles similar to those in the Brussels Regulation Recast. In all other cases, where the defendant is not domiciled in the EEA, the English courts operate their own jurisdictional rules set out in the Civil Procedure Rules Pt 6.

60 Article 4(1).

61 Article 5(1).

employment contracts, the weaker party should be protected by rules of jurisdiction more favourable to his interests than the general rules."

11.39 Accordingly, an insurer domiciled in a Member State may be sued in another Member State, in the case of actions brought by the policyholder, the insured or a beneficiary, in the courts for the place where the claimant is domiciled.[62]

Moreover, the Brussels Recast Regulation also makes provision for the case in which a third party brings proceedings directly against a liability insurer. Article 13(2) of that regulation is worded as follows:

> Articles 10, 11 and 12 shall apply to actions brought by the injured party directly against the insurer, where such direct actions are permitted.

Consequently, the special insurance rules and the liability insurance rules are all applicable to the third party's action. The special provision for liability insurance states that a liability insurer may be sued, as an alternative to any of the places set out in the insurance rules, in the courts of the place where the harmful act occurred.[63] In the event that the injured party has brought proceedings against the assured, the insurer may be joined to those proceedings wherever they take place as long as the law of the jurisdiction in question permits joinder.[64]

11.40 It is not clear from the wording of Article 13(2) whether a third party victim who suffered loss as a result of the assured's conduct which resulted in liability is treated as the assured so that, for example, he has a right to sue in the place of his own domicile. In *FBTO Shadeverzekenngen NV v Odenbreit*[65] the CJEU ruled that Article 13(2) was available whether or not there was a dispute between the insurers and the assured in relation to a claim under the policy. In *FBTO* the victim was in injured in The Netherlands where the assured and his insurer were both domiciled. It was held that Article 11(1)(b) permitted an action to be brought in the domicile of the assured, beneficiary or policyholder, and Article 13(2) extended Article 11(1)(b) so as to permit an action by the victim in his own domicile. Consequently, the victim was held to be entitled to pursue the insurers in his own domicile, in Germany. Similarly, in *Maher v Groupama Grand Est*[66] the claimants, who were domiciled in England, were injured in a road accident in France in March 2005, commenced proceedings against the driver's insurers in England under the direct action set out in the Fourth Directive.

11.41 More recently, in *Hofsoe v LVM Landwirtschaftlicher Versicherungsverein Munster AG*[67] the claimant relied on the *FBTO* case mentioned above, but the CJEU distinguished these two cases. In *Hofsoe* a vehicle that belonged to a person domiciled in Poland was damaged in an accident that took place in Germany. The driver who was responsible for the accident and his insurer were both domiciled in Germany. The victim entered into a rental contract for a replacement vehicle. Although the cost of rent was in total about EUR 3,465, the victim recovered only EUR 665 from the German insurer's representative in Poland. Following that the victim assigned his claim to H who assumed

---

62 Article 11(1)(b).
63 Article 12.
64 Article 13(1).
65 *FBTO Schadeverzekeringen NV v Odenbreit* (C-463/06) [2008] Lloyd's Rep IR 354.
66 [2010] Lloyd's Rep IR 543.
67 (C-106/17) [2018] Lloyd's Rep IR 608.

responsibility for securing compensation from insurers to which a victim may be entitled. H therefore commenced an action in Poland against the insurer's representative in Poland. The CJEU drew attention to H's position who was not deemed to be a weaker party whose interest was aimed to be protected by Recital 18. A person such as H, who carries out a professional activity recovering insurance indemnity claims against insurance companies, in his capacity as contractual assignee of such claims, should not benefit from the special protection under the Article mentioned above.

Green Card

11.42 The Green Card is an international certificate of insurance which confirms that the visiting motorist has at least the minimum compulsory motor third party liability insurance cover required by the laws of the countries visited. Hence, the Green Card System is a protection mechanism for victims of cross-border road traffic accidents.[68] If the insurer, for whatever reason, does not reimburse the damage, the national bureau under which authority the Green Card has been issued will guarantee the reimbursement.

11.43 The Council of Bureaux (CoB) is the managing organisation of the Green Card System. It operates under the United Nations' guidance and coordinates the activities of the different National Motor Insurers' Bureaux that are members of the Green Card System.[69] The CoB was established in 1949 at an International Conference of Motor Insurers convened in London by UK Motor Insurers' Bureau.[70] Subsequently the Working Party on Road Transport of the Inland Transport Committee of the Economic Commission for Europe of the United Nations investigated the possibility of establishing uniform and practical provisions for insurance cover for cross-border accidents. The relevant work and recommendations concluded that the introduction of a uniform insurance document would be the best way to achieve that end and set out the basic principles of agreements to be concluded between insurers in the different countries. The Inter-Bureaux Agreement was adopted in November 1951 to form the basis of the relationship between the insurers in States which, at the time, had responded favourably to the recommendation.[71] In 1952 Resolution No. 43 adopted by the Economic Commission for Europe formally approved the Green Card System.[72] The Green Card System was implemented on 1 January 1953. Subsequent developments such as the abolition of the Green Card checks on the borders of the members of EEA by the Council Directive 72/166/EEC led the adoption of Internal Regulations to incorporate all provisions governing the relations between bureaux into a single document.[73]

11.44 Hence, the Consolidated Directive[74] refers to the Green Card as

> an international certificate of insurance issued on behalf of a national bureau in accordance with Recommendation No 5 adopted on 25 January 1949 by the Road Transport Sub-committee of the Inland Transport Committee of the United Nations Economic Commission for Europe.

---

68 *Jacobs v Motor Insurers' Bureau* [2011] Lloyd's Rep IR 355, [8].

69 www.cobx.org.

70 www.cobx.org.

71 www.cobx.org.

72 www.cobx.org.

73 Internal Regulations adopted by the General Assembly in Crete on 30 May 2002 and revised in Lisbon on 29 May 2008, in Istanbul on 23 May 2013, in Tallinn on 2 June 2016 and in Helsinki on 8 June 2017.

74 Art 1(5).

11.45 The Green Card System facilitates (1) the crossing of borders and (2) claims settlements.

11.46 (1) The crossing of borders: As mentioned above, the objective of this system is to have a motor third party liability insurance policy of an insurance undertaking in country A recognised in country B. The motorist is therefore released from the obligation of taking out a national insurance contract at the border for holders of a Green Card. Motorists should obtain Green Cards from the insurer who has issued their motor insurance policy. The form of the Green Card to be used in the UK is laid down by the Motor Vehicles (International Motor Insurance Card) Regulations 1971.[75]

11.47 The Green Card System is primarily, but not exclusively, a European system. It presently includes all Member States of the European Economic Area (EEA). Several countries in the Middle East and bordering the Mediterranean Sea also actively participate in the system.[76]

11.48 (2) Claims settlements: A third party victim of a road traffic accident is not prejudiced by the fact that injuries or damage sustained by them were caused by a visiting motorist rather than a motorist resident in the same country. The Council of Bureaux does not handle any individual claim. A National Insurers' Bureau – or Green Card Bureau – is established in each participating country to guarantee that a victim suffering damages from a road traffic accident caused by a foreign vehicle (from another participating country) will be compensated in the country of accident. First it should be noted that, under Art 4.1 of the Internal Regulations, each bureau shall set out the conditions under which it grants, refuses or withdraws its approval to correspondents established in the country for which it is competent.[77] In case of road traffic accidents in one of these countries, any victim (either resident of that country or not) has the right to address himself/herself to the national bureau of the country where the accident occurred in order to have his claim handled and settled.[78] The bureau proceeds to investigate the circumstances of the accident. If, in the course of this investigation, the bureau notes that the insurer of the vehicle involved in the accident is identified and that a correspondent of this insurer has been approved in conformity with the provisions in Article 4, it shall forward this information promptly to the correspondent for further action.[79] If there is no approved correspondent, it shall give immediate notice to the insurer who issued the Green Card or policy of insurance or, if appropriate, to the bureau concerned that it has received a claim and will handle it, or arrange for it to be handled, by an agent whose identity it shall also notify.[80] The bureau

---

75 SI 1971/792.

76 The full list is currently as follows: Austria, Albania, Andorra, Azerbaijan, Belgium, Bulgaria, Bosnia and Herzegovina, Belarus, Switzerland, Cyprus, Czech Republic, Germany, Denmark, Spain, Estonia, France, Leichtenstein, Finland, United Kingdom, Greece, Hungary, Croatia, Italy, Israel, Islamic Republic of Iran, Ireland, Iceland, Luxemburg, Lithuania, Latvia, Malta, Morocco, Moldova, F.Y.R.O.M., Montenegro, Norway, Netherlands, Portugal, Poland, Romania, Russia, Sweden, Slovak Republic, Slovenia, Serbia, Tunisia, Turkey and Ukraine. www.cobx.org.

77 Subject to any agreement to the contrary binding it to other bureaux and/or to any national legal or regulatory provisions.

78 Internal Regulations, Art 3.1.

79 Ibid.

80 Internal Regulations, Art 3.2.1.

is authorised to settle any claim amicably or to accept service of any extra-judicial or judicial process likely to involve the payment of compensation.[81]

11.49 The Council of Bureaux (CoB) offers secretarial services to compensation bodies, guarantee funds and Information Centres in order to allow co-operation between these bodies and to safeguard the proper application of the Motor Insurance Directives. The CoB co-operates with the European institutions such as the European Commission. The Directive's application covered compensation in respect of any loss or injury resulting from accidents occurring in third countries whose National Insurers' Bureaux as defined in Article 1(3) of Directive 72/166/EEC have joined the Green Card System so long as such accidents are caused by the use of vehicles insured and normally based in a Member State and the injured party is resident in a Member State. At the same time the Directive required Member States to put in place legislation to give those injured in road accidents a right to make a claim directly against the driver's insurer.

11.50 By way of example, where a citizen from Russia drives a vehicle registered and insured in Russia into Greece where he causes an accident as a result of which a Greek citizen suffers personal injuries, the Greek victim can raise their claim against the Greek National Insurers' Bureau. The Greek National Insurers' Bureau may compensate the victim's loss subject to Greek rules of liability and compensation.[82] The Greek National Insurers' Bureau may then seek reimbursement from Russian National Insurers' Bureau who then may recover its outlays from the insurer in Russia. Alternatively, when a claim is received by the Greek National Insurers' Bureau it may refer the victim to the correspondent of the Russian insurer in Greece.[83] The correspondent may compensate the victim's loss under Greek domestic rules on liability and compensation and then may claim reimbursement from the insurer in Russia.

11.51 Green Card at the same time provides a guarantee for the visited country B that the insurer of country A will reimburse according to the existing legislation and insurance guarantee limits of the visited country B.

11.52 As explained in this chapter before, for accidents occurring abroad in one of the Member States of the European Economic Area, the visiting victim could either address himself/herself to the claims representative or in some specific cases to the compensation body of his/her Member State of residence.

11.53 The MIB is the representative responsible for operating the Green Card System in the United Kingdom.

11.54 The guarantees provided for in the system are conditioned on the existence (for the vehicle involved in the accident) of a valid "Green Card" issued by the National Insurers' Bureau of the country of the vehicle or under that bureau's responsibility. For countries belonging to the European Economic Area (EEA): the Consolidated Directive Article 14 provides that a motor third party liability insurance must cover, on the basis of one single premium, the entire territory of the EEA. Andorra, Serbia and Switzerland,

---

81 Internal Regulations, Art 3.3.

82 Internal Regulations, Art 3.4 provides "All claims shall be handled by the bureau with complete autonomy in conformity with legal and regulatory provisions applicable in the country of accident relating to liability, compensation of injured parties and compulsory insurance in the best interests of the insurer who issued the Green Card or policy of insurance or, if appropriate, the bureau concerned."

83 Safeguards the victim's rights in case the correspondent does not respect the rules of the system. www.cobx.org.

although not members of the EEA, also belong to this area of a single premium. This means that the normal price of motor third party liability insurance in these countries will allow travelling to all other mentioned countries. The presentation of the Green Card is not necessary anymore to cross the borders between:[84]

- the 28 Member States of the European Union;
- 3 additional European countries participating to the European Economic Area: Iceland, Liechtenstein and Norway;
- 3 additional countries participating to this system by way of agreement: Andorra, Serbia and Switzerland.

11.55 Between these countries, a guarantee mechanism applies on the basis of the origin of the vehicle ("the Member State in which a vehicle is normally based"). This guarantee will apply between the Green Card Bureaux of both countries, even if, in violation of the law, the vehicle that caused the accident turns out to be uninsured.

11.56 For the other participating countries, an additional premium can be asked for obtaining a Green Card. This means that in these countries an additional price can be asked to travel to another country belonging to the Green Card System, but it also means that a motor third party liability insurer in the EEA can ask for an additional premium for a vehicle, originating from the EEA to travel to a non EEA-country with a Green Card.

11.57 The conditions to visit countries not belonging to the Green Card System depend on the national rules of the country to be visited. If motor third party liability insurance is compulsory in that country, the conclusion of a frontier insurance, giving cover for the country visited, may be required.

---

84 Agreement between the National Insurers' Bureaux of the Member States of the European Economic Area and other Associate States www.cobx.org.

CHAPTER 12

The public policy doctrine

12.1 The Latin expression of the doctrine is *"Ex turpi causa non oritur actio,"*[1] and its shorter form is used as *ex turpi causa*. The doctrine may apply from contract, tort and criminal laws point of view and rather than applying a single test for the *ex turpi causa* defence, a broad approach which takes into account the different circumstances of each case has been adopted by the Courts.[2] This chapter will define the doctrine and discuss it within the motor vehicle third party insurance context.

12.2 One of the several forms of describing the doctrine is it deals with the enforcement of rights by the Courts whether or not such rights arise under contract.[3] In Diplock LJ's words,

> All that the rule means is that the courts will not enforce a right which would otherwise be enforceable if the right arises out of an act committed by the person asserting the right (or by someone who is regarded in law as his successor) which is regarded by the court as sufficiently anti-social to justify the court's refusing to enforce that right.[4]

Hence, as a branch of the principles of ethics,[5] and a principle of common law,[6] it is a public policy that a person may not stand to gain an advantage arising from the consequences of his own iniquity.[7] Permitting otherwise would be reaping the fruits of his own crime and profiting by his own wrong.[8] This may appear in two different forms: (1) broadly – no person can recover for damage that which is the consequence of their own criminal act;[9] (2) narrowly – damages cannot be claimed for loss of liberty lawfully imposed in consequence of the claimant's own unlawful act.[10]

12.3 The wider rule is imposed because it is offensive to public notions of the fair distribution of resources that a claimant should be compensated.[11] It will only operate

---

1 *Gardner v Moore* [1984] AC 548, Lord Hailsham, at 558.

2 *Clerk & Lindsell on Torts*, 22nd ed, [3–06].

3 *Hardy v Motor Insurers' Bureau* [1964] 2 QB 745, 767, Diplock LJ.

4 Ibid.

5 *James v British General Insurance Co Ltd* [1927] 2 KB 311, at 322, Roche J.

6 *Hall (Deceased), Re* [1914] P 1.

7 *Gardner v Moore* [1984] AC 548, Lord Hailsham, at 558; *Cunigunda, In the Estate of* [1911] P 108; *Hall (Deceased), Re* [1914] P 1; *Amicable Society for a Perpetual Assurance Office v Bolland* (1830) IV Bligh, N. S. 194.

8 *Hardy v Motor Insurers' Bureau* [1964] 2 QB 745, 762, Diplock LJ.

9 *Hardy v Motor Insurers' Bureau* [1964] 2 QB 745, 760, Lord Denning; for an illustration of this wider rule see *Vellino v Chief Constable of Greater Manchester* [2002] 1 WLR 218.

10 *Gray v Thames Trains Ltd* [2009] 1 AC 1339.

11 Ibid, [51].

252

THE PUBLIC POLICY DOCTRINE

if there is a causal link between the crime and the claim.[12] The narrow rule prevents a person from seeking an indemnity for wrongdoing because of "the inconsistency of requiring someone to be compensated for a sentence imposed due to his own personal responsibility for a criminal act."[13] Consequently, a liability policy cannot give an indemnity for criminal fines.

12.4 This distinction between the narrow and broad interpretation of the rule was observed in *Gray v Thames Trains Ltd*[14] where the claimant suffered post-traumatic stress disorder as a result of involvement in a major railway accident for which the defendant was responsible. While suffering from this disorder he killed a man. His plea of guilty of manslaughter by diminished responsibility was approved, and he was detained in a mental hospital. He claimed damages for negligence against the defendant. Application of the wider principle in *Gray* meant that the claimant's knowledge of what he was doing and that it was wrong was sufficient to bar a claim against the defendant who was responsible for causing the claimant's mental disorder.[15]

Various applications of the doctrine

12.5 Lord Halsbury said in *Quinn v Leathem*[16] that "every lawyer must acknowledge that the law is not always logical at all." In *Tinline v White Cross Insurance Association Ltd*[17] Bailhache J acknowledged Lord Halsbury's statement where the judge said "and everyone concerned with the administration of the law knows this. If the law is not logical, public policy is even less logical." The reflection of these observations was then explained more mildly by Roche J in *James v British General Insurance Co Ltd*[18] that the principles of public policy are themselves unchanging, but their applications may be infinitely various from time to time and from place to place. Moreover, it was held *Cleaver v Mutual Reserve Fund Life Association*[19] that in some cases the doctrine should be applied narrowly and ought not to be carried a step further than the protection of the public requires. This statement was supported in *Hardy v Motor Insurers' Bureau*[20] where Pearson LJ interpreted *Cleaver* as deciding that the doctrine "should not be wider than is necessary to effectuate its object."

12.6 If the right in question is contractual, the rights given to the parties by the contract must be ascertained according to the ordinary rules of construction,[21] and it is only after such ascertainment that the question of public policy arises.[22] It therefore appears that if the claim in question is contractual, the effect of the doctrine is not necessarily in all the cases to render the whole contract illegal,[23] but the wrongdoer is under a disability

---

12 Ibid.
13 *McCracken v Smith* [2016] Lloyd's Rep IR 171, [32].
14 [2009] 1 AC 1339.
15 See *Clerk & Lindsell on Torts*, 22nd ed, [3–18]–[3–21], [3–31].
16 [1901] AC 495, 506.
17 [1921] 3 KB 327, 331.
18 [1927] 2 KB 311, at 322.
19 [1892] 1 QB 147.
20 [1964] 2 QB 745.
21 *Beresford v Royal Insurance Co Ltd* [1938] AC 586.
22 Ibid.
23 Ibid, Lord Atkin.

precluding him from imposing a claim.[24] This is a personal ban[25] which may be invoked against the wrongdoer as well as persons who are regarded in law as his successors (or those who step into the wrongdoer's shoes).[26] It was stated in *Beresford v Royal Insurance Co Ltd*[27] that to enforce payment in favour of the assured's representative would be to give him a benefit, the benefit, namely, of having by his criminal act provided for his relatives or creditors. However, the doctrine cannot be invoked against an innocent third party whose claim is not through that of the wrongdoer.[28] This issue will be revisited in the following paragraphs.

12.7 A further point worth noting is that although the Courts had previously held that questions of public policy must develop nationally,[29] and it would be unreasonable to expect identity of outlook in the Courts of all countries, recently this opinion seems to have been varied, as in *Patel v Mirza*[30] a number of references were made by the Supreme Court to several other common law jurisdictions. In this case the Supreme Court discussed illegality in the context of a payment that was made by P to M to bet on the basis of the inside information that M was expecting to obtain through his contacts at RBS. P transferred £600,000 to M for this purpose; however, M's expectation about the inside information did not materialise and the money was never used for the purpose that it was paid. When M did not return the amount that he previously had received for this purpose, P sued M. Two conflicting interests were before the Supreme Court: first, P made the transfer of £600,000 for an illegal purpose. Second, if M had been permitted to retain the amount, M would have been unjustly enriched. The Supreme Court, after a careful analysis of the history of the development of the public policy doctrine in the context of illegal contracts – that contracts made for illegal purposes at the outset – and lengthy discussions involved in references from different common law jurisdictions including Canada, Australia, New Zealand and USA, decided in favour of P. The considerations on which the Supreme Court's reasons grounded were that the money was never used for the purpose for which it was paid, disallowing P's claim would not be a just and proportionate response to the illegality, but it would have been capable of producing results which may appear arbitrary, unjust or disproportionate. The issue of proportionality was seen in *Patel* as linked to the seriousness of the claimant's criminal conduct rather than the seriousness of the damage sustained and therefore the value of any damages that would be lost if *ex turpi causa* is applied.[31] Hence, allowing P's claim would not be undermining the integrity of the justice system but it would seem to be penal on P. The claim did not seek to enforce or profit by the illegality; it would simply return the parties

---

24 *Hardy v Motor Insurers' Bureau* [1964] 2 QB 745, Lord Denning; *Cleaver v Mutual Reserve Fund Life Association* [1892] 1 QB 147.

25 *Hardy v Motor Insurers' Bureau* [1964] 2 QB 745, 765, Pearson LJ.

26 *Cunigunda, In the Estate of* [1911] P 108; *Cleaver v Mutual Reserve Fund Life Association* [1892] 1 QB 147.

27 *Beresford v Royal Insurance Co Ltd* [1938] AC 586, Lord Macmillan; *Total Graphics Ltd v A.G.F. Insurance Ltd* [1997] 1 Lloyd's Rep 599.

28 *Gardner v Moore* [1984] AC 548, Lord Hailsham, at p 560.

29 *Beresford v Royal Insurance Company* [1938] AC 586, 600 in response to the argument that relied on a case from the USA. See also *James v British General Insurance Co Ltd* [1927] 2 KB 311, at 325, in respect of a decision in Ontario, Canada.

30 [2017] AC 467.

31 *Clerk & Lindsell on Torts*, 22nd ed, [3–44].

to the *status quo ante* where they should always have been. Their Lordships approved Gloster LJ at the Court of Appeal and the distinction she drew there between a claim to give effect to a right derived from an illegal act, and a claim to unpick the transaction by an award of restitution.

12.8 In *Patel v Mirza* the Supreme Court expressly overruled *Tinsley v Milligan*.[32] In *Henderson v Dorset Healthcare University NHS Foundation Trust*[33] the Court of Appeal discussed whether there are any other cases in other areas of the law which the Supreme Court in the *Patel* case held by necessary implication that they should no longer be followed. *Gray* was one of those cases that the Court of Appeal addressed and found still binding after *Patel*. Drawing a particular attention to the actual contractual and unjust enrichment issues in *Patel*, the Court of Appeal urged a considerable caution in determining whether any other cases than *Tinsley* were overruled by the Supreme Court. It is submitted that the approach in *Henderson* is not in conflict with *Patel* especially for the reason that in the latter the Supreme Court recognised that the common law principles develop from time to time and the application of the *ex turpi causa* doctrine may vary in each case.

Limitations to the doctrine

Life insurance references

12.9 One of the most often cited cases in this matter is *Cleaver v Mutual Reserve Fund Life Association* in which the murder of J by his wife F would not afford a defence brought by the executors of J. The contract of insurance on the life of J was enforceable by his executors although the right arising out of the statutory trust in favour of his murderer, F, under section 11 of the Married Women's Property Act 1882 was unenforceable, and since enforceability is the badge of a trust, the Court held that the statutory trust had come to an end.

12.10 *Cleaver v Mutual Reserve Fund Life Association*[34] was applied in *Hall (Deceased), Re*[35] where the death of the testator was due to the act of B who was found guilty of manslaughter. The Court refused to distinguish manslaughter from murder. B, who was the cause of the death of this man, and was convicted of felony in respect of that, could not claim an interest under any will made in her favour by the testator.

12.11 In *Beresford v Royal Insurance Co Ltd*[36] the question was whether the life insurance policy that M took out entitled the assignees to claim against the insurers after M's suicide. The policy in question was taken out in 1925 with a condition: "If the life or any one of the lives assured . . . shall die by his own hand, whether sane or insane within one year from the commencement of the assurance, the policy shall be void."

---

32 [1994] 1 AC 340 a mutual understanding or informal agreement case, in which the House of Lords laid down what subsequently became known as the "reliance principle" that a claim is barred by illegality if the claimant has to rely on his or her own illegality to prove his title to disputed property.

33 [2018] 3 WLR 1651. Similar to *Gray*, *Henderson* was a case of manslaughter by diminished responsibility. The claimant's killing of her mother could have been prevented but for the defendant hospital trust's negligent breaches of duty in caring for her, but the claim failed as a result of applying the wider principle in *Gray*.

34 [1892] 1 QB 147.

35 [1914] P 1.

36 [1938] AC 586.

The assured shot himself for the purpose of the policy moneys being made available for the payment of his debts. The jury found that the assured was sane at the time of the suicide. The policy was interpreted as under which the insurance company have agreed with the assured to pay to his executors or assigns on his death the sum assured if he dies by his own hand whether sane or insane after the expiration of one year from the commencement of the assurance. That obligation was not enforceable[37] if the claim was made by the assured's representatives. However, Lord Atkins said there is no objection to an assignee for value before the suicide enforcing a policy which contains an express promise to pay upon sane suicide, at any rate so far as the payment is to extend to the actual interest of the assignee.

Careless driving and *ex turpi causa*

12.12 Inevitably, there will be a tension between the objective of the compulsory insurance regime (including the MIB) and the public policy doctrine where the driver's conduct is criminal (whether careless, grossly negligent or deliberate). Careless driving is a criminal offence; nevertheless, drivers may still recover damages that they suffered as a result of the negligence of the other driver where both drivers are partly to blame. The claimant driver is not compensated for the consequence of his own criminal act.[38] As a result of a reduction from the compensation as appropriate, on account of contributory negligence, each driver is compensated only for that part of the damage which the law regards as having been caused by the other's negligence. No socially desirable consequences flow from denying the liability for public policy reasons in those examples.[39] Consequently, the recovery of damages does not offend public notions of the fair distribution of resources and poses no threat to the integrity of the law.[40]

12.13 Gross negligence is a more serious offence as the driving falls far below what would be expected of a competent and careful driver. It is called "dangerous driving" as it would be obvious to a competent and careful driver that driving in that way would be dangerous.[41] It is likely that such gross negligence amounts to breach of relevant enactments either by breaking the speed limit or drink driving, but it is not of the same seriousness as manslaughter by diminished responsibility.[42]

12.14 Whether careless or grossly negligent, arguing a public policy defence in the abovementioned examples was found as diminishing the purpose of motor vehicle insurance and standing the principle of public policy on its head.[43] However, as will be explained in the following paragraphs, where the claimant and the defendant motorists engaged in a joint illegal enterprise at the time of the accident, the claim may be barred by *ex turpi causa*. Otherwise the *ex turpi causa* argument in a claim where the drivers

---

37 References were made to *Fry L.J.* in *Cleaver v Mutual Reserve Fund Life Association* [1892] 1 QB 147; *Amicable Insurance Society v Bolland* (1830) IV Bligh, N. S. 194; *Hall (Deceased), Re* [1914] P 1; *Cunigunda, In the Estate of* [1911] P 108.
38 *Wallett v Vickers* [2018] EWHC 3088 (QB), [38].
39 *Gardner v Moore* [1984] AC 548, 561–562, Lord Hailsham.
40 *Wallett v Vickers* [2018] EWHC 3088 (QB), [38].
41 Ibid, [39].
42 Ibid, [39].
43 *Gardner v Moore* [1984] AC 548, 561–562, Lord Hailsham.

THE PUBLIC POLICY DOCTRINE

were careless was always rejected, even before the RTA 1930, irrespective of the degree of the negligence involved. *Tinline v White Cross Insurance Association Ltd*[44] discussed the doctrine in the context of exceeding the speed limit. The assured was driving his car at an excessive speed and knocked down three persons who were crossing the street. Two of the victims were injured, and the third was killed. Upon his counsel's advice the driver pleaded guilty to manslaughter, and he was so convicted. The insurers denied indemnity to the victims of the accident on the ground that the negligence was so gross and excessive that as a result of it a man was killed. They argued that under the circumstances it was against public policy to indemnify a person against the civil consequences of his criminal act. Bailhache J decided in favour of the claimants. The judge put emphasis on the wording of the policy and the nature of an accident within the meaning of the policy. The insurer agreed to indemnify the assured against sums which he shall become legally liable to pay to any other person as compensation for "accidental personal injury." The policy was an insurance against negligence whether slight or great which is different to an intentional act by the assured to cause harm to third parties. Bailhache J recognised that many of these accidents were due to driving at excessive speed of this type which amounted to a breach of an enactment which subjects the person guilty of it to fine or imprisonment. The policy was against claims for accidents due to negligence, without negligence there was no liability. Precisely the same negligence which injured the two persons killed the third; the fact that one of the persons was killed made no difference for this purpose. *Tinline* was applied in *James v British General Insurance Co Ltd*[45] where the driver was drunk at the time of the accident. Roche J found *James* indistinguishable from *Tinline* that in both cases the assured's act amounted to gross or reckless negligence, which constitutes criminality, but nevertheless it was negligence and was not the wilful or advertent doing of the act.[46] Roche J found that on the part of the wrongdoer there was not that degree of criminality which in the doing of a known unlawful act makes it against public policy that the perpetrator should be indemnified in respect of it.[47]

Joint illegal enterprise

12.15 It was mentioned above that where drivers who were involved in the same accident may make a claim against each other subject to their contributory fault to the accident, their claim may be barred for public policy reasons where their contribution to use of the vehicle is qualified as a "joint legal enterprise." In other words, in the absence of a criminal joint enterprise, dangerous driving by the claimant will not bar a claim pursuant to the *ex turpi causa* principle. That is because a person who assists or encourages another to commit a crime[48] is equally responsible in law for the crime committed by the principal.[49] Consequently an accessory who is injured by the principal's criminal conduct cannot sue the principal to recover compensation for his injuries.[50] This is a

---

44 [1921] 3 KB 327.
45 [1927] 2 KB 311.
46 Ibid, 323.
47 Ibid, 323.
48 Accessory or secondary party.
49 *Re v Jogee* [2016] UKSC 8 [1].
50 *Wallett v Vickers* [2018] EWHC 3088 (QB), [44]; *Re v Jogee* [2016] UKSC 8.

particular application of the *ex turpi causa* principle as explained above: if he were allowed to sue the principal, he would be claiming damages for conduct for which in law he is himself responsible.

12.16 To determine whether the claimant engaged in a joint illegal enterprise with the defendant motorist a two-stage test has been applied consistently:[51]

(a) Did the claimant's conduct amount to "turpitude"?
(b) If so, is the claim against the defendant (negligent motorist) founded on that turpitude?

(a) above deals, on the facts of each case, with the classification of the claimant's conduct: Was the claimant a party to a joint enterprise with the defendant driver/rider? The civil standard of balance of probabilities applies.[52] Some clear guidance and answers have been provided to (a) as will be mentioned below. On the other hand, the meaning of (b) is controversial.

Turpitude

12.17 This is a matter of fact to decide on the basis of the evidence, on the balance of probabilities. For the purpose of considering the issue of criminal joint enterprise what matters is the defendant's dangerous driving.[53] The question is whether the deceased was a party to a joint enterprise for the defendant to drive dangerously.[54] If he was, he was equally responsible with the defendant for the defendant's dangerous driving and therefore cannot sue to recover damages for the consequences of that driving. The question whether dangerous driving should amount to turpitude for the purpose of the *ex turpi causa* defence was considered in *McCracken v Smith*[55] where the test was satisfied towards only one of the defendants who was riding the motorcycle together with the claimant.[56] The claimant (Daniel) was the pillion passenger of a 16-year-old boy (Damian) riding a stolen trials bike at excessive speed when it crashed into a minibus negligently driven by Mr Bell. Two different claims were discussed in this case: one of them was against Damian which was barred because of the *ex turpi causa* principle. On the evidence the Court of Appeal found joint enterprise in dangerous driving: the motorcycle was kept at the claimant's house, and the claimant knew that that type of motorcycle was used for dangerous driving. The claimant and the rider were going for a ride together which entailed the very kind of dangerous riding that in fact took place on this occasion.[57] That was the kind of activity that youngsters on trials bikes had been engaging in on the roads of Carlisle, as illustrated by the YouTube footage (including the footage of this very bike). The claimant knew about trials bikes and the way they were being used on the road. This particular bike had been stored at his home on the day of the accident. It was being ridden by his

---

51 *McCracken v Smith* [2016] Lloyd's Rep IR 171, [43–44]; *Clark v Farley* [2018] EWHC 1007 (QB), [33]; *Clerk & Lindsell on Torts*, 22nd ed, [3–36].
52 *McCracken v Smith* [2016] Lloyd's Rep IR 171, [25]; *Clark v Farley* [2018] EWHC 1007 (QB).
53 *Wallett v Vickers* [2018] EWHC 3088 (QB), [50].
54 *Wallett v Vickers* [2018] EWHC 3088 (QB), [50].
55 [2016] Lloyd's Rep IR 171.
56 Similarly, see *Pitts v Hunt* [1991] 1 QB 24.
57 [2016] Lloyd's Rep IR 171, [20].

close friend Damian. When Damian picked him up on it, then, as the judge found, "he must have known that the bike was likely to be ridden on the road and too fast." The proper inference was that the two boys were parties to a joint enterprise the essence of which was that the bike was to be ridden dangerously.[58] The claim against Bell, however, was not barred. The issue in the claim against Bell was viewed in terms of the duty of care that the dangerous driving of the bike had no effect on the duty of care owed by and reasonably expected of Bell. There were two causes of the accident: the dangerous driving of the bike and the negligent driving of the minibus by Bell. Cases involving a claim by one party to a criminal joint enterprise against another party to that joint enterprise (claim between Daniel and Damian) are materially different to the claim against Bell by either Daniel or Damian. The fact that the criminal conduct was one of the two causes was not a sufficient basis for the *ex turpi causa* defence to succeed. As consistent with what was stated above as general principles of law in this regard, it was held that if negligence was established, any recoverable damages from Bell would be reduced in accordance with the principles of contributory negligence so as to reflect Daniel's own fault and responsibility for the accident.

12.18 The question of whether the fact that the bike was being ridden dangerously provides a defence to the claim has to be approached with caution. This has potentially wide ramifications as it is capable of affecting any driver involved in an accident with a negligent third party in circumstances where he or she is driving dangerously or is committing any other road traffic offence of sufficient seriousness to amount to turpitude for the purposes of the *ex turpi causa* defence.

12.19 *McCracken* was important for the determination of *Wallett v Vickers*[59] where Males J held that *McCracken* was a binding authority that in the absence of a criminal joint enterprise between the claimant and the defendant, dangerous driving by the claimant will not bar a claim pursuant to the *ex turpi causa* principle.[60] *Wallet v Vickers* reaffirms the principle stated above in introduction that permitting a claim between drivers who were involved in an accident may still give effect to the requirements of justice and public policy.[61] In order to achieve this result, the matter is to be determined in accordance with principles of causation, namely, "Has the conduct of the defendant made a material contribution to the claimant's injuries?" If so, the damages may be reduced by reason of the claimant's own fault. *In Wallett v Vickers* both the deceased and the defendant were undoubtedly guilty of dangerous driving as principals.

12.20 Recently, in *Clark v Farley*,[62] although the criminality in question was dangerous driving, *McCracken* was distinguished by a fairly narrow margin. The claimant, L, was a pillion passenger on a motorcycle being driven by E that collided with another motorcycle driven by F. The accident occurred on the "Mad Mile," a footpath in a park that had

---

58 [2016] Lloyd's Rep IR 171, [21], [24]. There was no evidence of Daniel giving express encouragement to Damian to ride as he did, but the judge found that the inference can and should be drawn that he gave implied encouragement by getting on the bike and by remaining on it in the circumstances already covered. He was more than a mere passenger. His presence on the bike must have been, and have been intended to be, an encouragement to Damian to ride as he did.

59 [2018] EWHC 3088 (QB).

60 [2018] EWHC 3088 (QB), [43].

61 Ibid.

62 [2018] EWHC 1007 (QB).

signs banning motorcycles. Each motorcycle was neither insured nor roadworthy. Both riders were riding carelessly, and there was no doubt that such negligence was causative of the accident. Having referred to *McCracken* and the Supreme Court decision in *R v Jogee* Yip J held that both cases considered if the person allegedly to be a party in the joint enterprise was "to encourage or assist the perpetrator to do the prohibited act, with knowledge of any facts and circumstances necessary for it to be a prohibited act."[63] On the facts Yip J found that the claimant did not intend to encourage or assist the rider to ride dangerously. There was no evidence of deliberate or reckless thrill seeking or risk taking on the Mad Mile. Nor did the evidence indicate that the path was used as a race track, rather it was used to ride bikes up and down. The claimant, like other youths in the area, would have known that people went to the Mad Mile to ride their off-road motorcycles. However, on a balance of probabilities, Yip J found no evidence that the claimant had been to the Mad Mile for that purpose before.[64] *McCracken*, although looking similar, was to be distinguished: in *McCracken* the Court of Appeal found it clear that the ride was going to entail the very kind of dangerous riding that in fact took place on that occasion; both boys were responsible for the way in which the bike was being ridden.[65] The claimant clearly knew about trials bikes and the way they were being used on the streets. The stolen motorcycle had been stored at his home on the day of the accident. The judge found that "he must have known that the bike was likely to be ridden on the road and ridden too fast" and that it was likely to be ridden in a dangerous manner. Further, there was evidence that when it was in fact being ridden dangerously he did not avail himself of opportunities to get off. On the other hand, as mentioned above, in *Clark*, the judge found no evidence as to L's intention to encourage the rider to ride dangerously with knowledge of the facts and circumstances necessary for it to be dangerous.[66]

Mental element

12.21 The conduct necessary to establish an accessory's liability as a party to a joint enterprise must be accompanied by the necessary mental element that "is an intention to assist or encourage the commission of the crime and this requires knowledge of any existing facts necessary for it to be criminal."[67] In *Wallett v Vickers*[68] the two drivers were driving at a speed well above the speed limit of 40 mph. Each was attempting to be the first to reach the point where the road narrowed to a single lane. As they approached the single lane, the deceased lost control of his vehicle and swerved across the central reservation into two vehicles on the opposite carriageway. The deceased and the two children in his vehicle were seriously injured. The other vehicle that exceeded the speed limit (defendant's vehicle) was not involved in the collisions. The claimant sought damages for bereavement and loss of dependency under the Fatal Accidents Act 1976. In order to succeed, the claimant had to prove that the deceased would himself have been

---

63 Which was also expressed as "community of purpose and action" in *R v Baldessare* (1931) 22 Cr App R 70 which was referred to in *McCracken* [2016] Lloyd's Rep IR 171, [22].
64 [2018] EWHC 1007 (QB), [53].
65 [2016] Lloyd's Rep IR 171, [22].
66 [2018] EWHC 1007 (QB), [61].
67 *Re v Jogee* [2016] UKSC 8 [7], [9].
68 [2018] EWHC 3088 (QB).

entitled to succeed in a claim for damages for negligence against the other driver. This then brought the discussions on the *ex turpi causa* doctrine which would apply in this case only if the parties were engaged in a criminal joint enterprise. Since the accident took place in a couple of seconds, Males J noted the difficulties in determining the mental element that the deceased was holding at the time, considering, however, that rather than working together or encouraging each other to achieve a shared objective, each driver would have preferred that the other should slow down and give way. Consequently, the judge held that there was no basis for any finding that the deceased intended to encourage the defendant to drive dangerously.

Causation

12.22 As stated in element (b) above, if there is turpitude, the next question will be whether the claim is founding upon such turpitude. Beldam LJ said in *Pitts v Hunt*[69] it has been a rule of public policy since the days of Lord Mansfield that a Court will not lend its assistance to a person who founds his cause of action on an illegal or immoral act. It appears that there is no need to discuss causation (b) unless turpitude (a) is present. How close should the link between the claimant's turpitude and the loss he suffered be in order to find that his claim is founded on that turpitude? Is the proper question to ask "whether the injury was the consequence of the claimant's unlawful act?"[70] Or is it sufficient to ask "if the criminal activity merely gives occasion for tortious conduct of the defendant?" Alternatively, should it be looked for if "the facts which give rise to the claim must be inextricably linked with the criminal activity"? In other words must the injury be "a consequence of the claimant's unlawful act only in the sense that it would not have happened if he had not been committing an unlawful act"? Can one say that, although the damage would not have happened but for the tortious act of the defendant, it was caused by the criminal act of the claimant? Or is the position that although the damage would not have happened without the criminal act of the claimant, it was caused by the tortious act of the defendant?[71]

12.23 In *Delaney v Pickett*[72] although the purpose of the journey was the transportation of cannabis intended for resale and the two men were acting in concert in a joint enterprise for illegal purposes, their illegal act was held to be incidental. It meant that the damage suffered by the claimant was not caused by his or her criminal activity but was caused by the tortious act of the first defendant in the negligent way in which he drove his motor car.[73] The Court viewed it as a matter of causation. A distinction was drawn between the criminal activity merely giving occasion for the tortious act of the first defendant to be committed and the fact that the immediate cause of the claimant's damage was the negligent driving (although the accident would never have happened had they not made the journey which at some point involved their obtaining and/or transporting drugs with the intention to supply).

---

69 [1991] 1 QB 24, 38. By referring to *Holman v Johnson* (1775) 1 Cowp. 341.
70 See *Vellino v Chief Constable of Greater Manchester* [2002] 1 WLR 218.
71 See *Gray v Thames Trains Ltd* [2009] 1 AC 1339.
72 [2013] Lloyd's Rep IR 24.
73 The evidence showed the defendant was speeding and lost control after overtaking another vehicle and attempting to cross back to the correct side of the road.

12.24 In *Joyce v O'Brien*[74] the facts were similar to *Delaney*, but the ruling of the Court was somewhat different. In *Joyce* the claimant's injury took place when he fell off the van which was carrying the ladders that he stole together with his uncle. The claimant was standing at the back of the van, which had one of the doors open, and was holding onto the van. It turned sharp left and the claimant was unable to stabilise himself. The judge was satisfied that the claimant and the first defendant had been involved in a joint enterprise for the theft of the ladders and that the accident occurred in the course of the two men making a speedy getaway. With regards to the link between the joint enterprise and the loss, Elias LJ held that after *Delaney v Pickett* the relevance of the established jurisprudence on joint enterprise cases did not cease. That means, the claimant may still be denied recovery not merely where the injury results directly from his own criminal conduct, but also where it results from the action of a joint participator carried on in furtherance of the joint enterprise. In other words, in certain cases the injury will still be treated as having been caused by the claimant even though the immediate cause was the act of a partner in crime. By reflecting the underlying wider public policy considerations the injury can properly be said to be caused by, rather than occasioned by, the criminal act of the claimant even if it results from the negligent or intentional act of another party to the illegal enterprise. Elias LJ did not suggest that this necessarily exhausts situations where the *ex turpi causa* principle applies in joint enterprise cases, but the judge was expecting it to cater for the overwhelming majority of those.[75] Elias LJ also noted that where the character of the joint criminal enterprise is such that it is foreseeable that a party or parties may be subject to unusual or increased risks of harm as a consequence of the activities of the parties in pursuance of their criminal objectives.[76]

12.25 This test was approved in *McCracken* where Richards LJ said that he had to follow *Joyce* rather than try to backtrack.[77] In holding the existence of the turpitude, in *McCracken* the Court of Appeal noticed that, on the facts of the case, the claimant could have foreseen the dangerous nature of the ride. The claimant's injury can properly be said to have been caused by his own criminal conduct even though it resulted from the negligent act of the actual rider of the motorcycle. The claimant was jointly responsible in law for the dangerous ride and he cannot bring a claim in respect of his own negligent act.[78] In *McCracken* the motorcycle collided with a minibus whose driver, B, was also found negligent. In respect of the claim against B, the issue was resolved by the finding of two causes of the accident: the claimant's joint enterprise in dangerous riding of the motorcycle and B's negligence. The causation test in (b) above was problematic: it was neither "although the damage would not have happened but for the tortious act of B, it was caused by the criminal act of the claimant"; nor "although the damage would not have happened without the criminal act of the claimant, it was caused by the tortious act of B." Some authorities discussed the defendant's duty of care where the defendant and the claimant were both parties to a joint illegal enterprise.[79] It was held in *Ashton v Turner*,[80] where the claimant and the defendant

---

74 [2013] Lloyd's Rep IR 523.
75 Ibid, [29].
76 Ibid, [29].
77 [2016] Lloyd's Rep IR 171, [47].
78 Ibid.
79 *Revill v Newberry* [1996] 1 All ER 291; *Pitts v Hunt* [1991] 1 QB 24.
80 [1981] QB 137.

THE PUBLIC POLICY DOCTRINE

were jointly participating in a burglary that involved the use of a getaway car at the time of the accident, it was held that, on the ground of public policy, the defendant did not owe duty of care to the claimant during the course of the burglary and during the course of the subsequent flight in the getaway car. Under the duty of care analysis, it was clear that the dangerous driving of the bike had no effect whatsoever on B's duty of care or on the standard of care reasonably to be expected of him. The facts of *Ashton* were to be distinguished from those of *McCracken* that in the former the claimant was a passenger in a car which was driven by the defendant and they were both being involved in a burglary and getaway car. Richard LJ's focus in *McCracken* with regards to the claimant and B was on the two different causes of the accident: the dangerous driving of the bike and the negligent driving of B – and it would be wrong to treat one as the mere "occasion" and the other as the true "cause." For an *ex turpi causa* defence it was not sufficient that the claimant's criminal conduct was one of the two causes, in which case the claimant's contributory negligence was to be considered instead of *ex turpi causa*.

12.26 It is submitted that when one asks towards B whether the claimant's claim founding on his participation to the enterprise, the answer would be in the negative. Hence, the analysis against B could have relied on the finding that the claimant's participation to the illegal enterprise did not cease the duty of care owned by B. Richards LJ referred to this, but his ratio in denying the *ex turpi causa* was the question of causation. Rejecting the *ex turpi causa* defence against B seems to be the most appropriate solution in this case considering that the actual rider of the motorcycle was not the claimant. Hence, *McCracken* is not inconsistent with the wider context of the public policy doctrine.

12.27 Should these cases be read differently, or should the principles applied now be modified after *Patel v Mirza*? An argument of this line was rejected by the judge in *Clark v Farley*. The judge was inclined to accept the argument that the authorities on this issue were settled and there was no need for modification after *Patel v Mirza*. Moreover, in any case, the judge found no policy considerations that might be relied upon following *Patel v Mirza* to produce any materially different outcome in *Clark v Farley*.[81]

12.28 Where the victim is not a part of a joint enterprise but his action was irreprehensible the Courts still applied the causation principle. In *Clarke v Clarke*[82] the victim arrived at the place where the accident occurred armed with the machete; had used cocaine at some stage, probably within 18 hours prior to the accident; and had arrived at the scene in a car containing a number of offensive weapons. The Court rejected the *ex turpi causa* defence raised by the motorist who caused J's injury. The Court required causation and proportionality as well as the claimant's action being reprehensible. HHJ McKenna said[83]: "When one asks the question What is the proximate cause of the claimant's injury? it is the first defendant's tortious management of the Jeep, and not the claimant's involvement, however serious that might have been, in the preceding fracas." The claimant's action was reprehensible, but it was not sufficient particularly because in the case the proportionality requirement was not satisfied.

---

81 The judge found it unnecessary in the context of *Clark v Farley* [2018] EWHC 1007 (QB), [35] to discuss *McHugh v Okai-Koi* [2017] EWHC 1376, where it appears to have been common ground that *Patel* should apply in a personal injury tort claim.

82 [2012] EWHC 2118 (QB).

83 Ibid, [30].

Turpitude not found – contributory negligence

12.29 If turpitude is not found there might be room to discuss the claimant's contributory negligence. In both *McCracken* (in a claim against the minibus driver as mentioned below) and in *Clark* the Courts discussed the amount of contributory negligence on the claimant. Foreseeability, rather than intention, was the relevant consideration in the assessment of contributory negligence.[84] In *Clark,* L was not wearing a helmet at the relevant time, and it was held that he ought to have foreseen the inherent risk in riding pillion along the path which was narrow and must have known that it was not designed to ride motorcycles on. The judge found him still young (15 at the time of the accident) but old enough to be conscious of the general risks associated with motorbikes.[85] Similarly, in *McCracken* the Court allowed some deduction from the compensation sought against the minibus driver. Most recently, in *Wallett v Vickers*[86] Males J held that the deceased bore a greater responsibility for the collision (60%): the defendant was also driving dangerously and culpably, but at least he did so in a way which enabled him to maintain control. Moreover, although he left it until the very last moment, he did at least permit the deceased to pull ahead when the road did narrow.

The nature of claims again the MIB and public policy

12.30 The public policy doctrine is available against the motorist driver. Invoking such a defence to an innocent victim of a motor vehicle accident, in the view of the English Courts, would be to stand the principle of public policy on its head.[87] Further, a claim against the MIB is, in a number of respects, different to a direct action by a third party victim against the defendant motorist's insurers. The former is a claim which is independent to an insurance contract; hence, it is a claim that arises out of an accident caused by either an uninsured or untraced driver. This nature of claims against MIB was discussed in several cases, the most cited of which is *Hardy v Motor Insurers' Bureau*[88] which adopted a purposive interpretation of the compulsory liability insurance and compensation scheme as discussed in this book. This case was brought against the MIB as a result of the injury that P caused when he deliberately drove off, dragged along H while H was leaning into the van with the door open and was holding on to the van with both hands. P was uninsured and unable to satisfy the judgment awarded against him and in favour of H. The question here was whether the MIB had to compensate H even though the injury was as a result of P's own wilful and deliberate criminal act.

12.31 A comparison is to be made here with the position that would have applied if P had been insured. If P took out the policy with the intention from the beginning of the contract to make a criminal use of the vehicle and the insurers knew of his intention, it would render the insurance contract illegal.[89] If the policy was valid from the outset in

---

84 [2018] EWHC 1007 (QB), [45].

85 Ibid, [75].

86 [2018] EWHC 3088 (QB).

87 *Gardner v Moore* [1984] AC 548, 561–562. The claimant sustained injuries as the result of being deliberately run down by a motor vehicle driven by the defendant. The sole question for decision by the House of Lords was accordingly whether *Hardy v Motor Insurers' Bureau* [1964] 2 QB 745 was correctly decided.

88 [1964] 2 QB 745.

89 *Gardner v Moore*, [1984] AC 548, 559, Lord Hailsham.

the case of no criminal intention from the beginning, but was used for criminal purposes after the contract was made, a claim by the *assured*[90] against the insurer would not be maintained for the public policy doctrine. When a third party makes a claim directly to the insurer, if this claim is defined as that of *through*[91] the assured, the third party could not claim under the same insurance. The same considerations are valid where the third party's claim falls under the TPA 2010 because the assured is bankrupt or under the 2002 Regulations without a judgement obtained against the assured – under both circumstances the third party cannot be placed in a better position than the assured is.[92] However, as analysed in Chapter 8 the scheme under the RTA 1988 section 151 is not to effect a statutory assignment of the assured's rights under his contract of insurance but to confer on a third party, who suffers bodily injury as a result of the tortious act of the assured and obtains judgment against him, a direct right of action against the insurers.[93] Claims under the MIB Agreements are of the same character. The third party's right is an alternative and independent right to the motorist, therefore it is not affected by the motorist's disability to claim from his own wrongdoing. Holding otherwise would have diminished the third party victim's rights, for which purpose the public policy doctrine should not be used.[94] In *Hardy* P was uninsured. As a result, the only other option available for the victim was a claim against the MIB. H's claim was upon a judgment obtained against the motorist P, in respect of the liability which arose from P's intentional criminal act, but that was the act of using a vehicle on a road. The compulsory insurance requirement under the RTA insured against "use" of a motor vehicle wide enough to cover, in general terms, any use of the vehicle, including innocent or criminal use.[95]

12.32 It is submitted that this exception is well justified by the Court in *Hardy*. It is true that the principle to be given effect is "no Court ought to assist a criminal to derive benefit from his crime"; put it in another form that "no Court ought to enforce stipulations tending to induce the commission of a crime."[96] However, there were no socially desirable consequences flowing from the doctrine's application.[97] Furthermore, as Diplock LJ noted in *Hardy*, this exception would not add significantly to the statistics of crime. What *Hardy* decided was (at least very clear from Diplock LJ and Pearson LJ) that the third party had an independent right to that of the motorist and the third party did not commit the anti-social act.

Claim against insurers under the 2010 Act

12.33 If the third party victim's claim falls outside the scope of the statutory compulsory motor vehicle insurance regime, and therefore the victim's right of direct action against the insurer is under the TPA 2010, whether the abovementioned analysis that involved *Hardy* and *Gardner* will apply to such a case is not clear. However, although

---

90 Emphasis added.
91 Emphasis added.
92 Note below paragraph 12.33.
93 [1964] 2 QB 745, 768,769.
94 [1964] 2 QB 745, 765, Pearson LJ.
95 *Gardner v Moore*, Lord Hailsham, page 559.
96 *Beresford v Royal Insurance Co Ltd* [1938] AC 586, Lord Macmillan.
97 *Gardner v Moore* [1984] AC 548.

obiter, the judiciary tends to adopt the same approach that the public policy is a personal matter to the assured and that defence does not transfer in a claim by the victim. The majority in *Charlton v Fisher*[98] supported this view. Moreover, in *Total Graphics Ltd v AGF Insurance Ltd*[99] Mance J, once again obiter, expressed that public policy created a personal disability to recover and there was no reason why the third party victim should be affected by any defence of public policy that would have affected the assured. On the other hand, in *Charlton v Fisher* Rix LJ found that because of the applicable regime to the accident involved, the injured third party was also affected by the disability which attached to the motorist himself. Rix LJ said an assignee with a merely derivative claim stands in the guilty person's shoes for the purpose not only of an ordinary contractual defence, but also of the *ex turpi causa* defence which is personal to the guilty party: and that this is so despite the innocence of the assignee himself.[100]

12.34 The third party victim's claim for compensation against either the insurer under the RTA 1988 s 151 or the MIB is not through the assured but through the entitlement provided by the RTA 1988 and the MIB Agreements, respectively. The assured's (wrongdoer) position is that his wrongdoing caused the injury, and the law provides a compulsory liability insurance regime to protect the third party victim. The MIB Agreements were entered into to provide protection against the uninsured and untraced drivers. Within this context the identification of the "relevant liability" is crucial that the MIB's liability may be argued only when the claim is covered by the Road Traffic Act compulsory liability insurance regime. As discussed in Chapter 10 the relevant liability is that of arising out of the use of the vehicle. Moreover, as held in *Hardy v Motor Insurers' Bureau*, it includes criminal use. The difference between *Charlton v Fisher*[101] and the other relevant authorities discussed is that in *Fisher* the claimant was injured when the assured deliberately drove his car towards the claimant's vehicle. The incident took place at the car park in a hotel, ie off road, thus it fell outside the RTA compulsory insurance regime as applicable at the time. The claim was therefore brought via the TPA 1930 and it was through the assured. If Rix LJ's view in *Carlton* is to be followed, whilst in an action under the compulsory insurance regime the public policy defence will be regarded as a personal ban, a claim under the TPA 2010 will treat it differently. In the latter context it derives from the claim in question and is carried to the third party victim through the assured. In other words, under the TPA 2010, the claim against the insurer is the assured's claim and the victim obtains it from the assured together with the public policy defence.

---

98 [2002] QB 578.
99 [1997] 1 Lloyd's Rep 599.
100 *Charlton v Fisher* [2002] QB 578, [97] Rix LJ.
101 [2002] QB 578.

Vehicles used in the course of a crime

12.35 Clause 6.1(e) under the 1999 UDA excluded claims where

(iii) the vehicle was being used in the course or furtherance of a crime, or
(iv) the vehicle was being used as a means of escape from, or avoidance of, lawful apprehension.

Although clause 6.1(e) (iii) and (iv) were added in the 1999 Agreement, which was adopted after the enactment of the Second Motor Insurance Directive (now consolidated by the 2009 Directive), such exclusions had no counterpart in the Directive. It was stated to be far from obvious why it was thought necessary to add provisions not authorised by EU law.[102]

12.36 In *Delaney v Secretary of State for Transport*[103] the Court of Appeal upheld D's claim against the Secretary of State for Transport, contending that (1) the exclusion in clause 6.1(e)(iii) of the 1999 Agreement was incompatible with the EU Directives, and the United Kingdom was thereby in breach of EU law; and (2) the breach was sufficiently serious to give rise to liability to damages on the principles in Case C-6/90, *Francovich v Italy* [1991] ECR I-537. In *Delaney* on 25 November 2006 D was the passenger in a car driven by P and was seriously injured in an accident caused by P's negligence. A substantial quantity of cannabis was found in the car at the time of the accident. P had a policy of insurance, but his insurers successfully avoided the policy for non-disclosure of material facts. The MIB argued that D knew or ought to have known that the vehicle was being used to transport cannabis for the purpose of drug-dealing, as developed in the case law considered later in this judgment. Jay J adopted (the Court Appeal upheld) the strict interpretation of the exclusion clauses within the meaning of the Directive. Although *Bernaldez* focused on the insurance cover, not on the obligation to set up or authorise a national body providing compensation for damage or injury caused by unidentified or uninsured vehicles, the Court of Appeal accepted that *Bernaldez* was still relevant in a more general context. The Court of Appeal held that the Second Directive gave Member States a legislative choice as to the means by which they fulfilled the obligation to set up or authorise the body provided for by Article 1(4); but the scope of that body's obligation to pay compensation, including the permitted exclusions, was clearly defined by Article 1(4) itself and there was no discretion to adopt additional exclusions. The only exclusions permitted by the Second Directive Article 1(4) were the monetary limits set out as well as the payment of compensation by the national body in respect of persons who voluntarily entered the vehicle which caused the damage or injury when the body can prove that they knew it was uninsured. The text of the Article did not suggest any other permitted exclusion. The Court of Appeal also accepted the claim for damages in favour of D under the *Francovic* principles: (1) the rule of law infringed is intended to confer rights on individuals; (2) the breach is sufficiently serious (The seriousness of the breach lay in the circumstances that existed at the time when clause 6.1(e)(iii) was introduced into the Agreement in 1999); and (3) there is a direct causal link between the breach of the obligation and the damage sustained by the injured party.

12.37 The 2015 UDA omitted the exclusion that previously appeared under clause 6.1(e)(iii).

---

102 *Delaney v Secretary of State for Transport* [2015] Lloyd's Rep IR 441.
103 [2015] Lloyd's Rep IR 441.

CHAPTER 13

Insurance of automated vehicles

13.1 SAE International's report[1] classifies vehicles into six categories in line with their level of automation. Accordingly, where a vehicle is driven by a full control of the driver there is no automation. One step ahead of this type of conventional vehicle is where the driver and the vehicle share the control of driving in the form that "driving assistance" is provided by the vehicle and active driving is performed by the human driver. The assistance may be in terms of the driving environment or steering or accelerating or decelerating the vehicle. It is very common for vehicles to provide a warning sound in terms of the closeness of other properties surrounding in parking the vehicle. The next stage is "partial automation" where the human driver performs active driving, but more assistance is provided by the vehicle compared to level two stated before. A further level is "conditional automation" which is described as specific performance by an automated driving system of all aspects of the dynamic driving task with the expectation that the human driver will respond appropriately to a request to intervene. A more advanced automation is specific performance by an automated driving system of all aspects of the dynamic driving task. In this "high automation" form, the vehicle performs the task even if a human driver does not respond appropriately to a request to intervene. Finally, where all aspects of the dynamic driving task are performed by an automated driving system under all roadway and environmental conditions that can be managed by a human driver occurs where there is full automation.

13.2 One of the obvious questions that such developments have brought into daily life is insurance of liability for use of automated motor vehicles. The UK Department for Transport and the Centre for Connected and Autonomous Vehicles carried out a consultation seeking views on proposals for people and businesses in the UK to use automated vehicle technologies and advanced driver assistance systems.[2] The objective of the consultation was to propose making amendments to primary legislation to ensure insurance products will be available for arrival. The consultation period was followed by the government's response to feedback from business and the public across the UK along with the associated impact assessment which provided details of the government's

---

1 SAE International J3016_201806. SAE, the Society of Automotive Engineers, is a U.S.-based, globally active professional association and standards developing organisation for engineering professionals in various industries.

2 Pathway to Driverless Cars: Proposals to support advanced driver assistance systems and automated vehicle technologies. https://assets.publishing.service.gov.uk/government/uploads/system/uploads/attachment_data/file/536365/driverless-cars-proposals-for-adas-and_avts.pdf.

next steps for each of the proposals on which the consultation was carried out.[3] The final development on this matter for now is the Automated and Electric Vehicles Act 2018 which received Royal Assent in July 2018 (AEVA 2018). The Act will come into force "on whatever day or days the Secretary of State appoints by regulations"[4] which is exercisable by statutory instrument.[5]

Automated vehicles defined by the Act

13.3 AEVA 2018 applies to vehicles which allow the driver to disengage from the driving task, handing full control to the vehicle when the automated systems are active. As SAE's definitions above reveal, automated vehicles (AV) technologies are different to Advanced Driver Assistance System (ADAS) where the driver must monitor and remain ready to take control from the vehicle at all times. AV, on the other hand, when the Automated Driving Function (ADF) is active, does not require any intervention by any person. This happens where the vehicle operates in a mode in which it is not being controlled, and does not need to be monitored, by an individual.[6] Hence, amongst the different levels of automation listed above, only the last two will fall under the scope of the AEVA 2018, and insurance of the rest will be subject to the conventional insurance regime as examined throughout this book.

13.4 As discussed elsewhere in this book so far, in the UK what is required to be insured is not the vehicle, but the user of the vehicle. Further, for the purposes of the compulsory MTPL insurance, the user must be liable to the third party for their negligent use of the vehicle. The obvious question with regards to AV is how can the compulsory insurance requirements be extended to cover traffic accidents resulting from a malfunction or failure of the automated system? In the conventional insurance context what is looked for to establish liability, among other things, is an element of human error in the way the accident has occurred. In the AV, how can it be determined if there was an error? Who would take the responsibility for the error? The absence of an actual human being driving the vehicle causes the main hurdle at this stage.

13.5 The first requirement under the AEVA 2018, which would enable the Act to be applicable, is that the Secretary of State must prepare a list of all motor vehicles that are designed and capable and may lawfully be used when driving themselves on roads or other public places in Great Britain. As a result of the recent developments in the EU law,[7] if the UK will still be under the obligation to implement the EU law in the near future, this section is required to be amended given that the compulsory insurance requirement under the RTA 1988 will have to be extended to private lands as well as public places.[8]

13.6 Section 1(1) of the Act also stipulates that the list is to be updated by the Secretary of State. Further, the Secretary of State is required to prepare a report assessing the impact and effectiveness of the list made under section 1 and to what extent the provisions

---

3 www.gov.uk/government/consultations/advanced-driver-assistance-systems-and-automated-vehicle-technologies-supporting-their-use-in-the-uk.

4 AEVA 2018 s 21(1).

5 AEVA 2018 s 21(3).

6 AEVA 2018 s 8(1)(a).

7 See Chapter 3.

8 See Chapter 3 and paragraph 3.69 et seq.

of the Act is appropriate in insuring liabilities for use of AVs within two years after the first publication of the list under section 1.[9]

Liability

13.7 For the reasons highlighted above, the initial questions to raise with regards to insurance of automated vehicles is who is the user of the vehicle and how can insurance of automated vehicles fit in the conventional motor vehicle third party liability insurance?

13.8 The AEVA 2018 stipulates a single insurer model which covers the driver when they are driving and when they have activated the ADF. The insurer will pay out to the third party victim where[10]

(a) an accident is caused by an automated vehicle when driving itself on a road or other public place in great Britain,

(b) the vehicle is insured at the time of the accident, and

(c) an insured person or any other person suffers damage as a result of the accident.

13.9 Insured person is any person whose use of the vehicle is covered by the policy in question.[11] Schedule to the AEVA 2018 paragraph 19 amends section 145 of the RTA 1988 in this respect that[12]

> in the case of an automated vehicle, the policy must also provide for the insurer's obligations to an insured person under section 2(1) of the AEVA 2018. . . . In this subsection "insured person" means a person who is covered under the policy for using the vehicle on a road or public place in Great Britain.

13.10 When the abovementioned conditions are present the insurer will be liable for the damage suffered, whether death, personal injury or damage to property.[13] If the vehicle was not insured at the time of the accident, section 2(2) places the same liability on certain types of owners where the vehicle is not insured due to being exempt from compulsory third party insurance under the RTA 1988 s 144(2) (such as in the case of vehicles owned by a local authority, a police body, a health authority or NHS trust).

13.11 The injury suffered by the user himself falls outside the scope of the conventional compulsory insurance. If a human is in charge of the automated vehicle, the loss suffered by that person falls outside the scope of the AEVA 2018 as the compulsory insurance provided under the AEVA 2018 leaves the following losses outside its scope:[14]

(a) damage to the automated vehicle;

(b) goods carried for hire or reward in or on that vehicle or in or on any trailer drawn by it, irrespective of being coupled or not;

---

9 AEVA 2018 s 7.
10 AEVA 2018 s 2(1).
11 AEVA 2018 s 8(2).
12 Paragraph 19 adds 3A to the RTA 1988 s 145(3).
13 AEVA 2018 s 2(3).
14 Ibid.

(c) the person in charge of the automated vehicle at the time of the accident.

13.12 Damage to the insured vehicle itself may be covered by a first party insurance; however, in line with the conventional compulsory insurance regime, the AEVA 2018 similarly excluded the cover for the damage suffered by the insured vehicle itself from the scope of compulsory insurance. Again, exclusion (b) is in line with the regime applicable under the RTA 1988. Since the AEVA 2018 applies to vehicles which are completely disengaged from the persons inside the vehicle, in the case of a person being in charge and control of driving, not the AEVA 2018 but the RTA 1988 will apply.[15]

13.13 Further, it is noticeable that the AEVA 2018 section 2(1)(a) used the expression "driving itself" rather than "user." This may be interpreted that the AEVA 2018 applies only where the vehicle is being actively driven by an ADF. Moreover, the words "arising out of," which were held to cover broader circumstances than "caused by,"[16] do not appear in the wording of section 2. It was argued that the AEVA 2018 seemingly departs from this by negating the words "arising out of" and "use" and including the term "when driving itself."[17] However, before coming to a conclusion as such, section 2 of the AEVA 2018 should be considered together with its section 8(1)(b) which provides that insurance of AV should cover the matters that are analysed under section 145 of the RTA 1988.[18] Schedule to the AEVA 2018 amends section 145 but not with respect to the scope of the insurance cover required under section 145(3)(a). Chapter 4 discussed the meaning and scope of section 145, and it will not be repeated here. Therefore, reading the AEVA 2018 section 2(1)(a) and section 8(1)(b) together, the words "arising out of" should not be taken as to have been omitted from the scope of the AEVA 2018. Moreover, new subsection 3A of the RTA 1988 section 145, as noted above, uses the word "also" with respect to what an insurance contract should provide in addition to s 145(3)(a). Hence, new subsection 3A reiterates that section 145(3)(a) is also applicable to insurance of autonomous vehicles. There is no express exclusion of the words "arising out of" from the scope of the insurance coverage required by the statute either. It is however noteworthy that the factual scenarios where the words "arising out of" have been tested were in the context of conventional insurance where only human users were involved in accidents. Therefore, how the wordings of "caused by" and "arising out of" will be illustrated in the context of autonomous vehicles is yet to be observed.

13.14 Section 2(7) of the AEVA 2018 states that the imposition of liability by this section on the insurer or vehicle owner does not affect any other person's liability in respect of the accident. The AEVA 2018 clearly provides that what is insured is the use of a vehicle by AV; the user is AV who cannot be physically identified, hence, what is insured is the vehicle namely, the third party injuries suffered as a result of the use of the vehicle by the vehicle itself. Where a third party makes a direct action against insurers under section 151(2) the third party's right grounds on the established liability to the owner. In this respect how a vehicle's liability will be established where the ADF is active raises a question. It was argued that AEVA 2018 section 2(1)

---

15 The wording of section 3(2) of the AEVA 2018 reiterates the same.
16 See Chapter 4.
17 See Channon/McCormick/Noussia, *The Law and Autonomous Vehicles (Contemporary Commercial Law)*, 2019, Informa Law, 2019, Chapter 3.27.
18 AEVA 2018 s 8(1)(b).

(and section 2(2) for vehicle owners) connote that payment is made regardless of fault.[19] This is because AEVA 2018 does away with liability and simply makes the insurer liable for injuries and damage caused by remote vehicles. As there is no human defendant, a claim is to be brought directly against the insurers, and the insurers then have various rights of recourse against those with responsibility for the losses, including manufacturers of products or suppliers of software.

13.15 It is arguable that where a vehicle is regarded as a product, under the Consumer Protection Act 1987 a strict liability may be imposed on the manufacturer of the product.[20] However, in this case, it has to be clarified whether the motor insurer is also a product liability insurer.

13.16 A further matter which AEVA 2018 does not touch upon is the liability of passengers. As demonstrated by *BTA Baltic Insurance* Company' *AS v Apdrošināšanas Nams' AS* (Case C-648/17) passengers' liability[21] falls under the compulsory MTPL insurance regime under the conventional insurance. This leaves another gap under the AEVA 2018 which, if the UK still retains the EU regime in the near future, needs to be amended to cover liability of passengers in the vehicle.

13.17 Exceptions for conventional insurance under the RTA 1988 section 144 were retained so that the crown and public sector are allowed to self-insure.[22] The limit for damage to property as permitted by the EU Directives and the RTA 1988 s 145(4)(b) also applies to insurance of AV.[23]

Defences available for the insurer

13.18 As discussed in Chapter 7 compulsory insurance regime leaves very limited space for contractual exclusions from the cover to be provided by the insurer. The AEVA 2018, clearly defines what types of defence and also exclusion clauses are permitted from the regime provided by the Act.

Contributory negligence

13.19 Liability under section 2 is subject to the contributory negligence defence available under section 3.[24] Section 3(1) refers to the Law Reform (Contributory Negligence) Act 1945 and expressly provides that where the injured party who claims against the insurer or the vehicle owner to any extent caused the accident that his claim derives from, a deduction from the injured party's claim as permitted under the 1945 Act would be made.

13.20 The person in charge of the vehicle can claim against the insurer as a passenger so long as he was not in control of the vehicle at the time of the accident. If this person allows the vehicle to begin driving itself when it was not appropriate to do so, and the accident was caused wholly by this negligence, section 3(2) of the AEVA 2018 excludes liability of the owner or insurer of an automated vehicle to the person in charge of the

---

19 Channon/McCormick/Noussia, [3.28].
20 See Channon/McCormick/Noussia, Chapter 4.
21 See Chapter 5, paragraph 5.78.
22 AEVA 2018 s 2(2).
23 AEVA 2018 s 2(4).
24 AEVA 2018 s 2(5).

vehicle. The word "wholly" is used here as under s 8(3)(b) an accident that is partly caused by an automated vehicle is also an accident caused by an automated vehicle for the purposes of the AEVA 2018.

Software

13.21 The AEVA 2018 expressly states that insurance policies may not include any other exceptions than that is expressly worded under section 4.[25] This is a welcome provision considering the controversies with respect to the enforceability of exclusions other than those listed under section 148 of the RTA 1988.[26]

Section 4 of the AEVA 2018 permits the insurer to exclude liability in circumstances defined under the section. The definition is based on the identity of the claimant. Where the claimant who suffered loss as a result of a traffic accident that the automated vehicle caused is the person insured under the single policy as referred to above, the insurer may exclude or limit liability if the claimant had made unauthorised modification to their AV, or if they had failed to install required updates to the software which in either case had resulted in the AV causing the accident. The successful operation of this exclusion depends also on the accident being a "direct result" of the alterations that are prohibited or a failure to install safety-critical software. Where it is the former, the act looks for the knowledge of the insured person with respect to prohibited alterations made to the vehicle. With respect to the latter, the act requires that either the insured person knows or ought reasonably to know, that updates were safety critical.[27] Where the insured person is not the holder of the policy, where a prohibited alteration was made to the vehicle, the defence is arguable only where at the time of the accident, the person knows that the alterations to the software were prohibited.[28] A number of cases have discussed and clarified the meaning of the words "know" and "ought reasonably to know" as examined in Chapter 8.

13.22 As set out under section 151 of the RTA 1988 and discussed in Chapter 8, an insurer may have to compensate losses caused by use of the vehicle by someone who is not insured under the policy in question. In the AV context, section 4(4) should be read by considering conventional insurance. Where the accident is caused by a person it is not the AEVA 2018 but the RTA 1988 that governs the compulsory liability insurance regime. If the insurer will have to pay in the case of the accident caused by an uninsured person under the insurance contract and either the prohibited alteration was made by the insured person or the safety critical update was not installed, the insurer may have to compensate the injured person because under the RTA 1988 the insurer's liability may not be excluded to the victim. The insurer, however, may recoup against the person who caused the accident. This is basically a mirror section to section 151(8). A mirror provision to the exclusion for passengers under the RTA 1988, the insurer's recovery from an

---

25 AEVA 2018 s 2(6).

26 See Chapter 7 for detailed discussion of section 148. It was stated in [3.40] in Channon/McCormick/Noussia "Section 148 lists certain exclusion clauses which cannot be used against a third party, meaning that other exclusion clauses can be utilised." However, the matter and a statement as such should be approached with care as analysed in Chapter 7 of this work.

27 AEVA 2018 s 4(1).

28 AEVA 2018 s 4(2).

insured person who is not the policy holder is available only where the insured person knew, at the time of the accident, that the software alterations were prohibited.

Subrogation

13.23 Section 5 regulates insurer's right of subrogation. Where liability is established under section 2 but also there are some other parties liable for the accident and therefore the loss, the insurer may subrogate the assured's rights against that person to the extent they caused the injured party's loss. These other parties' liability is limited to the amount by which they are liable to the insured party's loss. The owner, the injured party or the insurer may not claim any higher amount than their liability to the injured person.[29] Section 5(2)(c) recognises a settlement as proof of evidence of liability, as well as a judgment, decree or an arbitration award. If the injured party's loss is more than what any other person paid to the him, the loss of the injured party exceeding that amount is to be compensated by either the owner or the AV or its insurer.[30]

13.24 The Limitation Act 1980 section 10A sets a special time limit for actions by insurers etc in respect of automated vehicles

> (1) Where by virtue of section 5 of the Automated and Electric Vehicles Act 2018 an insurer or vehicle owner becomes entitled to bring an action against any person, the action shall not be brought after the expiration of two years from the date on which the right of action accrued (under subsection (5) of that section).

The limitation period commences when the amount of the insurer's or vehicle owner's liability to the injured party in respect of the accident is settled.[31]

Motor Insurers' Bureau

13.25 Not surprisingly, the AEVA 2018 does not provide any special provisions with regards to the MIB's liability. The single insurer principle seems to be the most appropriate as the Act adopted. The single insurer will insure the vehicle when ADF is active and inactive. In the former the AEVA 2018, in the latter RTA 1988 will govern the insurance issues. The insurer, under the RTA 1988,[32] will be obliged to be a member of the MIB and will pay levies to fund the MIB. It is likely that the MIB will adjust their levies for the reason of insuring the vehicle under two different regimes. The MIB Articles of Association and the relevant MIB Agreements will need to be amended to reflect such an expansion of the MIB's liability.

13.26 The MIB's liability should only be discussed after section 151(2)(b) of the RTA 1988 and Article 75 of the MIB's Articles of Association. A detailed examination of both of these measures is presented in Chapter 8. It suffices to say here that today there is only very limited availability to argue MIB's liability for uninsured drivers where the insurer is identified. Where the driver is untraced the MIB may be liable under the Untraced

---

29 AEVA 2018 s 5(4).
30 AEVA 2018 s 5(3).
31 AEVA 2018 s 5(5) and s 5(1)(a).
32 The RTA 1988 ss 145(5) and 95; also See Chapter 10.

Drivers Agreement. However in a case where the vehicle is not traced, it is not known whether it was an automated vehicle that caused the accident. Practical difficulties will reveal themselves after automated vehicles appear on the road. It should be noted here that given the overall objective of the compulsory MTPL insurance regime, the fallback system provided by the MIB will be needed and therefore the necessary measures are likely to be adopted to enable that opportunity for victims of traffic accidents where automated vehicles are involved.

INDEX

absence of insurance or security: deposited sums 2.31

admission of liability 7.46

age or physical or mental condition: defence that may not be argued against third party victims 7.4–7.6, 7.31

alcohol *see* driving under the influence of drink or drugs

Andorra: Green Card guarantee 11.54, 11.55

apparatus carried on vehicle: defence that may not be argued against third party victims 7.4–7.6, 7.38

arbitration: clauses 7.104, 7.105; Untraced Drivers Agreement 10.90–10.92

area of vehicle's use: defence that may not be argued against third party victims 7.4–7.6, 7.36

associated equipment and machinery 4.26, 4.37

assured user: definition 7.75, 7.76

authorised insurer: meaning 4.1; policy of insurance *see* policy of insurance or security

Automated and Electric Vehicles Act 2018: application 13.3; "arising out of" and "use" terms 13.13; contributory negligence 13.19, 13.20; crown and public sector 13.17; damage to the vehicle 13.11, 13.12; defences available to insurer 13.18; defined vehicles 13.3–13.6; direct right of action 13.14, 13.15; "driving itself" interpretation 13.13; excluded liability 13.21; insured person meaning 13.9; introduction of 13.2; liability 13.7–13.17; limitation period 13.24; list of all motor vehicles capable of driving themselves on roads /public places 13.5, 13.6; passengers' liability 13.16; single insurer model 13.8, 13.25; software installations 13.21, 13.22; subrogation 13.23, 13.24; unauthorised modifications to vehicles 13.21

automated vehicle insurance: classification of vehicles 13.1; "conditional automation" 13.1; consultation and feedback 13.2; development of legislation 13.2; "driving assistance" 13.1; "high automation" 13.1; legislation *see* Automated and Electric Vehicles Act 2018; Motor Insurers' Bureau Articles of Association and Agreements 13.25, 13.26; "partial automation" 13.1; responsibility for error 13.4

avoidance of insurance contract 6.30, 6.31, 7.107, 8.116, 8.123, 10.31

bankruptcy: breach of statutory duty 6.14; cancellation of policy and surrender of certificate 4.8; civil liability 6.40, 6.55; claims against MIB 10.96; insurer in other Member States 10.121; Third Party (Rights against Insurers) Act 1930 1.8–1.10

beach car parks 3.64

breach of claims 7.41, 7.42

breach of conditions 7.12, 7.13, 7.16, 7.28

breach of statutory duty 6.4–6.6

breach of warranty 7.12–7.14

bringing proceedings *see* legal proceedings

broken down vehicles: immobilisation 5.40–5.45; "moving" a motor vehicle 5.34–5.39; towage 5.46–5.62

Brussels Regulation Recast, European Parliament and Council Regulation 1215/2012 11.36–11.41

burden of proof: insurance cover on driver 2.11; MIB Uninsured Drivers Agreement 10.48

Burns test 3.42, 3.49

caravan parks 3.63

careless driving: *ex turpi causa* 12.12–12.14

car hire *see* credit hire agreements

car parks: beach car parks 3.65; hospital car parks 3.63; hotel car parks 3.63n143; overview 3.60, 3.61; public house car parks 3.63; railway station car parks 3.64; retail commercial enterprises 3.63; staff car parks 3.64

277

car-sharing arrangements 7.72–7.74

carried in or upon a vehicle: meaning 4.24–4.26

carrying goods: defence that may not be argued against third party victims 7.4–7.6, 7.33–7.35

causation: breach of statutory duty 6.16, 6.17; turpitude 12.19, 12.22–12.28; use of a vehicle 5.10–5.15

certificate of insurance or security: accident victim's request for information 2.17; burden of proof 2.11; confirmation of cover 2.12; defaced 4.3; delivery and effectiveness of cover 4.5–4.8, 8.6, 8.7; Deregulation Act 2015 4.5–4.8; electronic transmission 4.3; European Communities (Rights against Insurers) Regulations 2002 4.9; false statements/withholding information 2.18; form of 2.12; Green Card 11.42, 11.44; issue of 2.12; keeping a record of 2.19; lost or destroyed 4.3; not a "policy of insurance" 4.4; offences 2.13–2.18; production by driver on police request 2.13; requirement 2.12; seizure of vehicle on failure to produce 2.14–2.16; transfer of policy or security 4.10

champerty 9.11–9.13

civil liability: avoidance of the insurance contract 6.30, 6.31; breach of statutory duty 6.4–6.6; causation 6.16, 6.17; economic loss 6.39–6.45; exclusions from cover 6.19–6.26; impecuniosity 6.24–6.26, 6.54; interpretation of "permit" and "cause" 6.27–6.29; limitation period 6.46–6.55; *Monk v Warbey* liability 6.11–6.18, 6.22, 6.25, 6.30–6.38, 8.57–8.68; motor insurance 6.7–6.10; Motor Insurers' Bureau and *Monk v Warbey* liability 6.35–6.38; nature of liability 6.11–6.18; overview 6.1–6.3; owner is passenger in his own vehicle 6.18; owner is also user together with the driver 6.32–6.34; right of direct action 8.57–8.68; right of recourse 8.74–8.80

claim co-operation clauses 7.45–7.47

claims history statement 2.37–2.39

claims provisions 7.40–7.43

claims representatives: appointment under Fourth Directive 1.20, 11.3, 11.6, 11.7, 11.15, 11.16

clamping vehicles: vehicle not meeting insurance requirements 2.22

compensation amounts: minimum/maximum levels in Member States 4.12–4.16, 7.83, 7.84

condition of the vehicle: defence that may not be argued against third party victims 7.4–7.6, 7.32

conditional permission to use vehicle 3.6–3.8

Consolidated Motor Insurance Directive 2009/103/EC: *Article 4 Checks on insurance* 1.25; claims history statement 2.37–2.39; definition of vehicle 3.46; evaluation 1.24; exceptions to compulsory insurance or security 2.35–2.39; exclusion clauses 7.77–7.82; interpretation 1.23; liability for failure to implement 1.26–1.32; loss or injury during direct journey between two territories 2.6; minimum amount of indemnity 4.14–4.16; Motor Insurers' Bureau 10.14, 10.15; obligations to insure under 2.5–2.7; overview 1.22; proposal for amending directive 1.24, 4.16; scope of cover provided 4.44; where vehicle is normally based 4.45

contract of insurance: exclusion clause 2.25–2.28; extension clauses 3.15–3.23; rateable proportion clauses 3.35–3.39; void and voidable 2.23, 2.24

control of policy terms: arbitration clauses 7.104, 7.105; avoidance or cancellation of exceptions 7.2, 7.3; breach of claims 7.41, 7.42; breach of conditions 7.12, 7.13, 7.16, 7.28; breach of warranty 7.12–7.14; car-sharing arrangements 7.72–7.74; claim co-operation clauses 7.45–7.47; claims provisions 7.40–7.43; condition precedent 7.12, 7.14, 7.28, 7.40, 7.42; definition of assured 7.75, 7.76; deliberate acts by insured 7.96–7.103; domestic law 7.2, 7.3; driving licence conditions 7.39; essential character of journey 7.59–7.69; EU law 7.77–7.82; exclusions to conditions that may not be argued against third party victims 7.4–7.6, 7.30–7.38; hire and reward 7.70–7.71; Insurance Act 2015 section 10 and 11 7.13–7.21, 7.28; "insured vehicle" term 7.49; insurer v third party victim 7.1; insurers' liability to the assured where limitations in policy 7.12–7.15; limitation of liability 7.12; minimum coverage 7.83, 7.84; notification provisions 7.43; not relevant to actual loss 7.14–7.21; passengers 7.7–7.10; passenger's contribution towards accident 7.11; permitted exclusions 7.51–7.58; schedule particulars 7.48; single premium 7.94, 7.95; suspensory conditions 7.22–7.27; territorial scope of cover 7.94, 7.95; unfair terms 7.109; use for social/domestic or pleasure purposes 7.54–7.58; void or voidable contracts 7.106–7.108; warranties 7.12–7.14, 7.21, 7.23, 7.26, 7.40; what and who is insured 7.48–7.50

councils: exemption from compulsory insurance 2.32, 2.33, 4.27–4.30, 10.38

courts *see also* legal proceedings: discretion to set aside default judgment 8.142; Member State's liability for failure to implement directives 1.26–1.32; obligation to construe domestic legislation consistently with EU law 1.35, 1.36; principle of consistent interpretation 1.34–1.37

covering note 4.2

credit hire agreements: ancillary expenses included in repair cost 9.4; assessing basic hire rate 9.25–9.36; basic hire rate and actual credit hire rate 9.22–9.24; calculating damages 9.22–9.24; capital account loss 9.1; car hire 9.8–9.10; champerty 9.11–9.13; claimant not paying for cost of hire himself 9.47, 9.48; claimant's no claim discount 9.46; contingent liability 9.14; cost of car hire 9.6, 9.7; delay in arranging repair 9.45; different forms of arrangement 9.54–9.56; diminution in value 9.3; double recovery impediment 9.49–9.51; *ex turpi causa* 9.52, 9.53; failure to examine policy documents 9.38; failure to mitigate loss 9.37–9.46; free of charge replacement 9.49–9.51; impecuniosity 9.28–9.36; insuring the credit hire charge 9.49–9.51; legal statutes of 9.11–9.21; mitigation 9.6, 9.15–9.21; non-pecuniary losses 9.5; offer of replacement vehicle by defendant's insurer 9.41–9.44; pre-accident value 9.2; proof of need for replacement vehicle 9.39, 9.40; public policy considerations 9.11–9.13; repair costs 9.1–9.5; subrogation of insurer 9.47, 9.48; Uninsured Drivers Agreement 10.46, 10.46n86

Criminal Injuries Compensation Authority 10.40, 10.67, 10.75n130

criminal use of vehicle 4.60, 7.58, 7.96

cross-border movement: claims history statement 2.37–2.39

cul-de-sac 3.53n124, 3.60

dangerous driving 7.99, 10.112; 12.17–12.20

declaration to avoid insurance contract 8.122–8.124

default judgment: setting aside 8.142

deliberate damage caused by assured 7.96–7.103, 8.51–8.56

deposited sums: replacing insurance-security requirement 2.31, 2.32

Deregulation Act 2015 4.5–4.8

dispute resolution: Untraced Drivers Agreement 10.90–10.92

double insurance 3.34–3.36; 8.129

driverless cars *see* automated vehicle insurance

driving licences: conditions in relation to 7.39

driving under the influence of alcohol or drugs: contribution to accident 7.11; control of policy terms 7.81; fitness to use vehicle 7.31;

gross negligence 12.13; knowledge of 10.48; public place 3.63n150

drugs *see* driving under the influence of alcohol or drugs

drunk drivers *see* driving under the influence of alcohol or drugs

dumper trucks 3.43, 3.49

economic loss: claims under *Monk v Warbey* liability 6.39–6.45

effectiveness of cover 4.5–4.8

electric vehicles *see* Automated and Electric Vehicles Act 2018

emergency treatment of traffic casualties 4.47

employees' position: carried in or upon a vehicle 4.23–4.26; compulsory employers' liability insurance 4.20; employee driver 4.23; Employers' Liability (Compulsory Insurance) Act 1969 4.17, 4.21, 4.22; exempted institutions 4.27–4.30; history of insurance cover 4.17–4.22; passengers 4.21–4.23; subrogation in employment cases 4.38, 4.39; Third Council Directive 4.21; use of vehicle in course of employment 3.12; vicarious liability of employer 4.31–4.37; worker's compensation scheme 4.17

Employers' Liability (Compulsory Insurance) Act 1969 4.17, 4.21, 4.22, 4.22n32

employment: employees *see* employees' position; subrogation in employment cases 4.38, 4.39; use of vehicle in course of 3.12; vicarious liability of employer 4.31–4.37

essential character of journey: borderline cases 7.61–7.63; determination 7.59, 7.60; driver's intention 7.68; dual purposes 7.64–7.67; incidental deviations 7.69; motive to determine 7.68; multiple characters of journey 7.64–7.67

EU law: application of directives in Member States 1.14; consistent interpretation principle 1.34–1.37; Consolidated Motor Insurance Directive *see* Consolidated Motor Insurance Directive 2009/103/EC; control of policy terms 7.77–7.82; definition of vehicle 3.46–3.49; exceptions to compulsory insurance or security 2.34–2.39; exclusion clauses 7.77–7.82; First Directive *see* First Council Directive 72/166/EEC; Fifth Directive *see* Fifth Council Directive 2005/14/EC; Fourth Directive *see* Fourth Council Directive 2000/26/EC; historical progression of relevant directives 1.14–1.25; implementation of directives into national legislation 1.34–1.37; injuries suffered in other Member States *see* Fourth Council

Directive 2000/26/EC; insolvency of insurer 10.119–10.127; interpretation 1.23; "knew or ought to have known" in context of the Directives 10.104–10.111; limitation period 1.33; Member State's liability for failure to implement directives 1.26–1.32; minimum amount of indemnity 4.12–4.16, 7.83, 7.84; normal function of vehicle confined to use as means of transport 5.22–5.33; notification of third party claimant 8.136–8.141; "other public place" 3.66–3.72; owner of the vehicle 7.85–7.93; passenger as user 5.78–5.82; primary direct action against insurers under 8.143–8.151; reliance on a Directive in claims against MIB 10.129–10.133; Second Directive *see* Second Council Directive 84/5/EEC; single premium 7.94, 7.95; Third Directive *see* Third Council Directive 90/232/EEC; use of a vehicle 3.66–3.68

European Communities (Rights against Insurers) Regulations 2002 4.9

European Economic Area (EEA): accidents occurring in other Member States *see* Fourth Council Directive 2000/26/EC; Green Card guarantee 11.54, 11.55; jurisdictional rules 11.36–11.41

European Free Trade Association (EFTA): jurisdictional rules 11.36–11.41

evidence of insurance *see* certificate of insurance or security

excepted institutions or authorities 2.32, 2.33; 4.27–4.30

exceptions to compulsory insurance or security 2.31–2.33, 4.27–4.30

exclusion clauses: claims by owner of vehicle 7.85–7.93; contracts with 2.25–2.28; deliberate acts by insured 7.96–7.103; EU law 7.77–7.82; not to be argued against 7.4–7.6, 7.30–7.38; permitted 7.51–7.58, 8.50–8.56

extension clauses: challenge to enforceability 3.16; continuing ownership 3.24–3.33; definition of insured 7.76; differences between "instead of" and "succession" 3.26; doctrine of privity 3.16, 3.17; indemnification 3.15–3.33; insurable interest requirement 3.16, 3.18, 3.19; permitted users for the scheduled vehicle 3.15–3.33; temporary use of another car 3.27–3.33

*ex turpi causa se*e public policy doctrine

Financial Services Compensation Scheme 10.4, 10.5n197

Fifth Council Directive 2005/14/EC: exclusion from insurance obligations 2.35n67;

introduction and purpose of 1.21; Member State's liability for failure to implement 1.26–1.32; minimum amount of indemnity 4.13; Motor Insurers' Bureau 10.12, 10.13

First Council Directive 72/166/EEC: aims 1.16; exceptions to compulsory insurance or security 2.34; introduction 1.15–1.17; Member State's liability for failure to implement 1.26–1.32

foreign motor accidents: Fourth Council Directive *see* Fourth Council Directive 2000/26/EC; Green Card System *see* Green Card System

forklift trucks 3.42

Fourth Council Directive 2000/26/EC: accidents occurring in other Member States 11.1–11.4; appointment of claims representative 1.20, 11.3, 11.6, 11.7, 11.15, 11.16; entitlement to compensation where insurer identified 11.15; establishment of information centres 11.4; identification of insurer and vehicle 11.8; implementation procedure 11.10–11.14; introduction and purpose of 1.20; Member State's liability for failure to implement 1.26–1.32; Motor Insurers' Bureau as compensatory body under *see* Motor Insurers' Bureau as compensatory body under the Fourth Directive; prompt settlement of claims 11.6; time scale for legal action 11.7

Francovich damages: limitation period for claims 1.33

"gentleman's agreement" 4.38, 4.39

go-karts 3.42

goods carried in vehicle: defence that may not be argued against third party victims 7.4–7.6, 7.33–7.35

Go-peds 3.44

Green Card System: additional premium for obtaining 11.56; claims representative 11.52; claims settlements 11.45, 11.48; co-operation between bodies 11.49, 11.50; Council of Bureaux (CoB) 11.43, 11.49; countries using the system 11.47, 11.47n75; crossing borders 1.16, 11.45, 11.46; form of 11.46; guarantee funds 11.49; guarantee for the visited country 11.51; guarantee mechanism in EEA and EU Member States 11.54, 11.55; history of 11.43; information centres 11.49; international certificate of insurance 11.42, 11.44; local guarantee fund 11.32; managing organisation 11.43; Member State residents 11.9; Motor Insurers' Bureau 11.53; origin of the vehicle

INDEX

11.55; secretarial services 11.49; subscribing State 11.18, 11.18n29; validity of green card 11.54; visiting non-participating countries 11.57

hamburger van 5.18, 5.19, 5.33
haulage contractors 4.31n44
highways *see* road or other public place
Highways Act 1896 1.5
hire and reward: goods carried for 4.11, 7.51; passengers carried for 4.18, 4.56, 7.70, 7.71
hiring vehicles *see* credit hire agreements
history of insurance obligation: domestic law 1.3–1.7; early twentieth century 1.3–1.7; employees 4.17–4.20; EU law *see* EU law; first commercial policy 1.3; Highways Act 1896 1.5; Motor Car Act 1903 1.5; nineteenth century insurances 1.3; Road Traffic Act 1930 1.6, 1.11; Road Traffic Act 1988 1.7, 1.12; Third Parties (Rights Against Insurers) Act 1930 1.8–1.10; workmen's compensation scheme 4.17
horsepower/cylinder capacity of vehicle: defence that may not be argued against third party victims 7.4–7.6, 7.37
horses: history of insurance 1.3–1.7
hospital car parks 3.63
hospital treatment of traffic casualties 4.47
hotel car parks 3.63n143

Iceland: Green Card guarantee 11.54, 11.55
identification means: defence that may not be argued against third party victims 7.4–7.6, 7.38
immobilisation of vehicles 5.40–5.45
impecuniosity: civil liability 6.24–6.26, 6.54; credit hire agreements 9.28–9.36; right of direct action against insurer 8.122
insolvency: breach of statutory duty 6.14; cancellation of policy and surrender of certificate 4.8; civil liability 6.40, 6.55; claims against MIB 10.96; Financial Services Compensation Scheme 10.4; insurer in other Member States 10.121; insurers 10.4, 10.119–10.127; Third Party (Rights against Insurers) Act 1930 1.8–1.10, 6.2
institutions: exemption from compulsory insurance 2.32, 2.33, 4.27–4.30, 10.38
Insurance Act 2015: breach of terms 7.13; breach of warranties 7.13; conditions and conditions precedent 7.14, 7.28; terms not relevant to actual loss 7.16–7.21
insurance policy *see* policy of insurance
"insured vehicle" rather than driver 7.49, 7.50

joint criminal activity: public policy doctrine 12.15–12.26; use of stolen or unlawfully take vehicle 8.40, 8.41
joint liability of identified/unidentified persons 10.74
joint venture: use of vehicle 5.68–5.75
jurisdictional rules 11.36–11.41

knock-for-knock agreements 7.45, 7.47

legal proceedings: bringing of the proceedings 8.102–8.111; formality and content of notice 8.101–8.113; timing of notice of the bringing of proceedings 8.96–8.100
liability: civil liability *see* civil liability; contingent liability 9.14; Member State's liability for failure to implement directives 1.26–1.32; right of direct action *see* right of direct action against insurer; strict liability offence under RTA 1988 2.8–2.10; vicarious liability 4.31–4.37
Liechtenstein: Green Card guarantee 11.54, 11.55
lifts: passenger accepting 4.56n78, 5.63, 5.69, 5.73, 7.65, 7.69
limitation period: automated vehicles 13.24; claims against the UK 1.33; claims under *Monk v Warbey* liability 6.46–6.55
Lister principle 4.38, 4.39
local authorities: exemption from compulsory insurance 2.32, 2.33, 4.27–4.30, 10.38

manslaughter 8.42, 12.4
material damage: minimum amount of indemnity 4.12–4.16; 7.83, 7.84
maximum amount of cover required 4.11
means of transport: whether normal function of vehicle confined to use as 5.17–5.33
military vehicles: definition of vehicle 3.46; use of vehicle 3.67
miniature motor cycles 3.42
minimum amount of indemnity 4.12–4.16, 7.83, 7.84
Ministry of Defence: exemption from compulsory insurance 10.38
misrepresentation 2.10
Monk v Warbey liability *see* civil liability
Motor Car Act 1903 1.5
motorcycles: dangerous driving 12.17; passengers 5.72, 5.74, 5.75, 7.27, 12.20
Motor Insurers' Bureau: authorised insurer 4.1; automated vehicles 13.25, 13.26; claims against 10.6; company limited by guarantee 10.2n6, 10.26n60; emanation of the state 10.21–10.26; formation 10.2; history of 10.1,

281

10.2; Green Card System representative 11.53; independence from members insurers 10.27, 10.28; insurer's obligation to be a member of 10.5; legal nature of 10.21–10.26; obligation of 10.3; recovery from Financial Services Compensation Scheme 10.4; unnecessary involvement 10.29

Motor Insurers' Bureau agreements: "any liability" arising out of use of the vehicle 4.61, 4.61n95, 4.62, 8.46; automated vehicles 13.25, 13.26; avoided insurance cover 8.123; between Secretary of State for the Environment and 1.13; claims against 4.55, 4.59; complaints 10.70; criminal acts 4.61n95, 8.46; defences available to 10.99–10.111; EU Consolidated Directive 10.14, 10.15; EU Fifth Directive 10.12, 10.13; EU Fourth Directive 10.16, 10.17; EU law's influence on 10.9–10.17; EU Second Directive 10.9, 101.10, 10.16, 10.17; EU Third Directive 10.11; excluded liability 10.99–10.111; *ex gratia* payments 10.8, 10.8n18; insolvent insurers 10.119–10.127; "knew or ought to have known" in context of the Directives 10.104–10.118; legal anomalies 10.95; legal status 10.18–10.20; *Monk v Warbey* liability and 6.11, 6.35–6.38; nature of claims against 10.95–10.98, 12.30–12.32; protection provided by 1.13, 10.128; public policy doctrine 12.30–12.32; reliance on a Directive in claims against 10.129–10.133; stolen vehicles 10.99–10.103; uninsured drivers agreement *see* Motor Insurers' Bureau Uninsured Drivers Agreement; untraced drivers agreement *see* Motor Insurers' Bureau Untraced Drivers' Agreement

Motor Insurers' Bureau Article 75 insurer: appointment 8.125, 8.126; avoidable or cancelled policies 8.126, 8.133; burden of proof 8.128; ceasing to be 8.127; disputes and appeals 8.132; double insurance 8.129; payment with right of recourse 8.130; satisfying the creditor 8.130; uninsured/untraced driver 8.131

Motor Insurers' Bureau as compensatory body under the Fourth Directive: appointment of claims representative 11.15; indemnifying the injured party 11.17; jurisdiction matters 11.36–11.41; level of compensation – applicable law 11.24–11.35; requirements 11.13; response to claims 11.16, 11.17; right of recourse 11.22; unidentified insurer or vehicle 11.18–11.23

Motor Insurers' Bureau Uninsured Drivers Agreement: application 10.30, 10.31; authorities excluded 10.38; bringing of proceedings 10.59–10.65; claim form 10.55, 10.68; claims made by dependants 10.53, 10.54; duties of claimant 10.55–10.68; excluded liability 10.102; exclusions removed by 2017 Supplementary Agreement 10.43, 10.44; hire agreement/hire-purchase agreements 10.45n86; history 10.7; influence of drink or drugs 10.48; insurer's right of recourse where passenger as owner permitted uninsured driver 10.52; joined as additional defendant to relevant proceedings 10.59–10.63; "knew or ought to have known" in context of the Directives 10.104–10.118; legal status 10.18–10.20; other sources of recovery 10.39–10.42; passengers 10.45–10.50; relevant liability 10.33–10.36; response to claim 10.69, 10.70; right of recourse against Article 75 insurer 8.131; scope of 10.31; terrorism 10.44; unsatisfied judgment 10.37, 10.67; waiver of condition precedent 10.62, 10.63; withdrawn consent 10.51; voluntary acceptance of risk 10.51

Motor Insurers' Bureau Untraced Drivers Agreement: application 10.30, 10.31; arbitration 10.90–10.92; compensation payments 10.80–10.88; costs 10.89; damage to property 10.76; dispute resolution 10.90–10.92; duties of the claimant 10.78, 10.79; enforcement of payment 10.94; *ex gratia* payments 10.8, 10.8n18; history 10.8; joint liability of identified and unidentified persons 10.74; legal advice 10.88; legal status 1.29, 10.18–10.20; other sources of recovery 10.75; passengers 10.77; right of recourse against Article 75 insurer 8.131; right to set-off 10.93; scope of 10.71–10.73

Motor vehicles: adapted for use on roads 3.40, 3.41; associated equipment and machinery 4.26, 4.37; Consolidated Motor Insurance Directive definition of vehicle 3.46; definition 3.40, 3.46; dumper trucks 3.43; employees *see* employees' position; EU law 3.46–3.49; forklift trucks 3.42; go-karts 3.42; Go-peds 3.44; intended for use on roads 3.42; meaning of use of a vehicle 3.66–3.72; miniature motor cycles 3.42; RTA 1988 definition 3.40; scramble motorcycle 3.45; tractors 3.43

Motor Vehicles (Third Party Risks) Regulations 1972: certificate of insurance requirements 2.12, 2.19

"moving" a motor vehicle 5.34–5.39

national courts *see* courts

National Health Service: exemption from compulsory insurance 10.38

no claim discount 9.46

non-material damages: national law 4.49–4.52; persons who can claim compensation 4.53, 4.54; recovery 4.49–4.54

normal base of vehicle 4.45, 4.46

normal function of the vehicle: any use of vehicle consistent with 5.16, 5.17; domestic law 5.17–5.21; EU law 5.22–5.26; hamburger van 5.19, 5.33; machine for carrying out work distinct from means of transport 5.31; period of time for assessing purpose of use 5.29; policy wording 5.28; relevant use of vehicle on the road 5.18, 5.19; repairs on private property 5.27; taxi 5.20, 5.21; tractors 5.23–5.26, 5.32; vehicle parked on private land taken and driven without owner's permission 5.30; whether confined to use as means of transport 5.17–5.33

Norway: Green Card guarantee 11.54, 11.55

notice of the bringing of proceedings: formality and content of 8.101–8.113; timing 8.96–8.100

notification provisions: "as soon as possible" 7.44; example of claims provision 7.43; notifying insurer of action against the assured 8.92–8.95; notifying third party claimant 8.134–8.141

number of persons carried in vehicle: defence that may not be argued against third party victims 7.4–7.6

objectives of motor third party liability insurance 1.11–1.13

obligation to insure: burden of proof 2.11; certificate of insurance *see* certificate of insurance or security; continuing ownership 3.24–3.33; double insurance 3.34–3.39; exceptions to compulsory insurance or security 2.31–2.39; exclusion clauses in contracts 2.25–2.28; extension clauses 3.15–3.33; no obligation on insurer to accept insurance proposals 2.29, 2.30; permission or cause use *see* permission or cause use; rateable proportion clauses 3.35–3.39; road or other public place *see* road or other public place; strict liability 2.8–2.10; under Consolidated Motor Insurance Directive Article 3 2.5–2.7; under Road Traffic Act 1988 provisions 2.1–2.4; vehicle not meeting insurance requirements 2.20–2.22; void and voidable insurance contracts 2.23, 2.24

offences: absence of compulsory insurance 1.1; certificate of insurance 2.14, 2.17, 2.18, 5.2; employees' position 4.33; knowledge of 10.115; not having valid insurance 5.2; "other public place" 3.64; stolen or unlawfully taken vehicles *see* stolen or unlawfully taken vehicles; strict liability 2.8–2.10; use of vehicle 5.2, 5.2n3; vehicle not meeting insurance requirements 2.20–2.22

off road accidents 3.66–3.72

"other public place": meaning 3.63 *see also* road or other public place

"owner of the vehicle": driver injured by own negligence 7.86; exclusion clauses covering claims by 7.85–7.93; passenger in own vehicle 4.59, 6.18, 7.87–7.90; pedestrian is owner 7.91–7.93; victim is owner 7.85

passenger as user of the vehicle: accepting a lift 4.56n78, 5.63, 5.69, 5.73; common law 5.65–5.77; concept of use 5.63; control/ management or operation of vehicle element 5.66, 5.67, 5.75–5.77; EU law 5.78–5.82; interpretation of "user" 5.63, 5.64; joint venture 5.68; opening vehicle doors 5.78; ownership interest 5.76, 5.77; pillion passenger 5.72, 5.74, 5.75; pre-determined joint purpose 5.70–5.75

passengers: carried for hire or reward 4.18, 4.56, 7.70, 7.71; car-sharing arrangements 7.72–7.74; chauffeur driven 4.57; contribution towards an accident 7.11; employees' position 4.21–4.23; insurance policy requirements 4.56–4.59; owner of vehicle injured as passenger in own vehicle 4.59, 6.18, 7.85–7.90; restrictions in policy terms 7.7–7.11, 7.33; Uninsured Drivers Agreement 10.45–10.50; Untraced Drivers Agreement 10.77; use of the vehicle *see* passenger as user of the vehicle

pedestrians: owner of vehicle injured as 7.91–7.93

penalties: vehicle not meeting insurance requirements 2.21

permission or cause use: civil liability 6.27–6.29; conditional permission 3.6–3.8; continuing ownership 3.24–3.33; death of person who granted permission 3.9; employees using vehicle in course of employment 3.12; expressed or inferred 3.2; extension clauses 3.15–3.33; meaning of "permit" and "permitted" 3.13, 31.14; the offender 3.10, 3.11; permitted users for the scheduled vehicle 3.15–3.23; proof of *mens rea* 3.4, 3.5; restrictions 3.3; scope of RTA 1988 provisions 2.1. 2.2, 3.1–3.5

personal injury: both physical and psychological suffering 4.48; emergency treatment 4.47; meaning 4.48; minimum amount of indemnity 4.12–4.16

"physical location" of accident: other public place 3.66–3.72

physical or mental condition: defence that may not be argued against third party victims 7.4–7.6

pillion passenger 5.72, 5.74, 5.75, 7.27

"ply for hire" operations 2.27

police authorities: exemption from compulsory insurance 2.32, 2.33, 4.27–4.30, 10.38

policy of insurance or security: "any liability" arising out of use of the vehicle 4.60–4.62; "any person" to be covered 4.42, 4.55; authorised insurer 4.1; "bodily injury to any person" 4.55; cancellation of policy 8.120; certificate of insurance *see* certificate of insurance or security; control of policy terms *see* control of policy terms; covering note 4.2; declaration to avoid 8.122–8.124; Deregulation Act 2015 4.5–4.8; effectiveness of cover 4.5; employees *see* employees' position; European Communities (Rights against Insurers) Regulations 2002 4.9; meaning of "use" 4.43; minimum amount of indemnity 4.12–4.16; non-material damages 4.49–4.54; normally based in Great Britain 4.46; passengers 4.56–4.59; requirements in respect of 4.40–4.48; personal injury 4.47, 4.48; risks not required to be covered 4.11; schedule to 7.48; scope of cover provided 4.44; subrogation in employment cases 4.38, 4.39; terms *see* control of policy terms; transfer 4.10; use of vehicle 4.43; vicarious liability of employer 4.31–4.37; where vehicle is normally based 4.45, 4.46

private land: use of vehicles on 3.66–3.72; vehicle parked on private land taken and driven without owner's permission 3.68, 5.30

private road with public access 3.53–3.56

privity doctrine 3.16, 3.17

public bodies: exemption from compulsory insurance 2.32, 2.33, 4.27–4.30,10.38

public house car parks 3.63

public liability insurance 5.57

public place 2.1n1, 3.63 *see also* road or other public place

public policy doctrine: applications 12.5–12.8; careless driving 12.12–12.14; causal link between crime and claim 12.3; causation 12.22–12.29; claims against insurers under

Third Parties (Rights Against Insurers) Act 2010 12.33, 12.34; contributory negligence 12.29; cost of hire vehicle 9.52, 9.53; gross negligence 12.13, 12.14; interpretation 12.1–12.4; joint illegal enterprise 12.15, 12.16; life insurance references 12.9–12.11; limitations 12.9–12.11; meaning of *ex turpi causa* 12.1; mental element 12.21; nature of claims against MIB 12.30–12.32; principles of ethics and common law 12.2; turpitude 12.17–12.20; use of stole vehicle 8.40–8.42; vehicles used in the course of crime 12.35–12.37

purpose of journey *see* essential character of journey

railway station car parks 3.64

rateable proportion clauses 3.35–3.39

repair costs: ancillary expenses included in repair cost 9.4; capital account loss 9.1; diminution in value 9.1, 9.3; measure of loss 9.2; non-pecuniary losses 9.5; pre-accident value 9.2

retail commercial enterprises: public access and car parking 3.63

right of direct action against insurer: cancellation of policy 8.120; "causing or permitting use" 8.65–8.68; claimant the assured 8.48, 8.49; claimant the third party victim 8.48, 8.49; declaration to avoid insurance contract 8.122–8.124; delivery of certificate 8.6, 8.7; excluded liability 8.17–8.20; discretion of court to set aside a default judgment 8.142; EU law 8.143–8.151; liability covered 8.8–8.15; *Monk v Warbey* liability 8.57–8.68; Motor Insurers' Bureau appointment of Article 75 insurer *see* Motor Insurers' Bureau Article 75 insurer; "notice of bringing of the proceedings" 8.96–8.113; notifying the insurer of action against the assured 8.92–8.95; notifying the third party claimant 8.134–8.141; permitted exclusions 8.50–8.56; policy restrictions 8.43–8.47; primary direct action against insurers under EU law 8.143–8.151; requirements to be satisfied 8.5; right of recourse 8.69–8.80; RTA 1988 8.1–8.5; state of mind 8.28–8.39; stay of execution 8.121; stolen or unlawfully taken vehicles 8.17–8.39; timing for bringing proceedings 8.96–8.100; unlicensed driver exclusion 8.16; untraced driver 8.81–8.91; waiver 8.114–8.119

right of recourse against assured: amount that may be recouped 8.69; civil liability 8.74–8.80; EU law 8.74; MIB Article 75 insurer

8.131; national rules 8.74, 8.75; "the other side of the bargain" 8.71; owner as passenger 8.73; uninsured driver 8.70, 8.72
risks not required to be covered 4.11
road or other public place: car parks *see* car parks; definable way between two points 3.57–3.59; definition of road 3.50; EU law 3.66–3.72; off road accidents 3.66–3.72; "on" the road 3.51, 3.52; other public place 3.62–3.72; private road with public access 3.53–3.56; public place 2.1n1, 3.63; RTA 1988 provisions 2.1, 2.3; use of vehicle 3.66–3.68
Road Traffic Act 1930: history of 1.6, 1.7; main aim of 1.11; position of employees 4.18
Road Traffic Act 1988: burden of proof 2.11; caravan park roadways 3.63; certificate of insurance requirements *see* certificate of insurance or security; history 1.7; obligation to insure under 2.1–2.4; permit and cause use *see* permission or cause use; proof of act or default 2.8; regulation of third party liabilities 1.12; strict liability 2.8–2.10; vehicles failing to meet insurance requirements 2.20–2.22
road worthiness of the vehicle: defence that may not be argued against third party victims 7.4–7.6, 7.32
Royal Commission on Transport 1928 1.6

sale of vehicle: lapse of policy 3.24
"Scott v Avery" clause 7.104
scramble motorcycle 3.45
Second Council Directive 84/5/EEC: introduction and purpose of 1.18; Member State's liability for failure to implement 1.26–1.32; minimum amount of indemnity 4.12–4.16; Motor Insurers' Bureau 10.9, 10.10, 10.16, 10.17, 10.20
Secretary of State for the Environment: agreements between Motor Insurers' Bureau and 1.13
security against third-party risks: certificate of security *see* certificate of insurance or security; exceptions to 2.31–2.39; rules governing 1.12, 2.1, 2.3
seizure of vehicles: failure to produce certificate of insurance 2.13–2.16
shifting insurance from vehicle to vehicle 3.25, 3.26
sidecars 2.28
single premium charge 7.94, 7.95
social/domestic or pleasure purposes: purpose of the use 7.54–7.58 *see also* essential character of journey
"SORN" declaration 2.20

state of mind: "had reason to believe" 8.30–8.39; "turning a blind eye" 8.28, 8.29;
statistical information: accidents in the twentieth century 1.5n12
stay of execution 8.121
stolen or unlawfully taken vehicles: excluded liability 8.12, 8.17–8.27; exclusion clauses 7.80; *ex turpi causa* 8.40–8.42; joint criminal activity 8.40–8.42; "knew or had reason to believe" 8.30–8.39; "knew or ought to have known" 8.31–8.39; Motor Insurers' Bureau excluded liability 10.99–10.103; not meeting insurance requirements 2.20; "turning a blind eye" 8.28, 8.29; turpitude 12.17
subrogation right: assured's deliberate act 7.99, 8.51; automated vehicle insurance 13.23, 13.24; credit hire agreements 9.47, 9.48, 9.51; double insurance 8.129; employment cases 4.38, 4.39; Fourth Directive 11.10; insolvency 1.10; vehicle parked on private land driven without owner's permission 3.68, 5.30
suicide attempts 7.99, 8.51
suspensory conditions 7.22–7.27
Switzerland: Green Card guarantee 11.54, 11.55

taxicabs: hire and reward 7.71; sexual assaults 5.20, 5.21, 5.33; suspensory conditions 7.22; third party rights 1.8, 4.56
terms *see* control of policy terms
territorial scope of cover 7.95
terrorism 10.44
test certificate: use without 5.3n3
theft *see* stolen or unlawfully taken vehicles
Third Council Directive 90/232/EEC: employees' position 4.21; introduction and purpose of 1.19; Member State's liability for failure to implement 1.26–1.32; Motor Insurers' Bureau 10.11, 10.129
Third Parties (Rights Against Insurers) Act 1930: history of 1.8–1.10
Third Parties (Rights Against Insurers) Act 2010: claims against insurers under 12.33, 12.34; history and application 1.10
time of vehicle's use: defence that may not be argued against third party victims 7.4–7.6, 7.36
towage: control or management of vehicle the operative test 5.49, 5.54, 5.62; driver having no control over vehicle being towed 5.46–5.49; vehicle not used under its own power 5.50–5.62
tractors: defined as a motor vehicle 3.43, 3.46, normal function of the vehicle 5.16, use as a means of transport 5.23–5.25, 5.32

trailers 2.27n59, 5.16, 5.39

tramcars 1.3

trustee for a third party 3.17n48

"turning a blind eye": stolen or unlawfully taken vehicle 8.28, 8.29

turpitude: causation 12.22–12.29; dangerous driving 12.17–12.20; joint illegal act 12.23–12.27

tyres: worn down and defective 5.41, 5.41n82, 5.61n106

unfair terms 7.109

uninsured drivers: civil liability *see* civil liability; deliberate behaviour 8.51; "knew or ought to have known" 8.31; loaning a vehicle to 8.12; *Monk v Warbey* liability 8.57–8.68; Motor Insurers' Bureau arrangements 2.27; owner as victim 4.59, 7.89, 7.90, 7.93; permit and cause 3.5, 3.6, 3.14; pre-determined joint purpose 5.70, 5.72, 5.73; right of recourse against 8.70, 8.72; taxi driver 3.12; vicarious liability 4.33

Uninsured Drivers Agreement *see* Motor Insurers' Bureau Uninsured Drivers Agreement

unlawfully taken vehicles *see* stolen or unlawfully taken vehicles

unlicensed driver 8.16, 8.23

untraced drivers: judgment against 8.81–8.91; limitation period 1.33; *Monk v Warbey* liability 8.57, 8.82; Motor Insurers' Bureau liability 8.84–8.91; statistics 10.6

Untraced Drivers Agreement *see* Motor Insurers' Bureau Untraced Drivers Agreement

use of a vehicle: "arising out of the use" 5.10–5.15; causation 5.10–5.15; EU law 3.66–3.68; immobilised vehicles 5.34–5.45; identifying the user 5.1, 5.2; liability of user 5.2; meaning 4.43, 5.4–5.9; "moving" a vehicle 5.34–5.39; normal function of the vehicle 5.3, 5.16–5.33; not confined to act of driving the vehicle 5.9; parked on private land but no longer driven by owner 3.68; passengers 5.63–5.82; policy must cover "any liability" arising out of use of the vehicle 4.60–4.62; principal use as means of transport 5.17–5.33; private land 3.66–3.68; relevant use of vehicle 5.17–5.21; social/ domestic or pleasure purposes 7.54–7.58; towage 5.46–5.62; valid test certificate 5.3n3

value of vehicle: defence that may not be argued against third party victims 7.4–7.6

vehicle used in the course of a crime 12.35–12.37

void and voidable contracts 2.23, 2.24, 7.106–7.108

waiver: by affirmation 8.116, 8.117; by insurers' conduct 8.114, 8.115; promissory estoppel 8.118, 8.119

warranties 7.12–7.14, 7.21, 7.23, 7.26, 7.40

weight of goods carried in vehicle: defence that may not be argued against third party victims 7.4–7.6, 7.33–7.35

winding up: third party rights 1.8–1.10

workmen's compensation scheme 4.17, 4.18